JAPAN'S EXPANSION on the continent of Asia is a part of today's news; but it is also an ancient story, and its present phase cannot be understood apart from preceding events. The present volume covers the events up to the end of the sixteenth century, when Hideyoshi attempted to conquer all Asia. A second volume will take the account past the middle of the nineteenth century and will dwell especially upon the "Seclusion" period and its effect upon the future expansion of Japan. A third volume will begin with the emergence of the New Japan in 1868 and will close with Japan's self-establishment in Manchuria in 1932 and her preparation to make North China her new field of operation.

Each of these volumes, like the present, will consist of a monographic text and an appendix of documents. Japanese, Chinese, and Korean documents, monographs, and standard histories have been utilized in their preparation and the key documents have been translated from the originals in the Oriental languages. Through a careful comparison and investigation of these materials, Professor Kuno has endeavored to present an account that is accurate and free from bias.

With the present volume begins the publication, under the general editorship of Professor Robert J. Kerner, of researches and investigations undertaken by the Northeastern Asia Seminar of the University of California. Works projected include: the history of the eastward expansion of Russia, by Professor Kerner; the history of Japanese expansion on the continent of Asia, here begun, by Professor Kuno; at least two volumes on China's policy in the northern borderlands; and a selected bibliography. The histories are intended to be read and enjoyed by the interested laymen as well as by the student who has northeastern Asia for his special field.

JAPANESE EXPANSION ON
THE ASIATIC CONTINENT

HIDEYOSHI (1536–1598)

Who planned the expansion of Japan to the continent of Asia

JAPANESE EXPANSION
ON THE
ASIATIC CONTINENT

*A Study in the History of Japan with Special
Reference to Her International Relations with
China, Korea, and Russia*

⌒

By YOSHI S. KUNO

SOMETIME CHAIRMAN OF THE DEPARTMENT OF ORIENTAL
LANGUAGES IN THE UNIVERSITY OF CALIFORNIA

In Three Volumes

VOLUME I

University of California Press
Berkeley, California
1937

PUBLICATIONS OF THE NORTHEASTERN ASIA SEMINAR
OF THE UNIVERSITY OF CALIFORNIA

EDITED BY ROBERT J. KERNER
PROFESSOR OF MODERN EUROPEAN HISTORY

UNIVERSITY OF CALIFORNIA PRESS
BERKELEY, CALIFORNIA

———

CAMBRIDGE UNIVERSITY PRESS
LONDON, ENGLAND

PRINTED IN THE UNITED STATES OF AMERICA
BY SAMUEL T. FARQUHAR, UNIVERSITY PRINTER

TO
ROBERT JOSEPH KERNER

**WITHOUT WHOSE ENCOURAGEMENT AND ADVICE
IT WOULD NOT HAVE BEEN POSSIBLE
TO WRITE THIS WORK**

CONTENTS

Chapter II

Chapter III

CONTENTS

Chapter IV

CONTENTS

LIST OF ILLUSTRATIONS

LIST OF MAPS

EDITOR'S PREFACE

THE PUBLICATION *of the present volume begins the presentation in print of researches and investigations which were undertaken by the Northeastern Asia Seminar of the University of California following its inception in February, 1931, by members of the Faculty representing the Departments of Political Science, Economics, History, Oriental Languages, and Slavic Languages.*

The plan of research and publication agreed upon includes a bibliography and a series of volumes projected upon the following general topics:

(1) Northeastern Asia: A Selected Bibliography—Contributions to the Bibliography of the Relations of China, Russia, and Japan in Manchuria, Mongolia, Korea, and Eastern Siberia, edited by Professor Robert J. Kerner with the assistance of the members of the Northeastern Asia Seminar. Two volumes, about 1700 pages. Some 13,500 titles of books and articles are included, of which 2500 are in Chinese, 2500 in Japanese, 3500 in Russian, and 5000 in Western languages. Chinese, Japanese, and Russian titles are given in the original language, transliterated, and translated. This work has been completed and will be published if the Social Science Research Council and the American Council of Learned Societies, through their Joint Committee, can obtain enough subscriptions to make it possible.

(2) The history of the eastward expansion of Russia to the Pacific from its origins to the present time and an analysis of Russia's present position in Asia and on the Pacific, by Professor Robert J. Kerner. The first volume on this topic, carrying the account to the eighteenth century, is almost ready for the press.

(3) The history of Japanese expansion on the continent of Asia from its origins to the present time, by Professor Yoshi S. Kuno. This work is planned in three volumes, of which the

present volume is the first. The second volume, continuing the account to the middle of the nineteenth century, is almost ready for the press.

(4) China's policy in the northern borderlands. It is planned to publish at least two volumes on this subject, of which the first, by Dr. T. C. Lin, of Nankai University, Tientsin, China, is almost ready for the press.

It will be seen from the foregoing that the purpose is to subject the imperial triangle of Northeastern Asia—the meeting of the three empires of Russia, China, and Japan—to a series of thorough and unbiased investigations with a view to exposing the manner of expansion, the policies, and the interests of these Powers in this region, as objectively as possible.

Professor Kuno, in the present volume, has put Western scholarship into a position not only to understand Japan's historical evolution in relation to the main problem, but also to judge the conditions out of which Japanese expansion emerged.

Each volume will consist of a monographic text presenting the research, and translated key documents pertinent to the investigation.

It is hoped in this way to contribute to a better understanding of the greatest problem in the Far East and to give a sounder and more objective basis on which to judge events in that important and awakening region of the world.

ROBERT J. KERNER

AUTHOR'S PREFACE

THE PRESENT VOLUME *is the first of three which will be written on Japanese expansion on the continent of Asia. It covers the events up to the end of the sixteenth century, when Hideyoshi attempted to conquer all Asia. The second volume, the manuscript of which is now almost finished, will take the account past the middle of the nineteenth century and will dwell especially upon the "Seclusion" period and its effect upon the future expansion of Japan. The third volume will begin with the emergence of the New Japan in 1868 and will close with Japan's self-establishment in Manchuria in 1932 and her preparation to make North China her new field of operation.*

Each volume, like the present, will consist of a monographic text and an appendix of documents. Japanese, Chinese, and Korean documents, monographs, and standard histories have been utilized in their preparation and the key documents have been translated from the originals in the Oriental languages. Through a careful comparison and investigation of these materials, the writer has endeavored to present an account which is accurate and free from bias. It is his hope that thereby some light will be shed upon the conflicting and often puzzling international relationships existing in the Orient.

The concomitance of a Chinese empire existing more or less feebly, a Russia expanding eastward, and a Japan carrying on a continental expansion, was bound to bring about a conflict. It came to a head in the Russo-Japanese War (1904–05), which still remains one of the greatest wars fought between two nations. The end of this conflict is not yet in sight. The advance of Russia on the continent of Asia is a movement of recent centuries, but Japan's desire to expand on the continent has been manifested again and again for more than a thousand years. In the early centuries of her national life, Japan frequently came into conflict with China, Korea usually being the victim, until, finally, Korea found herself annexed to Japan. In more

[xv]

recent times, Japan has come into conflict with Russia, and the victim has always been China. It remains to be seen what will be the future course of events in Northeastern Asia.

 I am grateful to the Institute of Social Sciences of the University of California for supplying the necessary financial assistance, both from its funds and from those which have been received from the Rockefeller Foundation, for the work on this and subsequent volumes. Professor Robert J. Kerner, who planned the work of the Northeastern Asia Seminar of the University of California, first encouraged me to undertake this task and he has assisted me with advice and editorial suggestions throughout the preparation of the present volume.

Y. S. K.

THE EMPRESS JINGO
Traditionally the first Japanese conqueror of Korea

CHAPTER I

Early National Expansion of Japan, Ending in the Seventh Century, A.D.

ACCORDING TO NATIONAL TRADITION, the first emperor, Jimmu, having conquered several wild tribes, established his throne on February 11, 660 B.C. The empire thus founded consisted of Yamato and four small districts in the central part of Honshu Island. Its area was only a few hundred square miles. In the early period, which covered 563 years, nine emperors ruled but nothing of note took place. Imperial accessions to the throne, imperial marriages, proclamations of the heirs-apparent to the throne, and imperial deaths and burials were the only events recorded in the national annals.

In the reign of Sujin, the tenth emperor, Japan gradually emerged from the Mythological Age. Sujin is reputed to have ruled for sixty-eight years, his reign ending in 30 B.C. He is known as the "Emperor of the Beginning of the National Life."[1]* This emperor, it is said, sent four princes of the imperial blood, with strong military support, in four different directions to subjugate the wild tribes. Thus did Japan enter upon a period of national expansion which extended her domain to the coast of the Sea of Japan.[2] In the early part of the reign of the Emperor Suinin, who is said to have ruled for ninety-nine years, his reign ending in 70 A.D., an envoy came to Japan from Kaya, a small district in the southern tip of Korea. He made the following request:

"Kaya has been in continuous war with the kingdom of Shinra. Both the state and the people have suffered greatly. It is our desire to place the entire district under the rule of the emperor of Japan. We therefore request that the emperor send an able military general with a strong force."[3]

* Superior figures refer to notes which will be found on pp. 179–90.

[1]

As a result, the kingdom of Mimana was established as a protectorate of Japan, and the Japanese government-general[4] set up in that kingdom. This is the first entry in the history of Japan concerning either international relations or national expansion on the continent.[5] In the succeeding two hundred years, however, no mention is made of Japan's relations with Korea or any other nation.[6]

In the reign of Chuai, who ruled Japan for eight years, his reign ending in 200 A.D., the Kumaso tribe in Kyushu threatened the existence of the empire of Japan. The emperor, accompanied by the Empress Jingo, at the head of a large army proceeded to the south end of Honshu, which afforded a direct approach to Kyushu. There he held a military council on the campaign against the Kumaso. The Empress Jingo, guided by divine inspiration, insisted that he should entirely ignore the military activities of the Kumaso and should immediately invade the kingdom of Shinra in Korea, which was noted for its gold, silver, and other treasure. If the emperor should make a surprise attack, she declared, he would win a bloodless victory in Shinra. She further maintained that the Kumaso would be subjugated automatically because the uprising of that tribe was to be attributed to the financial and military support of Shinra. The emperor ignored this advice and invaded Kyushu, where he waged war against the Kumaso. He was killed by a stray arrow in the first battle.[7]

At the time of the unnatural death of the emperor, the Empress Jingo was an expectant mother. The imperial army of Japan therefore remained inactive for lack of a military leader. However, according to the records, within two months after the death of her husband, the Empress Jingo, in accordance with divine instructions, decided to invade Shinra in Korea in person. In September, 200 A.D., the empress mustered the military and naval forces. In October, she took the entire fighting force across the Korean Channel by way of Tsushima (Tsu island), and swooped down upon the coast of Shinra. The king of Shinra found it impossible to cope with this sudden invasion, and surrendered without a battle. The Empress Jingo permitted Shinra to maintain its national existence under the suzerainty of Japan. Korai and Kudara followed the example of Shinra, and became voluntary tributary states of Japan. In December, the Empress Jingo[8] returned in triumph to Japan, and on the day of her landing the posthumous son of the Emperor Chuai was born to her, fourteen months after conception.

The first foreign conquest of Japan was thus made by a woman, who in three months' time subdued the three kingdoms[9] in Korea, namely, Shinra, Kudara, and Korai. This Korean conquest was long regarded as the greatest and most glorious national accomplishment in the history of Japan. The Empress Jingo was worshiped as the guardian goddess of the nation. Ojin, her posthumous son and the fifteenth emperor, was a born conqueror, and was therefore long revered as the god of war. For about fifteen hundred years after their deaths, the Empress Jingo and her son were reverently worshiped, and whenever Japan was at war, especially with foreign nations, their divine souls were invoked because they were the first conquerors of a foreign nation.

This conquest of Korea by the Empress Jingo is a much mooted question in the history of Japan. Some historians regard it as fiction, for the following reasons:

(1) This invasion of Korea by Japan is mentioned in neither Chinese nor Korean histories.

(2) The only accounts of this invasion of Korea by the Empress Jingo are to be found in the two oldest standard histories of Japan, written in 712 and 720 A.D., respectively, but these accounts are mere fairy tales.[10]

(3) The Empress Jingo, who is said to have conquered Korea in 200 A.D., actually lived in the fourth century A.D.[11]

(4) For more than a thousand years after the founding of the Japanese nation, its history was mythical rather than truly historical. According to tradition, the empire of Japan was

founded in 660 B.C.; in the early part of the fifth century A.D., Japan came into possession of the Chinese written characters, but because of the lack of an educated class, the Japanese nation[12] depended upon Koreans who were permanent residents of Japan for all literary and intellectual work. It was not until the eighth century A.D. that the Japanese were able to use the Chinese characters with any skill. The *Kojiki,* the first Japanese history to be written by a Japanese, was composed in 712 A.D. It was the result of dictation taken from the court historian, whose duty it was to commit the national history to memory. In this way, in 712 A.D., the history of Japan for a period of 1372 years, beginning with the assumed date of the founding of the nation in 660 B.C., was transmitted by word of mouth from one historian to another.

(5) Although February 11, 660 B.C., is recognized as the day on which the empire of Japan was founded, and although even today all state documents and state papers have this date as the beginning of their calendar, modern historians believe that the actual date of the founding of the empire was about the beginning of the Christian era. In 712 A.D., when the first national history was written, the Japanese historians, guided by the *Yisho,* a Chinese work on historical theory and philosophy, expanded about seven hundred years of the national life to fourteen hundred years, and distributed the national historical events hit or miss through this period. Consequently, the history of Japan in the ancient period cannot be conclusively studied or determined until an accurate historical chart has been made. During the past quarter-century, Japanese historians have been making a detailed, comparative, chronological study of the history of the three countries, China, Japan, and Korea, and have succeeded in producing some historical charts that are reliable. Before judgment is passed upon the authenticity of the Empress Jingo's invasion of Korea and of other early international relations and events, some such chart should be referred to.[13]

However, taking it for granted, for the foregoing reasons, that the conquest of Korea by the Empress Jingo is fiction, nevertheless it is probable that, both before and after her time, the Japanese crossed the water and made numerous inroads with varying success upon the kingdoms in Korea. This is substantiated by the records in standard Korean histories of a number of Japanese invasions of Korea in a period of 550 years beginning in 50 B.C. and ending in 500 A.D. Sometimes the Japanese took Koreans prisoners and at other times they compelled Korea to send hostages to Japan. Strange to say, most of these events, although mentioned in Korean history,[14] are not recorded in Japanese history.

In the latter part of the nineteenth century, Chinese government authorities excavated a large stone monument near the border line of Korea and Manchuria. This monument proved to be one that had been erected in honor of a famous king of Korai about fifteen hundred years before. The inscriptions on this monument shed light on many disputed historical events; for example, in one inscription it is stated that Japan had reduced both Shinra and Kudara to tributary states.[15]

Again, it is recorded in Chinese history though not in Japanese history that in the fifth century A.D. Japan on many occasions sent envoys to the imperial court of China to request recognition of her authority to rule in Shinra, Kudara, Mimana, and other states in Korea.[16]

Taking into consideration all these records in China and Korea, together with the available records in Japanese history (which should be studied in connection with a reliable historical chart), one concludes that, either in the latter part of the fourth century or in the early part of the fifth century, Japan established her suzerainty over Shinra and Kudara, extended her military power over Korai, and finally established her government-general in Mimana for the purpose of supervising affairs in the Korean peninsula.

In the fifth and sixth centuries, because of the annual tribute

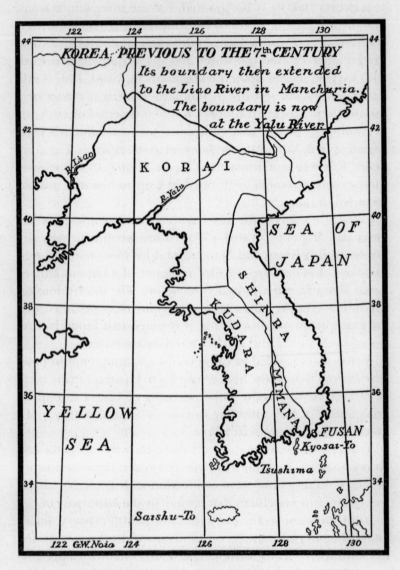

KOREA PREVIOUS TO THE 7th CENTURY
Its boundary then extended
to the Liao River in Manchuria.
The boundary is now
at the Yalu River.

R.Liao

K O R A I

R.Yalu

SEA OF

JAPAN

SHINRA

KUDARA

MIMANA

YELLOW

SEA

FUSAN
Kyosai-To

Tsushima

Saishu-To

G.W.Noia

KOREA PREVIOUS TO THE SEVENTH CENTURY

sent by the kingdoms in Korea, the national wealth of Japan was greatly increased. The continuous introduction of Chinese civilization by way of Korea and the intellectual and industrial works contributed by Korean emigrants to Japan did much to advance the social conditions and national life of Japan. While the foundation of Japanese civilization was thus being laid, however, the country was undergoing radical changes.

From time immemorial, the military authority had been regarded in Japan as a sacred imperial prerogative. The command of the imperial army had never been entrusted to any but persons of royal blood." This is why, after the death of the Emperor Chuai, the Empress Jingo, in spite of the fact that she was an expectant mother, had to assume command of the army that she took to Korea. As a result of this highly centralized military organization, Japan developed, in the fourth and early fifth centuries, into one of the strongest military powers in Asia. Because of this strength, even though she was the youngest of the nations and the Japanese people as a whole were still illiterate, she was able to bring the kingdoms in Korea under her military rule. In the second half of the fifth century, however, because of the increase of national wealth and the advent of the easy, luxurious mode of living of the continent, and because warfare was conducted far from home across the water in Korea, the emperor and the princes of the royal blood began to take less and less interest in military affairs. Finally, the military authority was entirely delegated by the throne to powerful families. Jealousies and rivalries sprang up among them, the Japanese military leaders in Korea frequently disagreed, and eventually Japan lost her national prestige.

While Japan was thus losing ground abroad, loose morality prevailed at home. In the reign of Yuryaku, the twenty-first emperor, there was a military man named Kibi-no-Tasa who had a beautiful wife. One day, in the imperial court, Tasa boasted of the great beauty and grace of his wife, saying that no woman like her was to be found in Japan or in any other country. The emperor overheard this remark and had an audience with the wife of Tasa. He was greatly attracted by her.

In 463, the emperor appointed Kibi-no-Tasa[18] as governor-general of Mimana, with instructions to proceed to Korea without delay to take up his official duties. After his departure, the emperor ordered Tasa's wife to make her home at the imperial palace. Soon a son was born to her. When this news reached Tasa in Mimana, Korea, he rebelled against the emperor. At that time, the kingdom of Shinra had not sent tribute to Japan for seven years and was therefore in fear of military punishment by Japan. Tasa took advantage of this situation and formed an alliance with Shinra, in the hope of creating a new kingdom of Mimana and making himself its ruler. The allied armies of Shinra and Mimana invaded Kudara, which had remained faithful to Japan. Taking advantage of this disturbed condition in southern Korea, the king of Korai in northern Korea, who had long nursed an ambition to establish a single united Korean state, sent a large army south.

The three kingdoms, Shinra, Kudara, and Korai (Kokuli), had maintained independent existence for several centuries. They had long been rivals and had frequently engaged in warfare. Shinra, the oldest kingdom, was also the weakest. Because of her geographical proximity to Japan,—she was situated in the eastern part of the Korean peninsula, facing the Sea of Japan,—Shinra was the first state to be conquered and the first to be made a tributary state of Japan in Korea. Shinra, however, frequently ignored the authority of Japan, formed alliances with one state or another, and encroached upon neighboring states. She had even dared to invade Mimana, a Korean state under the direct control of Japan.[19] Shinra was always observant of changes in China, Japan, and Korea, and availed herself of every possible advantage in advancing her national standing. Although she sent tribute to Japan, she did so at her own convenience or, if pressed for it, only in response to military threats from Japan.

Korai (Kokuli) was the largest state of the three, occupying the whole of northern Korea. At one time, the territory of Korai included that part of Manchuria which is now known as Kwan-Tung and Mukden. As Korai was a great distance from Japan, being far to the north and adjoining China, she was naturally more closely in touch with China than with Japan. Although she sent envoys to Japan to show due respect, in general she acted as an independent state. As a matter of fact, Chinese histories in those days contained statements that the ruling dynasties in China recognized the authority of Japan in Shinra, Kudara, and Mimana, but none[20] of them mentioned that Japan had any authority over Korai.

Kudara had Korai and Shinra on her northern and eastern boundaries, respectively, and she was separated from China by the Yellow Sea. Kudara was a faithful tributary state of Japan, and many of the kings of Kudara[21] kept their crown princes in Japan in order to show due respect to the imperial court. On the whole, Kudara maintained her national existence by depending in large part upon Japan.

Mimana was a small state, triangular in shape. Its sides adjoined the borders of Kudara and Shinra, and its base formed the coast line of the Korean Channel.

In 465, these three kingdoms and Mimana entered upon a most complicated military struggle. Kudara was attacked from the east by the allied armies of Shinra and Mimana, the latter being under the control of Tasa, the Japanese governor-general who had rebelled against the emperor. At the same time, Kudara was attacked from the north by Korai. Because Kudara, the most faithful tributary state of Japan, was thus endangered, and because of a desire to crush the rebellious governor-general, the Emperor Yuryaku of Japan had planned to proceed to Korea in person at the head of a large imperial force. Domestic conditions in Japan compelled him to abandon this plan,[22] but he sent a large army under the command of Ki-no-Oyumi and three other generals, with the hope of saving Ku-

dara and of inflicting due punishment upon both the king
of Shinra and the rebellious governor-general. When the
Japanese troops reached Kudara, its capital had already been
stormed and it was occupied by the army of Korai, the king,
queen, and their children had been taken prisoners, and the
kingdom of Kudara[23] was virtually destroyed. The Japanese
generals sought out Bunshu, a younger brother of the king,
placed him on the throne at a newly selected capital in Kudara,
and proceeded to crush the governor-general in Mimana.
Shinra was likewise defeated. Finally, Shinra, Kudara, and Mimana, under the direction of the Japanese generals, formed an
alliance against Korai, the purpose being to form a united front
in southern Korea against northern Korea.

The alliance of Kudara, Mimana, and Shinra against Korai
did not accomplish its ends. Its failure was partly owing to disturbances in the newly established kingdom of Kudara; but
the main cause of its failure is to be found in the unscrupulous acts of the Japanese leaders and their lack of loyalty to
the throne. Disregarding their duties and the work entrusted
to them by their emperor, some of them supported Kudara,
and others approached Shinra and even Korai for the purpose
of advancing their personal interests.

The critical condition in Korea reached its climax when
Ouiwa, the son of Ki-no-Oyumi, became the governor-general
of Mimana. He first established himself firmly in Mimana and
came to a secret understanding with Korai, their aim being to
place the whole of Korea under their joint control. In 487,
Ouiwa openly rebelled against the emperor of Japan, and entered into a secret agreement with Korai[24] whereby Ouiwa was
to be made king in southern Korea and the king of Korai was to
be ruler of all northern Korea, including the greater part of the
former kingdom of Kudara. Ouiwa began building a strong
fortress in order to isolate Kudara from both Shinra and Japan.
Before this plan could be matured, the king of Kudara sent his
entire fighting force against Ouiwa. He risked the fate of his

kingdom in this battle and was successful. Ouiwa suffered a crushing defeat and left Korea for parts unknown.

Thus, within less than a quarter-century, the Japanese governors-general in Korea twice rebelled against their emperors and twice betrayed the allied states in Korea. They also forfeited the respect and confidence of the Koreans for all Japanese and brought their country into disrepute. Even the faithful kingdom of Kudara took advantage of the situation and requested that Japan cede to her four large districts in Mimana in recognition of the service she had done Japan by destroying Ouiwa, the rebel governor-general of Mimana, together with his army. The imperial government did not immediately consider this demand of Kudara, which seemed to it both extraordinary and unjustifiable. Kudara persisted and finally, in 523, she gained these districts by bribing high officials of the imperial court of Japan.[25]

When it became known that Japan had ceded four districts of Mimana to Kudara, the people of Mimana expressed dissatisfaction with the division of their state; they even threatened to appeal to arms. The kingdom of Shinra likewise opposed the cession on the ground that it disturbed the balance of power in southern Korea. Finally, Shinra entered into alliance with Korai and invaded Mimana with the object of annexing that state to her kingdom.

Japan sent an envoy by the name of Kenu to southern Korea with instructions to settle the problem in Mimana to the satisfaction of Korai, Shinra, and Mimana. Kenu, lacking both tact and ability, not only failed in his mission, but also incurred the ill will of both Shinra and Kudara. War ensued. In 532, Shinra had virtually occupied the greater part of Mimana. Then Korai and Shinra formed an alliance and threatened even the existence of Kudara. The king of Kudara earnestly requested that Japan send strong reënforcements, and Japan responded promptly to this request. Many dissatisfied men from Mimana also rallied round the standard of Seimei, the king of

Kudara, and in 554, he declared war on Shinra. In the beginning of the war, Kudara was quite successful; her king forced
his way far into the interior of Shinra. But eventually his army
was completely routed and the king himself was killed. This
victory made it possible for Shinra to occupy the whole of
Mimana. Upon hearing of this, Japan sent a large army, which
was defeated by Shinra. In 562, the Japanese government-general in Mimana was uprooted and the entire state was annexed
to Shinra.[26]

In 552, that is, ten years before the Japanese disaster in
Korea that ended with the annexation of Mimana to Shinra,
Buddhism had been introduced from Kudara into Japan.
Whether or not Buddhism should be adopted in Japan became
a serious national problem, and Japanese leaders were divided
in opinion. The history of Japan during the reign of the Emperor Kinmei, the twenty-ninth sovereign, who ruled the
empire for the thirty-one years ending in 571, is therefore concerned mainly with Japan's military disasters in Korea and her
subsequent unsuccessful attempt to regain Mimana, together
with the disputes over Buddhism.

The Emperor Kinmei had felt the loss of Mimana in his
reign to be a great disgrace. On his deathbed, he requested that
his successor should make the restoration of Mimana to Japan
the latter's personal ambition as well as a national objective.[27]
The maintenance of Japan's sovereignty over Korea was no
longer a national question; Japan's ambition in the second half
of the sixth century was to regain her power over Mimana.
However, because of domestic troubles she was not able to
send an army to Korea and therefore made but little headway.
The most important of these troubles was the Buddhist question. The Buddhist and the anti-Buddhist factions made the
choice of a religion a leading national problem. The struggle
was serious, and finally they decided to settle their differences
by an appeal to arms. In 587, civil war broke out; it ended in
a complete victory for the Buddhist party.

The establishment of Buddhism as the national religion was thus definitely settled after thirty-five years of continual dispute and struggle. But Japan was not yet in a position to wage war against Shinra and thus comply with the dying request of the Emperor Kinmei. So she merely protested to Shinra against the occupation of Mimana and indicated that she might appeal to arms if Shinra failed to meet the Japanese demand. At the same time, Japan gave all possible assistance to Kudara in the rehabilitation of that kingdom. In this way, Japan[28] prepared to avenge herself on Shinra, with the coöperation of Kudara, while she awaited an opportunity to regain her power to rule over Mimana.

Toward the close of the sixth century, when Korea was temporarily enjoying peace and Shinra was a rising power in the peninsula, conditions in China were changing rapidly. China was emerging from centuries of chaos, and forging her way toward national unification. Ever since the middle of the third century, when the great Han dynasty came to an end, China had been divided into small kingdoms that were continuously at war with one another. Later, several powerful northern tribes crossed the Gobi Desert and invaded China, establishing kingdoms there. Finally, China came under the rule of what are known as the Northern and Southern dynasties. One weak dynasty succeeded another.

Although none of these rapidly changing ruling houses was strong enough to invade Korea, this long-continued chaos in China was very disquieting to the Korean peninsula. In those days, the small states in Korea sent envoys with a sort of tribute to the ruling houses in China and to Japan as well, for the twofold purpose of ensuring the good will of the one nation and recognizing the sovereignty of the other. Most of the small kingdoms in Korea maintained their national existence by thus pledging loyalty to both China and Japan. These chaotic conditions in eastern Asia made it possible for Japan to establish and maintain her authority in southern Korea for nearly three hundred years, beginning in the fourth century A.D. and ending in the middle of the seventh century.

Not long before the close of the sixth century (589 A.D.), an indigenous movement for the national unification of China proved successful and the whole of China came under the rule of a single imperial house, the Sui dynasty. This unification of China had a marked effect upon Korea, for the Sui emperor planned to extend his successful military campaign into Korea. Korai,[29] the largest kingdom in Korea, and adjoining China, was naturally his military objective. But Korai was the ally of Shinra, so that this military threat from China against Korea greatly weakened the national standing of Shinra.

Thus the long-awaited opportunity came to Japan and made it possible for her to comply with the dying request of the Emperor Kinmei. In 591, the Japanese emperor completed his preparations for the military campaign. He sent an army 20,000 strong to Kyushu under the leadership of five military men, there to await further instructions before moving against Shinra. Having thus made complete military preparation, Japan entered into diplomatic negotiations with Shinra and demanded a satisfactory settlement of the long-pending problem in Mimana. But nothing was accomplished, because of the sudden death of the Japanese emperor almost immediately after the negotiations were started. In 600 A.D., Japan planned another attempt to regain Mimana. Before taking actual steps against Shinra, however, Japan unofficially sent a national representative to the newly risen Sui empire of China, to ascertain the attitude of China toward Korea.

While Japan was thus preparing to regain her power over Mimana, the people of Mimana in 600 A.D. rose against Shinra. Japan promptly sent a large army to Korea and waged war against Shinra in coöperation with the Mimana forces. This campaign was successful and the king of Shinra sued for peace, pledging to restore Mimana to Japan. Because Shinra failed to make good this pledge, in the fourth month of 602 A.D. the

Japanese army invaded Shinra and forced her to surrender the entire state of Mimana. In recognition of the changing conditions in Korea, instead of establishing a government-general in Mimana, Japan[30] entrusted the authority over Mimana to Kudara, stipulating only that the king of Kudara should send tribute annually to Japan from both his own kingdom and the kingdom of Mimana.

In 604 and again in 607 A.D., two national events of signal importance took place in Japan, namely, the adoption of a calendar in 604 and the sending of an envoy to China in 607. The calendar was first introduced into Japan from Korea in 553 A.D., but Japan, lacking an educated class, had not been able to use it. In 602, a Korean Buddhist priest who was well versed in astronomy and calendar-making came to Japan bringing with him the calendar and a book on astronomy. In the next two years, the imperial regent, Shotoku, who is known in history as the "Founder of Japanese Civilization," made a careful study of the calendar and its use. In the first month of 604, he established a new national custom, in accordance with which all state papers and government documents should bear dates. This action indicates that, for 1264 years, counting from the assumed date of the nation's founding, Japan had had no calendar and that historical events had apparently been recorded undated.[31]

In 607, Japan sent an envoy to China. He carried a personal letter from the "Emperor of Japan" addressed to the "Sui Emperor of China." This was a most significant event in the history of Japan, for the following reasons:

(1) This was the first international intercourse between the two nations, Japan and China. The envoy represented in person the imperial court of Japan.

(2) This was the first time that a state paper was sent from Japan to China in which the equality of the respective national standings and rights was strictly maintained, the title of "Emperor" being used for the rulers of both Japan and China.[32]

(3) This was the first historical event in Japan that was correctly recorded by contemporaries both in Japan and in China.

Chinese history records that an envoy arrived from Japan in the third year of the Taiyeh era. Japanese history records that an envoy was sent to China in the fifteenth year of the reign of Suiko. Both the third year of Taiyeh in China and the fifteenth year of the reign of Suiko correspond to 607 A.D. in the Occidental calendar. Here is evidence that, beginning in 607 A.D., the entries in Japanese history become trustworthy; from that date on, Chinese, Japanese, and Korean history may be studied on a contemporary basis.

The purpose of Japan in sending the envoy, historians generally believe, was to ascertain definitely the policy of China in dealing with the kingdoms in Korea. At that time, although Japan was rapidly losing her authority in Korea, yet her sovereign rights in that country apparently still obtained. The history of the Sui states that both Kudara and Shinra regarded Japan as a great nation and served her with due respect.[33]

In 612, the Sui emperor of China invaded Korai with an army 300,000 strong, but he met disastrous defeat, only a few thousand of his men returning to China.[34] The Sui dynasty was short-lived, and in the seventh century the great T'ang dynasty began to rule China. A T'ang emperor likewise unsuccessfully invaded Korai. But Korai's successful defense cost her dear and after the war with China she was exhausted both militarily and financially, and could no longer maintain her prestige.

Shinra, intellectually the most advanced state in Korea, foresaw the inevitable fate of Korea before the might of a united China. So she deserted Korai, her former ally, recognized the authority of Sui, and later made ready submission to the emperors of the great T'ang dynasty. Shinra entertained the hope of establishing a united kingdom in Korea under a Chinese protectorate.[35] This attitude on Shinra's part caused Kudara and Korai, which formerly had been enemies, to make an alliance against Shinra under the supervision of Japan.

In 642, Kudara, supported by Korai and helped by Japan, had successfully invaded Shinra and occupied several districts in that kingdom. In 645, the T'ang emperor invaded Korai and the king of Shinra sent an army to Korai in order to strengthen the latter's forces. Kudara, in turn, invaded Shinra. In this way the entire Korean peninsula was plunged into serious strife.

In the middle of the seventh century, Japan, as well as all the kingdoms in Korea, foresaw the coming change in the Korean peninsula and prepared for the inevitable struggle. Korai, weakened, as has been noted, by invasions from China and deserted by Shinra, formed an alliance with Kudara against Shinra. In order to satisfy Kudara, Japan entrusted to her the authority to rule in Mimana, thus cementing the sovereign and tributary relationships between herself and Kudara. Her hope was to extend her power to Korai through the influence of Kudara. In this way, Japan planned to regain her rapidly declining authority in Korea. She apparently succeeded, though but temporarily: it was about this time that Korai for the first time in her history began to send tribute-bearing envoys to Japan whenever Kudara sent her annual tribute thither.

Shinra was completely isolated and was even threatened by Japan and the other two kingdoms in Korea. Nevertheless, Shinra remained both the most powerful and the most intellectual state in Korea, and still held fast to her traditional ambition to effect the unification of Korea under her domination. China, under the rule of the T'ang, was beginning to rise as the greatest financial, military, and intellectual power on the Asiatic continent. In 657, Shinra openly severed her tributary relations with Japan and recognized the sovereignty of the T'ang emperor of China. Thus did Shinra make her final move in preparation for her military campaign in Korea.

In 660, the T'ang government of China and that of Shinra entered into an understanding with respect to Kudara. In the summer of the same year, a T'ang army 200,000 strong, convoyed by a strong naval force, crossed the Yellow Sea, effected a landing on the west coast of Kudara, and marched toward the capital of Kudara, defeating the enemy in every engagement. At the same time Shinra invaded the eastern border of Kudara with like success. The kingdom of Kudara was thus attacked from both sides at the same time.[36] A decisive battle of three days' duration ended in the complete rout of the army of Kudara, the capital being stormed and occupied. In the winter of 660, 13,000 Kudara prisoners, including the king, the queen, and other members of the royal family, were sent to the imperial court of China to bear witness to the magnitude of the victory.

After the conquest of Kudara, the allied armies of the T'ang and Shinra proceeded to Korai, where they hoped for a like success. In the meantime, surviving subjects of Kudara had gathered their forces and reoccupied their strongholds. They had also sent an envoy to the imperial court of Japan to announce the great national disaster and to request that Japan send back Hosho, the crown prince of Kudara, who had been stationed in Japan as a hostage, so that the kingdom of Kudara might be reëstablished under the military protection of Japan.

Japan realized that she must act promptly if she would maintain her authority in Korea, and decided to muster her national strength. The ruling empress, Saimei, was well past sixty years of age, yet nevertheless she made preparations to cross the water and command the imperial army in person. In the fifth month of 661, the empress, accompanied by the crown prince, proceeded to Kyushu and stationed her army on the coast of the Korean Channel where she awaited a naval convoy. Unfortunately, because of her advanced age, she died within two months.

The death of the empress caused Japan to delay her military campaign and to modify the original plan. To meet the emergency, Japan sent strong military and naval forces to

Korea to help the struggling forces of Kudara in reëstablishing their kingdom. At home, the crown prince, in compliance with the prescribed national mourning, escorted the body of the deceased empress back to the imperial capital, where both the imperial burial and the imperial succession were duly observed.

Two months after the death of the empress, Hosho, the Korean prince, was sent back to Korea with additional troops,[37] but it was May, 662, before the rehabilitation of Kudara was sufficiently advanced to permit of the crowning of Hosho as king. About the same time, Korai sent an envoy to Japan asking for military assistance. In March, 663, Japan sent an army 27,000 strong to invade Shinra, hoping to relieve Korai from Shinra's military pressure. In the summer of 663, warfare in Korea reached its final and most critical stage. The allied armies of the T'ang and Shinra concentrated on Kudara with the object of crushing both the Japanese and the Korean troops and uprooting the reëstablished kingdom of Kudara. Another strong T'ang fleet reached the coast of Korea, and in August a great naval battle was fought at the entrance of Hakuson-ko Bay. Through four successful maneuvers, the T'ang fleet won a decisive victory, hundreds of Japanese war vessels being either sunk or destroyed by fire. According to the records in all the histories, Japanese, Chinese, and Korean, because of the conflagration and the blood of the Japanese killed, both the sky and the water became crimson.[38]

The land battle likewise resulted in a complete victory of the allied armies. The capital of the new Kudara was again stormed and occupied. Hosho, its king, accompanied by a few faithful followers, escaped to Korai. The fifteen months of desperate struggle had come to naught; the kingdom of Kudara was completely destroyed. On the 24th of August, the Japanese gathered the remnant of their fighting force and, accompanied by about four thousand of the Kudara people, left Korea for Japan.

In 668, five years after the destruction of the kingdom of Kudara, Pyeng Yang, the capital of the kingdom of Korai, capitulated. Hozo, its king, together with all the military and civil officers, surrendered to the T'ang forces. Thus did the kingdom of Korai likewise come to an end.[39]

After the destruction of the kingdoms of Kudara and Korai, the T'ang emperor of China stationed a trusted general as a sort of resident-general in each of the conquered districts. However, the T'ang empire gradually withdrew from the direct exercise of authority over those districts and transferred it to the king of Shinra. It was under King Bunbu, who reigned in Shinra from 661 to 680, that the unification of Korea was effected, and the entire peninsula united into a single kingdom under the suzerainty of the T'ang emperor of China.[40]

Her military and naval forces annihilated, Japan was forced to withdraw completely from the Korean peninsula, and her authority in Korea was entirely swept away. She retained not a single inch of Korean territory;[41] nor had she in the Korean peninsula a single Korean subject who looked to her for protection and guidance.

After the destruction of the kingdoms of Kudara and Korai, several thousands of citizens of those two states felt it disgraceful and unsafe to live under the rule of Shinra and the T'ang. They left Korea and went to Japan. There they were received kindly, and the Japanese government allotted to them several districts in different parts of Japan. Two places in particular, one in eastern Japan and the other in western Japan, were allotted exclusively to these Korean refugees. These were called the "Counties of Kudara and of Korai."[42] Even today, there are several places in Japan that are known as Kudara and Korai villages, Kudara and Korai districts, and Kudara and Korai fields, especially in or near the vicinity of the present prefectures of Osaka and Tokyo. They are historic landmarks, concrete evidence that in Korea there once existed the prosperous kingdoms of Kudara and Korai. They also bear witness to the fact that in her ancient period, ending in the seventh century, Japan had a sort of sovereign and tributary relationship with the kingdoms in Korea.

Never at any time, however, did Japan exercise authority over the whole of Korea. Prior to the eighth century, the several kingdoms into which Korea was divided dealt with China and Japan individually and sent them tribute at their own convenience. After the unification of Korea under the rule of Shinra, China, for the first time in Oriental history, established a sort of suzerainty over the whole of Korea. This suzerainty of China in Korea following the eighth century was gradually widened with each change of dynasty in China. Finally, over a period of about six hundred years, ending in 1895,—that is, the period during which China was under the rule of the Mongol (Yuan), the Ming, and the Manchu (Ching) dynasties,—actual sovereign and tributary relationships were established between China and Korea. Especially during the Ming dynasty and the greater part of the Manchu dynasty, Korea considered it a great national honor to be a tributary state of so superior a nation as China. In those days, Korea and Japan maintained international relations on an equal footing. Notwithstanding that this is a well-established historical fact, most Occidental historians seem to believe that, prior to 1895, Korea was under the joint suzerainty of Japan and China. Some of these Occidental scholars have made statements in the histories they have written to the effect that the struggle between China and Japan in 1894 was centered around the question of their respective sovereign rights in Korea. Other scholars have stated clearly that the immediate cause of the Sino-Japanese War was the relationship of the two powers to Korea and that Korea was a kingdom over which both China and Japan claimed suzerainty.[43] In actual fact, none of the Chinese, Japanese, or Korean histories contains any record to the effect that Korea was tributary to Japan after the middle of the seventh century.[44]

CHAPTER II

National Unification and International Relations of China, Japan, and Korea (Seventh to Fourteenth Centuries)

THE SEVENTH CENTURY was an epoch-making period in the Orient. In this century, China, Japan, and Korea completed their national unification and reorganization. This activity was occasioned by the rise of the great T'ang dynasty in China. The rise of China in the seventh century affected other nations in the Orient just as later the rise of Japan was to do in the twentieth century. China, Japan, and Korea are so closely connected geographically, intellectually, and politically that the rise of either China or Japan always affects the other two, and small, weak Korea, the military roadway between the two greater powers, always suffers when supremacy in the Orient is transferred from one to the other.

For two hundred years, beginning in the fifth century, China was in chaos resulting from a series of domestic and foreign wars. On many occasions, the wild tribes of the north and internal rebel bands established kingdoms in China, thus dividing her into several independent states. National unification was finally effected by the Sui dynasty in 589, but, unfortunately, it was short-lived. In 618, the great House of T'ang arose. China entered upon a new national existence and soon became the greatest intellectual, military, and political center in the Orient. The T'ang government was recognized by all the surrounding nations, and its superiority was respected. This rise of the T'ang in China had immediate effects upon Japan and Korea.

Up to that time—some recapitulation here may help the reader to synthesize the situation—Korea had never been a single state, but had long been divided into separate kingdoms and separate states. In the latter part of the sixth century, the kingdom of Shinra, which was rapidly gaining power in the peninsula, began to foster an ambitious plan. She undertook a military campaign in southern Korea with the hope of destroying the kingdoms and states there and of driving the Japanese out of Korea. She was successful, but with the progress of the campaign Shinra realized that she could not accomplish her ends without military aid from the outside. It was at this time that China became a united nation and decided to extend her authority into northern Korea. This common interest of China and Shinra brought the two nations together.[1] In the second half of the seventh century, the joint armies of Shinra and the T'ang destroyed the kingdoms of Kudara and Korai after having annihilated the military forces of Japan in Korea. Thus, in the seventh century, for the first time in her history, Korea became a united nation.[2] Moreover, it was the first time that China's supremacy had extended over the entire peninsula.

As for Japan, during the reigns of the first nine emperors this country remained in seclusion, barely maintaining an existence in Yamato and surrounding districts in the central part of Honshu, the entire area of which covered but a few hundred square miles.[3] In the reigns of the tenth, eleventh, and twelfth emperors, Japan gradually entered upon a period of national expansion. The domain of the empire was greatly increased, the authority of the emperor being extended over nearly the entire southwestern half of the island of Honshu.

Seimu, the thirteenth emperor, ruled Japan for sixty-one years, peaceably and wisely. He directed all his energy to domestic administration and the amalgamation of the old Japanese homeland and the newly conquered districts.[4] When the Emperor Chuai ascended the throne as the fourteenth sovereign of Japan, as a result of the long, peaceful administration of the Emperor Seimu the empire was firmly established and the national wealth and strength had been greatly aug-

mented. Therefore, in the beginning of the reign of the
Emperor Chuai, Japan was both militarily and financially
strong enough to proceed with a new national undertaking.
The need was awaiting the opportunity. Because of the remarkable increase of the population, national expansion
seemed imperative, and it became a great national problem
in Japan whether to expand westward and annex Kyushu, or
to expand eastward and conquer the northeastern half of Honshu so that the whole of this main island might be under the
imperial rule. In one direction it would be necessary for Japan
to wage war upon the Ainu, in the other direction upon the
Kumaso. The Ainu was by far the more powerful of these two
tribes. The northeastern half of Honshu, and Yezo and the
other northern islands under the control of the Ainu, although
extensive, were barren and cold. Moreover, to wage war
against the Ainu would be more difficult and dangerous than
to wage war against the Kumaso. Kyushu, the homeland of the
Kumaso, was mild in climate, possessed a fertile soil, and
would provide an ideal place for the overflow of Japan's population. But Kyushu is separated from Korea only by a narrow
strip of water, and for centuries the Kumaso in Kyushu had
been friendly with the Koreans in southern Korea. The real
strength of Kumaso therefore lay in the fact that she could
readily get military aid from a rich kingdom in southern
Korea.[5] Unless Japan should first establish her authority in
Korea, she would not be able to conquer the Kumaso and
annex Kyushu. In the time of the Emperor Chuai, Korea, the
reader will remember, was divided into three small kingdoms
and several separate states, and quite unable to present a
united front against Japan. China was likewise divided into
many separate states; and furthermore, she was invaded time
and again by wild tribes from the north, and was therefore
in no position to interfere with Japan's military undertakings in Korea.[6] These conditions in eastern Asia invited Japan
to extend her power into Korea. So it came about, under these

special circumstances, that Japan extended her authority to the Asiatic continent before she had brought the whole of Japan proper under her rule. According to Japanese history, Japan's first conquest of a Korean kingdom took place in 200 A.D. Modern historians, however, are agreed that this notable event took place either in the latter part of the fourth or in the early part of the fifth century. In the fifth and sixth centuries, she continued her successes in the Korean peninsula and became a recognized ruling power in southern Korea. At the same time, in accordance with the original plan, the Kumaso were conquered and Kyushu was made an integral part of the Japanese empire.

In the seventh century, the unification of China was completed. About the middle of the seventh century, the Japanese power in Korea was completely wiped out by the joint forces of the T'ang and Shinra, and Korea became a single state under the rule of Shinra. The defeat of the Japanese arms in Korea in 663 was so decisive and her military situation there became so hopeless that, as we have seen, no other course was open to her except to abandon entirely her traditional suzerainty over Korea.[7] She wisely made it her policy, however, to maintain friendly relations with China. She did more: she reaped benefit for herself through the introduction and adoption of the T'ang method of organization in accomplishing certain domestic reforms in Japan.

With respect to the war in Korea, from the very beginning Japan had neither cause nor ambition to take up arms against the T'ang. Unfortunate circumstances, however, forced her to do so. After the destruction of the kingdom of Kudara, Japan had neither obligation nor military strength to continue the war in Korea. Japan, at that time, was in the midst of a great national transformation (see p. 28) in which China and the T'ang civilization were the dominating influence. Japan needed at this time the aid of China,[8] not war with her.

As for China's position, the T'ang sent troops to Korea for

the sole purpose of making it possible for Shinra to unify Korea. The military clash with Japan in Korea was only a side issue. Furthermore, as is evidenced by history, China has always been a peace-loving nation. In her imperial days, what China wanted was not territorial gain but supremacy over neighboring nations so that they would revere the imperial throne and maintain a safe and quiet national existence under the protection of China. After the war in Korea in the seventh century, which ended in the crushing defeat of Japan, the T'ang emperor had no desire to carry his victories farther;[9] on the contrary, he showed a strong inclination to continue friendly relations with Japan. Even before the unification of Korea was effected, he twice sent envoys to Japan to let Japan know that he would not carry hostilities to that country. He did this in a most dignified and impressive manner.[10] When his envoy went to Japan in 665, the party consisted of 254 persons. The second envoy went to Japan in 669 with a party of more than 2000 persons. Japan took advantage of this attitude of the T'ang emperor and sent an envoy in return to show due reverence to the imperial throne of China.[11]

The war of 663 did not disturb the friendly international relations between Japan and China. The latter showed magnanimity, and the former made ready submission. When Japan withdrew from Korea she retained Kyushu. Her ruling power at home in Japan, however, scarcely covered the southern half of the chain of the Japan Islands, and the northern half was under the control of the Ainu.[12] Pursuing her purpose of effecting national unification, Japan now planned to drive the Ainu from at least the northeastern half of Honshu, and thus to make Kyushu, Shikoku, and Honshu (which are now known as Japan Proper) the domain of the empire of Japan. The Ainu were a courageous and physically powerful tribe and possessed, in addition, great numerical strength. From the seventh century on, successful military campaigns were conducted against them, but the ambitious undertaking of conquering the whole of Japan Proper was not accomplished until the close of the ninth century.

Although the military campaigns against the Ainu proved slow and dangerous undertakings, the national transformation was successfully accomplished; not, however, through a natural demand of the people, but rather forced upon the people by the government and the ruling class. In those days, every new thing and every new idea that appeared in China, bad as well as good, was seized and introduced into Japan. To the Japanese in the seventh and eighth centuries, this seemed the quickest and surest way to uplift their nation. This period lasted about two hundred years, beginning in the seventh century; it is known in Japanese history as *Tosei Mobo-Jidai* ("The Period of Imitation and of the Copying of the Ideas, Methods, and Organization of the T'ang"—that is, of China and of things Chinese).[13]

The imperial government and all the local governments under its control, together with the methods of national administration, were completely reorganized simply by duplicating those of the T'ang in China. The organization of cities and towns was likewise modeled after that in China. Chinese customs and manners, even to dwellings and garments, were introduced into Japan. Finally, an attempt was made to replace the Japanese language by the Chinese classical language, and it was made a national regulation that all official communications, documents, and histories should be written in Chinese. Moreover, in addition to sending young Japanese to educational institutions in China, Japan decided to provide some educational facilities at home in Japan. So schools and colleges modeled on those in China were established in Japan. The curricula were composed exclusively of Chinese subjects, such as Chinese Composition, Chinese Classics, Chinese History, and Chinese Philosophy; no Japanese subjects were included. The Civil Service examinations were all conducted in Chinese and were on Chinese subjects.

In 645, the Laws and Statutes of Japan were completed. They were not only exact copies of those of China; they were written, moreover, in the Chinese language exclusively.[14] In 650, China revised her laws and codes; in 670, Japan revised her laws and codes to embody the new ideas adopted in China. China again made revisions of her laws and codes in 664, in 681, and in 686; Japan likewise revised her laws and codes in 681, in 701, and in 717. Thus each revision of the national laws and codes in Japan was made after changes and modifications had been made in the laws and codes of China.

It has already been told how, in 607, when Japan sent her first envoy to China, she assumed an equal national standing with China. In state papers, the title of "Emperor" was used for the ruler of Japan as well as for the ruler of China. However, after Japan had entered the Period of the Imitation of China and of Things Chinese, she abandoned this assumption of equality, discontinued the use in state papers of the title "Emperor" for the ruler of Japan, and gave full recognition to the supremacy of China. She even depended solely upon China's example in her attempt to develop as a nation.

Nevertheless, Japan considered that it would be a great national disgrace were a state paper to be written with a humility acceptable to the T'ang government; or in the same way as papers sent by tributary nations, such as Korea, in which the title of "Emperor" was given to the ruler of China, and the title of "King" to the ruler of the tributary country.[15] So, making the best of the situation, Japan sent her envoy to China without providing him with any state papers.[16] China, however, gave the envoys from Japan the same treatment that she extended to envoys from countries ranked as tributary states. Often there were handed to the Japanese envoys Chinese state papers in which the title of "Emperor" was used for the Chinese ruler and that of "King" for the ruler of Japan, with its implication that Japan was a nation tributary to China. The Japanese envoys not only made no objections, they humbly accepted the papers; but, upon returning to Japan, they never presented these papers to the imperial throne. These Chinese state papers therefore never became national documents. It is an important fact in the history of Japan that there are no entries regarding the exchange of state papers by China and Japan in the medieval period, despite the fact that a number of envoys were sent from Japan to China within that period.[17] Some historians declare, however, that no matter what attitude or precautions were taken by Japan in her international dealings with China in those days, it is undeniable that envoys sent by Japan to China were of tributary capacity.[18]

In summary of Japan's national development to the eighth century, it may now be said that prior to the fifth century, when Japan came into contact with Korea, she was a military nation without any elements of civilization. During the fifth and sixth centuries, the country came under the intellectual influence of Korea and of Korean émigrés to Japan. In those centuries, if Japan had anything worthy of the name of civilization, it was to be attributed to Korean efforts. In the seventh century, Japan came into contact with China and entered the Period of Imitation of China and of Things Chinese.[19] She made noteworthy progress both intellectually and industrially. But the Japanese civilization of that time was merely a transplantation of Chinese civilization. Soon Japan began to suffer by reason of the corruption induced by this continental civilization. Luxury, effeminacy, idleness, and even licentiousness gradually undermined her national life. The emperors took less and less interest in national affairs,[20] and at last began to delegate all military authority to the more powerful families.

At this point in the national development the Fujiwara family rose to power. It became inseparably related to the imperial family and finally not the military authority alone but all imperial authority was delegated to it. So matters stood at the beginning of the eighth century. In the middle of the eighth century, the forty-fifth emperor, Shomu, married a daughter of the Fuji-

wara and made her his empress. This was a most unusual event
in Japan. It had been an inviolable unwritten law that no
woman could be empress unless she were a princess of the imperial blood. This tradition had been faithfully adhered to in
order to prevent the sacred blood of the imperial family from
being polluted by that of families that could not claim direct
descent from the Sun Goddess.[21] After the Emperor Shomu
had violated this sacred tradition and had thus set a new prece-
dent, the Fujiwara became a family especially privileged to be
empress-providers. Over a period of twelve hundred years up
to the present time, seventy-eight emperors have ascended the
throne; sixty-three of these, including Hirohito, the present
emperor, have had daughters of the Fujiwara for mothers.
This union of the imperial family brought about the political
ascendancy of the Fujiwara. Because of the marriage relationship, the head of the Fujiwara was virtually always either the
father-in-law or the grandfather of the ruling emperor. In such
capacity, the Fujiwara began to conduct national affairs in the
name of the emperor. It soon became an inviolable tradition
that (1) the empress and the court ladies who were eligible to
be imperial consorts must be of the Fujiwara blood;[22] (2) the
crown prince must be an imperial prince who had a Fujiwara
mother;[23] and (3) whether the emperor on the throne were an
infant or a man of maturity, he was obliged to have the head
of the Fujiwara as his regent. In this way, for nearly two hundred years, beginning in the tenth century, Japan was under
the rule of the Fujiwara regency.[24]

As the Fujiwara began to feel their power, they found it
embarrassing to have a grown man on the throne who might
ask a question or two with respect to national affairs. They
therefore established a new custom; namely, the ruling emperor should abdicate the throne almost immediately after a
son was born to him by a daughter of the Fujiwara, in favor
of the infant.[25] When barely beyond the age of childhood, the
young emperor was provided with Fujiwara daughters to be

either empress or consorts. As soon as he begot a son, the emperor was advised to follow the example of his father and abdicate the throne. In those days, it was the essential duty of the emperor to marry a daughter of the Fujiwara and to become a father. If he failed to have a son, he was advised to abdicate the throne in favor of an infant brother who had a Fujiwara mother. At the height of the power of the Fujiwara regency, the imperial throne was generally occupied by infants. Two or three, or even four or five retired emperors, none of whom was beyond his prime, sometimes were living at the same time. They usually spent their lives in the quiet of Buddhist monasteries.

Under the Fujiwara regency, Japan began to develop intellectually and industrially somewhat independently of Chinese civilization. However, the development of that period (the tenth and eleventh centuries) was confined to the capital city and its surrounding districts, rather than being nation-wide. City dwellers enjoyed a high degree of civilization, but dwellers in the provincial districts still lived as their forefathers had in primitive times. Naturally, with the progress of the nation, the gap between the country and the city districts widened; neither the country nor the city dwellers sympathized with or understood each other. Strange though it may seem, the advance of civilization in Japan gradually brought about disintegration in the nation.

The administration of the Fujiwara aggravated this situation. Theirs was an exceedingly selfish family; it had no ambition to rule the nation well, but thought only of self-aggrandizement. All government positions of any importance were monopolized by members of the Fujiwara.[26] The imperial capital (Kyoto), although the center of national civilization, was also a city of luxury and pleasure-seeking. Since only in Kyoto was civilized living possible, all the Fujiwara officials managed to reside in Kyoto. Soon, even the governors of the provinces ceased to go to the provinces that they administered, but sent deputies and themselves enjoyed luxurious ease in Kyoto.[27] Finally, the military officers likewise remained in Kyoto instead of going to their military stations. Everything was left to underlings. The high officials gathered the taxes from provincial districts without making any return in service. The people in the provinces, forced to support an idle horde of Fujiwara officials without receiving any benefit therefrom, suffered by reason of the ever-increasing taxation. Their condition became so unbearable that numbers of them left their homes and joined bands of brigands or pirates, so as to free themselves from government bondage.

The Fujiwara administration thus unwittingly became responsible for the rise of new and forceful elements in the empire. With the complete monopoly of government posts by the Fujiwara, men of education and ability could not get positions unless they had Fujiwara blood. Now in those days, the Fujiwara as well as the emperor were devoted Buddhists, and Buddhism exerted great influence over people of all classes. Buddhism was a religion based originally upon a principle of equality, with entire disregard of both rank and blood, and the Buddhist Church afforded opportunity to all to rise in accordance with their attainments and abilities. So persons who were ambitious and disappointed because they could not obtain government appointments began to enter the Buddhist ministry,[28] and the Buddhist Church became the center of intelligence and learning. Even the Fujiwara, when confronted by difficult national problems, always sought assistance from the Buddhist Church. Consequently, the Buddhist Church became a great political, as well as religious, power in Japan.

Persons of genius and ability, even including princes of the royal blood, provided they were strong physically, began to leave the capital for provincial districts, where they reclaimed the wilderness and became owners of great tracts of land. These new landowners, fresh from their contact with civilization in the imperial capital, were, as a rule, men of ability as well as of aristocratic blood, and they soon became centers of respect and authority among the poverty-stricken people by whom they were surrounded. These people were glad to offer them their services, and with the steadily growing numbers of these self-invited tillers of the soil, the landowners extended repeatedly their estates thus reclaimed. In the course of time, the relationship of lord and serf developed from that of land-owner and tenant farmer,[20] and the pioneers of the wilderness became local magnates of influence and power. The Fujiwara as well as the imperial government foresaw a danger in this newly risen power in the provincial districts, and the government repeatedly decreed, though quite ineffectively. that the people should not disgrace themselves by becoming serfs of local landowners.

As a result of the century of maladministration under the Fujiwara, the nation became increasingly disorderly. Pirates infested the sea; brigands ravaged the land.[30] The brigands established headquarters here and there wherever there was a geographical advantage. They swooped down upon villages and cities, plundering as they went. The Fujiwara were entirely powerless to give any protection to the suffering people. In easy, licentious living they had lost all their fighting spirit and strength, and could devise no means of coping with the marauders. It became necessary for all landowners to provide their tenant farmers with military weapons; also, in order to meet the ever-increasing peril from bandits, the landowners augmented their fighting forces. Before long, every landowner was a military power in his own district, and the mass of the people came to regard the landlords as their sole source of protection against the bandits. To the care of the landlords they entrusted their property and the welfare of their families, and soon, in all parts of Japan, there was to be noted the rise of numerous military families.

At first, the brigands operated only in the provincial districts, but after the weakness and helplessness of the govern-

ment became apparent, they extended their operations even
into the capital city.[31] In the eleventh century, the great mansions of the Fujiwara and even those of the imperial family
were not spared. Since neither the government nor the Fujiwara had either military or police power sufficient to protect
themselves or their property, the Fujiwara requested the private military families in the provincial districts to proceed to
Kyoto and to station their fighting men in that city, and both
the Fujiwara and the imperial government were completely
dependent upon these military families. Nevertheless, the
Fujiwara were able to use these military men to serve their
own ends, for the following reason. The military men in the
provinces were descendants of men who had left Kyoto because
of their disappointment in not obtaining official positions. But
these descendants had inherited the desire of their ancestors
for official position, a desire which became stronger as their
wealth and power increased in the provincial districts. So this
was the situation in the eleventh century: all the military families in the provincial districts which had fighting strength,
coveted official titles; the Fujiwara lacked military strength,
but had complete control of official appointments: and so the
Fujiwara and the military families found it mutually advanta-
geous each to supply the other's needs.

The military men from the provincial districts began their
service in the capital as bodyguards of a sort to the leading
Fujiwara, but their function was not confined to this family
service. The national chaos was increasing, and as local uprisings became more frequent either the military men in Kyoto
or others who still remained in the provincial districts were
requested to proceed to the seat of disturbance and suppress
the uprisings. Thus the military men gradually became figures
of national power and dignity, and finally the Fujiwara began
to ask them to help settle their personal quarrels. After the
Fujiwara in their rise to power in the tenth century had succeeded in either destroying or exiling all the powerful rival

families that opposed them, and had secured a firm monopoly of government positions, rivalry sprang up among themselves. It started with the problem of whose daughters should be the empress and the imperial consorts. Disputes and disagreements developed ill feeling and enmity. In the middle of the eleventh century, the regency and other high government positions became bones of contention, even between brothers and between fathers and sons.[32] Sometimes, they went so far as to appeal to arms to settle their disputes. The once powerful Fujiwara families were greatly weakened by this internal strife, and toward the close of the eleventh century the control of the imperial government was rapidly slipping from their hands.

Taking advantage of the change in national conditions, the retired emperors living in the Buddhist monasteries began to hold a sort of imperial court and to take up important national questions. Gradually they encroached upon the imperial authority delegated to the regency, and finally they demanded that the work of the actual imperial court should be placed under their control on the ground that the infant emperor on the throne should respect the findings and advice of his father rather than that of his Fujiwara father-in-law.[33] The Fujiwara lacked power to dispute the demand of the retired emperors, and thus, although they were nominally permitted to retain the regency, as well as other government offices, they became mere figureheads, like the emperor on the throne.

The monastic rule of the retired emperors lasted for about three-quarters of a century, ending in the latter part of the twelfth century, but it was no better than that of the Fujiwara. The retired emperors lived, it is true, in Buddhist monasteries, but they did not adhere to Buddhist rites and practices. On the contrary, they were usually surrounded by young women and led lives of luxury and licentiousness. Most of these retired emperors, after abdicating, raised new families. When a son was born to a favorite woman, the retired emperor generally attempted to force the ruling emperor to abdicate the throne

in favor of this infant son.[34] Sometimes, in the event of the
death of the ruling emperor, two retired emperors would each
present a son as candidate for the throne. Indeed, during the
monastic rule, succession to the throne was a matter of serious
dispute, even to the point of military struggle and bloodshed.

The retired emperors, however, like the Fujiwara, had no
military forces. They, too, were obliged to ask the military
families in the provincial districts to come to the capital and
fight for their cause.[35] No matter which side won, each struggle
for the imperial cause resulted in the ascendancy of one military family or another. During the Fujiwara regency, there
were numerous military families in the provincial districts of
Japan, but as a rule they were not on friendly terms and so
they lacked unity. It was the policy of the Fujiwara, when a
military family became independent and arrogant, to pit some
other family against it, thus lessening the fighting strength of
both. In the beginning of the twelfth century, the families
known as the Taira and the Minamoto emerged as the two pre-
eminent military powers. Both of these families had originally
been founded by imperial princes who had become landowners in the provincial districts and, later, military leaders. Because of their imperial blood, the Taira and the Minamoto
were the most distinguished, and with their gradual ascendancy all the minor military families in the various provinces
gathered under the standard of either the one or the other.
So it came about that the entire fighting strength of Japan was
controlled by these two military families.

By the middle of the twelfth century Japan was completely
dependent for military strength upon the aid of either the
Taira or the Minamoto. Naturally, the rivalry between these
two military families became more intense, and upon any opportunity, whether in their own cause or in that of either the
imperial family or the Fujiwara, they plunged readily into
bloody struggle. In the early twelfth century several battles
were fought between the Taira and the Minamoto, with vary-

ing success on either side. In the middle of the twelfth century
there arose a serious national problem in respect to the succession to the imperial throne. In this, both the imperial family
and the Fujiwara were peculiarly involved. The Taira and the
Minamoto had to fight for these respective parties, and the
side taken by the Taira won a decisive victory. All the leaders
of the Minamoto were killed in battle, or captured and put to
death, or exiled. Their followers were scattered and the existence of the Minamoto as a fighting unit was ended. As rivals,
it had been the sole aim and ambition of the Taira and the
Minamoto to gain the imperial favor, each one hoping thus
to become superior to the other. The Minamoto having been
destroyed, the Taira became the unrivaled power in the empire, not only militarily but also politically.[36] Where there is
strength, there is power. Shirakawa II, the only living retired
emperor, could no longer retain control of national affairs,
and, like the emperor on the throne and the Fujiwara regent,
he became only a figurehead.

Kiyomori, the head of the Taira, was a man of ambition and
genius. Patterning after the Fujiwara,[37] he accomplished within
a decade what it had taken the Fujiwara more than a century
to bring about.[38] The emperor was obliged to take as his empress a daughter of Kiyomori. Immediately upon the birth of
a son to her, the emperor was advised to abdicate the throne
in favor of the infant, and Kiyomori became the grandfather
of the ruling emperor and the prime minister of the empire.
Soon, because of Kiyomori's high-handed policy and his ex-
cessive power, the Taira became the object of jealousy and
hatred. Like the Fujiwara, the Taira occupied all offices of any
importance in the imperial court, and within less than a quarter-century all the Taira became addicted to luxury and extravagance and lost not only their strength but even their will
to fight.

Encouraged by the increasing unpopularity and weakened
military condition of the Taira, the widely scattered Minamoto

family gathered its strength together and rose against the Taira
in various parts of Japan. In a series of successful battles, the
Taira were driven from Kyoto to wander from one part of
Japan to another until finally the entire Taira family was
annihilated in a decisive naval battle fought in 1185. The
ascendancy of the Minamoto was supreme. It was marked by
the introduction of feudalism into Japan,[39] although a formal,
feudal government was not completely organized until 1192,
when the emperor appointed Yoritomo, the head of the Minamoto, to the office of shogun.

Feudalism brought about the second fundamental national
transformation of Japan. The feudal government of Japan is
unique in the world's history. It was called the Dual Form of
Government because both the imperial government and the
feudal-military government, or shogunate, coexisted throughout the Feudal Period. It may be more properly spoken of as
the military representative form of government because the
emperor always requested the military men, who controlled
both the military situation in Japan and the military families,
to rule the empire in his stead.

The head of the imperial family was the emperor (the mikado), and the head of the shogunate was usually known as
the shogun. The emperor was the object of national honor and
respect; the shogun was the representative of administrative
authority.[40] However, the shogun was subject to the emperor,
who alone had the right to confer the title of shogun, although
he could not select the man who should be the shogun. Moreover, after the shogun was once appointed, the emperor had
absolutely no power over him; he could neither remove the
shogun nor request him to resign; he could neither issue instructions to the shogun nor demand explanations from him.
The emperor had to appoint as shogun the head of the military
family that controlled all the feudal lords and other military
men in the empire, who would, it was assumed, in the capacity
of shogun, be able to organize the shogunate, that is, the feudal-

military government. As long as a particular family was able
to maintain the military supremacy in the empire of Japan, the
emperor had to appoint as shogun the head of the newly risen
family, generation after generation. If a new military family
rose to power and overthrew the ruling military family, the
emperor had to appoint as shogun the head of the newly risen
military family. The emperor nominally reigned over the empire, but the shogun was the real ruler. With the sole exception
of the power of conferring official titles, the emperor had to
entrust to the shogun all authority over affairs of state, including civil, military, financial, and diplomatic affairs. In Japan
throughout the Feudal Period, the power was in the hands of
the shogun. The only thing that the shogun could not do was
to appoint his successor, but he could nominate a man to succeed him. Thus deprived of all authority and power, the emperor was always placed above all political and military strife,
and, as feudalism developed, the imperial throne was more
and more revered as sacred and inviolable. It is still a sacred
national tradition that the throne shall be kept aloof from national change and disturbance.⁸

The Feudal Period in Japan lasted for nearly seven hundred
years, having begun in 1192 and terminated in 1867. It is identified with the successive rise and fall of five military families,
who founded, after bloody military struggles, five feudal-
military governments, known as the Kamakura shogunate
(1192–1333), the Ashikaga shogunate (1338–1573), the Oda
Period (not a shogunate; 1574–1582); the Toyotomi Period
(not a shogunate; 1585–1600); and the Tokugawa shogunate
(1603–1867).

In the twelfth century, Kyoto, which had been the imperial
capital of Japan for more than five hundred years, was the center of civilization, and of luxury and licentiousness as well.
The imperial government and the nation as a whole were corrupt and degenerate. Any leader, any authority established in
Kyoto, always became a victim of that city's vice. None could

hold his own. Yoritomo, the founder of the first feudal-military government (the Kamakura shogunate) therefore selected for his military capital Kamakura, in the "Wild East" of Japan three hundred miles from Kyoto.[42] There, in a new environment, he started a new sort of national life. Simplicity, frugality, self-respect, straightforwardness, and the holding of the interests of the state and the interests of their lord above their own constituted the virtue of the military men of the Feudal Period. Loyalty and strict military discipline were required of them, and consideration and kindness were always shown to the mass of the people. Prompt attention to the affairs of the people and the meting out of justice were the aim and practice of the government. The Kamakura shogunate thus provided an admirable administration and thereby gained nation-wide support and gratitude.

From the middle of the seventh century, when the Emperor Tenchi abandoned Korea and changed the national policy from one of expansion abroad to one of domestic unification and national betterment, down into the thirteenth century, Japan had looked upon China as her guide and tutor, and she long remained in the merely imitative stage. After the introduction of feudalism in the thirteenth century, Japan became intellectually and politically independent. Her laws and codes were greatly simplified so as to meet the needs of the people, and the government was organized in conformity with the life and intellectual status of the nation.

As for international relations with China, throughout the entire period of the T'ang, which began in the seventh century, Japan sent envoys to China continuously and showed the greatest reverence to the T'ang imperial throne. In 884, Michizane, who was the most distinguished scholar and statesman of his time, was appointed the Japanese envoy to China. At that time, the T'ang dynasty was nearing its end. Japan was accordingly informed that China was just entering upon a period of great national disturbance and that, in consequence,

Japan would no longer benefit by sending envoys and students. The imperial government of Japan therefore decided to discontinue the traditional custom of showing reverence to the throne of China,[43] and the newly appointed envoy and his party remained at home.

Twenty-two years later, in 906, the T'ang dynasty was overthrown and China fell into national chaos. In the short space of fifty-three years, five empires and twelve kingdoms rose and fell. Finally, in 960, the Sung came to rule China. This new dynasty maintained its existence for more than three hundred years, ending in 1279; but its rule was weak, its power was limited to China Proper, and its territory was continually invaded and encroached upon by Mongols and Tartars. The Sung dynasty was finally destroyed by Kublai Khan.

Throughout the rule of the Sung, Japanese students and traders crossed the water to China of their own accord, and Japan was thereby enabled to benefit from the newly developing Sung civilization in China. Nevertheless, Japan had no formal international relations with China. The Sung emperor, however, in order to show the superiority of China over Japan, on several occasions sent rich gifts to the emperor of Japan; and in some of the state papers of the Sung, the emperor of Japan was addressed as "You, the Chief of the Barbarian People in the East." Although Japan accepted the gifts sent by the Sung emperor, she never acknowledged any of the state papers. She would show that she was too dignified to acknowledge papers in which the Japanese emperor was addressed as "Chief of the Barbarian People of the East."[44]

In the thirteenth century, after Japan had entered upon the Feudal Period, China came under the rule of the Yuan (Mongol) dynasty. The new emperor, Kublai Khan, demanded that Japan recognize his superior power and send an envoy to show due reverence to his throne. Japan refused to comply with these demands and as a result she suffered from international controversy and warfare that lasted half a century.

As for Korea, for a period of approximately two hundred years after her unification in the seventh century, she enjoyed peace and prosperity under the rule of Shinra. Through all these years she sent envoys to China in recognition of China's superiority. Toward the close of the ninth century, the rule of Shinra began to decline. The new kingdoms of Korai and the Later Kudara were founded within the domains of the former kingdoms of Korai and Kudara, which had been destroyed in the seventh century. Thus, in the tenth century Korea was again divided into three kingdoms. In 935, the king of Shinra surrendered his ruling power to the king of Korai, and in the following year, the kingdom of Later Kudara was destroyed. In 936, Korea was again united under the rule of Korai.[45]

With the destruction of the T'ang dynasty, five short imperial dynasties rose and fell in China Proper. At the same time, powerful Tartar imperial dynasties came into existence in Mongolia and Manchuria, thus geographically separating China and Korea. This condition continued after the Sung dynasty came to rule China Proper, and for three hundred years, beginning in the tenth century, Korea sent tribute-bearing envoys to the imperial governments in Mongolia and Manchuria. At the same time, as has been noted, Korea sent envoys time and again to the Sung government in China Proper. In this way, by showing a dual loyalty to both the Chinese and the Tartar governments, Korea was able to maintain her national existence. In the middle of the thirteenth century, the Mongols destroyed the Tartar government. They also invaded and conquered the greater part of China Proper, after which the Sung government was barely able to maintain an existence in southern China. In 1271, the Mongols adopted the name "Yuan dynasty" and became the greatest ruling power in Asia. Korea was completely subjugated by the Mongols and maintained but a nominal existence. In addition to sending tribute to the Mongol throne, Korea was requested time and again by the Mongol emperors to contribute to the Mongol military undertakings against other nations. The crown prince of Korea was requested to reside in Peking. Most of these crown princes, generation after generation, were obliged to marry the daughters of Mongol emperors.[46] Moreover, the kings of Korea were permitted to ascend the throne solely by the consent of the Mongol emperors, and they were often forced to abdicate by orders from the same source.

It was at the time when this forced relationship obtained between the Mongols and Korea that Japan's national existence was threatened. Kublai Khan had been grossly misinformed with respect to affairs in Japan.[47] He believed that Japan was the wealthiest nation in the world, a nation teeming with gold and other treasure. He also thought that Japan was situated geographically very close to the Asiatic continent. He once told an envoy from Korea that if one should leave the continent in the morning, he could reach Japan in the evening, and that in sailing to Japan rice might be carried to eat but that fish could be easily caught.[48]

In 1266, Kublai Khan decided to reduce Japan to a tributary state. He sent an envoy provided with personal letters in which Kublai Khan intimated that he might appeal to arms should Japan fail to recognize his supremacy and imperial authority. This envoy and his party were ordered to proceed through Korea, and the king of Korea was instructed to provide guides and all necessary provisions.[49] In the spring of 1267, Kublai Khan's envoy, accompanied by the envoy of the king of Korea, sailed for Japan; but they were overtaken by a great storm and had to return to Korea without reaching their destination.[50] The king of Korea thereupon sent a special envoy to the court of Kublai Khan to advise him to abandon his plan of sending an envoy to Japan because in order to reach Japan it was necessary to cross millions of miles of water swept by storms and full of many other dangers.[51] Kublai Khan was greatly offended. He accused the king of Korea of making up this explanation filled with bombastic words, and was angered by his lack of sincerity and loyalty. Kublai Khan instructed the king of Korea to make all possible diplomatic connections with Japan so that his letter might be speedily sent to its king.[52] He further ordered the king of Korea to build a thousand large warships for military purposes. In 1268, accordingly, the king of Korea sent an envoy to Japan bearing the personal letter of Kublai Khan as well as a state paper from Korea to the ruler of Japan.[53]

Although the Korean envoy stayed in Japan for five months, he returned without having obtained either a reply to the letter or any explanation. In 1269, Kublai Khan again sent an envoy to Japan accompanied by an envoy from Korea with instructions to demand a reply to the letter sent in the preceding year. Failing to receive any satisfactory explanation, they took two Japanese as prisoners and carried them to China in order to prove to Kublai Khan that they had really been in Japan.[54] Kublai Khan received these Japanese kindly and facilitated their return home.

In December, 1270, Kublai Khan appointed a trusted statesman, Chao Liang-Pi, as his personal representative to Japan, and planned to send with him a military guard of three thousand men. Chao accepted the appointment but, in order to show a friendly feeling to Japan, Chao left Peking accompanied by but twenty-four followers. In September, 1271, he and his party, accompanied by the envoy of the Korean king, left Korea for Japan. Chao carried to Japan the second personal letter of Kublai Khan. Upon his arrival, he insisted that he would proceed to the national capital of Japan and there present the state papers in person to the "Ruler of Japan," but Chao was not permitted to do this. After long discussion, a copy of the original paper was sent first to Kamakura and then to Kyoto. Because Kublai Khan's letter contained undiplomatic terms and military threats, Japan refused to acknowledge it,[55] and both the Chinese and the Korean envoys were finally driven from Japan.

In 1273, Kublai Khan again sent Chao as his envoy to Japan, charged, also, with demanding an explanation with respect to the state paper sent to Japan in 1271. After a lengthy stay, Chao was obliged to leave Japan without having accomplished anything.[56] Upon his return to Peking, Chao had a long personal interview with Kublai Khan. He first gave a description of Japan, its climate, manners and customs, local products, and general conditions. In reply to an inquiry by Kublai Khan concerning the possible results of a military undertaking against Japan, Chao spoke as follows:

"I have stayed in Japan more than a year and have come to know that the Japanese are both a courageous and a bloodthirsty people, but that they do not know how to observe human relationships and the duties and obligations therein involved. The country is very mountainous and has an abundance of water. There is but little opportunity for either agricultural or industrial development. Even though we might subjugate the people, we should not be able to employ them in any beneficial way. Even though we should conquer the land, we could not make it productive. Moreover, there are insurmountable dangers in crossing the water to Japan. Therefore, to employ our nation and people for the sake of such a country as that of Japan would be similar to an attempt to fill a deep and vast valley by pouring into it our national treasure. I therefore earnestly beseech Your Majesty to give up the contemplated invasion of Japan."[57]

Kublai Khan, having for seven years planned and prepared to subjugate Japan, and having been successful in all his military and diplomatic undertakings hitherto, could not so easily give up his plans against Japan, a nation that had repeatedly driven away his envoys and had entirely disregarded his state papers. Finally, in the winter of 1274, Kublai Khan sent 900 war vessels to Japan with 25,000 men aboard. This immense naval force started from the Korean coast. Kublai Khan's army, which was made up of Mongols, Chinese, and Koreans, attacked and occupied almost all the islands in the Korean Channel. In a desperate military struggle lasting about two weeks, Kublai Khan's men won victory after victory and effected a landing on the coast of Kyushu. One morning, however, the entire army had disappeared. In the midst of their success, a great storm had arisen in the night and Kublai Khan's armada was broken in pieces, and half his men were drowned in the sea. The terror-stricken remnant hastily left Japan in the remaining ships and sailed to Korea.

This war was viewed quite differently by Japan and by Kublai Khan. Japan attributed the destruction of Kublai Khan's armada and the disaster to his army to divine intervention, and was convinced that a nation thus divinely protected could never be conquered by a foreign enemy.[58] After the war of 1274, both the government and the people were firm in the belief that the national honor and existence of Japan would be maintained by their fighting men, with divine aid. They awaited with calm confidence any future Mongol invasion.

As for Kublai Khan, he was informed by the returned military men that his 900 war vessels with 15,000 men aboard had defeated and routed Japanese forces 8000 strong on one occasion and 102,000 strong at another time, but that his imperial army, after ravaging, frightening, and destroying both the enemy forces and their land until the arrows were exhausted,[59] had been obliged to return home because of lack of preparation and equipment. Kublai Khan believed that the victory so brilliantly won must have convinced the Japanese of their hopeless military situation and that Japan would therefore readily recognize the authority of his empire.[60] In February, just three months after the return of his ships, he sent a trusted statesman named Tu Chung-Shih as an envoy to Japan, with instructions to establish tributary relations with that nation.

This envoy, also accompanied by an envoy sent by the king of Korea, arrived in Japan in April. Japan took most drastic action. She arrested both the envoys and their followers and beheaded them all.[61] In this way, Japan, confidently relying on divine protection, manifested her determination both to Kublai Khan and to her own people that the question pending should be decided only by appeal to arms. At this time, Kublai Khan had virtually conquered China Proper. In 1277 and again in 1279, Kublai Khan required that a letter to Japan should be written by the Sung general who had surrendered to him, in which the general must say that the Sung had been destroyed by the Mongols and that the same fate would come to Japan.[62] Japan was thus indirectly advised to recognize the authority of Kublai Khan in order to save her nation. Nevertheless, upon their arrival the envoys bearing these letters were likewise beheaded.[63] In 1279, the Sung dynasty was finally destroyed after having ruled China for more than three hundred years, marking the virtual completion of Kublai Khan's conquests on the Asiatic continent. In the following year, Kublai Khan was informed that Japan had beheaded both his envoy and the accompanying party, concerning whose fate he had worried for the past five years.[64] Kublai Khan thereupon decided to subjugate Japan by employing his entire military resources. The king of Korea and the rulers of other tributary states visited the court of Kublai Khan in person, pledged their loyalty, and placed their military forces at his disposal.[65]

In 1281, all the necessary preparations had been completed. Kublai Khan's great armada consisted of about 4500 large war vessels. It was in two divisions, one of which sailed from Korea and the other from Chiang-Nan, a district in China. Japan had been expecting this Mongol invasion for nearly a decade, and she had prepared for it in three ways, as follows: (1) a nationwide mobilization had been effected, thus giving military training to all able-bodied men;[66] (2) high stone walls had been built on all coasts approachable from the continent in order that the landing of the invaders might be prevented;[67] and (3) the entire nation was united and placed under divine protection, the grace of Heaven being invoked.[68]

On May 3, 1281, the first division of Kublai Khan's armada of 900 war vessels with 40,000 men aboard left the Korean coast. Upon reaching Japanese waters, they occupied most of the small Japanese islands. The Japanese on the main islands bravely defended their coasts, and the invaders spent two months on the water without achieving any marked success. Meanwhile, an epidemic broke out on the ships, thousands of men lost their lives, and the food was nearly exhausted. In July, the long-expected main division of the armada, 3500 war vessels carrying more than 100,000 men, which had sailed from the coast of China, finally joined the first division in Japanese waters. There followed a series of bloody battles between the Japanese on the land and the invaders on the sea. In the dead of night, hundreds of desperate Japanese sallied forth in small boats and succeeded in boarding the enemy's war vessels, where they engaged in hand-to-hand combat. The Japanese were fighting in the enemy's field, but this was the only course open to them as they had no war vessels. In general, the high stone walls along the coasts, in the building of which the Japanese had spent more than a decade, served their intended purpose. The men garrisoned behind them fought bravely and foiled every attempt at landing made by Kublai Khan's men.

While the outcome was still doubtful, on the last day of July, 1281, a vapor, supposedly sulphuric in composition, rose from all parts of the sea at once, the waters being overhung by heavy rain clouds. While Kublai Khan's men were wondering at this strange phenomenon, a strong southwest wind swept the entire coast. It continued to blow both day and night on August 1. When on the second day the storm had partly subsided, Kublai Khan's great armada was well-nigh a total wreck.[69] After a series of desperate struggles with the Japanese, whose courage was heightened by faith in divine assistance, Kublai Khan's men selected some 200 half-wrecked ships out of the original 4400 and returned to the continent. According

to Chinese and Korean historical records, of the more than
100,000 men who had left the Chinese coast in the main division of the armada, but three individuals returned to China.[70]
Sung-Lien, a famous Chinese historian of the time, gave a
detailed account of this disaster in the *Imperial Authorized
Edition of the History of the Yuan Dynasty*, in which one reads
the statement:

"On August 1, 1281, a great storm crushed and destroyed
the armada. Wen-Hu and other leading generals selected the
strongest of the half-wrecked ships and sailed for China, thus
deserting troops to the number of one hundred thousand who
had left the coast of China with them in the main division of
the armada. These abandoned troops requested a man named
Chang Pai-Hu to be their leader. Under his direction, they
felled trees and began to build ships in the hope of being able
to return home. On the 7th day of August, the Japanese came
to the island and attacked and killed most of them, the remaining twenty to thirty thousand being taken prisoners. They
were taken to a place called Hakata, where all who were Chinese, Koreans, or Mongols were killed. Only the lives of the
men of the Sung, who had been forced to join the Mongol
forces after the destruction of the Sung dynasty, were spared."[71]

The first division of the armada, 900 vessels with 40,000
men, which had sailed from the Korean coast, encountered
this same great storm. Although ships and men were almost
all of them lost, they fared better than those in the second
division. The destruction of Kublai Khan's armada is the most
complete disaster recorded in world history. It is the only
instance in which the term "annihilation" can be used in its
real sense. The account of the armada of Kublai Khan, its
preparation, strength, and final destruction as given in the
records of Japan agrees in all essentials with the records of
both China and Korea.

Kublai Khan's invasion of 1281 was the culmination of thirteen years of international controversy and military threats,

during which Japan had continuously expected a serious national calamity. Throughout this period all the native and Buddhistic deities were invoked and their divine protection and revelations besought. The national temple at Ise, where the Sun Goddess was worshiped, became the center of national devotion and reliance. It was not strange, after a great storm destroyed Kublai Khan's armada in 1274 and again in 1281, that the nation and the people believed that the great winds had been sent in response to their prayers. These winds are known in Japanese history as *Ise no Kamikaze* or *Shinpu* ("the Divine Wind from Ise Sent by the Sun Goddess"). Ever since this destruction of Kublai Khan's armada by the divine wind in the thirteenth century, it has been the national belief that Japan is a divinely protected nation and that she can never be conquered by a foreign power. So strongly are the people imbued with this faith that there is absolute national confidence in the ultimate success and justification of all her causes and claims in any dealings with foreign nations.[72]

The annihilation of Kublai Khan's armada and of his troops in Japanese waters in 1281 was the first great military disaster that the Mongol empire had suffered since it was founded by Genghis Khan. Unless Japan were crushed, therefore, Mongol prestige and dignity would be lost on the continent, especially in China, that country having been conquered only a few years earlier. Immediately upon receipt of the disastrous news, therefore, Kublai Khan prepared for a third invasion on a far larger scale. In 1282, he ordered that 3000 large war vessels be built. The king of Korea voluntarily offered to build 150 war vessels for the same purpose.[73] In 1283, Korea was ordered to gather all needed provisions and to muster tens of thousands of men to be trained for naval service. It was planned to complete the preparation for the third invasion by August of that year.[74] The plan for this new invasion was so extensive, the military requisitions were so heavy, and the mustering of men was so strictly carried out that local uprisings broke out here and there in various parts of the empire and Kublai Khan was forced temporarily to abandon his campaign of revenge.[75] The local governments were accordingly permitted to discontinue building the war vessels.

Kublai Khan now conceived the idea that, because Japan was a Buddhistic nation, she might be induced to send tribute through the influence of prominent Buddhist priests. On two different occasions, he sent eminent Chinese Buddhist priests and their parties to Japan, provided with his personal letters, but storms prevented them from reaching their destination.[76]

In 1285, Kublai Khan again prepared to invade Japan. He first established a new administrative office called the "Department for the Invasion of Japan," which was charged with the supervision of all matters connected with the invasion. All large ships were confiscated from private owners both in China and in other parts of the empire. In addition to the great number of war vessels built by Kublai Khan's government, the king of Korea was commanded to build 650 vessels and to train 10,000 men for naval service.[77] It was planned that by August, 1288, everything would be ready for the third invasion.

In China, special war taxes were levied and various kinds of military requisitions were made. The people thereby suffered greatly. Finally, the governors of the various provinces appealed to the central government and asked that the condition of the people be taken into consideration. Because of the military campaigns against Japan in both the past and the present, they stated, the people had suffered extremely, and the affairs of the local governments had become greatly confused. When, in the spring of the preceding year, the government had announced the abandonment of the military campaign against Japan, the people had been so relieved that their exclamations of joy had resounded like thunder from district to district. Now that the government had renewed the preparations for a third campaign against Japan, all classes of people, including farmers, merchants, and artisans, had been obliged to give up their lines of work and prepare for military service.[78] The poor had deserted their homes to seek places of safety. The rich had exhausted their wealth in meeting the continuous demands of the government.

In 1286, Liu Hsuan, an eminent Chinese statesman, presented a memorial to the throne, appealing to Kublai Khan and noting that recently the government had reëstablished the "Department for the Invasion of Japan" and had begun to engage diligently in preparations for a campaign against Japan. He continued:

"This state of affairs has serious bearing on the welfare of the nation and even upon the very existence of our empire. . . . Japan is separated by millions of miles of sea and ocean from China. Even though our troops might reach that country without encountering destructive storms, nevertheless, because Japan has extensive territory and a teeming population, our fighting men might be surrounded. If our troops should once be defeated, how could they receive reënforcements? Our army on the continent certainly cannot fly across the waters to Japan. In preceding generations, the Sui invaded Korea with disastrous results to themselves. The T'ang emperor, Tai-Tsung, the greatest military genius of his time, personally commanded his immense army and invaded Korea. Although he gained initial success, he finally abandoned regretfully his campaign. Despite the fact that Korea is a nation not far from China, both the Sui and the T'ang invasions ended in total failure. In renewing our military campaign against Japan, therefore, we should take into serious consideration the fact that Japan is situated far beyond the waters which separate us from her by millions of miles."[79]

Kublai Khan approved of Liu's memorial and immediately issued an imperial edict ordering the discontinuance of all military preparations.[80] But he could not bring himself to abandon altogether the campaign against Japan, nor could he free himself from his desire for revenge.[81] Taking advantage of the geographical proximity of Korea to Japan, Kublai Khan instructed his son-in-law, the king of Korea, to undertake the pending campaign. In 1288, the king of Korea was appointed "State Minister for the Invasion of Japan" and was ordered to supervise all the work of that department. In 1289, Kublai Khan sent several trusted officers to Korea for the purpose of inspecting the military equipment and provisions in Korea. Later, he sent another party to supervise the building of war vessels and the manufacture of military weapons.[82]

The national resources of Korea were almost exhausted and the demands of Kublai Khan were severe and exacting. Moreover, the king of Korea became fully convinced that the work assigned him by Kublai Khan was entirely beyond the power and resources of his kingdom. In 1292, the king of Korea sent an envoy to Japan in the hope of settling the international difficulties between Japan and Kublai Khan. In the personal letter entrusted to the envoy, the king of Korea stated that after an existence of three hundred years the Sung empire in China had been destroyed solely because the Sung emperor had stubbornly refused to recognize the ruling power of Kublai Khan, whereas the kingdom of Korea, having readily entered into sovereign and tributary relations with the Mongols, had been able to retain its national existence. Both the ruler and the people, he said, had enjoyed peace and prosperity under the "Great Emperor of China and of the Mongols."

By taking into consideration, the letter of the king continued, how and why the Sung empire had been destroyed, and how and why the Korean kingdom had been able to maintain its prosperity and existence, the "Ruler of Japan" should be convinced of the necessity of sending an envoy to the court of Kublai Khan to pay due homage to him. By doing this, Japan would lose nothing and she would gain great benefits in the future. History evidenced the fact, the king concluded, that any nation which relied upon its geographical isolation and failed to pay due homage to great neighboring nations would sooner or later meet a sad fate. This Korean envoy remained in Japan for fifteen years, dying in 1307 with his mission unfulfilled.[83]

In 1293–94, Kublai Khan sent officials to Korea to inspect the progress of the preparation for the "Campaign for the Invasion of Japan." Upon their arrival, these officials were greatly surprised and filled with sympathy at Korea's having been so reduced and impoverished. Encouraged by the attitude of these officials, the king of Korea decided to proceed to Peking in person and present the entire situation to Kublai Khan.[84] However, before the arrival of the Korean king, Kublai Khan died in January, 1294, at the age of 80 years, having ruled his empire for thirty-five years. Ko Shao-Min, a noted Chinese historian, has written that Kublai Khan was the greatest ruler in Asia. Notwithstanding his brilliancy, historians regret the fact that, even after throwing 100,000 of his fighting men into Japanese waters, he still planned to invade Japan; nor did he ever discover the blindness and folly of this ambition. His son, Cheng-Tsung, succeeded him.

Even after the death of Kublai Khan, some of the prominent Mongols tried to carry out the plan of again invading Japan.[85] In 1298, several prominent Mongol statesmen presented a memorial[86] to the throne and requested that preparations be started for the invasion of Japan in order to carry out the dying request of Kublai Khan. The emperor declined the proposal, saying that the nation was not yet ready to undertake so great a project. In the following year (1299), the emperor planned to approach Japan in two ways; namely, through diplomatic channels and through military action. In the spring of 1299, the emperor sent a most distinguished Chinese Buddhist priest, whose name was Issan, as his personal representative to Japan, and reëstablished the "Department for the Invasion of Japan." First he would try, through his diplomatic representative, to settle peaceably the difficulties with Japan; but if this should fail, he was ready to resort to arms.

The Emperor Cheng-Tsung was not successful with either plan. Upon reaching Japan, though at first harshly dealt with, Issan was gradually able to impress the Japanese with his scholarly attainments and personality. He became a naturalized citizen of Japan and made notable contributions, both literary and religious, to the national life. Issan lived in Japan for twenty years, but he was not able to carry out the mission upon which he had been sent.[87]

Cheng-Tsung was no more successful with his military plan than with his diplomatic effort. History records that nothing was accomplished by the "Department for the Invasion of Japan" established under the Korean king in 1299.

In December, 1301, some 200 war vessels made a sudden inroad upon a small island off the southern coast of Kyushu. Before an actual military engagement started, a great storm swept the entire coast and the war vessels hurriedly sought safety. The Japanese thought that these war vessels had come from either China or Korea, and that they were part of the long-expected third Mongol armada. Chinese historians definitely deny that these war vessels had any connection whatever with the Mongol government in China.[88]

At any rate, this is the last entry in historical accounts with respect to Mongol invasions in China, Japan, or Korea. For thirty-three years, beginning in 1266 and ending in 1299, the Mongol emperors in China were persistent in their efforts to reduce Japan to a tributary state. During these thirty-three years, and even in the following decade, Japan was never free from fear of possible invasion from the continent. The whole nation felt unsettled. All able-bodied men were stationed in Kyushu and on islands in the Korean Channel. When, in June, in the twenty-sixth year of the Oyei era (1419), war vessels numbering more than 200, manned by nearly 18,000 fighting men, invaded Tsushima (Tsu island) in the Korean Channel, imperial envoys were sent to the leading shrines and temples in Japan to pray for a divine wind,[89] and at the same time the entire fighting force in Kyushu was mobilized. Fortunately, before the arrival of an army from Kyushu, the coast guards of Tsushima had forced the enemy to withdraw after he had suffered great loss.

The Yuan dynasty was nearing its end. Having been assimilated through the vitality of Chinese culture and manner of living, the Mongols had lost both fighting spirit and strength. This so-called Third Mongol Invasion was merely a minor military undertaking started by Korea in the hope of destroying the headquarters of the Japanese pirates who from time to time swooped down upon her coasts.

This invasion of Tsushima took place one hundred and thirty-eight years after the destruction of the armada of Kublai Khan in 1281. It provides proof that Japan had felt it necessary to prepare for further Mongol invasion for scores of years after her decisive victory in the thirteenth century. The government had made this preparation in both military and religious ways, but after the actual experience of what was to them divine intervention, both the government and the people generally put more emphasis on religious services than on military preparation. Japanese history records that, throughout the entire period of the Mongol military threats and invasions, the religious expenditures were far in excess of the amount spent for military preparation.

The decisive victory in 1281 placed the government, however, in a most delicate and serious situation. Military men asserted that the victory had been won through their courage and skill because they had coped successfully for two months with Mongol invaders to the number of 150,000. The noncombatants who had built the stone walls claimed credit for the victory because these coast defenses had prevented the landing of the invaders. Finally, the priests and other religious workers said the victory was theirs, because the armada had been completely destroyed by the divine wind. The pressing problems fronting the government were: how to continue the

military and religious preparation for the third Mongol invasion; how to satisfy the demands of the numerous seekers of
rewards; and how to rehabilitate the nation.

In 1284, Tokimune Hojo, the originator of the plan for
national defense and Japan's most constructive statesman, died
at the age of 33 years. His untimely demise virtually sealed the
doom of the government. After his death, every plan and de-
vice adopted for the purpose of meeting the situation only
aggravated conditions. The rate of taxation reached an un-
precedented height, and nearly all commodities were made
subject to taxation. Nation-wide economy was enforced. Food,
clothing, and housing were made subject to government inter-
ference and supervision, causing great inconvenience, dissatisfaction, and humiliation. The victory of 1281 had brought
neither benefit nor safety to the nation. There had been absolutely no war prizes either in the form of indemnity or of territorial gains. Japan's only gains in winning this victory were
the sending of Kublai Khan's armada to the bottom of the sea
and the freeing of the coast from hostile invaders. After this
war, the national coffers were empty, and both the government
and the ruling families, particularly, were impoverished. In
1297, a most unheard-of policy was adopted. A Law of Repudiation was promulgated,[20] by which all debtors and creditors
were instructed to consider their respective financial obligations and claims as cancelled. Estates and properties held as
securities were ordered to be returned immediately to their
owners, without compensation. When this law was put in
force, the people became fearful lest laws of a similar nature
might be promulgated at any time. Mutual trust and confidence were overthrown and the stability of the national
finances was undermined.

The extreme national poverty and the maladministration
that accompanied it caused the once popular Kamakura
shogunate to become a center of dissatisfaction and hatred.
Finally, in 1333, this shogunate came to an end, after a most

admirable administration of approximately one hundred and fifty years. The financial exhaustion consequent upon the glorious defense against Kublai Khan's invasions and his continued military threats was the main cause of this regrettable ending[91] of an able family.

During the last century of the existence of the Kamakura shogunate, the actual authority in Japan had been exercised by the Hojo family. The Hojo had saved the nation, but they could save neither themselves nor the Kamakura shogunate.

CHAPTER III

The Dark Age in Japan—Piracy—Chinese Diplomatic Supremacy

WITH THE DOWNFALL of the Kamakura shogunate and the destruction of the Hojo family, the ruling authority was restored to the Emperor Godaigo, the ninety-sixth sovereign of Japan. This period of imperial restoration was of exceedingly short duration; it began in June, 1333, and ended in December, 1336.[1] Many reasons have been advanced for the failure of the rule of the Emperor Godaigo. The first reason is twofold: the imperial government was not restored to power because the people desired an imperial restoration; and the Kamagura shogunate was not overthrown because the people disliked the feudal-military rule—the political change was brought about by certain persons who hated the Hojo, the ruling family in the Kamakura shogunate;[2] and the destruction of the Hojo incidentally put an end to the power of the military families. Second, the imperial restoration was not accompanied by a national reformation, but was established upon the existing feudal foundation; in other words, the imperial restoration merely replaced the Kamakura shogunate.[3]

Although brought about in this somewhat abnormal way, the imperial restoration made it possible for the emperor and the court nobles, long deprived of power, again to take hold of national affairs. Unfortunately, they revived the old complicated and impractical methods of administration, thus causing the people great inconvenience. Furthermore, in the hope of gaining the respect of the people and impressing them with the imperial dignity, the building of grand imperial palaces and many state buildings, like those of the former imperial days, was immediately undertaken. The rate of taxation, which had already reached an unbearable height under the

Hojo rule, was multiplied, yet the national revenue was insufficient to meet the expenditures. For the first time in the history of Japan, the government issued paper currency without any metallic reserve behind it.[4] With the national financial integrity thus shaken, the cost of living soared.

The group which had brought about the downfall of the Kamakura shogunate consisted of military men and priests, disappointed because they had received no reward for service rendered either before or after the invasion by Kublai Khan. They wanted to avenge themselves upon the Hojo, but they also sincerely wished to improve conditions, and toward this end the downfall of the Hojo was necessary. So they gathered under the imperial standard, expecting not only to achieve these purposes but also to receive compensation for fighting in the cause of the emperor. After the imperial restoration, the court of award swarmed with hundreds of thousands of claimants, but only the court nobles and a few of the outstanding military lords received rewards. Personal favoritism and bribery were in complete control.[5] Moreover, the cases were handled in a most unsystematic way. Sometimes a single estate would be awarded to several persons, out of which arose of course great confusion and many quarrels. Sometimes after a certain district had been granted to a family, it was shortly taken away again on the ground that adjustment was necessary. Affairs became even more serious than they had been after the invasion by Kublai Khan. On the whole, most of the claims were either ignored or left unrecognized,[6] and dissatisfaction and disappointment prevailed among all classes. The mass of the people suffered by reason of the heavy taxation and the high cost of living, and the nation was confronted with national bankruptcy because of the reckless financial undertakings by inexperienced court nobles. After two years of this disorder under imperial rule, the people longed for a return to at least the stability of a military administration.[7]

This grave national condition was aggravated by the riv-

alry and enmity between the two most distinguished feudal-
military families, the Ashikaga and the Nitta. Although both
were branches of the Minamoto and although both had been
founded by brothers, these families had long been unfriendly.
Under the stress of prevailing conditions, both families had
joined the imperial army and both had given outstanding
service: one had stormed the Kamakura fortress, and the other
had occupied Kyoto. After the imperial restoration, their rivalry became more and more intense, and the Nitta and the
Ashikaga became the military centers of the opposing interests. Finally, Takauji, the head of the Ashikaga, left Kyoto
with all his followers under the pretense of suppressing a rebellion in eastern Japan. Later, he established a military government at Kamakura and requested the Emperor Godaigo
to appoint him shogun with full military authority. When the
emperor refused, Takauji marched upon Kyoto with his entire
force, with the express purpose of reorganizing the imperial
government by removing the Nitta and by getting rid also of
other undesirable leaders. The emperor declared Takauji to
be both a national and an imperial enemy and sent the Nitta
and other military leaders to check his advance.

Although Takauji gained initial success and occupied Kyoto, he finally met with crushing defeat, his entire army being
dispersed. Takauji was resourceful and prompt. Believing that
he was defeated because he had fought against the throne, and
still convinced that the restoration of the military government was the prevailing desire of the people, he first reorganized his army with the support of the leading military families
in Kyushu, and at the same time approached an imperial
prince who had long cherished ill feeling against the Emperor
Godaigo, and induced the prince to declare himself emperor.[3]
In this way, the second attempt to reëstablish the shogunate
was made under the guise of the "War Between the Two Emperors." The opposing forces were the Emperor Godaigo, supported by the Nitta and other loyal military families, on the

one side, and on the other, the "Pretender" (the new emperor) supported by the Ashikaga and their followers. As Takauji had hoped, the people considered it an imperial war.[9] This time, he was successful. All the military families and all the fighting men who were dissatisfied with the imperial rule of Godaigo and who longed for the return of the shogunate, joined his army. The imperial army under the command of Nitta, Kusunoki, and other loyal military men, was completely defeated. The Emperor Godaigo was forced to abandon Kyoto, the imperial capital, and the new emperor established his court there under the military protection of the Ashikaga.

The Emperor Godaigo, after abandoning Kyoto, proceded to the mountainous district of Yoshino, where he established his new court with the support of the court nobles and the military men who were still loyal to him. The districts in which Kyoto and Yoshino were situated, adjoined each other, the one to the north and the other to the south. The period of the coexistence of the two imperial courts, the one at Kyoto and the other at Yoshino, is therefore generally known as the "Period of the Northern and Southern Dynasties."[10]

In 1338, Takauji, the head of the Ashikaga family, was appointed Sei-i Tai-shogun by the new emperor at Kyoto. The second shogunate, known in history as the Ashikaga shogunate, was established only five years after the downfall of the first shogunate established at Kamakura.[11] The Ashikaga had made Kyoto its military capital so as to provide the necessary military protection for the imperial court there. The military and geographical needs of the nation made it necessary to provide, also, a separate military government at Kamakura, the former military capital.

The Ashikaga shogunate at Kyoto and the Ashikaga military government at Kamakura were headed, respectively, by the elder and the younger sons of Takauji, yet, because each of these governments possessed absolute ruling power in the separate districts which had been assigned to it, they were

virtually independent, and, in the course of time, rivalry and
enmity sprang up between them. Thus, with the founding of
the Ashikaga shogunate, Japan came to have four separate
governments; namely, the imperial government at Yoshino (the
Southern dynasty), the imperial government at Kyoto (the
Northern dynasty), the Ashikaga shogunate at Kyoto, and the
Ashikaga military government at Kamakura. As a result, the
nation was disrupted. Partisans and sympathizers with one or
another of these four governments, especially with the Northern and Southern dynasties, were to be found everywhere. In
some families the father was loyal to the imperial government
at Yoshino, and the sons had a strong inclination to fight in
behalf of the imperial government at Kyoto. Nowhere in
Japan did peace and harmony exist. National conditions became more and more serious.[12] The disorderly and weak rule
of the Ashikaga may be accounted for by the complementing
facts. When Takauji ambitiously planned to reëstablish the
shogunate, he was not strong enough to undertake the work
single-handed and so he solicited military assistance from several leading military lords. The Ashikaga shogunate had come
into existence, indeed, only through the coöperation of many
powerful military families. These military families had considered the Ashikaga more as their allies than as the ruling
power in Japan. Furthermore, Takauji had realized that the
main cause of the downfall of the Hojo as well as of the imperial government that had been restored by Godaigo, was to
be traced to the failure of both to give due compensation to
their men for their services. After founding his shogunate,
therefore, Takauji rewarded all the military men most liberally. Several of them were even made lords of from two to
three provinces. A family by the name of Yamana was given
as many as ten provinces, thus becoming master of one-sixth
of the area of Japan.

As a result of this liberality, there were in Japan, during the
Ashikaga Period, a number of military lords whose financial

and fighting strength was sufficient to enable them to cope
with the shogunate government. These lords were not only
unruly and arrogant, but they were also always ready to rebel
against the shogun.[13] Whenever they nursed a grievance, they
deserted both the Ashikaga shogunate and the imperial court
at Kyoto and joined forces with the imperial court at Yoshino.
Under these circumstances, the shogun did not, as a rule, fight
these rebellious military men to a finish. After a few battles,
the shogun would induce them to come back to his side by
offering liberal terms and making generous concessions. Naturally, the military men came to believe that rebellion was a
most profitable undertaking, and military lords shifted from
one side to another for the sake of material gain. Throughout
almost the entire Ashikaga Period, which lasted nearly two
hundred and fifty years, intrigues, conspiracies, rebellions,
battles, reconciliations, and assassinations followed one another in cycles.

In history, the Ashikaga Period is known as *Ka-koku-Jo*,
which means, "The lower rule and conquer the higher";[14] in
other words, "The Period of the Usurpation." Political ethics,
the relation of master and subject and that of elder and younger,
were entirely disregarded. Loyalty and sincerity were no longer
observed. Family and blood relationships no longer constituted parts of the social organization. Might was power, and
conspiracy and intrigue became controlling elements. The
overthrow of families and the rise of others were matters of
common occurrence.

Moreover, positions of higher authority were frequently
created by persons of lower rank for other persons to occupy
as might suit the former's convenience. Persons of higher rank
therefore came to have, as a rule, neither dignity nor authority
over the lower. *Ka-koku-Jo* was really originated by Takauji
when he made the imperial prince declare himself emperor
under Takauji's military protection. He took this step so as to
get a chance to fight against the Emperor Godaigo without

being declared an imperial enemy, and so that he might be appointed shogun by the new emperor. After the founding of the Ashikaga shogunate, the shogun Takauji and other Ashikaga men openly declared that, although the emperor had conferred the title of shogun upon the head of the Ashikaga family, yet it was the shogun who, in fact, had created the emperor. The people in general said that the head of the imperial court at Kyoto was a most fortunate person, because he was made emperor by the shogun without having to fight for his position.[15] Similarly, the military lords said that, although it was the shogun who had given them the territory, it was solely through their coöperation and military assistance that the head of the Ashikaga was made shogun. The retainers of the feudal lords held the same attitude toward their lords. Throughout the long rule of the Ashikaga this peculiar national situation obtained, in which persons of lower rank looked down upon those of higher rank. In course of time, treachery, plunder, and intrigue on the part of the lower against the higher became a common practice throughout the nation.[16] To extend one's own estate and to augment one's wealth regardless of the means employed seemed to be the chief ambition of persons of all classes.

Because of the anarchical conditions in Japan, China and Korea also suffered.[17] As the national chaos increased, most of the disorderly military men along the coast and on the small islands turned pirates. They invaded the coasts of China and Korea, plundering, killing, and taking prisoners wherever they went. Finally, their inroads became so frequent and were conducted on so large a scale that the problem of how to cope with the marauders became a serious national question in both China and Korea. Failure to solve this problem ultimately caused the downfall of the ruling dynasties in the two countries.

Strange as it may seem, these inroads of the plundering Japanese in China and Korea had their origin in the destruction of the armadas of Kublai Khan and his subsequent unsuccessful attempts to conquer Japan. Prior to the fourteenth century, when the Mongol emperors had completely abandoned the invasion of Japan because of lack of both financial and military strength, no Japanese had even dreamed of so ambitious an undertaking as the invasion of continental nations such as China and Korea. After the middle of the seventh century, when the military and naval power of Japan was crushed by the joint forces of China and Korea, Japan[18] had (1) abandoned her ruling authority in Korea; (2) made herself *Kyo-To-byo,* which means "Sick Man Who Continuously Fears the T'ang [China]"; and had (3) exposed herself to *Shina Suhai-Netsu,* which means "Fever to Worship and Revere China." For nearly two hundred and fifty years Japan had admired, imitated, and adopted almost everything to be found in China, intent upon making out of Old Japan a new nation modeled upon China under the T'ang.

After the downfall of the T'ang dynasty in the early tenth century, Japan had, it is true, discontinued her humble practice of sending envoys to China. Nevertheless, throughout the three hundred years from the tenth to the thirteenth centuries, when China was under the rule of the Sung dynasty, she had continued to regard her as a most enlightened nation and had acknowledged her supremacy. In those days the Japanese were trained from childhood to fear China, a nation that had four hundred states while Japan had but sixty states. When any religious or intellectual problem arose in Japan, it was the custom of Japanese scholars to lay it before prominent men in China. China, for her part, considered Japan as a nation only partly civilized. In 1118, the Chinese emperor sent a communication addressed to the emperor of Japan in which he said that the Japanese ruler, who was the "Chief of the Tribe of Eastern Barbarians," had not adhered to the practice of showing respect to the court of China, and that therefore he "was [hereby] advised to learn how to revere a nation of great and supreme power."[19] After a long discussion of this communication, Japan decided not to answer it, on the ground that it was not written in accordance with diplomatic usage. About half a century later, in 1172, Japan received another letter of similar nature from China. This time, according to the entries in both Chinese and Japanese records, Japan not only acknowledged the letter, but also sent to China a gift of the products of her land, which Chinese historians called tribute.[20]

In those ancient times, to consider China as a nation of unapproachable standing and dignity was second nature to the Japanese. However, after the armadas and the men of Kublai Khan had twice been annihilated by the divine wind, the Japanese, convinced that their nation was under divine protection and therefore could not be conquered by a foreign enemy, radically changed their attitude toward China; and in the fourteenth century, when Japan learned that China had abandoned her plan of invasion and had decided to keep her hands off Japan because it was impossible to conquer her, the ancient feeling of fear and respect for China was changed to one of contempt and defiance. China did not feel the effects of this change of attitude so long as Japan was under the rule of a strong central government and her people remained at home; but toward the latter part of the Kamakura Period, when the Hojo family lost its authority and the people began to suffer hardship and poverty, men of venturesome inclination began to cross to the continent, where they pirated merchant ships and ravaged the coast.[21] In the beginning, these inroads were limited almost exclusively to the southwestern coast of Korea and the neighboring waters, which were of easy access to the Japanese.

The warfare between the Northern and Southern dynasties in the Ashikaga Period (fourteenth century) spread all over Japan. In each important battle, many leading military families were destroyed, and their followers became destitute. With the increase of national chaos, Japan was overrun with bandits, some of whom even sought fortune beyond the sea. When they returned with shiploads of treasure, others followed suit, and at last the military men who lived along the coast and on the small islands became professional pirates. Even noted military families together with their entire followings made piracy their profession. They established their headquarters on the numerous small islands in the Inland Sea, and subheadquarters on three different groups of islands in the Outer Sea.[22] They systematically ravaged not only the ships but also the villages and cities along the coasts of China and Korea. Tsushima and Iki Island in the Korean Channel were their first outposts. From these headquarters, the Japanese pirates swooped down upon the entire length of the coast of northern and southern Korea as well as upon the coast of southern Manchuria. The Goto Islands, off the northwestern coast of Kyushu near Nagasaki, constituted their second base, from which they attacked and ravaged the coasts of Chihli, Shantung, Chekiang, and Kiangsi provinces in China. A group of small islands off the southwest coast of Kyushu near Kagoshima was their third base, and the coasts of Kwangtung, Fukien, and other Chinese provinces their fields of operation.

In this way, the entire coast of China and Korea was continuously at the mercy of the Japanese pirates. Merchant vessels were also objects of prey, but the main field of operation was in the prosperous cities, towns, and villages along the seacoast. These pirate bands were not mere casual groups of men of venturesome inclination; they were well-organized bodies. The fleets numbered from 50 to 60 ships, as a rule, and sometimes there were more than 200. According to official records in Korea, each pirate ship carried 100 or more men. A Japanese pirate band, although generally consisting of several hundred men, sometimes numbered as many as 10,000. Although most of these pirate bands had great fighting strength, the acquisition of territory was not their object; plunder was their main purpose.[23] They fought bravely and desperately, and their attacks were both sudden and of short duration. They moved from town to town, ransacking houses and carrying off things of value in much the same fashion as the honey bee gathers nectar from one flower after another.

The Japanese pirates usually operated with a fleet of numerous small vessels. Upon effecting a landing, they conducted themselves as organized troops while they robbed and plundered one settlement after another. Sometimes these pirate troops marched far into the interior and attacked even fortified cities. On rare occasions, even the national capital of Korea was threatened. The Chinese and the Koreans, who in their long enjoyment of peace and prosperity had neglected to keep up military training, were unable to cope with Japanese who had been born and raised in a disorderly environment and who had made bloody struggles their profession. Furthermore, the pirates plundered at will any part of the long stretch of coast, so that neither the Koreans nor the Chinese could build defensive works that would be of any use. How to rid their coasts of Japanese pirates and to safeguard their subjects who dwelt near the coasts became grave national problems in both countries.[24]

The Korean coast, because of its proximity to Japan, was in the beginning the main field of operation. By the middle of the fourteenth century, the condition of Korea was very serious. The government being unable to afford protection from the pirates, the people deserted their homes and fled to the mountainous districts, thus converting the greater part of the districts along the coast into a No Man's Land. Finally, the Korean government, realizing that it was powerless to deal with the Japanese pirates in a military way, adopted two plans: (1) the removal of the national capital to a mountainous district far from the coast, so that it could not possibly be reached by the Japanese pirates; and (2) the sending of an envoy to reëstablish friendly relations with Japan, that country having been regarded as an enemy nation since the time of Kublai Khan, and to request that the Japanese government control its subjects and prohibit their sailing to Korean waters for the purpose of piracy.[25] The first plan ended in total failure. After several years of investigation, no district was found that would be sufficiently convenient for the national capital and sufficiently secluded to be safe. As for the second plan, the Korean government sent envoys a number of times to Japan without results. The war between the Northern and Southern dynasties was in progress and the Korean envoy was unable to find any real authority to whom his problem might be presented. Later, envoys were sometimes fortunate enough to gain interviews with representatives of one or the other of the two imperial governments. Yet, because of the chaotic conditions in Japan and because several of the provinces were outside the control of either of the imperial governments, these representatives could neither give nor promise any assistance to Korea.[26] In 1385, according to Korean records, one hundred and fifty Japanese pirate vessels invaded the northwestern province of Korea near the border of Manchuria, plundering and ravaging almost the entire district. In the following year, the southwestern coast of Korea was visited by the same sort of disaster. So in 1389, the Korean government, in desperation, gathered all its war vessels and invaded Tsushima and the island of Iki in the Korean Channel, determined to destroy the headquarters of the Japanese pirates and thus to remove the source of trouble. This expedition, however, ended in failure.[27] The main troubles with Korea in the fourteenth century were long-continuing maladministration, corrupt government, and financial exhaustion. The Korean army was composed of mercenary troops of the old type, and neither the men nor the officers had fighting spirit. Even food and equipment were lacking. The expedition therefore only revealed the impotence of the Korean government and its complete lack of prestige.

At this time, Li Cheng-Kui, one of the generals of the Korean army, came into prominence as a national hero. Of unusual military genius and magnetic personality, he was a statesman of rare ability, and the men under his command had not only implicit confidence in him, but also both admiration and affection for him. Naturally, his army became the most important fighting unit in Korea.

In May, 1377, Li Cheng-Kui successfully defended the southeastern coast of Korea, along the Korean Channel, from Japanese pirate bands of great fighting strength. This was virtually the first victory won by the Koreans over the marauding bands. In September of the same year, Li again defeated the Japanese pirates when they invaded the northwestern district along the coast of the Yellow Sea.[28] Three years later, however, in 1380, Japanese pirate troops many thousands strong effected a landing on the southern coast along the Korean Channel. They defeated the Koreans in every engagement. Nine commanding generals of the Koreans lost their armies, and two of the generals were killed. Finally, to the great consternation of the Koreans, the Japanese invaders prepared to advance upon the Korean capital. Li and his army, which was then stationed in the northeastern part of Korea, were sent for. Upon arrival, Li made his troops the fighting center, and reorganized the defeated, downhearted Korean forces. In a last desperate stand against the Japanese pirates, Li challenged the pirate leader to single combat, killed him, and put to rout the entire force of the pirate troops. This was the only notable victory won by Koreans over the Japanese marauders. After this battle, when Li returned in triumph to the national capital, the state minister Tsui, accompanied by all the court officers, received and welcomed him at the gateway of the city and expressed the gratitude of the nation, saying that if Korea had not had a man of Li's ability at this critical time, her national fate would have been sealed. His victory had not only saved the nation but had also revived it, and had inspired the people with hope and courage.

Li's reputation became nation-wide. The reorganization of the Korean army was begun at once, in accordance with a plan suggested by him. In 1385, Japanese pirate troops again invaded Korea and defeated the Korean armies led by various commanders, but finally were defeated by Li's forces. Li was the only military man in Korea able to cope with the Japanese pirates. He became the idol of the nation and was made the leader in both civil and military affairs in Korea. He continued to be successful in both his civil and his military undertakings, and won the admiration and respect of the government officers as well as of the people. In 1392, the king was forced to surrender all his authority to Li Cheng-Kui, and the Wang dynasty of the kingdom of Korai came to an end, after having ruled Korea for 456 years. The chief contributory cause of its downfall, however, was the continued incursions of the Japanese pirates.[29]

In 1392, Li Cheng-Kui began to rule Korea under the name of King Tai-Tsu, thus becoming the founder of the Yi dynasty. The Yi dynasty ruled Korea for 518 years, their sway ending in 1910 when Korea was annexed to Japan. Throughout the first two hundred years of the rule of this dynasty, Korea enjoyed the best administration in her history. The country made remarkable progress both intellectually and industrially, and was regarded as one of the highly civilized nations in Asia. The successful establishment of the Yi dynasty was accomplished through the wise diplomatic policy adopted by King Tai-Tsu, its founder, in his dealings with China and Japan. The effective Korean administration in the fifteenth and sixteenth centuries[30] is also to be attributed to the change for the better in Japan in the second half of the fourteenth century. Though it proved of brief duration, peace was restored, national unification was effected, and a strong centralized government was established. Furthermore, Japan showed a happy readiness to comply with the Korean request that Japanese pirates be prevented from sailing to the Korean coast.

In 1367, Yoshiaki, the second of the Ashikaga shoguns, died at the age of thirty-seven years, leaving an only son, Yoshimitsu, who was but nine years of age. On his deathbed Yoshiaki summoned his son, and summoned also Yoriyuki, one of the most eminent statesmen of the time. To the latter, the dying shogun entrusted the family affairs of the Ashikaga and the administration of all national matters. He especially requested that his boy be raised and educated to become a capable ruler. He said, "After my death, the relation between Yoriyuki and Yoshimitsu should be that of father and son, and not that of lord and subject." In 1368, Yoshimitsu was appointed shogun by the emperor.

Yoriyuki was a scholar, statesman, and soldier of real ability. He was also a man of much sincerity and caution. He had been greatly inspired by the dying words of the second shogun, and he gave to Japan, in the capacity of military regent for the boy shogun,[31] a very successful administration.

Yoshimitsu was trained and educated along military, civil, and other lines of work designed to fit him to rule Japan. When he became old enough to conduct national affairs, he was a man of strong will and good judgment and possessed both military and administrative ability. He always asserted that, although his grandfather and father had been made shoguns through the military coöperation of leading feudal lords, as for himself, he had been born to be appointed shogun and had grown into manhood as a shogun should, and therefore he was a shogun whose dignity should be respected and whose authority should be obeyed. In this way, Yoshimitsu made it clear that he would not tolerate the independent and selfish undertakings of the military men, as had his grandfather and his father. He planned to place all the military lords under the authority of the Ashikaga shogunate,[32] which should be centralized in himself. At the same time, he showed a readiness to accept the challenges of any military men who might rise against him.

In 1391, the Yamana, the most daring and most powerful military family of Japan, ruling one-sixth of the empire and lord of ten provinces, a family ever ready to rise against the government, began to make great military preparations. Yoshimitsu regarded this as an act of rebellion. He also saw in it an excellent opportunity to put his new policy to a test. It was both a serious and a risky undertaking for Yoshimitsu, but he won a decisive victory. After the close of the war, with noticeable tact and ability he exercised a commendable combination of severity and magnanimity in dealing with the Yamana. He confiscated nine of their ten provinces, thus reducing their fighting strength, but he permitted the family to maintain its status as lord of one province, on the ground that the meritorious work of the Yamana's ancestors should be recognized. Later, another military family by the name of Ouchi, rebelled. The Ouchi family, with six provinces under its rule, was lord of a tenth of the area of Japan. Yoshimitsu was likewise successful in conquering this family, which, like the Yamana, he permitted to maintain its status as lord of two provinces. This elimination of the two most powerful and arrogant military families in Japan fully established the indisputable authority of Yoshimitsu in the empire.

Yoshimitsu now realized that the coexistence of the two imperial courts, one at Yoshino and the other at Kyoto, was the main cause of national disturbances. The merging of these two imperial governments into one was seen to be essential to the establishment of a centralized authority in Japan. At that time, in striking contrast to the military ascendancy of Yoshimitsu, all the military families, including the Nitta and the Kusunoki, which had been loyal to the Southern dynasty, had either been destroyed or shorn of their fighting strength. Although the imperial court at Yoshino had virtually no military backing, it was the legal imperial ruling power, and as such commanded nation-wide respect. In 1392, Yoshimitsu therefore sent trusted representatives to the Yoshino court with the proposal that the two imperial dynasties should be united under the condition that their members should enjoy equal imperial dignity and rights, including succession to the throne. The Emperor Gokameyama, head of the Southern dynasty, at Yoshino, actuated solely by a desire to save the people from further military suffering, accepted this proposal. In October of the same year, the Emperor Gokameyama left Yoshino for Kyoto, where he handed the three sacred imperial insignia to the Emperor Gokomatsu, head of the Northern dynasty. Thus, after fifty-six years of antagonism and warfare, the two imperial courts were united. In this half-century, five emperors in succession had been heads of the Kyoto imperial government, and three emperors had ascended the throne at Yoshino. Notwithstanding the fact that all the emperors of the Northern dynasty reigned over almost the whole of Japan under the military protection of the Ashikaga, while the authority of the emperor of the Southern dynasty extended only over two or three provinces, yet, in Japanese history, the emperors of the Southern dynasty alone are mentioned in the line of the imperial succession, the existence of the five emperors of the Northern dynasty being completely ignored. In Japan, the sacred imperial insignia are identified with the throne.[33] Therefore, no matter how long a person might remain in power or how completely he might control the empire of Japan, if he ruled without having in his possession the sacred imperial insignia, he would not, even though he were a prince of the imperial blood, be recognized as a sovereign of the empire of Japan. With the unification of the two imperial governments, the organization of the Ashikaga shogunate was completed, and the shogunate was recognized as the central ruling authority.

This notable historical event took place in the same year that the Yi dynasty was established in Korea by Li Cheng-Kui, who is known in history as King Tai-Tsu (the "Founder King"). Li had announced the general Korean national policy as follows: "Our kingdom should always pay reverence to the West [i.e., maintain with China the relationship respectively of suzerain and tributary nation] and should always command the trust and confidence of the East [i.e., secure the friendship of Japan]. The successful rule of our kingdom and the safe existence of our dynasty depend entirely upon how effectively we maintain this national policy."[34] In the fifteenth century, this policy received the approval of the dying Shen Shu-Chou, the most distinguished Korean statesman of his time, who, when requested by King Ting-Tsung to give him his final advice, replied, "My humble advice to the king and to his descendants is to maintain peace with Japan in order to safeguard the national existence of our kingdom."[35]

The great necessity of the new Korean government to maintain peace with Japan was of course created by the fierce attacks of Japanese pirates upon the coasts of Korea. The "Founder King," Tai-Tsu, in spite of his earlier success in repelling these invaders, found that the military strength of Korea was unequal to the unremitting task. He therefore gave a definite formulation of the national policy as: (1) to establish friendly relations with Japan and, with the coöperation of the Japanese government, to check the invasions of the pirates; and (2) to conciliate the Japanese pirates by offering liberal terms such as trade privileges, or by directing the pirates to more fruitful fields elsewhere.[36]

In 1392, that is, in the first year of the new kingdom, King Tai-Tsu sent a special envoy to Japan with instructions to make some arrangement with the Japanese government in respect to the pirate raids. This envoy arrived in Japan at a very opportune time. The Northern and Southern imperial governments had been united, and the Ashikaga shogunate ruled the empire. His task was therefore quite unlike that of the other envoys, all of whom had found Japan in a most disorderly condition and had uniformly failed in their respective missions because there was no real national authority in Japan with which they might deal.

The Korean envoy sent in 1392 was very successful. He readily approached the authority in power in Japan, by whom he was kindly received. When he related how, during the preceding half-century, Korea had suffered because of the repeated inroads and plundering of the Japanese pirates, the Japanese government expressed deep regret and sympathy and said that such barbarous and inhuman acts of its people had not only caused great disaster in Korea, but had also greatly disgraced Japan in the eyes of the world.[37] In every way, Japan showed a readiness to punish the pirates and to prevent them from again sailing to Korean waters. She also promised to return all the Koreans that had been carried away by the Japanese pirates. The Korean envoy returned home with great satisfaction and hope. When, in 1398, six years later, Korea sent a second envoy to Japan, the Japanese government informed him that all the pirate bands in Kyushu had been suppressed, and that those in the distant islands of the Outer Sea had been outlawed, and before long the government would send fleets to disband and punish them. The Japanese government then expressed a desire to establish friendly relations between Japan and Korea so that ships of trade might freely enter each other's harbors.[38] Japan also requested that Korea would provide her with certain valuable books, for which Korea was especially noted. Korea willingly complied with all these requests of Japan. On one occasion, she sent to Japan the complete set of standard Buddhistic sutras which comprised seven thousand volumes and was both rare and expensive.[39]

The Ashikaga shogunate sincerely endeavored to carry out its pledge to Korea with respect to the pirates, and by the beginning of the fifteenth century the pirate inroads on the Korean coast had been considerably reduced. Nevertheless, Korea as a whole was far from being free from their ravages. The truth was, the Japanese pirates had a well-established organization. Piracy in those days was not considered to be robbery, but rather a military activity on the water. Military families and their followers never felt it a disgrace to be pirates. Indeed, they sometimes proudly declared themselves "Chiefs of the Pirates," and even signed letters and contracts in that way. For nearly five hundred years, to as late as the beginning of the eighteenth century, the term "pirate organization" was gen-

erally used in place of "navy organization." Military families
and their men who engaged in military affairs were known as
Samurai (men carrying swords), a word which in modern terms
might be translated as "army men." Military families and men
who engaged in fighting on the sea were called *Kaizoku* (plun-
derers on the sea). This, in our modern sense, would mean
"naval men."

In the fourteenth, fifteenth, and even in later centuries, it
is clearly evident, piracy in Japan was a regularly recognized
profession.[40] The Ashikaga government in the fifteenth century, in keeping with its pledge to Korea, might have interfered with and regulated the pirates and their undertakings,
but it was entirely beyond that government's power completely
to destroy them. Moreover, on many occasions in Japanese history the government requested the assistance and coöperation
of the pirates in military undertakings. Sometimes the government even entrusted to the pirates work of great national importance. As a matter of fact, the Japanese navy developed out
of the pirate organization.

Considering all these conditions, the Korean government
finally realized that it could not depend upon the self-imposed
efforts of Japan alone to check and suppress the pirate activities. Two or three times, in the fifteenth century, Korea therefore attacked, with all her available naval force, the Japanese
island of Iki and Tsushima, important headquarters of the
Japanese pirates,[41] situated in the Korean Channel. These Korean expeditions, unfortunately, always ended in disastrous
failure, and the Korean government was forced to adopt a
conciliatory policy in dealing with the pirates. This policy, as
we have seen, was formulated by Li Cheng-Kui (King Tai-Tsu)
and approved by Shen Shu-Chou, the distinguished Korean
statesman. Shen Shu-Chou once explained Japanese piracy in
Korea as follows:

"The Japanese are brave and courageous. They excel people
of other nations in fighting with the sword and with the hal-

berd. They are adept in sailing on the ocean in small boats. Korea and Japan are close neighbors, being separated only by a narrow strip of water. If we should deal with the Japanese righteously and justly, meeting their demands, they would act properly and prove themselves to be desirable neighbors. If we should deal with them otherwise, they would pursue their own wild course, plundering and ravaging as they go. In the latter part of the rule of the Wang dynasty, because of long maladministration Korea entered upon a period of great national disorder. We therefore failed to deal with the Japanese properly. This caused them to invade our kingdom. They have reduced our coast districts almost entirely, laying them waste and making several thousand miles uninhabitable."

In accordance with the conciliatory policy, the Korean government treated the Japanese marauders as national guests rather than as pirate bands, and met their demands and needs for food, clothing, and other things. They were also induced to engage in trade with the Koreans on very liberal terms. If they so desired, they were provided with guides who directed them to rich fields of operation outside of Korea. On some occasions, the Korean government concluded something like treaties of trade with the "Chief of the Pirates" on most liberal terms. This conciliatory policy on the part of Korea, together with the good will of Japan and the responsibility assumed by that country for the suppression of the pirates, gradually produced the expected results. Year after year the pirate inroads in Korea became less and less frequent,[42] and toward the end of the reign of King Shih Tsung, the fourth sovereign of the Yi dynasty, who ruled Korea from 1419 to 1450, there were scarcely any pirate attacks on the Korean coast. However, this cessation of the Japanese pirate attacks in Korea did not mean that the pirates had been destroyed; they had merely shifted their field of operations. With the gradual decrease of the pirate raids on the Korean coast, their activities along the coast of China correspondingly increased.

Toward the close of the thirteenth century, China for the first time in her history came under the rule of a foreign dynasty. During the reigns of the Mongol, Kublai Khan, and his successors, because of the Mongol invasions of Japan and other military undertakings against her, as well as military activities against other nations, the Chinese suffered greatly from unbearable taxes and continuous military requisitions. These things undermined her financial strength. Later, the Chinese empire was visited by a series of inundations, famines, earthquakes, and other catastrophes. Moreover, because of their complete assimilation to Chinese life and ways of living, the Mongols had lost their strength and fighting spirit. China was ravaged and plundered by Japanese pirates, but the Mongol government was powerless to protect the Chinese people. All these things made the Chinese more and more dissatisfied with being under the rule of a foreign dynasty. In the middle of the fourteenth century, taking advantage of the weakened condition of the reigning dynasty as well as of its unpopularity, all the Chinese leaders in the various provinces rose against the Mongol government. Chu Yuan-Chang, a Buddhist priest in the province of Anhui, was one who rose against the government. He won a series of brilliant victories, and finally, in 1368, as the head of a united China, Chu succeeded in driving the Mongols and their emperor beyond the Great Wall. Thus was China wrested from the rule of a foreign power. In that same year, Chu founded a new Chinese empire and ascended the throne at Nanking.[48] Chu Yuan-Chang is known in history as the Emperor Tai-Tsu, the founder emperor of the Ming dynasty.

In the first year of his reign, that is, in 1368, the Emperor Tai-Tsu issued an imperial edict to the rulers of Annam, Chan-Cheng (Cochin China), Japan, and Korea, demanding that all these four nations recognize the suzerainty of the Ming over them. In his imperial edict, the emperor stated that he had destroyed the power of the Mongols in China and had come himself to rule the Great Middle Nation as the founder of the great Ming dynasty. Consequently, he further said, the chiefs of all the four barbarian nations [meaning Annam, Cochin China, Japan, and Korea] should promptly recognize his authority. In the following year, 1369, Annam, Cochin China, and Korea sent tribute to the imperial court of the Ming and willingly became tributary states of China. However, in this state paper of China the emperor of Japan was addressed as "Chief of the Barbarian Nation." Because of this violation of international courtesy, Japan completely ignored the edict, even going so far as to fail to acknowledge it.[44]

Although the first approach to Japan by the Emperor Tai-Tsu ended in failure, yet, because the plundering of the Japanese pirates became increasingly serious, the emperor found it necessary to settle this grave national problem with Japan in one way or another.[45] In 1369, the second year of his reign, the emperor sent his second envoy to Japan. In his state paper, the emperor first bitterly complained of the brutal and destructive acts of the Japanese pirates. He concluded by saying:

"Upon the receipt of our imperial instructions, the King of Japan should style himself a humble subject of our empire.[46] He should present a memorial to our throne and send an envoy to our court. Otherwise, he should make military preparation to defend his country against the inevitable. If he should permit his unruly subjects to continue their plundering on our coasts, we will send our military men with a strong fleet, with instructions first to capture all those disorderly persons in his country and then to proceed to his capital city in order to take up this matter with him directly. I hereby present the entire matter for his consideration."

This Ming envoy reached Kyushu and gained an interview with the imperial prince, Kanenaga, who is mentioned in Chinese histories as "King Lianghui" and who was the military governor-general representing the Southern imperial government in Japan. Prince Kanenaga was greatly offended by the threats in the state paper. He ordered that the envoy and all the members of his party be immediately imprisoned, but three months later he permitted them to return home to China. Thus the second attempt of the Ming emperor had ended in failure.

In the third year of his reign, the plundering of the Japanese pirates extended from Shantung in the north to Fukien in the south. In that year, the Emperor Tai-Tsu sent Chao Yi, a most renowned statesman, as his third envoy.[47] The state paper that the emperor sent by Chao Yi read, in part, as follows:

"The accumulated evils and the continuous violation of the laws of humanity by your subjects do certainly offend Heaven, from whose punishment Japan is destined to suffer. The day is not far off when we shall comply with Heaven's will and send a punitive force to your country."[48]

Prince Kanenaga was offended by the contents of this letter also, and accused Chao, the envoy, saying:

"Although Japan is a close neighbor of China, yet she has never shown any reverence to the Chinese imperial throne. In the past, the Mongols ranked our country as a barbarian nation and attempted to reduce us to subjects and dependents. We entirely ignored their demands. Later, the Mongol ruler sent his envoy, Chao, to express good will on one hand, although on the other the Mongol armada with a fighting force 100,000 strong suddenly appeared off our coast. This act of the Mongols offended Heaven. Thunder and great winds completely annihilated them. Now, the new emperor in China has sent an envoy, also named Chao, with instructions to approach us in a similar way. Are not you and also your emperor, blood relatives of the Mongols, our national enemies?"[49]

Chao explained to Prince Kanenaga that he had absolutely no blood connection with the Mongols, nor had the Emperor Tai-Tsu, who was a noble and brilliant man noted for his military genius. It was Tai-Tsu who had succeeded in wresting the Chinese from the rule of the Mongols, who had restored China to the Chinese, and who had founded the great Ming empire. So the envoy, Chao, was permitted to return to China. Although it had not been possible for him to accomplish his mission, he was allowed to take back with him seventy of the Chinese prisoners who had been rescued by Prince Kanenaga from the pirates.[50] In 1372, the Emperor Tai-Tsu despatched another envoy to Prince Kanenaga, to whom he sent, together with other gifts, the Chinese national calendar. But the gift of the national calendar signified that the Ming emperor held Japan as a tributary state, so that Prince Kanenaga was again greatly offended and gave orders that the envoy and his party should be imprisoned.[51] After two years of suffering in prison, they were permitted to return home to China. In spite of these failures, the Emperor Tai-Tsu continued to send envoys to Japan year after year, and to demand that the pirates be controlled and suppressed. If this demand was not complied with, he said, Japan would be invaded and punishment inflicted upon the nation as well as upon the disorderly persons. Finally, in July, 1381, the emperor sent a state paper to Kanenaga, in which he said, in part:

"You live in a country far out in the ocean, and you have not yet learned how to fear Heaven. You live at the bottom of the well and you measure the size of Heaven by this limited field of vision. You therefore arrive at erroneous conclusions. As you believe that deep water is impassable and that mountain ranges constitute strong national protection, you have dared us and have permitted your people to plunder and rob. The time will soon come when the Emperor Above will use human hands as his instruments and severely punish you and your country."[52]

Prince Kanenaga replied that Japan was both geographically and militarily well prepared to go to war, and that the Ming emperor should take into consideration the fact that war was a risky undertaking and that China and Japan each had equal chance of victory.[53] Upon reading this letter, the Emperor Tai-Tsu was wroth. However, fearing that if he should send a fleet to Japan it might meet the same fate that befell Kublai Khan's armada in the thirteenth century, he abandoned his plan of invasion.

In 1380, the year before Kanenaga wrote to the Ming emperor, Hu Wei-Yung, one of the most prominent state ministers in the Ming government, rebelled and planned to overthrow the Ming dynasty. It was later discovered that Hu had entered into a secret understanding with Japan to the effect that the latter would send to the court of the Ming, under the guise of a tribute-bearing vessel, a strong ship manned by four hundred armed men. On the reception day, these armed men should suddenly attack all the court officers and even the emperor himself. Hu's army on the outside was to coöperate with this uprising within.[54] The successful suppression of this rebellion was wholly owing to the discovery of the plot before it could be carried out. The Emperor Tai-Tsu concluded that Japan was a most untrustworthy and dangerous country, with which the Ming should have no further dealings.

The Emperor Tai-Tsu ruled China for a period of thirty-one years, his reign ending in 1398. He always maintained that one of China's greatest national problems was how to deal with the Japanese pirates who so continuously attacked the Chinese coast. After all his strenuous diplomatic negotiations with Japan had ended in failure, he decided that the only way to cope with the situation was to build extensive works of defense along the entire coast of China from the extreme north to the south.[55] Accordingly, in the latter part of his reign, the entire coastal area was divided into five military districts, Chihli, Shantung, Chekiang, Fukien, and the two Kwangs (East and West). At various points in each of these districts, strong fortresses and military stations were built and troops stationed therein. At places of minor importance, fire-signal stations were established, manned with coast guards of varying strength. By this arrangement, near-by fortresses and military stations were notified by fire signals of any approach of Japanese pirate ships.

All these elaborate works of defense were ineffective because the military men of the Ming lacked fighting spirit, and so the Chinese coast was left at the mercy of the pirate bands.

In the late fourteenth and early fifteenth centuries the gravest and most difficult problem that confronted China and Korea was how to deal with Japan in respect to the Japanese pirates. In this matter, the dealings of Korea with Japan were decidedly more satisfactory than were those of China. Korea's success was mainly owing to the fact that the Korean government entered into negotiations with Japan in strict accordance with international rulings. Korea first recognized Japan as a nation of equal standing with herself. She appealed to Japan's national dignity and pride and on this basis asked her to assume the responsibility of suppressing the piracy along the Korean coast; and offered, in return for this friendly effort,[56] to make trade and other concessions. This diplomatic approach by Korea gained the sympathetic coöperation of Japan, and by the end of the fifteenth century Korea was almost entirely free from the plundering of the pirates.

In striking contrast to the dealings of Korea with Japan, China entirely disregarded international courtesy and rulings. She assumed that she was the supreme nation in the world, and she regarded Japan as her vassal state. The Ming emperor instructed the "Ruler of Japan" to destroy the pirate bands so that the coast of China might be free from their plundering. He threatened Japan, saying that if she failed to comply with this imperial instruction he would send a strong military force to inflict punishment upon her. This demand being ignored by Japan, the Ming emperor found it impossible to carry out his military threat because he feared disaster in Japanese waters similar to that encountered by Kublai Khan's armada. Thus, throughout almost the entire reign of the Emperor Tai-Tsu, which lasted more than a quarter-century, the same diplomatic procedure was repeated over and over again: (1) China claimed suzerainty over Japan; (2) the Chinese emperor instructed Japan to control her disorderly subjects; (3) China made military threats; and then (4) failed to carry them out.

Finally, the Emperor Tai-Tsu, as a last resort, built extensive works of coast defense. This step likewise ended in failure, because, in the first place, the Ming dynasty was the weakest ruling house in the history of China, especially in respect to military strength, and in the second place, the pirate bands that made inroads into the districts along the Chinese coasts were entirely different in composition from those that attacked the Korean coast. The bands that invaded Korea were entirely Japanese without any admixture of other nationals. The pirate bands that invaded China were composed in large part of Chinese.[57] Chinese histories relate that only about 30 per cent of the men in the "Japanese" pirate bands were Japanese, and that the remaining 70 per cent were Chinese who had been forced by the Japanese marauders to join them. After once joining a Japanese pirate band, because of the observation of strict military discipline the Chinese usually fought with no regard for danger. This was in striking contrast to the attitude of the soldiers in the Chinese army, who, when danger threatened, deserted at the first opportunity. One of the Chinese histories gives the following account:

"On one occasion, a Japanese pirate band of from sixty to seventy men effected a landing. This band of small fighting strength advanced upon the armies of the Ming, which melted away in one engagement after another. The Japanese marauders advanced with ever-increasing strength because of the steady stream of Chinese that joined them. They continued to advance, covering thousands of miles and killing and wounding more than four thousand Chinese. At the close of three months of bloody struggle, they finally threatened Nanking, the national capital of China."[58]

The negotiations of the early Ming with Japan were conducted almost exclusively between the Ming government at Nanking and the military governor-general in Kyushu, who

was the head of the Seisei-Fu, the separate establishment of
the Southern imperial government in Japan. After the Emperor Tai-Tsu, in the latter part of his reign, learned of the
coexistence of the two imperial governments,[59] and that the
Northern imperial government was the more powerful, he
made several attempts to negotiate with the Northern imperial
government with respect to the pirate question. That government apparently showed a willingness to look into the matter.
However, according to the records in Chinese history, all the
state papers and communications sent to the Ming government by the Northern imperial government or by its representatives, in 1374, 1376, 1379, 1380, 1381, and 1386, were rejected by the Emperor Tai-Tsu on three grounds; namely: (1)
these Japanese state papers were not dated according to the
Chinese national era; (2) they failed to observe the traditional
usages that tributary states were bound to observe when addressing suzerain nations; and (3) they did not show due reverence to the Ming emperor as the ruler of the "Supreme Nation
in the Orient."[60] Chinese history through four thousand years
consistently bears evidence that the Ming dynasty, as well as
all the other imperial dynasties in China, looked down upon
foreign nations either as tributary states or as barbarian nations, and attempted to exercise suzerainty over them.

In the fifteenth century, however, China succeeded in getting Japan to recognize the suzerainty of China over her, thus
reducing the national standing of Japan to that of a tributary
state. This was effected in a most unusual way. It was not
brought about by military conquest, nor by diplomatic or international pressure, but voluntarily by Yoshimitsu, who bartered the national honor and dignity of Japan for his own
selfish ends. Yoshimitsu, the third shogun of the Ashikaga government, was a man of great military genius, and of statesmanship as well. He succeeded in uniting the two imperial governments, the one at Yoshino and the other at Kyoto, thereby uprooting the chief source of national disturbance; and forced

all the powerful military families to recognize his authority. Of the fifteen Ashikaga shoguns, Yoshimitsu was the only one who could wield the shogunal power. Throughout his life, he ruled Japan with a masterful hand, and kept the people of all classes under his control. But with his rise to power Yoshimitsu fell a victim to extravagance and luxury. He was especially fond of building magnificent palaces and temples. He built one of his numerous palaces in the foothills of Kyoto, and one of its buildings, three stories high, was covered inside with heavy gold leaf. To meet his ever-increasing expenditures, Yoshimitsu sought out all possible sources of revenue, and when Japan could yield no more, he turned to China.[61]

China was a large and rich nation, yet because of her military weakness she could not afford protection to her own people against the continuous ravaging and plundering of the Japanese pirate bands. Therefore, disregarding the national policy of the first Ming emperor, Tai-Tsu, which was to keep away from Japan, his successors earnestly desired to enter into some sort of agreement with Japan on the pirate problem. In Japan, Yoshimitsu, the only person in power who could control and suppress the piracy, was seeking some source of revenue. The Ming emperor and Yoshimitsu were thus in a position to meet each other's needs. However, there had long been insurmountable obstacles in the way of international intercourse between China and Japan. Since the founding of the Ming empire, the emperors had strictly adhered to the time-honored national traditions of China and had proclaimed that if Japan could do anything in China's behalf, she should do it as the bounden duty of a tributary state to a suzerain state; that is, if Japan could suppress her pirates, she should do so in compliance with the instructions of the Ming. In Japan, both the imperial government at Yoshino and that at Kyoto had long ignored the claims of China and had even disregarded her military threats. However, by the fifteenth century, when Yoshimitsu rose to power, the conditions in Japan had become entirely changed.

Yoshimitsu was arrogant, egotistic, and self-centered. He recognized neither the dignity nor the authority of others. He dictated to the emperor not only in government affairs, but in the latter's personal and private affairs as well. He treated all the court officers, including the imperial regent and the state ministers, as if they were his house servants. Nevertheless, because of his imperative need of money, Yoshimitsu was ready to bow low before a possible source of revenue, and even to barter the national honor and dignity of Japan for the trade privileges and other pecuniary concessions and grants that the Ming emperor was able to offer.[62] For these reasons, in 1401, Yoshimitsu sent an envoy to the Ming court provided with a personal letter written in a most humble fashion. At the same time, he sent various products of Japan as a sort of national tribute to the imperial throne of the Ming. In 1402, in a reply to Yoshimitsu, the Ming emperor expressed great satisfaction and praised Yoshimitsu, especially for the loyalty he had shown to the throne and his observance of the relationship of subject and lord. Along with this letter, the Ming emperor sent Yoshimitsu a copy of the Ming national calendar, with instructions that thenceforth state papers, memorials, and other communications sent by Yoshimitsu to the Ming throne should bear the date of the national era of the Ming, as was fitting from the ruler of a tributary state. Later, the Ming emperor invested Yoshimitsu with the title of "King of Japan," and later presented to him the official garment of the Ming court and the golden seal to be used by Yoshimitsu in his capacity as king of Japan; and throughout the rest of his life, Yoshimitsu, in all his state papers and memorials addressed to the Ming emperor, always used the title, "King of Japan, a subject of the Ming Emperor."[63]

In further recognition that Japan was a tributary state of the Ming empire, all these papers were dated as of the Ming national era. Thus, in the beginning of the fifteenth century, suzerain and tributary relationships between China and Japan were established and observed. These international agreements were all entered into without the consent of the emperor of Japan, but not without his knowledge. For Yoshimitsu, dressed in the official garments of the Ming court, which had been sent to him by the Ming emperor, was accustomed to be present at the imperial court of Japan. Thus Yoshimitsu recognized the emperor of Japan in domestic affairs, although he ignored him entirely in international dealings with China. By so doing, he gave the Ming emperor and other rulers on the continent the impression that he was the sole ruler of Japan.[64] It was evident to all that his purpose was financial gain. However, some Japanese historians believe that Yoshimitsu's dealings with the Ming emperor had, also, political ends. As he lived in the period of *Ka-koku-Jo* ("The Period of the Usurpation"), Yoshimitsu, they assert, fully intended to force the emperor of Japan to surrender the imperial authority to him both in name and in fact. His investment by the Ming emperor with the title of "King of Japan" was, they say, a first step in this ambitious plan, and he hoped thereby to establish his standing and gain the recognition of all the nations in the Orient, headed by China. It is generally believed that Yoshimitsu would have usurped the throne of Japan had he lived a few years longer.

Although state papers had been exchanged between the Ming government and the Ashikaga shogunate some years earlier, it was not until 1403, when Cheng-Tsu, the third emperor of the Ming dynasty, ascended the throne and Yoshimitsu sent state papers congratulating him upon his succession and pledging the national reverence and loyalty of Japan to the Ming throne, that the suzerain and tributary relationship between China and Japan was established. It was in one of these state papers that the title "King of Japan, a subject of the Ming Emperor," was used for the first time. Yoshimitsu began by eulogizing the new Ming emperor. When the sun rose high in the heavens, he said, no place in the world remained dark. When a timely, gentle rain blessed the earth, everything grew. When a great sage appeared, all the nations in the world were benefited, and people from all directions turned to him and placed themselves under his protection. Now, he continued, there had ascended the throne as the second founder of the empire, the "Great Emperor of the Ming," whose virtue as a sage had been inherited from the "Great Yao" and whose wisdom and courage surpassed even that of the "Great T'ang." Yoshimitsu concluded his state paper with these words: "Although the Emperor lives in a well-secluded imperial palace, his authority and virtue have reached the country in the waters [Japan] far beyond the eastern shore of his empire. The King of Japan, a humble subject of His Majesty, hereby reverently sends his envoy bearing local products as tribute to the throne."[65]

In the same year (1403), the Emperor Cheng-Tsu recognized Yoshimitsu's memorial and expressed his appreciation, saying:

"Between Heaven and earth, China and various barbarian states maintain their existence. They are ruled by us as a single unit without discrimination. Our doctrines and authority enable those who live both far and near to enjoy the same imperial blessings. The King of Japan has learned Heaven's will and has followed in the way of righteousness. We ascended the great sacred throne, and, without delay, he has sent an envoy bearing tribute to our throne. We approve of and praise his prompt observance of obedience. Our official seal to be used by the King of Japan is hereby presented to him. We practice our imperial doctrine and virtues, which embody the blessings of Heaven and earth. The King of Japan is hereby instructed faithfully to serve the great power above him [the Ming empire] in order that he may enjoy everlasting prosperity and happiness."[66]

Immediately after China had in this way established her suzerainty over Japan, the Emperor Cheng-Tsu took up the pirate problem and issued an imperial edict instructing Yoshimitsu to seek out and subjugate all the Japanese pirates. Yoshi-

mitsu promptly acknowledged the relationship of sovereign
and subject between the Ming emperor and himself, and put
forth his best efforts either to capture or to destroy the Japanese pirates. From time to time, he sent captured pirate leaders
to China, where the pirates thus sent were generally put into
large boilers and steamed to death.[67]

Beginning in 1403, the Ming emperor Cheng-Tsu issued
regularly, year after year, instructions in respect to the pirate
problem. In 1404, he issued the following edict:

"The Emperor hereby issues a decree of instruction to the
King of Japan. We greatly approve of and praise the King of
Japan for his prompt compliance with the instructions of our
imperial court. We have been informed that the King of Japan
has strictly forbidden the people in Iki, Tsushima, and other
islands to commit piracy or to ravage the coast districts of our
empire. We would issue further instructions to the effect that
the people in those islands should henceforth surrender their
weapons and devote themselves to agricultural pursuits. If
they should do this, the King of Japan would gain an everlasting reputation for having taught them how to gain happiness
and prosperity. This decree is hereby issued by us."[68]

Probably because the pirates did not forsake their plundering and devote themselves to agriculture as was suggested by
the Emperor Cheng-Tsu, Yoshimitsu found it necessary to take
military action against them. He was successful in this undertaking. Consequently, in January, 1406, the Emperor Cheng-
Tsu issued an imperial edict, which read as follows:

"The Emperor hereby issues a decree to the King of Japan.
Because your disorderly subjects in Iki, Tsushima, and in several other distant islands had continuously ravaged and plundered our coast districts, and because our people living there
had long suffered from the inhuman and brutal acts of those
pirates, we instructed the King of Japan to destroy them. He
therefore sent troops and practically annihilated them. Their
ships were destroyed and their leaders were either killed or

captured. Those that were captured were sent to our imperial court. The King of Japan thus feared and revered the throne and carried out our instructions promptly. This evidences that, although he lives far beyond the waters, yet his heart is always with us in our imperial court. Henceforth, the people living in the coast districts of our empire will be free from the dangers and ravages of the pirate bands. . . . We hereby send an envoy to express our heartfelt appreciation and satisfaction and to confer honors upon the King of Japan."[69]

The annihilation of the Japanese pirates was as yet far from being an accomplished fact. Yoshimitsu had to continue his military operations against the pirates; and he was very successful. About six months later, in January, 1407, the Emperor Cheng-Tsu therefore issued another imperial edict, in which he expressed his high appreciation. It read, in part, as follows:

"The Emperor hereby issues a decree to the King of Japan. In the past, pirate bands ravaged and plundered our coast districts, thus causing great suffering among the people there. We therefore instructed the King to hunt out and destroy them. The King earnestly and promptly obeyed our commands. He dispatched troops and succeeded in destroying their fleets, and inflicted severe punishment upon them. The leaders that were captured were sent to us to deal with. However, some of their leaders together with many followers made their escape to far distant islands which were almost impossible to reach. Because of geographical disadvantages, our fleets were unable to penetrate these new haunts. Therefore, our brave men with their sharp weapons could not carry out their work effectively. Being of inhuman and desperate nature, the pirates could neither be brought to reason nor made to fear us. The King of Japan therefore devoted days and nights, even to the extreme of neglecting to eat or to sleep, in the hope of devising ways and means of coping with the pirates. Finally, his plan was completed. Because of his remarkable strategy and tactics, the King of Japan, with great skill and bravery, enabled his men to destroy or capture all the escaped pirate leaders. The pirates that were captured were sent to us for punishment. The memorial sent by the King, giving a detailed account of the experiences in capturing the pirates, has been read by us over and over with great appreciation and admiration. The King's loyal and faithful service approached divine protection. The work accomplished by him has gained Heaven's sanction and has afforded us great comfort, having met our every expectation. Henceforth, all our coast districts will be clear and safe, and the dwellers therein will no longer be alarmed by signal fires. Even the chickens, pigs, and dogs will henceforth find the place safe. All this is due to your remarkable and meritorious work. . . . From the time that Japan came into existence, there has never before appeared a man who has had such high attainments and wisdom as has the King of Japan. . . . We hereby send a special envoy to convey verbally our appreciation."[70]

During the early part of the reign of the Ming emperor Cheng-Tsu, China fully established her suzerainty over Japan and succeeded in compelling Japan to keep the Chinese coast districts free from Japanese bandits. For his services, Yoshimitsu, who was recognized by China as "King of Japan," received very liberal compensation from China.[71]

He also gained the privilege of sending tribute to the Ming throne, as well as the right to engage in trade. Strange though it may seem, during the time of Yoshimitsu, the sending of tribute to the Ming throne was regarded as a privilege and not as an obligation. Every time Japan sent tribute to China, in the form of local products, the Ming emperor showed great appreciation and sent back, by the Japanese tribute-bearing envoys, gifts of silver, copper, bronze, silk brocades, and other fine goods, the value of which was many times that of the tribute sent by Japan.

In fact, in those days, the sending of tribute to China on the part of Japan and the making of gifts on the part of China was really a private "trade" between the Ming emperor and the

"King of Japan." The balance was always greatly in favor of Japan.[72] Yoshimitsu ("King of Japan") was likewise privileged to monopolize all the trade with China. This trade was not conducted between nation and nation but between the Ming government and the "King of Japan." Tradesmen in China and tradesmen in Japan had absolutely no connection with it. According to the trade agreement, the Ming government issued one hundred trade licenses to the government of the "King of Japan."[73] Japanese ships entering the Chinese ports for trade purposes were permitted to engage in trade only after they had presented some of these trade licenses, thus identifying themselves as ships sent by the government of the "King of Japan." Although some feudal lords and some Buddhistic monasteries were occasionally permitted to use the trade licenses, the government of the "King of Japan" virtually monopolized the trade, and Yoshimitsu, throughout his life, regarded it as the greatest source of revenue of his government. The rewards received by Yoshimitsu from the Ming emperor for his service in subjugating the pirate bands further enriched him. Year after year, throughout his life, Yoshimitsu continued to capture pirate chiefs and to send them to the Ming emperor, who always rewarded him liberally. Of all the rewards thus sent, that given in May in the fifth year of the Yung-Lo era of the Emperor Cheng-Tsu (1407) was the most esteemed because of its great value.[74] Not only was Yoshimitsu rewarded, but also the envoys in whose custody he had sent the pirate prisoners to the Ming throne. The gift sent to Yoshimitsu in 1407 consisted of twenty-two different kinds of articles, numbering 535 pieces. It included 1000 *ryo* of silver, 15,000 *kan* of copper, and many pieces of rare silk brocades, together with other valuable woven materials.

The respective fundamental purposes of the international undertakings entered into by China under the Ming dynasty and Japan were, on the part of China, to suppress and conquer the Japanese pirates, thus keeping her coast districts free from being plundered; on the part of Japan, to strengthen her financial situation by gaining the privileges of trade and of sending tribute to the Ming throne, and to receive rewards for her services in subjugating the pirates. With the increasing activity of the pirates and the necessity of continuing military measures against them, the intercourse between the two nations naturally became much more frequent.[75]

In 1403, when the treaty with respect to trade and the sending of tribute was being negotiated, China was fearful lest pirate ships enter the harbors of China under the guise of trade ships from Japan, and fearful, too, lest Japanese trade ships carry concealed weapons to be used as opportunity might present itself. She was also concerned lest her financial burden in making liberal return for the tribute sent by Japan to the Ming throne should become increasingly heavy. Accordingly, the treaty gave Japan permission to send tribute-bearing and trade ships to China but once in every ten years.[76] It was further stipulated that Japan was not to send more than two ships at a time, that the number of men in these ships should not exceed two hundred, and that under no circumstances were the ships to carry military weapons of any description. However, after China and Japan had entered into these international agreements, conditions proved entirely different from what had been expected. Yoshimitsu showed great loyalty and sincerity. Year after year, he searched out the pirates, capturing their leaders and destroying their ships. The Ming emperor and all China realized that Yoshimitsu's service was invaluable both to the throne and to the nation, and they fully appreciated that he was China's savior and peace-giver.[77] In recognition of this, the Ming government entirely disregarded the terms of the treaty and permitted Japan to send tribute and trade ships every year. Moreover, the limitations on the number of ships and the men on board them were also disregarded. China welcomed the Japanese tribute and trade ships and gave them every possible accommodation.

But Yoshimitsu, when he entered into an agreement with the Ming government by the terms of which the national dignity and honor of Japan were tarnished,[78] had virtually sold the national independence of Japan to China. He faithfully adhered to all the duties and obligations and always tried to render full service for the money received. Furthermore, he showed great reverence to the Ming throne as a humble subject of his lord.[79] Whenever the Ming emperor sent an envoy bearing an imperial edict, Yoshimitsu always sent two of his officers of the highest rank to the outermost gates of the city to meet the envoy and his party and escort them to his palace. When the imperial edict was about to be handed to him by the Ming envoy, Yoshimitsu first burned incense in order to purify himself, and then prostrated himself three times in succession before receiving and reading the paper. Because of his success in suppressing the pirates, and because of his sincerity and attitude of loyalty to the Ming throne, the Emperor Cheng-Tsu time and again expressed his appreciation of his accomplishments as well as respect for his personality and his ability.

The service of Yoshimitsu to the Ming throne was, as it happened, of brief duration. In the late spring of 1408, Yoshimitsu was suddenly taken ill, and he died on May 6 after severe suffering of about a week. He was only fifty years of age. Yoshimitsu ruled Japan as shogun for twenty-six years. He then resigned the office of shogun, shaved his head, and continued to rule Japan for fourteen years as a Buddhist priest. (He is known in Chinese history by the name of Tao-i, this being his Buddhistic name.) During the last six of these fourteen years, under the title of "King of Japan, a subject of the Ming Emperor," he devoted himself to the service of the Ming throne. He lived a most extravagant and luxurious life, which could not be duplicated even by the emperor of Japan.

Yoshimitsu's untimely death in the prime of life was deeply regretted by Cheng-Tsu, the Ming emperor. On December 21,

1408, the Ming emperor sent an envoy to Japan for the special purpose of having him worship the departed soul of Yoshimitsu. The emperor himself addressed Yoshimitsu's soul by issuing an imperial edict in which he first expressed great admiration for the personality and accomplishments of Yoshimitsu, and then recounted the numerous services rendered by Yoshimitsu to the Ming throne. He concluded by expressing his personal grief and sadness because of Yoshimitsu's death, and consoled both himself and Yoshimitsu's soul by saying that the fame of Yoshimitsu would go down through history and that his great works would be remembered as long as Heaven and earth should exist.[80] At the same time, the Ming emperor issued an imperial edict to Yoshimochi, the successor to Yoshimitsu, in which he expressed condolence on the death of his father. As the first gift to Yoshimochi, the Ming emperor sent five hundred rolls each of silk and fine linen, and despatched another envoy to Japan to invest Yoshimochi with the title of "King of Japan."

Yoshimochi, the fourth shogun of the Ashikaga, possessed neither the ability nor the attainments of Yoshimitsu. He was a man of sincerity, uprightness, and principle, and he always regretted that the dealings of his father with China had disgraced and degraded Japan. When the Ming emperor, in 1408, desired to invest him with the title of "King of Japan" as the successor to Yoshimitsu, he promptly refused to accept the investiture. He even refused to grant the Ming envoy an interview,[81] and instructed his representative to inform the envoy that Japan would no longer maintain relations with the Ming empire, and would no longer either send tribute to the Ming throne or engage in trade therewith; nor would she feel it incumbent upon herself to comply with instructions of the Ming emperor with respect to suppression of the Japanese pirates; moreover, the Ming emperor should not send his envoys to Japan, as they would not be received. In spite of the fact that the Ming envoy sent in 1408 returned to China with such a report, the Ming emperor continued to send envoys and to demand that Yoshimochi adhere to all the regulations and perform all the duties and services that Yoshimitsu, his father, had pledged himself to perform. The Ming emperor even resorted to military threats; but Yoshimochi stubbornly maintained that Japan was not a tributary state of China.

After Yoshimochi had discontinued relations with China, he no longer made any effort either to control the pirates or to send his fleet to their haunts. This attitude of the shogunate government had a marked effect upon the coast districts of China. They suffered from the ravages and plundering of the pirates as they had before the time of Yoshimitsu. Standard histories of China contain accounts of these changes in conditions. According to the records contained therein, during the five years beginning in the first year of the Yung-Lo era of the Ming emperor, Cheng-Tsu, Japan sent tribute to the Ming court every year regularly, and no attacks by Japanese pirates were made on the Chinese coast. But 1408, the year in which Yoshimitsu died, was the last year in which the annual tribute was sent by Japan to the Ming court for a quarter-century. It was also the year in which the Japanese renewed their plundering. From that year on, the pirates made attacks on the Chinese coast every year. The histories of the Ming contain accounts of attacks in 1408, 1409, 1410, and 1411.[82]

The renewed plundering by the Japanese pirates became increasingly serious and dangerous. Almost the entire coast of China from Shantung in the north to Fukien in the south suffered from their attacks, and without the coöperation of Japan the Ming government found it impossible to cope with them in a military way. For the purpose of reopening negotiations, the Ming emperor sent envoys to Japan in 1417, 1418, and 1419, sometimes offering very liberal terms and sometimes complaining of the lack of courtesy shown his envoys. But Yoshimochi did not change his hostile policy toward China, the Ming envoy being driven away each time without having either been granted an interview or given a reply to the imperial state papers that he had brought with him.

When envoys came in 1418, 1419, and again in 1422, Yoshimochi instructed his representative on each occasion to explain to the Ming envoy why Japan would not enter into negotiations with China, and to ask that the Ming government entirely discontinue sending envoys. This matter being of serious import, Yoshimochi put everything in written form so that his representative might convey to the Ming envoy Yoshimochi's decisions in detail. This document first stated that Japan was the nation of the gods, and that the ruler of the nation had therefore never conducted national affairs without obtaining either divine instructions or consent. Notwithstanding this, his father, Yoshimitsu, had dared to violate this sacred national tradition by receiving the national calendar of the Ming empire, by accepting the official seal as "King of Japan" from the Ming emperor, and by even going so far as to style himself "a subject of the Ming court," thus revering the ruler of a foreign nation as his lord. Since the foundation of the nation, the document further stated, such outrageous and disgraceful acts as those committed by Yoshimitsu had never before been known in the history of the empire. All these acts of Yoshimitsu had offended the gods, and his death in the prime of life was a divine punishment. Yoshimitsu, on his deathbed, had deeply regretted what he had done and had pledged to all the gods that his descendants would be strictly prohibited from receiving any instructions from foreign nations, and that they would sever all relations with the Ming empire. Yoshimochi would neither grant an interview to the Ming envoy nor send an envoy to the Ming court: not because he relied upon the geographical advantages of Japan, but because he revered the instructions of the native gods and because he was complying with the dying request of his father.[83]

Instead of replying to the military threats of the Ming emperor, Yoshimochi harked back to historical events. Hundreds of thousands of Kublai Khan's fighting men and several thousands of his warships which had been sent to conquer Japan, had been sunk, he said, to the bottom of the sea by the winds sent by the gods, under whose guidance and protection Japan maintained her existence.[84] As for the complaint of the Ming emperor about the Japanese pirates and their plundering of the Chinese coast districts, Yoshimochi stated that, as the pirates were outlaws of Japan, the Ming government was free to capture them and to inflict due punishment, and that therefore the Ming emperor should not appeal to Japan with respect to conditions along the coast of his own empire. As for the complaint of the Ming emperor concerning the Japanese lack of courtesy in receiving his envoys, Yoshimochi denied that any discourtesy had been shown. He expressed it as his opinion that if both the Ming government and the Japanese government should refrain from sending uninvited envoys, the methods of dealing with them would never become national problems. He concluded by saying that, as it was his policy not to send envoys to the Ming court, it would be well for the Ming emperor to keep his envoys at home.

After the contents of the foregoing statement of Yoshimochi had been orally delivered by his representative to the Ming envoy, and after they had been conveyed to the Ming emperor, the hoped-for results were brought about. The Emperor Cheng-Tsu concluded that it was useless to attempt to deal with Japan on the pirate problem. Throughout the remainder of his reign and the reign of the Emperor Jen-Tsung, no envoys were sent to Japan.[85]

This condition persisted for a quarter-century, up to the time that the Emperor Hsuan-Tsung, the grandson of the Emperor Cheng-Tsu, came to rule China.[86] The Emperor Hsuan-Tsung discerned that a satisfactory solution of the pirate problem might be obtained only if China and Japan should come to an understanding about it. Being aware that Japan could not be approached directly because since 1408 she had repeatedly refused to receive envoys from the Ming court and had subsequently closed her door against China, the Ming emperor decided to employ the king of Liu Chiu as his diplomatic agent. Liu Chiu was a small island kingdom that had pledged allegiance to both China and Japan. In January, 1432, the Ming emperor, Hsuan-Tsung, issued an instruction to the king of Liu Chiu, in which he stated that, since his accession, all the states, both large and small, in various parts of Asia had been sending envoys to the Ming court, thus showing reverence to the throne, and that Japan was the only country that had not sent tribute-bearing envoys. Accordingly, the king of Liu Chiu was instructed to transmit to Japan the imperial desire of the Ming emperor that Japan should conform with the practice of other countries.

This attempt to renew international intercourse came at a very opportune time. In Japan the fifth shogun, Yoshikazu, the only son of Yoshimochi, died in 1425 after having ruled but two years. He left no son to succeed him. In 1429, after long consideration, a brother of Yoshimochi who had become a Buddhist priest was requested to lay aside his priestly robes to become the sixth shogun. Being a Buddhist, Yoshinori (this was the name taken by him when he reëntered secular life) neither believed that Yoshimitsu had died as the result of divine punishment, nor did he place any credence in the dying request of Yoshimitsu. Furthermore, being a great admirer of his father, he desired to reinstate his father's policy.[87] Like his father, Yoshinori was an egotistic man and of strong materialistic inclinations. He, too, hoped to gain trade concessions and grants from China, and thereby to enrich both himself and his government. Accordingly, when in 1432 he was informed by the king of Liu Chiu of the desire of the Ming emperor, he promptly sent an envoy to the Ming court to express his earnest desire to reëstablish relations with the Ming empire.[88]

The Ming emperor, Hsuan-Tsung, was highly pleased with his diplomatic success. In the following year (1433) he sent to

Japan an envoy bearing an imperial edict to Yoshinori, the "King of Japan." In this edict, the Ming emperor expressed high appreciation and praise for the loyal and distinguished service of Yoshimitsu, the father of Yoshinori, mentioned with regret the deplorable national course pursued by Japan since the death of Yoshimitsu in cutting off all communication with the Ming court, and concluded by expressing great satisfaction because Yoshinori had at last begun to walk in the footsteps of his father by sending a tribute-bearing envoy to the Ming court, thus showing that he feared Heaven and revered the "Great Nation." Along with this imperial edict, the Ming emperor sent to the king of Japan one hundred *ryo* of silver and to his queen one hundred *ryo* of silver, together with hundreds of rolls of valuable woven stuffs, as a sort of allowance from the throne to the ruler of a tributary state.[89] In order to impress Japan with the strength and power of the Ming empire and with the glory and dignity of the Ming throne, the Emperor Hsuan-Tsung sent about six hundred men as escort for his envoy. They sailed to Japan aboard five large vessels. On June 1, 1433, they reached Kyoto, the capital of Japan, and five days later they were received by Yoshinori with great reverence and honor. In accordance with the practice of his father Yoshimitsu, Yoshinori burned incense to purify both his soul and his body and then prostrated himself twice in succession in worship before receiving and reading the imperial edict.[90]

Now that the suzerain and tributary relationship was reestablished between China and Japan, Yoshinori had to observe all the duties and obligations to the Ming throne that had been observed by his father, Yoshimitsu. He was invested with the title of "King of Japan." All the memorials and state papers that he addressed to the Ming throne were signed, "Yoshinori, King of Japan and subject of the Ming Emperor."[91] The national calendar of the Ming was used in dating papers addressed to the Ming government, in evidence that Japan was a tributary state of China.

On June 17, 1433, Yoshinori concluded a sort of treaty with the Ming envoy on the pirate problem. It consisted of three articles: (1) Japan should henceforth strictly prohibit her subjects from committing piracy and should severely punish those who disobeyed; (2) Japan should keep several fleets of war vessels along her coasts to watch for pirate ships and prevent them from sailing from Japanese waters to the Chinese coast; and (3) all the subjects of the Ming emperor who had been taken prisoner by the Japanese pirates should be sent back to their respective homes in China.[92]

In thus reviving friendly relations with Japan, the Ming emperor made many liberal grants. The number of tribute and trade ships was increased from two to three. The number of men aboard these ships was increased from 200 to 300.[93] The number of trade licenses granted to the government of the "King of Japan" (the shogun) was increased from 100 to 200. A new usage was established, permitting of pecuniary gifts by the Ming throne to the "King of Japan" and his "queen." These gifts were respectively 200 *ryo* of silver to the "king" and 100 *ryo* of silver to the "queen" together with hundreds of rolls of valuable woven goods. This allowance by the Ming throne was sent each time that a Japanese envoy returned home from China. In addition to this allowance, Yoshinori, the shogun, under the name of "King of Japan," begged the Ming emperor time and again to give him large amounts of copper coins to help him financially in running the government, and the Ming emperor usually responded to these requests. Although there is no documentary evidence to substantiate the fact, historical records state that in 1434, the year following the renewal of the suzerain and tributary relationship with China, Yoshinori begged the Ming emperor to give him copper coins to the amount of 300,000 *kan,* which was 30,000,000 copper coins in the Ming currency, and that the request was complied with.[94]

The international relations between China and Japan during the fifteenth and sixteenth centuries, when China was under the rule of the Ming dynasty and Japan was under the rule of the Ashikaga, fall into two periods.[95] The first period was very brief; it covered less than ten years, beginning in 1403 when Yoshimitsu sent a memorial to the Ming throne, using the title "King of Japan, a subject of the Ming Emperor," and ending when Yoshimochi, the son of Yoshimitsu, repeatedly refused to receive the Ming envoys or to accept the Ming imperial edicts. He finally succeeded in making the Ming emperor realize that the door of Japan was closed to him. The second period covered 115 years, beginning in 1432 when Yoshinori sent a tribute-bearing envoy to China, thus renewing the suzerain and tributary relationship with the Ming empire, and ending in 1547 when the twelfth shogun, Yoshiharu, sent the last memorial to the Ming throne in which appeared the title, "King of Japan, a subject of the Ming Emperor."

During the first period, Yoshimitsu faithfully and sincerely carried out the obligations and duties that he had pledged to the Ming throne. Through his meritorious and energetic efforts, the Ming government was able to keep the entire coast of China free from attacks of the pirates, and he received from the Ming throne due recognition, compensation, and expressions of appreciation. In the second period, although the Ashikaga shoguns (as "Kings of Japan") received tribute-sending and trade privileges, as well as far greater throne allowances from the Ming emperor than had Yoshimitsu, neither Yoshinori nor the other shoguns ever sought to control or to subjugate the pirates. In the entire 115 years, neither the Chinese nor the Japanese histories contain any record that the "King of Japan" sent captured pirates to the Ming throne.[96]

In these circumstances, the treaty terms of 1433 remained quite unobserved. According to the historical records of the Ming, in 1439, only six years after the treaty had been concluded, a pirate fleet of forty vessels made destructive invasions of district after district. In those days, the Japanese pirates employed Chinese who had fled from China because of heavy taxation and compulsory unpaid labor, to spy out conditions in the coast districts which the pirates were about to attack. Furthermore, the Japanese went to the Chinese coast prepared for two lines of action: when opportunity presented, they made use of military weapons of various kinds and robbed and murdered as they went; at other times, when they found the Chinese coast well protected, they displayed various kinds of Japanese local products, which, they asserted, they had come to bring as tribute to the throne,[97] and under this pretext they demanded due courtesy and good treatment, and this Japanese ruse made it impossible for the Chinese to differentiate between tribute-bearing ships and pirate fleets. Conditions became so increasingly serious that local officials presented memorials to the throne, praying the emperor to place all ships coming from Japan under strict regulation and control.[98] This the emperor repeatedly refused to do, lest other peoples coming from far distant lands might be disappointed in their expectations and become estranged through such actions on the part of the imperial throne of the Ming. So fearful, too, was he lest China might suffer more extensively from the plundering of the Japanese pirates if her relations with Japan should be severed, and so strong was the desire of the Ming throne to maintain the dignity and honor of China's suzerainty over Japan, that the emperor permitted the "King of Japan" to continue the privilege of sending tribute-bearing vessels and trade ships to China. (See below, pp. 122–23.)[99]

Yoshinori's failure to keep his pledge to the Ming throne with respect to the pirates may be laid to unfortunate domestic conditions rather than to insincerity. Yoshimitsu and Yoshinori ruled Japan under entirely different conditions. When Yoshimitsu entered into the agreement with the Ming emperor, he was the sole master of Japan, both civil and military, there being not a single statesman or military lord who dared either to oppose or to criticize him.[100] Thus free to turn his entire military and diplomatic activities to the pirate problem, Yoshimitsu was able to fulfill his pledge to the Ming throne, and to secure thereby the much coveted financial and economic rewards.

When Yoshinori, in the middle of the fifteenth century, began to rule Japan as the sixth Ashikaga shogun, conditions were vastly different. As the result of a quarter-century of the weak and mild administrations of the fourth and fifth shoguns, the military families had again become arrogant and arbitrary. Yoshinori, who had great admiration for the achievements of his father, Yoshimitsu, decided to reorganize the shogunate government with the purpose of getting the ruling authority into his own hands as his father had done. This involved, as will be explained, several risky military expeditions against men closely related to him by blood.

The Ashikaga family at Kamakura was originally founded by the brother of Yoshiaki, the second shogun. It had been entrusted with authority over all of eastern Japan in order that the Japanese empire might be placed under the complete control of the Ashikaga family through the coöperation of the two military governments already established at Kyoto and Kamakura, respectively. Contrary to expectation, the Ashikaga at Kamakura and the military government in eastern Japan became strong rivals for the shogunate government at Kyoto. When the fifth shogun died without leaving a successor, Mochiuji, the head of the Ashikaga at Kamakura, believed that, as the nearest relative of the deceased shogun, he was the logical successor to the shogunate. When he was informed that Yoshinori, a brother of the fourth shogun, had been ordered to renounce his Buddhist priesthood so that he might be appointed as the sixth shogun, Mochiuji was both disappointed and angered. He refused to recognize Yoshinori's authority, nicknamed him the "Secularized Priest Shogun," and opposed his government in every possible way. The rebellious acts of Mochiuji became so threatening that in 1439 Yoshinori formed an alliance with a strong military family in eastern Japan and

waged war against Mochiuji and his military government at
Kamakura. Yoshinori's army was successful. Mochiuji was
killed, and gradually the rule of Yoshinori made headway in
eastern Japan.[101]

Yoshinori had another formidable rival for the shogunate
in his brother, Gisho, who had likewise been a Buddhist
priest. When the question was settled and Yoshinori had been
appointed sixth shogun, Gisho, much disappointed, left Kyoto
and went to Kyushu, where he planned to enlist the military
assistance of the feudal lords and to rise against the new shogun. Quick action by Yoshinori nipped this rebellion in the
bud. He destroyed some of the powerful military families in
Kyushu, thereby strengthening his authority.

Greatly encouraged by his success both in eastern Japan and
Kyushu, Yoshinori turned his attention to the powerful military lords in central Japan. He availed himself of all possible
opportunities to exercise his authority there, but his main
purpose was to create a number of smaller feudal families
through a subdivision of the existing large families. In this,
he was both arbitrary and self-willed. His policy[102] was to strike
at random and without warning. He succeeded in a measure,
quite a number of powerful military families being either deprived of parts of their estates or completely destroyed. However, as he accomplished his purpose, the situation of Yoshinori
became more and more insecure. The military lords, fearing
lest their turn might come next, watched his every move with
uneasiness and suspicion. A powerful military family named
Akamatsu, which had come into prominence with the founding of the Ashikaga shogunate, controlled three large provinces
in central Japan. Yoshinori had been planning to confer two
of these provinces upon a favorite member of the Akamatsu
family, thus creating two Akamatsu families. When the lord
of the Akamatsu learned of this secret plan of the shogun, he
realized that the Akamatsu family would either be reduced to
lower rank or be destroyed because of disobedience to the

shogun's command, and decided that Yoshinori should meet his fate before the Akamatsu confronted its destiny.

In the early summer of 1441, the shogun's army won a decisive victory in eastern Japan. Leading military families in Kyoto in turn gave banquets in celebration and in honor of Yoshinori. The lord of the Akamatsu prepared an especially great banquet at his mansion and requested that Yoshinori honor him with his presence. In the midst of the revelry, three hundred armed men sprang from a hiding place and disarmed the shogun's bodyguard. Two Akamatsu men seized Yoshinori by his feet and by his arms, and carried him to their lord, in whose presence he was beheaded like a common criminal. This took place on June 24, 1441.

Yoshinori was a man of great genius and ability, but he was hasty, dictatorial, and cruel. He tried to uproot social and political evils through his own will, without consulting others. Had he lived longer, he might have been the second founder of the Ashikaga shogunate.

After the murder of the shogun, the Akamatsu remained in Kyoto for five days, keeping watch on the general condition and attitude of the shogunate government. The government and its supporters had been taken by surprise by the assassination. They did nothing. On June 29, the lord of the Akamatsu set fire to his mansion and left Kyoto in broad daylight, taking all the members of his family with him to his province. There, he rebelled against the shogunate government. He was subsequently conquered, but only with great difficulty. The rule of the Ashikaga shogunate virtually came to an end with the assassination of Yoshinori.[103]

In 1442, Yoshikatsu, the seven-year-old son of Yoshinori, was appointed the seventh shogun. He died the next year. In 1444, Yoshimasa, the second son of Yoshinori, also seven years old, was appointed the eighth shogun. At this very critical time the Ashikaga shogunate was thus headed by mere boys. The administrative work of the government was entrusted to powerful feudal lords, among whom jealousy and rivalry soon sprang up. Most of the military men gathered around one or another of these military barons, ignoring the authority of the shogun and engaging in petty warfare among themselves. Large Buddhistic communities maintained military forces, thus making of themselves centers of disturbance.

Yoshimasa was shogun for more than thirty years, but he had neither the ability nor the will power of his father, Yoshinori. He permitted favorite men and women, among whom were his wife and his concubines, to take a hand in government work, and bribery and favoritism were rife everywhere. In the years of his rule, also, Japan was frequently visited by famines and epidemics.

Yoshimasa, unable to cope with the situation, finally gave up all political and military affairs and devoted himself entirely to the study of art, architecture, and literature. Gradually he fell a victim to luxury and licentiousness, and became a most extravagant and unsympathetic individual. He levied taxes upon everything. He established toll stations along the national roads and along the district roads, where road taxes were collected from pedestrians. Both the shogun and the military families borrowed money wherever they could, and after they had thus become heavily indebted, Yoshimasa would promulgate a law of repudiation. According to the historical records, Yoshimasa promulgated laws of repudiation thirteen times in twenty years.[104] All trust and confidence were thereby undermined. When all the national sources of revenue were exhausted, Yoshimasa followed the example of Yoshimitsu and Yoshinori and reëstablished the suzerain and tributary relationship with China. Time and again, in the name of the "King of Japan, a humble subject of the Ming Emperor," Yoshimasa disgracefully begged monetary allowances from the imperial court of China.[105]

In the second half of the fifteenth century, there were many coexisting figureheads in Japan, but there was no strong central

ruler. The historical reasons that made this situation possible
may be stated briefly. In the early ninth century, the emperor
had delegated all authority to the Fujiwara, and the head of this
family ruled the empire as imperial regent. In the eleventh
century, the retired emperor in the Buddhist monastery deprived the Fujiwara of all power, allowing them to retain only
the empty title of imperial regent. In 1192, with the founding
of the feudal government, the retired emperor in the Buddhist
monastery was again reduced to a figurehead, and the shogun
became the central authority in both civil and military affairs.
In the second half of the fifteenth century, Yoshimasa became
shogun, but in name only: he was quite incapable of holding
or exercising any power whatever. In all the nation there appeared no man of real genius and power competent to master
the situation, destroy the Ashikaga, and establish a new military government.

And so Japan plunged into her Dark Age. First came the
"Eleven Years' Civil War."[106] The great families of the Hosokawa
and the Yamana gradually became rivals. All the military men
joined themselves to one or the other, in accordance with their
local conditions and personal and family interests. Under the
standard of the Hosokawa were gathered 160,000 fighting men
and their leaders, and 90,000 men rallied to the standard of
the Yamana. Both groups marched upon Kyoto. Numerous
bloody battles were fought in Kyoto and surrounding districts, but none of them was decisive. Toward the close of this
prolonged warfare, the heads of both the Yamana and the
Hosokawa died from illness in the same year. The leaderless
military barons, tired and disgusted with the ineffective bloody
struggles, gradually left Kyoto and returned to their respective
districts. Nearly all the principal buildings, including the imperial palace, the palace of the shogun, state mansions, and
noted temples and shrines of the city had been destroyed. Kyoto, the imperial capital for about seven hundred years, was
reduced to a barren waste.

Meanwhile, Yoshimasa, the eighth shogun, continued to disregard both the chaotic condition of the nation and the sufferings of the people. He built an elegant mansion in the Higashiyama district of Kyoto and spent the remainder of his life in ease, relying chiefly upon the imperial court of China as his source of revenue. Because of his total lack of military strength, Yoshimasa did not pledge to the Ming emperor that he would destroy the pirates, as Yoshinori and Yoshimitsu had done, but he revered the Ming ruler as an emperor of supreme power and divine virtue. Under the title of "King of Japan, a subject of the Ming Emperor," he begged for copper coins, stating that because of the long period of warfare the copper coins had all been scattered, the national coffers had become empty, and there was no way to care for the interests of the people. In 1475 and again in 1478, Yoshimasa begged 50,000 *kan* (5,000,000 copper coins), and in 1483 he begged 100,000 *kan* (10,000,000 copper coins).[107] The *Standard History of the Ming* describes one of these money-begging affairs thus: "In 1476, in addition to the regular throne allowance, the King of Japan begged for 50,000 copper coins as an additional grant." The money thus obtained by Yoshimasa in behalf of the people was all spent extravagantly by himself.

Yoshimasa was, however, a person of exceptional ingenuity and of artistic and literary talent, and he surrounded himself with men of like talents. During his residence at Higashiyama, time and again he obtained books and fine art works from the Ming emperor. He studied them carefully and finally developed new types of artistic and literary works. Strangely enough, most of the Japanese schools of art of modern times had their origin and development during the civil war which marked the beginning of Japan's darkest age. The rule of Yoshimasa is known in the history of Japanese civilization as the Higashiyama Period. On the one hand, the Higashiyama was socially and politically a most destructive period; on the other, it was Japan's creative period in the realms of art and literature.

. The Eleven Years' Civil War had been brought about by many complicated social and political conditions. On the whole, it was not only caused by, but it also exposed, the impotency and hopeless degeneracy of the Ashikaga shogunate. Although the war apparently ended in 1478, in fact hostilities were merely transferred from the imperial capital of Kyoto to the provincial districts and Japan entered upon a period of nation-wide warfare. It is true that the Ashikaga still retained the shogunship through appointment by the emperor, but only because there was no military leader strong enough to claim the appointment. The laws of the Ashikaga shogunate had long been inoperative, but the shogun was still surrounded by a few military barons who were inseparably connected with the Ashikaga through family traditions. Seemingly loyal, they were often actually treacherous and undependable. Because of their scheming, Kyoto became a place no longer safe for the shogun, who was often obliged to leave the military capital and either take refuge in the provinces of sympathetic feudal lords or seek their aid in reëstablishing himself in Kyoto. The tenth shogun, Yoshitane, in his latter days found no place of safety except the small island of Awaji in the Inland Sea of Japan. He died there in exile and he is therefore known in history as the "Island Shogun."[108]

The Ashikaga shogunate family originally had a number of provinces and estates under its direct control. Most of these provinces the shoguns lost in the national chaos of the Dark Age, to the aggressive military barons. This loss involved them in great financial difficulties so that the shogun and his government were unable to meet their obligations to the imperial court and the imperial family. Consequently, even so important a national matter as the enthronement celebration of a newly ascended emperor frequently could not be observed until several years after the event. In fact, one emperor had to wait for twenty-two years for his enthronement, when the chief priest of a wealthy Buddhistic community was prompted by sympathy for the emperor to donate both his personal savings and the church funds so as to make the enthronement possible.[109] Two other emperors were forced to wait many years for their enthronement celebrations until rich feudal lords supplied the means. The one hundred and second emperor, Gotsuchi Mikado, who died in 1500 A.D., remained unburied for more than six weeks because of lack of funds at the imperial court and the inability of the shogun to provide what was required.[110] The court nobles, by begging funds from several feudal lords, finally got together enough money for the interment.

In the sixteenth century, because no provision could be made for them, most of the court nobles were obliged to leave Kyoto and wander from province to province until they found some rich and generous feudal lord who was willing to open his home to one or more of them. This resource was not open to the emperor and a few of the more prominent court nobles, who, because of the traditional and historical connections with the imperial capital, were compelled to stay in Kyoto. In those days, the imperial court was abandoned and all ceremonial rites and proceedings went unobserved. The imperial palace was virtually deserted and left at the mercy of the elements.[111] The wall surrounding the palace ground fell into a state of decay. On hot summer days, roadside vendors set up their wayside stands within the palace grounds, where they sold tea and light refreshments. Little children made the audience hall their playground and made mud pies on its steps. The emperor and his family were for a long time without any financial provision, so that the emperor was eventually forced to earn his own living. Since he had no trade or training, his education having been wholly cultural, he sold his poems and his autographs. Usually he inscribed poems of his own composition on several pieces of paper and fastened them on the bamboo screens in the front of the house where passers-by might read them and make selections. When someone found a poem that he liked, he would take it and leave a copper coin. If a person desired to have the emperor compose a poem on a specified subject or to autograph a particular selection from some standard literary work, he had only to write the subject on a piece of paper and to wrap it, together with a few copper coins, in a piece of cloth and hang it on the bamboo screen. A few days later, he would find the emperor's autograph or poem on the screen.[112] Both the poems and the autographs of the emperor sold well. Even though Japan was passing through its darkest and most trying period, the sacred national tradition that the emperor was a direct descendant of the Sun Goddess still had great weight with the people, and the possession of a work from the emperor's pen was regarded as an honor; even more, it was esteemed as a divine charm.

In the sixteenth century, the imperial court and the imperial family of Japan were reduced so low that they were barely able to maintain their existence. And the state of the shogun was a great deal worse. Although the head of the Ashikaga family was appointed by the emperor as shogun and although he was entrusted with the sole authority to rule Japan on behalf of the throne, in these times the shogun could not even be a figurehead—because there was no nation for him to rule. In Honshu, Shikoku, and Kyushu war was waged continuously, the stronger destroying the weaker, and newly risen families annihilating the old families. Some of these military families made themselves lords of from five to twelve provinces. Japan was thus virtually divided into many separate states, each of which was an independent ruling unit. In such circumstances, the Ashikaga ceased to be a national ruling power. Nevertheless, they remained a storm center for several reasons; namely: (1) the head of the Ashikaga was still the holder of the title of "Shogun," and (2) as such he always sought to remain in Kyoto in order to identify himself with affairs in the imperial capital; (3) the shogun had absolutely no military power of his own; nevertheless (4), such families as the Hosokawa, the Miyoshi, and the Matsunaga, among which rivalry

and enmity were rife, all professed to be loyal to the shogun;
however, (5) they sought to use him to advance their respective family interests; as a result, the shogun was frequently
driven out of Kyoto, and, at times, even his whereabouts was
unknown.

In March, 1489, the ninth shogun, Yoshihisa, died in a military camp when waging war against a rebellious lord. This
was the last time in the history of Japan that an Ashikaga shogun led an army in person.[113] The tenth, eleventh, and twelfth
shoguns were, indeed, appointed by the emperor, but were
immediately driven away from Kyoto by treacherous military
lords. With the aid of local military lords, they were able
briefly to reëstablish themselves in Kyoto, but only to be driven
out time and again. Yoshiteru, the thirteenth shogun, met a
most unusual death. The Matsunaga and the Miyoshi, the two
leading military families that were closely connected with the
Ashikaga shogunate, promised Yoshihide, a younger member
of the Ashikaga, that they would satisfy his ambition to become
shogun. In order to make room for him, in May, 1565, the
Matsunaga, assisted by men of the Miyoshi, made a sudden attack upon the thirteenth shogun, Yoshiteru, at his mansion in
Kyoto, and assassinated him.[114] The fact that the shogun was
thus killed neither for political reasons nor because of enmity
but merely for the purpose of satisfying the self-seeking ambition of a young man, gives one some idea of the condition of
Japan in the sixteenth century.

In February, 1568, Yoshihide was appointed by the emperor
as the fourteenth shogun, in compliance with the request of
Matsunaga. Yoshiaki, a brother of the thirteenth shogun,
escaped from Kyoto and wandered from one province to another, seeking the assistance of feudal lords in avenging the
death of his brother and making himself the shogun. He did
not succeed in his quest until he presented his case to Nobunaga, a rising military man of ability and ambition. Under the
military protection of Nobunaga, Yoshiaki, in 1568, made a

successful entry into Kyoto, and forced Yoshihide to flee. Yoshihide went to the island of Shikoku, where he died in September, 1568, after having been shogun for but seven months. In the same year, the emperor appointed Yoshiaki as the fifteenth shogun of the Ashikaga. Yoshiaki highly appreciated the service rendered by Nobunaga. Notwithstanding the fact that Nobunaga was many years his junior, he always addressed him as "Father" and he pledged himself to conduct not only the governmental affairs but his personal affairs as well in accordance with Nobunaga's advice.

Nobunaga, happily, was a man of both wise foresight and loyalty to his country. It was his ambition to effect national unification. He faced a situation in which all national order, as well as all political, social, and religious institutions, was either undermined or hopelessly degenerated. The sole surviving traditions—and they had survived only because they were so deeply rooted in the life and thought of the people—were the sacredness of the throne and the divinity of the emperor. Nobunaga therefore concluded that so great an undertaking as that of the restoration of peace and the unification of Japan could not be effected unless the movement were centered upon the emperor and his court. After establishing himself in Kyoto, Nobunaga placed the imperial capital under the control of the military police, thus assuring order there. He abolished all the toll stations and removed many of the unjust burdens from the people in order to make it possible for them to live happily. He rebuilt and repaired palaces for both the emperor and the shogun, and made suitable provision for them to live in comfort and maintain their dignity. He built many residences for the court nobles, thus making it possible for them to return to Kyoto from their places of refuge in the provincial districts. The emperor, surrounded by his court nobles, was able to resume regular court proceedings and to revive many important ceremonies that had long been unobserved.

Nobunaga, through all these wise acts, had become the central support of the emperor, the shogun, and the mass of the people. His increasing popularity caused Yoshiaki to become jealous of him. The frequent advice that he received from Nobunaga further estranged him, made him hate Nobunaga, and finally developed into active enmity. In the spring of 1573, Yoshiaki, the shogun, conspired against Nobunaga and made an unsuccessful attempt to destroy him and his forces by inducing the powerful military families in the provincial districts to form an alliance against him.[115] After the failure of this plot, Yoshiaki begged the forgiveness of Nobunaga, which was granted. Four months later, Yoshiaki made a second attempt to destroy him. This time, Nobunaga acted promptly: he besieged Yoshiaki at his palace, forced him to surrender, and permanently exiled him from Kyoto. Yoshiaki later became a Buddhist priest and died at a good old age. With the exile of Yoshiaki from Kyoto in the summer of 1573, the Ashikaga shogunate automatically came to an end. The Ashikaga Period covered 235 years, beginning in 1338 and ending in 1573. In this long period, fifteen Ashikaga shoguns ruled Japan, either actually or nominally. Of the fifteen shoguns, the third, Yoshimitsu, the fourth, Yoshimochi, and the sixth, Yoshinori, were the only ones that exercised ruling power. On the whole, the entire Ashikaga rule was the most chaotic and the most disgraceful in the history of Japan.[116]

In the half-century ending in 1547, when Yoshitane, Yoshizumi, and Yoshiharu held the titles of tenth, eleventh, and twelfth shoguns of the Ashikaga, the shogunate rule virtually ceased, even the form of government being sometimes nonexistent. Nevertheless, all these shoguns continued to send memorials to the Ming throne in China in the name of the "King of Japan, a subject of the Ming Emperor." In these memorials and under this name, the Ashikaga shoguns always reverently eulogized the Ming emperor as the great sovereign of a suzerain nation, possessed of great divine virtue and power. The shogun accompanied the memorial with products of Japan sent to the Ming throne nominally as tribute, but actually for the purpose of receiving a profitable return.

In 1506, when the eleventh shogun, Yoshizumi, sent a memorial to the Ming throne in the name of the "King of Japan, a subject of the Ming Emperor," he stated that under Heaven there existed only one ruler of suzerain power. Upon him alone shone the sun and the moon. Korea and a myriad of other nations, whether civilized or barbarous, reverently sent tribute and showed submission to the Ming throne. He said further:

"The sacred and divine virtue and the benevolent protection of His Majesty have reached our humble country. We hereby send Keigo as our envoy and Kogyo and Seido as assistant envoys to the imperial court for the purpose of presenting the products of our humble land as tribute to the throne. This memorial is reverently presented by Yoshizumi, the King of Japan, a subject of the Ming Emperor, with fear and awe, humbly bowing his head three times in succession."[117]

In 1527, the twelfth shogun, Yoshiharu, in a memorial to the Ming throne, first eulogized the Ming emperor, saying: "The grand administration and intellectual attainments of the great Emperor of the Ming have had no equal in the history of China. Nations from the east and the west and from the north and the south rival each other in sending their tribute to the throne." He then pitifully described conditions in Japan, saying that, because of long-continued warfare, the whereabouts of the golden seal given by the Ming throne to Japan had become unknown, and, he continued: "Therefore, I, the King of Japan, have signed my name in a special style of writing of my own without attaching the official seal. I hereby humbly request the gift of a new golden seal, and a new trade license to keep as a national treasure. The sacred virtue of His Majesty and his divine-like blessing reach us who dwell far from the throne to the same degree as they reach those who are closer. With ready obedience and heartfelt gratitude, the local products of our land, in accordance with the traditional usage, are hereby presented to the throne as a tribute."[118]

In 1547 the Ashikaga shogun sent his very last memorial in the name of "King of Japan, a subject of the Ming Emperor." According to official records, these tribute-bearing envoys sailed in four vessels, which left Japan in February, 1547, and reached Ningpo, China, in March, 1548.[119] The envoy and his party went by land to Peking, arriving there in April, 1549. They left the capital in August of the same year, and arrived home in Japan in the spring of 1550, thus consuming nearly three years on their official mission to the court of the Ming and in returning to Japan. It was a tedious, hazardous, and expensive undertaking, even in the sixteenth century, because of the lack of both water- and land-transportation facilities. However, Japan sent tribute-bearing envoys, at rather irregular intervals, for nearly one hundred and twenty-five years. She did this because the Ming court was a source of great revenue, and she broke off the relationship only when China's growing weakness made it no longer profitable.

On the part of China, the Ming emperor had been willing to make a very liberal allowance to the "King of Japan" (the shogun), first, because Japan's recognition of the Ming empire as a suzerain nation satisfied the traditional pride of China; and second, because, in the fifteenth and sixteenth centuries, the Ming empire was steadily declining. In this situation, China made it her national policy to maintain friendly relations with other nations, and she was well pleased to have Japan recognize her as its suzerain power, and especially to receive her promise to control the pirates. Even after China realized that Japan could not be depended on to restrain the pirates, she still honored the relationship lest Japan might encourage the pirates to greater excesses.

China paid dearly, however, for this attempt to maintain a proud position which, ironically enough, the judgment of later historians was to disavow (see below, pp. 126–27). Let

us return, however, to the special troubles of the fifteenth and
sixteenth centuries, in which China suffered one calamity
after another in quick succession, and because of which, in
part, she was willing to continue to receive Japan's tribute-
bearing envoys.

In the middle of the fifteenth century, the Wala, a branch
of the Mongolian tribe, invaded North China and completely
routed the imperial army of the Ming. In the following year,
the Emperor Ying-Tsung raised a very large army which he led
himself, and waged war against the Wala. His army was annihilated, and both he and his military staff were taken prisoners.
The emperor, however, was permitted to return to his imperial capital after living in disgrace with the barbarians for
more than a year.[120]

At the same time, the entire coast of China from the northern to the southern extremities was continuously ravaged by
Japanese pirates with ever-increasing seriousness. In the sixteenth century, conditions became even worse. Innumerable
dissatisfied Chinese joined the Japanese pirates, and Chinese
pirate leaders and their bands coöperated with the Japanese
pirates so that the people in southern China suffered unceasingly from these robbers.[121]

During the quarter-century from 1550 to 1573, in which
Yoshiteru, Yoshihide, and Yoshiaki were, respectively, the thirteenth, fourteenth, and fifteenth shoguns, no envoys from the
"King of Japan" arrived at the Ming court. The Ashikaga shogunate was so distressed that it could not even equip tribute-
bearing ships to send to China. Even before their time, the
shogun had frequently found it necessary to ask wealthy feudal
lords to advance money to cover the expense, on the condition
that it would be paid back from the throne allowance sent by
China. But in these years, because of the increased activities
of the pirates, even the ships of the "King of Japan" on their
way home from China were plundered, so that the feudal lords
naturally feared to risk their money.

About the middle of the sixteenth century, the pirates extended their field of operations. By the invitation of the Chinese outlaws, the Japanese pirates occupied a group of islands off the coast of China, where they established additional headquarters in Chinese waters and commenced invading even the far interior of China. In 1546, Shih-Tsung, the eleventh Ming emperor, therefore sent a special envoy to Japan requesting the thirteenth shogun, Yoshiteru, to suppress the pirates.[122] Yoshiteru replied in 1547 that China was suffering from the ravages of the pirates because Chinese outlaws had induced members of the unruly class of Japanese people to invade and plunder China, that this was therefore China's own problem, as it was caused by her own people; consequently, Japan had neither concern nor responsibility with respect to it. This was the final communication exchanged between Japan and the Ming government.

Eight years later, in 1565, the shogun Yoshiteru was assassinated. The *Standard History of the Ming* contains an entry concerning this event to the effect that the "King of Japan" and all his state ministers were killed; that domestic war was waged; and that all the islands of Japan were in a chaotic condition. The Ming government then realized that Japan could not be depended upon to suppress the pirates.

With the exile by Nobunaga of the fifteenth shogun of the Ashikaga in 1573, the Ashikaga shogunate, which was known in China as the "Government of the King of Japan," automatically came to an end. In the second half of the sixteenth century, after the relations of the Ming with the Ashikaga shogunate had been severed, the Ming government gradually gained in both strength and fighting power, and its army became better able to cope with the Japanese pirates. The complete suppression of the pirates was not accomplished, however, until peace was restored in Japan and a strong central government established.

In 1588, Hideyoshi, founder of the fourth military government in Japan, framed and promulgated laws with respect to the pirates. These laws were vigorously enforced. Hideyoshi took this step voluntarily in order to maintain the national standing and dignity; he did not do it at the request of the Ming government. The most important provisions of these laws were:

(1) The maintainence of pirate ships and the practice of piracy were strictly prohibited.

(2) All feudal lords and local magistrates were instructed to summon and examine all their subjects who were engaged in trade, in the fishery industries, or in other work on the sea. If any were found to be connected with piracy, they should be severely punished. Those who could prove that they were engaged in honorable work should be permitted to continue in it. However, all of them should be required to present written statements, sworn to, taking the gods as witnesses, to the effect that they would never either practice piracy or enter into any relationship with the pirates.

(3) All the feudal lords and the local magistrates should be held responsible for piracy committed by their subjects. If any of these should engage in piracy and be arrested and convicted, the feudal lord or magistrate of the district would be punished even to the confiscation of his estates.[123]

The last of these pirate laws was issued under date of July 8, in the sixteenth year of the Tensho era (1588). This law, promulgated by Hideyoshi, marks the final chapter in the Japanese piracy which had ravaged the coast of eastern Asia for more than two hundred years.

The memorial presented by the Ashikaga shogun ("King of Japan") to the Ming throne and the imperial edict issued by the Ming emperor to the "King of Japan" are still extant. They bear evidence that the suzerain and tributary relationship existed between China and Japan during the fifteenth and sixteenth centuries. However, Japanese historians do not consider the exchange of these state papers as anything but disgraceful diplomatic transactions by which the Ashikaga shoguns bartered the national independence for the sake of their own interests. Japanese historians have never given any recognition to the claim that Japan was ever a tributary state of China, for these reasons, namely:

(1) China never established suzerain power over Japan through military conquest as she had done over Korea and others of her tributary states.

(2) Even during the Ashikaga Period, the Ming throne never exercised ruling authority over the "King of Japan" or his kingdom; nor did it effectively impose any duties or obligations upon the "King of Japan."

(3) On the contrary, the Ming throne was time and again obliged to send silver and copper coins to the "King of Japan" in return for the so-called tribute. In fact, Japan actually exacted money from China under the guise of a tributary state.

The Chinese scholars and statesmen are in agreement with this view of the Japanese that Japan, as a national government, was never a tributary state of China. On September 29, 1870, a Japanese representative arrived at Tientsin. His mission was to sound out the Chinese government with respect to its willingness to enter into treaty relations with Japan. Ying-Han, the governor of Anhui, strongly opposed the conclusion of a treaty with Japan. He presented a memorial to the throne in which he stated that, because Japan had been one of China's tributary states, the conclusion of a treaty between them on equal terms would be a disgrace. He mentioned also the fact that, for two hundred years, during the Ming dynasty, Japanese pirates had harassed China's coast.

The Yamen of the imperial government of China referred the memorial to Li Hung Chang and to Tseng Kuo-Fan, the two greatest Chinese scholars and statesmen of the time, with instructions to make a report on the matter. Li replied on January 21, 1871. The Wo invasions (i.e., attacks of the Japanese pirates), he stated, had been partly occasioned through the unwise policies of the Ming emperors. Under the Ching dynasty, there had not been any trouble between China and Japan. As a matter of fact, in that period Chinese merchants had engaged in business in Nagasaki, and the Japanese had frequently come to Kiangsu and to Chekiang. In 1860–61, when both these provinces were being harassed by the Taipings, and when, at the same time, China was at war with an Occidental nation, Japan might have taken advantage of the situation to make trouble, had she so desired; but she had taken no such step. Li concluded his statement by emphasizing the fact that Japan was not a tributary state and therefore could not be classed with Korea, Liu Chiu, and Annam.

Tseng's reply reached Peking on March 29, 1871. It stated that Japan's desire for a treaty was only natural. If China should refuse when approached in a friendly way, the world would conclude that nothing could be done with China except by force. Japan was not in the same category with Korea, Liu Chiu, and Annam, and her desire to be treated like England and France was quite natural. Dr. T. F. Tsiang, of the Tsing Hua National University of China, in criticizing Ying-Han's memorial, wrote: "Ying-Han's knowledge is evidently defective. Japan was not a tributary to China. The troubles during the Ming dynasty, styled the Wei invasions in our history, were genuine enough, much like the invasions of the Northmen in mediaeval Europe, but three centuries had intervened."[124]

However, even today there are persons of the type of Governor Ying-Han who, without any comprehensive knowledge of the historical background, discuss historical events and draw conclusions based solely on fragmentary documents. Of such are those who state that Japan was a tributary state of China during the fifteenth and sixteenth centuries.

CHAPTER IV

The National Unification of Japan and Asiatic Conquest

THE ASHIKAGA SHOGUNATE, nominally at least, maintained an existence for approximately two hundred and fifty years. It actually exercised ruling authority, however, only during the half-century beginning in the early part of the rule of Yoshimitsu and ending in 1441 when Yoshinori was assassinated. After the Eleven Years' Civil War, in the second half of the fifteenth century, the Ashikaga lost its political, financial and military power completely. All the feudal lords and most of the leading Buddhist monasteries either established military governments of their own in the provincial districts or maintained military organizations. Japan was thus split up into hundreds of independent fighting units, which were continually at war with one another.

In the sixteenth century, the emperor not only had no palace in which to live, but even found it difficult to provide for the needs of his family. As for the shoguns, they found it impossible to reside in the military capital, and sometimes even their whereabouts was unknown. There were in Japan the emperor, the imperial regent, the shogun, the military regent, and other officers of high rank, but none of them was able to exercise authority, and no military man was powerful enough to elevate himself to the shogunate and to organize a central military government. In the middle of the sixteenth century the national status of Japan reached its lowest point. This proved to be the turning point.[2] In this black darkness, a faint light appeared which pointed the way toward national betterment. In this period of usurpation most of the old feudal families had been destroyed, either by their retainers or by persons of obscure origin,[3] and these newly risen families replaced those of former days. Total changes had thus taken place in the ruling units, and Japan was in a position to start her national life afresh. It was at this time that Japan first came into contact with Occidental nations. Association with Occidentals and an acquaintance with their civilization inspired the Japanese with new ambitions. The introduction of Catholicism gave them a new religion. It also stimulated the hopelessly degenerated Buddhism and brought about a reform in that faith. Foreign trade and the rapid increase in the output of the gold, silver, and copper mines consequent upon the adoption of Occidental methods of mining, augmented the national wealth. The first innovation accepted from the Occident was firearms. Their rapid adoption brought about radical changes in military tactics and methods of fighting.[4] Single combat was replaced by numerical strength, personal bravery gave way to strategy, the smaller military fighting units therefore ceased to exist, and so national unification was facilitated.

At this very time when Japan was thus entering upon a new national existence, three men of unusual statesmanship and military ability, Nobunaga, Hideyoshi, and Iyeyasu, made their appearance.[5] Nobunaga was born in 1534; Hideyoshi in 1536; Iyeyasu in 1542. Not only were these men contemporaries; they had been born in districts within a radius of less than fifty miles. They became well acquainted with one another in their early manhood, and throughout their lives they coöperated in the work of national unification.[6] They were men of similar inclinations, and they held one another in high regard. Yet each possessed an entirely different sort of personality and attainment from the other two, and consequently, their accomplishments differed greatly and in their work for the nation each made a distinct contribution. Nobunaga started the work and cleared the ground. Hideyoshi laid the foundation for national unification, and Iyeyasu completed the superstructure. Nobunaga, noted for his keen and correct judgment, was nevertheless of destructive inclination.

Hideyoshi was noted for his broadmindedness and his great tact. He possessed a remarkable ability to utilize everything, whether good or bad, to the national advantage. Iyeyasu was a man of constructive ability, noted for his patience and endurance but given to trickiness and scheming. Nobunaga, Hideyoshi, and Iyeyasu became the respective founders of the third, fourth, and fifth military governments.

In the middle of the sixteenth century, all national traditions and usages, with the sole exception of the sacredness and inviolability of the imperial throne, had been uprooted. Even during the darkest period of Japanese history, the emperor was still the center of national reverence, honor, and dignity. So great, however, was the national chaos and poverty that the people, although they greatly revered and deeply sympathized with him, were unable to render him any financial service. Any person, therefore, who worked for the imperial cause became, in a way, a representative of the people's attitude toward the emperor and a symbol of their support for him. Nobuhide, the father of Nobunaga, was one of the founders of the Oda family. As he was both loyal and farsighted, he readily perceived that so newly risen a family as his could best maintain its prosperity by showing loyalty to the throne and by rendering financial service to the emperor. Nobuhide, therefore, in 1541 and 1544 donated certain amounts of copper coin to the imperial court. These gifts made possible the reparation of the sadly neglected national temple at Ise and the wall surrounding the imperial palace at Kyoto. As this was an unusual thing for a military man of that time to do, the emperor expressed his deep appreciation of the donation made by Nobuhide by sending to him an envoy bearing a personal letter of gratitude. "To respect the emperor and to show loyalty to the throne," as Nobuhide had done, thereafter became a tenet of Nobunaga, Hideyoshi, and Iyeyasu, and the national unification, in the sixteenth century at least, was centered about the imperial throne.[7]

In 1567, after the death of Nobuhide, the emperor sent a special envoy to Nobunaga, his son and successor, expressing his appreciation of the loyalty and sincerity of Nobuhide, and instructing Nobunaga to follow in his father's footsteps. The emperor especially requested Nobunaga to restore the imperial estate by dislodging the unruly military barons who were wrongfully occupying it. He also expressed an earnest desire that Nobunaga should proceed to Kyoto and establish order there.[8] Nobunaga was greatly impressed by the honor of having thus been selected by the emperor from among a large number of military men, to serve the throne. Nobunaga faithfully carried out the imperial instruction, but he also utilized it for his military advancement. Whenever he was confronted by a formidable enemy, he encouraged his men by telling them that the military campaign was being conducted for the imperial cause against a national enemy. While Nobunaga was adding to his military fame and preparing to march upon Kyoto, subjugating, as he marched, the military families along the way from his province to the imperial capital, Yoshiaki appealed to Nobunaga to escort him to Kyoto in order that he might avenge the assassination of his brother, Yoshiteru, the thirteenth shogun, and to establish him as his brother's successor. In 1568, in compliance with the request of the emperor as well as with that of Yoshiaki, Nobunaga left his home province at the head of a large army and made a successful entry into the imperial capital. He thus fulfilled the pledge that he had made to the emperor some years earlier.[9] Moreover, at his instance, Yoshiaki was appointed shogun by the emperor. In 1573, with the permanent exile of the shogun, Yoshiaki, from Kyoto, the Ashikaga shogunate automatically came to an end. Possessing the unreserved trust and confidence of the emperor, Nobunaga now began the work of national unification.

Nobunaga was a great character, in whom destructive and constructive genius were peculiarly blended. He was never satisfied until he had completely destroyed everything that stood in his way. He possessed the wonderful faculty of discovering ability in men and usefulness in things. He gave all possible assistance and protection to the Catholics, on the one hand, and, on the other, he completely destroyed the militant Buddhist communities. A Catholic priest who lived in Japan at the time of Nobunaga described him, in a communication to his home church in Portugal, as a staunch friend of the Catholics, who had readily granted both money and estates to the Church.[10] The priest concluded, however, with the comment that he was not a Christian and that there was no possibility of converting him. Nobunaga was a man who would worship nothing but himself and who recognized no guiding spirit other than his own judgment. He took Hideyoshi from among his stable boys and made it possible for him to become the greatest military man in Japan. Nor did he overlook the value of the Occidental weapon, firearms. In fact, his great military successes and consequent rapid rise were mainly achieved through his use of firearms and the complete reorganization of his army.[11]

Two years after the downfall of the Ashikaga, Nobunaga undertook a great offensive against the Takeda, whose military power had long been recognized as invincible. The Takeda had a large and well-trained force which they had styled the "Ever-Victorious." Most of the military men of the Takeda, however, had been trained only in the military arts and methods of fighting of the old school, and they placed but little faith in firearms. In 1575, a great army under the personal command of Nobunaga, and including among its generals Hideyoshi and Iyeyasu, proceeded to the provinces of the Takeda. In May of that year, there was fought a great battle, the most significant and decisive of the sixteenth century in its effect upon Japan's future. This was the first battle in which the old weapons and military arts were pitted against the new. Nearly 100,000 men took the field. The men of the Takeda

exhibited marvelous fighting spirit and courage, and showed
both skill and training, but their struggle was hopeless. Bearing themselves with all the dignity and self-respect of knight-
hood, the Takeda fighting men melted away before the fire of
Nobunaga's army. At the close of the day, the great army of
the Takeda had no fighting strength left. This army, which had
been the flower of militarism in Japan for a quarter-century,
was thus, in a single day's combat, reduced to a negligible military element. The engagement is known in history as the battle of Nagashino, after the district in which it took place. It
is specially noteworthy because military men were all convinced by it that personal bravery and training could not com-
pete with weapons of destructive power.

Although firearms had frequently been used before in military engagements, it was in the battle of Nagashino that for
the first time in the history of Japan men in the ranks were provided with firearms to be used in conjunction with man power.
Nobunaga was the first military man in Japan to avail himself
of the use of firearms to its full extent. His success not only
proved their value, but also revolutionized the methods of
fighting. The battle of Nagashino marked a new epoch in warfare in Japan, and a victory made possible through the introduction of firearms into Japan restored peace to the nation.[12]

In the latter part of the sixteenth century, although Nobunaga gained ascendancy rapidly, his control was still limited
to the central part of Honshu. Not only were Kyushu and Shikoku wholly outside of his control, but also both the northeastern and the southwestern parts of Honshu were under the
rule of military families that were unfriendly to him. After
the battle of Nagashino, Nobunaga stood forth as the only
man able to bring about national unification. In 1576, just
one year after this famous battle was fought, the emperor
recognized the long and faithful service of Nobunaga, and
his ever-increasing military prestige, by appointing him Lord
Keeper of the Privy Seal. In the following year, 1577, the em-

peror appointed him as one of the two supreme state ministers. Thus the emperor entrusted to Nobunaga both civil and military authority, and requested that he rule Japan on his behalf. Nobunaga still had before him the task of conquering several powerful military families, but was, nevertheless, the founder of the third military government of Japan.

In 1576, Nobunaga selected the district of Azuchi as the seat of his military government. There he built a great stronghold, the first of its kind to be impregnable. Because of the extensive use of cannon and firearms, fortresses of the old type no longer sufficed for protection. The building of this castle, the strongest and most magnificent of its kind in Japan at that time, took four years and marked the beginning of a new epoch in military engineering in that country.[13] It was with Azuchi as his base that Nobunaga entered upon the final stage of his military campaign to effect national unification.

Nobunaga held that the national unification could not be effected until all the Buddhist communities had been shorn of their military power and the unruly feudal military barons destroyed. Accordingly, he completely destroyed the Buddhist community at Mount Hiyei by burning over the entire mountain, including hundreds of Buddhistic edifices, all the Buddhist priests together with their fighting men and dependants, and even all the trees. For approximately eight hundred years, the Buddhist monastery at Hiyei had been recognized as the most sacred Buddhistic center in Japan. In the sixteenth century, this monastery had not only become hopelessly degenerated, but it was also developing into a fighting unit, and thus becoming a center of national disturbance. In resorting to such drastic measures as the destruction of the Hiyei Buddhistic Community, Nobunaga was also giving warning to other Buddhists who might have militant inclinations. After inflicting due punishment upon other Buddhistic communities, Nobunaga finally turned his attention to the Honganji Community at Osaka. The Honganji sect of Buddhism originated in Japan in the thirteenth century. It is monotheistic, its followers worshiping only one Buddha, known as Amida. This Buddhist sect has been and still is the most powerful, as well as the richest, in Japan. The Honganji Buddhists declared that Nobunaga was the enemy of Buddha. They built a formidable castle at Osaka, in which they maintained thousands of fighting men. They formed alliances with several powerful military families, and even threatened Nobunaga's life. The military leaders to whom he entrusted campaigns failed him time and again. Finally, he conducted a military campaign in person. After a series of bloody engagements, he succeeded in isolating the Honganji Community by cutting off its sources of military and food supplies, and in 1580 the Honganji Buddhists surrendered to him. The Osaka castle, together with the surrounding districts, they transferred to him upon the condition that they might be permitted to engage in their religious work in some other part of Japan, provided they refrained entirely from any sort of military activity. In dealing with Honganji Buddhism, Nobunaga deviated from his fixed policy, because he realized that religious teaching so deeply rooted as that of the Honganji sect could not be entirely eradicated. Moreover, he had gained his main object, which was to deprive the Buddhist communities of military power. From that time on, the Buddhistic monasteries in Japan lost their military characteristics. The capitulation of the Honganji castle at Osaka constituted the final chapter in the history of militant Buddhism in Japan.[14]

In 1579, while successfully conducting a campaign against the Honganji, Nobunaga waged war also against the Mori, the strongest military family in western Japan; it occupied the entire southwestern part of Honshu. The Mori were devout Buddhists, and the strongest allies of the Honganji. Moreover, the territory of the Mori faced Shikoku and Kyushu, and the approach to these islands was possible only through the Mori territory. Unless the Mori could be subjugated, neither Shikoku nor Kyushu could be invaded. This important military undertaking was entrusted to Hideyoshi. He was eminently successful, one stronghold after another falling before him and province after province being occupied.[15]

In 1582, within less than a decade after the downfall of the Ashikaga, Nobunaga had become the undisputed master of thirty-three provinces, which constituted one-half the area of Japan. His future seemed very bright. The Honganji Buddhists had been conquered and the news of victories was steadily being received from Hideyoshi at the front. There was every indication that national unification would be effected within a year or two. While Nobunaga was thus rejoicing over his military prospects in 1582, word came from Hideyoshi that the Mori, having found their cause hopeless, had sued for peace. Hideyoshi asked instructions from Nobunaga, to tell him whether he should negotiate peace or proceed with the campaign. He also requested, if the peace proposal of the Mori should be rejected, that Nobunaga should come in person with a large military force, as he believed the campaign might be concluded very shortly if the present opportunity were availed of. Nobunaga promptly decided to continue the war with the Mori. He ordered his military leaders to proceed to Hideyoshi's war front with all available men. In June, 1582, Nobunaga went to Kyoto, the imperial capital, with a small bodyguard of about one hundred men, to have an interview with the emperor before proceeding to the front. On the following morning at dawn, Mitsuhide, one of Nobunaga's military leaders who had been on the road to join Hideyoshi, suddenly rebelled and turned his army of 20,000 fighting men toward Kyoto. He surrounded Nobunaga at the Honnoji monastery, where he had temporary headquarters. Nobunaga and his bodyguard fought bravely, but all were killed. Thus did Nobunaga lose his life in the prime of his manhood at the very time when a great and brilliant future was opening before him. He was only 47 years of age.

The untimely death of Nobunaga afforded Hideyoshi an

opportunity to rise and complete the unfinished work. Hideyoshi was a self-made man of unusual and magnetic personality and ability,[16] who, from a very menial position, and without education, training, or financial backing, struggled on to achievement. Throughout his eventful career, Hideyoshi was blessed with continual success. In his old age, one of his admirers asked him what was the secret of his success. He replied: "There is absolutely no secret. I have a set rule that I always adhere to. It is that in whatever occupation or position I may be, I always concentrate my attention and energy upon my work. While I am engaged in any task, I never think about what I am to do next."

Notwithstanding this habit of concentration, he was also a man who was never taken by surprise, no matter how unexpected a happening might be. He possessed the enviable ability to remain self-composed and quiet in emergencies and to judge quickly and correctly. This was well illustrated on the death of Nobunaga. At the time, Iyeyasu, two grown sons of Nobunaga, and several military leaders in the service of Nobunaga were within reaching distance of Kyoto, yet none of them took any steps after this unexpected happening. Hideyoshi's prompt action demonstrated his remarkable ability to master a situation.[17] Nobunaga was murdered on June 2. The news of his death reached Hideyoshi on the evening of June 3. Taking advantage of the fact that the Mori had already sued for peace, Hideyoshi entered into negotiations with them on June 4. Toward the close of the day following, the treaty of peace was concluded, on terms dictated by Hideyoshi.[18] The Mori ceded five provinces of the eleven controlled by them. They agreed immediately to withdraw all their troops from the war front, and to see that the commanding general of the troops that had confronted Hideyoshi's army should commit self-destruction with military honor in recognition of his defeat.

On June 6 and 7, all the terms of the treaty with the Mori having been carried out, Hideyoshi began a series of forced marches in the direction of Kyoto, where Nobunaga had been assassinated. On June 9, he established his military headquarters at Himeji. On June 12, he marched to a place called Amagasaki, near Kyoto. On June 13, he gave battle to Mitsuhide at Yamasaki, where Mitsuhide was making preparations for defense. In a combat of a single day, Hideyoshi completely routed the army of Mitsuhide. On the night of that same day (June 13), Mitsuhide and some of his followers were killed by a local mob while they were on the way to the provincial districts to raise a new army. Hideyoshi thus avenged the death of Nobunaga eleven days after the assassination, in this way making a remarkable military record not only in the history of Japan but indeed in that of any nation.[19] This promptness and success of Hideyoshi gave him standing. The entire nation, including the emperor and the leading men of the time, admired and praised his loyalty and quick action. He was a coming man and everything indicated that he would be the successor of Nobunaga.[20] The reputation that Hideyoshi thus gained, however, aroused great jealousy among the military men with whom he had served as a colleague under Nobunaga. But these men were soon split into two factions. Some of them gradually became reconciled to the situation and showed a readiness to recognize the authority of Hideyoshi; others decided to resort to arms. Within a remarkably short space of time, Hideyoshi dealt with them successfully. Those who strongly opposed him were either destroyed or subjugated;[21] others, who were inclined toward a peaceful settlement, were won over by his tact and diplomacy and came to be numbered among his friends.

Hideyoshi made his most phenomenal rise in the year beginning in the early summer of 1582 and ending in the summer of 1583. Within one year after the death of Nobunaga, Hideyoshi, who had been only one of Nobunaga's lieutenants, became his successor. All the military leaders in the service of Nobunaga were either overcome or became his loyal supporters. Not only did all the provinces that had been under the control of Nobunaga recognize the authority of Hideyoshi, but also even the Mori in southwestern Honshu pledged him their loyalty, and a number of military families in Kyushu and Shikoku expressed a readiness to coöperate with him in his future military undertakings.

The accomplishments of Hideyoshi in this one year were both far greater and more effective than those of Nobunaga in his whole lifetime. But Hideyoshi was a man of great ambition and achievement. He regarded this rapid ascent as only an initial success, and planned to make still greater contributions to the welfare of his nation.

In May, 1583, the emperor, in recognition of the rise and work of Hideyoshi, appointed him "Imperial Councilor of State." In July of the same year, Hideyoshi distributed twenty provinces among thirty-three of his military men, thus making them feudal lords. He selected Osaka as his military headquarters,[22] and built there the most commanding and impregnable stronghold in Japan. It is still standing and is considered the most marvelous military engineering accomplishment in Japan of the sixteenth century. From Osaka as his base, Hideyoshi started his work of national unification.[23] In 1585, Shikoku was conquered; in 1587, Kyushu was overcome. He completed the subjugation of all the minor military families and of the militant Buddhists and in 1590 entered upon his final military campaign, in which he either completely conquered or subjugated all the powerful military families in northeastern Japan. National unification was thus completed and peace restored within eight years after the death of Nobunaga.[24] The authority of Hideyoshi extended from the northern to the southern extremity of the empire of Japan.

With the progress of the work of national unification, the emperor's trust and confidence in Hideyoshi increased. In March, 1585, Hideyoshi was appointed "Lord Keeper of the Privy Seal." In July of the same year, the emperor made Hideyoshi the *Kampaku* ("Imperial Regent"). This was the first time in the history of Japan that a man not of Fujiwara blood was appointed to the regency. Only three years had elapsed since the death of Nobunaga when Hideyoshi began to rule Japan on behalf of the emperor. In December, 1586, the emperor appointed Hideyoshi the *Dajodaijin* ("Grand Supreme Minister of State"). The *Dajodaijin* was the highest official in Old Japan.[25] This position was as a rule left unoccupied save when the emperor found a man of high attainments and special merit. Hideyoshi began life as a peddler and rose to the highest rank attainable in his time. He was of obscure birth, lacking not only a family name but also not even knowing who was his father. With his appointment as *Dajodaijin,* in 1586, the emperor, in further recognition of the great service rendered by Hideyoshi to both the throne and the nation, therefore created a new family, called Toyotomi, of which he made Hideyoshi the founder.[26] Accordingly, Hideyoshi's rule in Japan is known as the Toyotomi Period. In 1588, all the leading military families, headed by Iyeyasu, in the presence of the emperor pledged loyalty to the throne and affirmed their readiness to serve the regent, Hideyoshi, stating that thenceforth they would act in strict accordance with all the instructions and commands of the regent. This pledge of 1588 made Hideyoshi the absolute authority in both civil and military affairs.[27]

In their conduct of national affairs, both Nobunaga and Hideyoshi made the throne the central source of authority. They always accepted appointments as court officers, and as officers in the imperial court they ruled Japan. The third and the fourth military governments, founded by Nobunaga and Hideyoshi, respectively, were not shogunate governments like the first, second, and fifth military governments, and neither Nobunaga nor Hideyoshi held the title of "Shogun."[28] Like Nobunaga, Hideyoshi possessed a marvelous ability to discover men of genius in various lines, but, unlike Nobunaga, he never looked on others as his rivals. He was a broadminded, self-controlled man, and never, as did Nobunaga, fell a victim to temper or to the impulse to exercise destructive power. Even his enemies fell under his spell and coöperated with him. He was a man of self-confidence and reliance. Once, when an admirer asked him if he feared rebellion, he replied: "None will rise against me, because a greater lord than myself is not to be found. Neither can any aspirant expect to make of himself a better ruler than I am."[29]

Hideyoshi, realizing his own lack of education, gathered about him men of attainments and genius and utilized their education, experience, and training to the best advantage. In this way, he was able to make numerous innovations in the national life; he even introduced a sort of self-government. By drawing a distinct line between the civil and the military classes and forcing the Buddhist priests, the merchants, and other civilians to surrender their weapons, he effected a nation-wide disarmament. He declared a policy of government monopoly over gold, silver, and copper mines and placed the entire output under national control. He coined gold, silver, and copper money, which was soon used throughout the nation.[30] Hideyoshi thus established a domestic system of coinage in Japan for the first time in the nation's history.[31] Prior to that time, Chinese copper coin had been the standard national coin of Japan. Throughout the Dark Age, Japan had been divided into hundreds of independent ruling units, each of which had different land measurements, as well as different rates of taxation. After the completion of her national unification, Japan was therefore sadly in need of uniformity in land measurements. Hideyoshi decided to establish a uniform system of land measurements throughout Japan.[32] This was a great undertaking and required several years for its completion. The standards of measurements adopted at that time are still in use in Japan, and upon the basis of the uniform land system a uniform tax system was worked out.

In Hideyoshi's later years three different conditions came

to a culmination, namely: (1) the wealth of the nation was greatly augmented by the steady increase in the output of the gold, silver, and copper mines, as well as by the increase in foreign trade; (2) the land was filled with men of fighting spirit and military experience, as a result of the centuries of warfare; and (3) Hideyoshi himself became, as he is often called, the "Napoleon of Japan." Such a man could not brook the spending of his life in so small an island empire as was Japan; in fact, while he was still in the service of Nobunaga, Hideyoshi had already revealed his plan of conquest on the Asiatic continent.[33] The foregoing conditions, following in the wake of the restoration of peace, brought about the great foreign war of the sixteenth century.

Hideyoshi's campaign on the Asiatic continent was not carried beyond Korea, because of his death and for several other reasons. It is therefore known in history as the "Korean campaign." However, neither the conquest nor the invasion of Korea were part of Hideyoshi's plan. His aim was to create a great Asiatic empire, including China, Japan, Korea, India, Persia, and such other Asiatic nations as were known to the Japanese in those days, as well as all the islands near the continent, such as Liu Chiu, Formosa, the Philippines, and other islands in the South Sea.[34] He planned first to extend his ruling authority over China, Japan, and Korea, together with the surrounding islands, and to make them the first unit of his new empire.

Now it was a well-known fact that China had always asserted that she was the "Heavenly Commissioned Supreme Nation" and had always looked down upon all other nations as being either barbarian states or tributary states. Hideyoshi was therefore convinced that China could be conquered by military force alone.[35] Nevertheless, it was his policy to establish his military authority over other nations either by military threat or by diplomacy, and he determined to adhere to it. So, after first completing his plan for the conquest of Tai-Min (China), he sent envoys to various other nations demanding either their

coöperation in his campaign or the sending of tribute to the
Japanese throne. In November, 1590, and in July and September, 1591, Hideyoshi sent personal letters to Liu Chiu, to India, and to the Philippines. In these letters he stated that it
had been his destiny from birth to become the sole ruler of
the world. In fulfilling this mission, he went on, he had within
a short time conquered all the unruly military barons in Japan
and had put an end to the national chaos of hundreds of years
by effecting the unification of that nation. He had completed
preparations for the conquest of Tai-Min, and therefore the
nations to which he was addressing these letters were now accordingly to recognize his authority either by sending tribute
or by meeting certain military requisitions.[36]

As for Korea, Hideyoshi entirely disregarded the time-honored suzerain and tributary relationship between China and
Korea, and took it for granted that Korea would make ready
submission to him and coöperate in his campaign against
China. In 1587, after he had subdued and conquered all the
unruly military barons in Kyushu and had extended his authority along the entire coast of that island (which faces Korea
beyond the Korean Channel), Hideyoshi decided to summon
the king of Korea to Japan to pledge loyalty to the imperial
throne. This plan did not succeed, but in 1590 the king of
Korea did send envoys to Hideyoshi to congratulate him upon
his military successes and his national unification of Japan. In
that same year, Hideyoshi wrote to the king of Korea, saying,
as in the letters to other nations, that he had been born with
the destiny of becoming the "Ruler of the World,"[37] that he had
already completed preparations for the conquest of China, and
demanding that the king of Korea send an army to be the vanguard. The Korean king promptly refused to coöperate in
Hideyoshi's military undertaking in China; China and Korea,
he said, had always maintained the relationship of suzerain and
tributary states as well as that of father and son, and he would
not bear arms against the nation of his lord and father merely

for the sake of satisfying an unjustifiable claim of a neighboring nation. The king of Korea also refused to open his kingdom to Hideyoshi's army, in order that they might march into China through Korea.[38]

In 1591, Yoshitomo, the lord of Tsushima, went to Korea and presented the demands of Hideyoshi for trade privileges and other concessions in written form. He requested that Korea forward this to the Ming throne, and threatened that Korea's refusal to comply with his request would bring about serious consequences both to herself and to China. The king of Korea ignored both his request and his threat.[39] Yoshitomo waited for two weeks without receiving a reply and then returned home, and Hideyoshi realized that he must crush Korea in order to open a road for the invasion of China. Toward the close of 1591, Hideyoshi completed the national mobilization. Without counting those engaged in transportation, commissary, and other manual work, the strength of Hideyoshi's army was 305,000 men. Of the sixteen divisions of his army, the first nine divisions, the total strength of which was 158,700 fighting men, were to proceed to China by way of Korea. Hideyoshi surrounded himself with prominent military leaders and kept with him the seven remaining divisions. He established his military headquarters at Nagoya Hizen, on the northern coast of Kyushu, facing the Korean Channel. The first nine divisions of the army Hideyoshi sent on in charge of their respective commanding generals, but the commanding general of the entire army did not go as commander-in-chief, because he, himself, planned to cross the water with additional troops whenever the way was opened for the invasion of China by the Japanese forces, and to take command in person.[40]

The army raised by Hideyoshi for this continental campaign was the greatest and strongest, both numerically and in fighting strength, ever mustered in Japan up to his time, but his naval force consisted of only 9200 men. The sole duty of this navy was to act as convoy to the army transports. Hideyoshi

thus failed to take into consideration the naval forces of Korea
and of China; it never occurred to him that a naval battle of
any seriousness might take place. This lack of a navy of real
fighting strength was one of the chief causes of the failure of
Hideyoshi's continental campaign.

On March 26, 1592, the vast army of Hideyoshi, accompanied by his navy, sailed for Korea. On April 13, Yukinaga and
his troops, the vanguard of the first division, effected a landing
at Fusan. They occupied a stronghold there without encountering any formidable resistance.[41] On April 18, Kiyomasa and
his troops, the vanguard of the second division, effected a successful landing at Fusan. They were followed by other divisions
of the army.

Korea, at the time of the invasion, had enjoyed peace and
prosperity for more than two hundred years. As a result, she
had not only lost all fighting spirit and power, but also, neither
her king nor his court placed any credence in Hideyoshi's
threat of invasion.[42] They made absolutely no military preparations, and Hideyoshi's army advanced through Korea as if that
country were an open field. His military forces attacked and
occupied strategic points and strongholds, one after another,
without meeting any considerable resistance. On April 17,
1592, the tidings of the landing of Japanese troops at Fusan
and of their occupation of one of Korea's strongest castles
reached the national capital. The Korean king and his court
were terror-stricken. The king raised as large an army as possible by enlisting men from the various provinces, and sent
them under General Shen Li, the most distinguished military
man in Korea, to check the invasion of the Japanese forces,
which were rapidly advancing. After he had left as commander
of the hurriedly raised army, the entire population of the capital waited daily for news of victory. Toward evening on April
29, three men on horseback galloped through the main gateway. They were soon surrounded by government officials and
crowds of people, to whom they imparted the information that

Shen Li, their commander-in-chief, had been killed and that the entire army had not only been routed but virtually annihilated.[43] This terrible news spread rapidly. The king held a hurried conference with his court and decided to abandon the capital. In the dead of night of that same day, the king left his palace, accompanied by his family and a few of his chief officers. After great hardship, they finally settled at Pyeng Yang, the ancient capital, which was situated in the northernmost part of Korea. After the capital had thus been abandoned, the people rushed into the palace and the government buildings, looting everywhere and starting fires, and the city was soon ruined and reduced to chaos.[44] Consequently, when on May 2 the Japanese army reached the national capital, they were well received by the people and the place was promptly surrendered to them. On May 16, the news of the capitulation reached Nagoya, the military headquarters in Japan. Hideyoshi thereupon made immediate preparations to cross the water to Korea, and take personal command of the entire army in the invasion of China.[45] The Japanese military leaders in the Korean capital decided to remain there until his arrival, and then under his personal command to march to the borders of China.

Hideyoshi outlined his continental campaign as follows: (1) before the end of May, 1592, he would make a triumphant entry into the Korean capital; (2) before the close of the year, he would occupy Peking, the national capital of China; (3) in 1593, the Kampaku ("Supreme Imperial Advisor of the Throne of Japan") would be requested to proceed to Peking, where he should assume the title of "Kampaku of China"; (4) in 1594, the imperial court would be removed from Kyoto, Japan, to Peking, China, and his majesty the emperor of Japan would ascend the throne of the newly created empire; (5) when China, Japan, and Korea were thus united into the first unit of the great Asiatic empire, Hideyoshi would establish himself at Ningpo, Chekiang Province, South China; and (6) all the military leaders would be privileged to carry their military under-

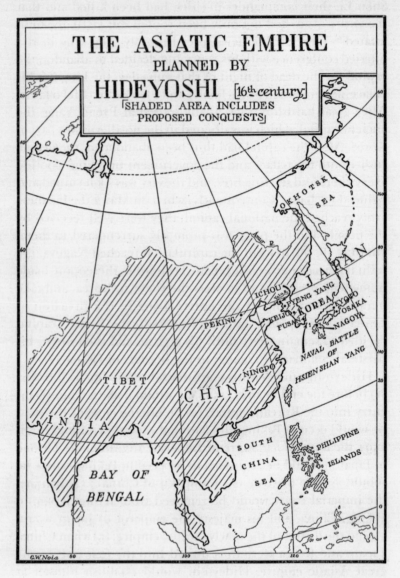

THE ASIATIC EMPIRE PLANNED BY HIDEYOSHI
IN THE SIXTEENTH CENTURY

takings into India and other Asiatic countries, thus to extend
their respective domains.[46]

In the latter part of May, 1592, Hideyoshi's preparations for
sailing to Korea were completed.[47] Iyeyasu and Toshiiye, the
two most distinguished military and political leaders, whose
opinions were always highly regarded by Hideyoshi, came forward and offered strong opposition to Hideyoshi's leaving Japan for the continent. Their reasons were two, namely: (1) as
Japan had just emerged from a long period of national chaos,
and had but recently entered into a period of peace, the
national unification was being maintained chiefly through
Hideyoshi's personality and magnetic power, and therefore
the national safety would be endangered by his absence; (2)
the annual stormy season was imminent and it would be a very
hazardous undertaking to cross the water—Hideyoshi should
at least postpone his sailing for the continent until the spring
of the following year, when weather conditions would be more
favorable.[48]

Opposition came also from another quarter. Hideyoshi's
mother was 80 years of age. Throughout his life, he and his
mother were devoted to each other. She of course strongly opposed the plan of Hideyoshi's leaving for the continent, and
later, when she feared that Hideyoshi had already sailed, she
became seriously ill from worrying about him. With the hope
of cheering her and quieting her by his presence, Hideyoshi
hurried from his military headquarters to Kyoto, traveling
hundreds of miles, only to arrive there on the day after his
mother's death. In agony of heart, he said, "I never thought
that my ambition to conquer the continent would bring this
curse upon me."[49] While speaking thus, he fainted. Although
this was solely a family affair, yet, so strong is Oriental filial
piety, the death of his mother greatly affected Hideyoshi's continental plans.

In final dissuasion, the emperor made a personal appeal to
Hideyoshi, in which he said that he depended solely upon

Hideyoshi, and that his personal presence was essential to the welfare of the nation. He requested that Hideyoshi abandon his plan of going to the continent in person, especially in the stormy season.[50] The imperial request caused Hideyoshi to postpone his sailing for Korea until March, 1593, when the sea would be calm. This decision proved to be a serious error, and adversely affected both his military campaign and his prospects of continental conquest.[51]

After his decision was made, Hideyoshi sent additional troops to the continent, reorganized his major fighting unit of 130,000 men,[52] and ordered that they immediately undertake the invasion of China, their first objective being Peking. He soon found it necessary to alter this plan. In the first place, when it became known that Hideyoshi would not sail for Korea to take personal command of his forces, all the military leaders were both disappointed and discouraged, and instead of coöperating and acting as a unit, each began to act independently. In the second place, the Koreans, even though they had been completely routed and dispersed, still continued military activities, engaging in guerrilla warfare and attacking the Japanese whenever opportunity presented, especially along the lines of communication. This brought about a shortage of food supply in the Japanese army. Hideyoshi therefore realized that there would be great danger in further extension of the line of communication, as most of the districts between the war front and the base of supplies were swarming with Korean bandits who were loyal to their country. So he decided to have his military men complete the conquest of Korea before undertaking the campaign in China. To accomplish this, he assigned the eight provinces into which Korea was divided to his leading military men and commanded that they establish their ruling power therein, thus placing Korea and her people under their complete control before they proceeded to the Chinese border.

In the year 1592, therefore, Hideyoshi changed the plan of

his military campaign three times. His first plan had been to cross the water himself in May, 1592, and to invade China and occupy Peking by the close of that year. His second plan had been to postpone crossing the water to Korea and taking command of his army there until March, 1593, his military leaders in Korea being ordered, in the meantime, to continue the campaign in accordance with the original plans, including the invasion of China and the occupation of Peking. His third plan had been a change from the military occupation of Korea by his military men to Korea's complete subjugation, the army advancing no farther than the Chinese border, where it was to remain until he should come to assume command of the entire army.[53]

The third plan was carried out with some degree of success. In June, 1592, Yukinaga, who commanded the vanguard of the first division of Hideyoshi's army, invaded Heian-Do, the northwestern province of Korea, adjoining the southern border of Manchuria. His army advanced rapidly toward Pyeng Yang, the ancient capital of Korea, where the king of Korea had taken refuge. Because of the steadily increasing military danger, the king and his court abandoned Pyeng Yang on June 11. Five days later, Yukinaga occupied that city. Pyeng Yang being the last stronghold in northern Korea, its occupation opened the road to Hideyoshi's army for the invasion of China. The king of Korea and his court escaped from Pyeng Yang to Ichou, a small border town adjoining Manchuria. From this place the king repeatedly made urgent appeals to the Ming throne, asking that a powerful army be sent to save his kingdom from total destruction at the hands of the Japanese.[54]

Kiyomasa, commander of the vanguard of the second division of Hideyoshi's army, invaded Kankyo-Do, the northeastern province of Korea, adjoining the southern border of Manchuria. On July 23, the Korean crown prince and his brother, together with their families and followers, were taken prisoners by Kiyomasa.[55] Within a period of only three months,

Hideyoshi's army had overrun the whole of Korea. But the instructions given by Hideyoshi to subjugate Korea were not strictly followed; the Japanese military leaders, instead of sub-jugating Korea, stopped with a military occupation of that kingdom. Contrary to the expectations of Hideyoshi, there-fore, Korea was far from being a conquered nation, and at every opportunity the Koreans rose up against the invaders.

In his continental campaign Hideyoshi had not entirely dis-regarded the need of a naval force, yet it is undeniable that he did not consider the navy an essential factor in his military organization.[56] In so thinking he was only following what had long been a military tradition in Japan. Throughout the seven hundred years of the feudal military period, all national diffi-culties were settled by land battles. During the two hundred years of Japan's Dark Age, it is true, the entire length of the coasts of Korea and China were ravaged continuously by Jap-anese pirates. However, those pirates did not commit piracy on the water; they were rather land bandits and marauders, professional fighting men born during Japan's war period. They went to the continent by crossing the water in small ships, and upon landing they ravaged and plundered the cities and towns.

In Korea, the point of view was quite different. During these two hundred years, ending in the latter part of the sixteenth century, while Korea was suffering from the ravages of pirate bands, she was building a strong navy with which to drive away the Japanese pirate bands and defend her coast. In Japan the navy might be regarded as merely supplementary to the army; in Korea the navy was esteemed the most important military factor in national defense. Korea, however, had en-tirely neglected her army. At the time of Hideyoshi's invasion, Korea's navy was one of the most powerful in the Orient. Her ships were large and strong, and her naval men were daring and well trained. Most of Hideyoshi's naval force, on the con-trary, was composed of military men.[57] They were, indeed, fighters of great spirit and experience. On land they fought like tigers; but on the sea, when engaged in naval battles with the Koreans, they could fight no better than a tiger could fight in the water against a shark.

The strength of Hideyoshi's navy was only about one-twentieth that of his army, and was composed, as has been noted, of land soldiers unused to the sea. The total number of war vessels was about 700. As most of them were small in size and poor in construction, they were not fit for naval engagements. On April 27, 1592, this entire Japanese naval force arrived at Fusan, the Japanese military base in Korea,[58] where it prepared to sail northward along the coast of Korea, keeping in touch with the rapidly advancing Japanese army on the land. Before leaving Fusan, the war vessels were divided into several fleets. A few days later, they encountered a large Korean fleet. The commander of this fleet, having heard of the remarkable fighting power of Japan on the land, concluded that she possessed equally great fighting power on the water. Instead of fighting, he sank his entire fleet! He and his naval staff escaped to the land in small boats, leaving several thousand Korean marines at the mercy of the enemy. Upon hearing of this first great naval disaster, the Korean king selected Yi Shun-Chen to be commander of the navy and placed Korea's entire naval force under his charge. Yi is known in history as the "Nelson of the Orient." He was a man of great naval genius and the outstanding engineer of his time. He both designed and built a large number of war vessels of a new type possessing great offensive and defensive power, known as the "turtle ship" because it was shaped like a turtle.[59] The fighting power of the turtle ship in those days was comparable to that of a dreadnaught against an ordinary cruiser in modern times. On May 7, 1592, Yi Shun-Chen sailed forth to search for the Japanese fleet. At Yu-Pu he encountered a Japanese fleet of 50 vessels, and a naval battle ensued. It ended in the overwhelming defeat of the Japanese fleet, entailing the loss of 40 vessels. In spite of this disaster, the main Japanese naval forces adhered to the original plan and continued to sail along the Korean coast, in order to co-operate with the army on the land.

On May 29, Yi, with a fleet of turtle ships, entrapped a strong Japanese fleet at Tang-Pu and engaged in a series of naval battles which lasted for nearly a week. In the battle of June 5, Yi destroyed, by fire, 43 Japanese war vessels, including the flagship. On July 8, another great naval battle was fought at Hsien Shan Yang, Japan losing 63 of her 70 war vessels that were engaged in the fight. On July 12, a most decisive naval battle was fought in the same waters, 42 out of 73 of the major Japanese ships being destroyed by fire. As a result of this naval battle at Hsien Shan Yang, Korea gained command of the sea. The Japanese naval leaders by this time fully realized that neither personal valor nor daring had any winning chance against the skill of the Koreans and their strongly constructed war vessels. The remnant of the Japanese fleet of about 470 vessels sailed south and took refuge in the harbor of Fusan, the Japanese military base in Korea.[60] They did not dare to venture out of that harbor for fear of encountering the Korean fleets.

The Korean naval commander, Yi Shun-Chen, entertained a daring ambition. In the hope of winning a complete victory over the invaders, he decided to destroy the Japanese military base at Fusan as well as the remnant of the Japanese fleet, thus cutting off entirely the Japanese forces in Korea from their military base at Nagoya in Japan. On September 1, 1592, Yi, in pursuance of this ambitious plan, took personal command of all the Korean fleets and attacked Fusan. Entering Fusan Harbor, he encountered both the Japanese fleet and their land forces. A severe naval and military engagement ensued. Although the Japanese lost 100 war vessels, yet by their combined fighting power on land and on sea they finally succeeded in forcing Yi to withdraw. The loss sustained by the Korean naval force in this engagement was so great that Yi was not able to repeat his attempt to destroy the Japanese military base at Fusan. The Japanese, by reason of their successful defense, were able to maintain their line of communication between Fusan in Korea and Nagoya in Japan.[61] Nevertheless, the loss of sea power seriously hindered Hideyoshi's plans for a military campaign on the continent, and the Japanese military campaign in Korea had to be continued without any naval support.[62] There remained as a line of communication between Korea and Japan only the Fusan-Nagoya line.

In Korea, the condition of the Japanese troops was now becoming unfavorable. They were beginning to suffer from a shortage of food supplies. Rivalries among Japanese military leaders were becoming increasingly serious. The line of communication between Japan's war front and her military base in Korea was continuously threatened by local uprisings. Consequently, the Japanese military force at Pyeng Yang, the northernmost post of the Japanese war front, did not dare to take the next step and actually invade China.[63] The Japanese were compelled to await the coming of the Chinese army and fight them on Korean soil. Instead of a continental campaign culminating in the invasion of China, the field of battle was confined exclusively to Korea.

In June, 1592, the Ming emperor Shen-Tsung, in response to a request from the Korean king, sent an army under the command of General Tai Chao-Pien to that distressed kingdom. Immediately upon crossing the Korean border, General Tai heard of the fall of Pyeng Yang. Fearing lest his army would not be strong enough to engage in battle with the victorious Japanese army, he turned toward Ichou, where the Korean king was holding his court, and announced his coming to Korea to rescue that country. In July, the Ming emperor sent a second large army to Korea under the command of Tsu Cheng-Hsun. Tsu was a noted military leader who had just won a victory against the northern tribes, and he felt sure of gaining a similar victory over the Japanese. Tsu crossed the

river Yalu to the northern border of Korea. There he made
an official announcement, saying: "To me [the general] who,
at the head of three thousand fighting men, have [has] annihilated a Tartar army of one hundred thousand, the Japanese
robber army in Korea will be but a group of ants and wasps.
They will soon be scattered to the four winds."[64]

In the midst of a storm on the night of July 15, 1592, Tsu
made a sudden attack on the Japanese army at Pyeng Yang.
The Japanese military force under the command of Yukinaga
was taken by surprise, but it was soon ready. Tsu and his army
were completely routed, most of his military leaders being
numbered among the dead. This great victory of the Japanese
was won mainly through their advantage in being well provided with firearms. The Chinese force was made up princi-
pally of cavalry, the men fighting with long spears in the narrow, muddy streets of Pyeng Yang. The annihilation of Tsu's
army brought home to the Ming emperor for the first time the
seriousness of the Japanese invasion of the continent. From
that time on, he regarded the invasion as a grave national question for China rather than as a mere local matter in Korea,
China's tributary state. After several days of discussion in the
Chinese imperial court, a proposal made by Shih Hsing, a
prominent statesman, was agreed upon.[65] The question was,
Should Korea be left to her fate, China building a strong line
of defenses along her northern border to prevent inroads of
the Japanese into China, or should China put forth her entire
national strength to save Korea from the Japanese invaders?

Shih[66] said: "If Japan should complete the occupation of
Korea, her next objects of conquest would be Liao-Tung and
other districts in Manchuria. Then the Shan-Hai-Kuan in the
Great Wall would be under her control. Our imperial capital,
Peking, would then be in danger. Therefore, Korea's present
national suffering is a serious national event to us. Were the
Emperor Tai-Tsu [founder of the Ming dynasty] on the throne
today, he would give serious attention to this matter."[67]

On September 2, 1592, the Emperor Shen-Tsung sent Pi Fan as envoy to Korea bearing the following imperial edict, which was addressed to the king:

"We have now sent our two state ministers in charge of civil and military affairs to Manchuria with instructions to take with them experienced troops one hundred thousand strong selected from Liao-Yang and other military stations, and then to proceed to your country in order to destroy the robber troops [the Japanese] that are ravaging your country. If the military force of Korea would coöperate with our imperial army and attack those atrocious creatures [the Japanese] from both sides, we should be able to exterminate them without allowing a single one to survive. We have ascended the throne in accordance with the command of Heaven and have come to rule both the Hua [Chinese] and the barbarian peoples. Peace has prevailed within the four seas and the myriad of nations therein are enjoying prosperity and happiness. Nevertheless, those insignificant and malignant brutes have dared to come forward and overrun your country. In addition to sending our troops to your land, we have issued imperial edicts to several military stations in the southeastern coast provinces as well as the Liu Chiu, Siam, and other nations. We have instructed them to muster several hundreds of thousand fighting men and invade Japan. These troops will soon cross the sea to that island country and destroy their haunts. The day will soon come when that whale-like monster Hideyoshi must submit his head and be slain. Then the waves will again become quiet."[68]

Although in his imperial edict of September 2, 1592, the Ming emperor outlined his plan of attacking and destroying the Japanese army in Korea and of invading Japan and putting Hideyoshi to death, China was not so situated at the time as to be able to undertake a military campaign of this magnitude. In fact, even then a great war was raging in the Ning-Hsia district, near the Mongolian border. The Ming emperor was therefore unable to finance an army of the size he had suggested in his edict; all he could do was to send an army of 35,000 men under the charge of Sung Ying-Chang, a noted military leader. On September 26, 1592, Sung left Peking and proceeded toward the Shan-Hai-Kuan to the defense of Manchuria against the Japanese invaders.[69]

In the meantime, the Japanese general, Yukinaga, and his troops at Pyeng Yang, after the destruction of Tsu's army, had contempt for the Ming troops, believing that these troops lacked fighting spirit as well as strength. Yukinaga sent a warning to the Korean people in which he said that Korea could not depend upon help from the Ming, because a single Japanese military man would be able to overcome and scatter a Ming army even as a tiger could destroy a flock of sheep.[70] Yukinaga realized, however, that there would be no advantage in invading Manchuria. His troops might occupy Manchuria and they might even take Peking, but neither achievement would be of any military advantage to Japan. On the contrary, the Japanese line of communication would have to be extended, and the army's source of supply would be threatened by Korean and Chinese uprisings along the line between the war front and the military base at Fusan. Yukinaga and his troops remained at Pyeng Yang to await the coming of the Ming forces. For the time being, the situation was a stalemate. The Japanese could only maintain their northernmost war front at Pyeng Yang, as if the plan of Hideyoshi's continental campaign had been entirely abandoned.[71] Likewise, the Chinese could not even approach the Korean border, but were only prepared to defend themselves in Manchuria and in other parts of the Ming empire against the possible invasion by Japanese troops, as if the promise of the Ming emperor to the king of Korea in his edict of September 2, 1592, had been completely forgotten.

Besides attacking and destroying the Japanese army in Korea, invading Japan, and putting Hideyoshi to death as outlined in his edict, the Emperor Shen-Tsung planned to make use of the individual services of some of his subjects toward ending the war in Korea. He therefore issued the following announcement:

"1. Any person who should either capture or kill the atrocious Hideyoshi, who had originated the trouble in Korea, would be elevated to nobility with the rank of marquis and would receive the corresponding reward.

"2. Any person who should either capture or kill Hidetsugu [the "Supreme Imperial Advisor of the Throne of Japan"] would be elevated to nobility with the rank of marquis.

"3. Any person who should kill Yukinaga, Hideiye, or other Japanese military leaders of similar rank in Korea would be rewarded with five thousand taels of silver.

"4. Any person who should propose and successfully carry out a plan for the restoration of peace in Korea would be elevated to nobility with the rank of count, and would receive a reward of ten thousand taels of silver."[72]

Notwithstanding the promise of these greatly coveted rewards, at first no one dared to volunteer. In the course of time, a man named Shen Wei-Ching presented himself before the supreme state minister Shih Hsing and proposed a plan for inducing Hideyoshi to conclude peace with China and Korea. In addition to being well versed in the affairs of Japan, Shen was a man of great eloquence and of impressive personality. State Minister Shih, who was greatly distressed by conditions in Korea, readily accepted Shen's offer.[73] In September, 1592, Shen Wei-Ching was sent by State Minister Shih to Pyeng Yang, financially well provisioned. Upon reaching Pyeng Yang, Shen held a series of interviews with Yukinaga and immediately began preliminary negotiations for peace. When Shen reached Pyeng Yang, Yukinaga and other military leaders had already become tired of the war; they could not advance, they could only await the arrival of the Ming army. Furthermore, they faced the prospect of resuming the war without the coöperation of the navy and their shortage of military supplies was keenly felt. Because of the almost inexhaustible man power of China, the Ming government would be able continuously to send reënforcements to Korea, but the Japanese at Pyeng Yang, because of the frequent uprisings of the Koreans, were in danger of being cut off from their military base at Fusan.⁷⁴ The Japanese felt that they could not look forward with any confidence either to success or to the termination of the war. Naturally, Yukinaga and his forces at Pyeng Yang welcomed the peace proposal of Shen Wei-Ching. Yukinaga and Shen drafted conjointly tentative terms of peace and agreed that they would present these terms to their respective governments. They hoped to gain the consent of both the Ming emperor and Hideyoshi to send duly authorized representatives to Korea to negotiate peace on the basis of the following tentative agreement:

(1) The Tatung Chiang (the large river that runs past Pyeng Yang) should be taken as the boundary line between the territory of Korea to remain under Japanese control and the territory to remain under Korean control. As the Tatung Chiang divides Korea into two parts, one of which is twice as large as the other, through this arrangement the southern two-thirds of Korea, which was at that time held in military occupation by the Japanese, would be ceded to Japan by Korea.

(2) The Ming emperor should allow Japan trade privileges in China.

(3) In order to show friendly feeling, the Ming emperor might send one of his daughters to Japan to marry the ruler of that nation.

(4) A fifty-day truce should be declared, and a large wooden post should be set up on the state road, at a point ten miles north of Pyeng Yang, the agreement to be that the Chinese and Koreans should not go south of the post and that the Japanese should not go north of the post.

(5) If the Ming emperor should conclude peace with Japan, on the basis of this tentative agreement, Shen was to return to

Pyeng Yang, accompanied by the imperial envoy and by the national hostage.

(6) Upon the acceptance of the hostage by Japan, Yukinaga with his troops would withdraw from Pyeng Yang to the national capital of Korea, where peace negotiations would be carried on between China and Japan.[75]

The agreement completed, Shen Wei-Ching left Pyeng Yang for Peking, promising to return by October 20, 1592, when the fifty-day truce would expire. October 20 came and went but Shen did not put in an appearance at Pyeng Yang. Many Japanese began to question the sincerity of Shen, but Yukinaga had full confidence in him and patiently waited for the coming of the Ming envoy whom Shen was to bring with him. One month later, on November 20, Shen arrived at Pyeng Yang and asked Yukinaga to grant additional concessions. Among these was the return to their homes, before the opening of peace negotiations, of the two royal princes and their families, who were being held prisoners by the Japanese army. Yukinaga stated that it would be impossible for him to make this concession, because these royal princes were under the charge of other military leaders and not of himself. After a few days, Shen again left Pyeng Yang assuring Yukinaga that the Ming envoys and the national hostages would shortly arrive at Pyeng Yang.[76]

While negotiations for peace were in progress, the great war in Ning-Hsia in northern China was successfully terminated. Li Ju-Sung, the commanding general of the victorious army, was the national hero. He soon came to be regarded as the man who could save Korea from the Japanese invaders and who would even carry the war overseas to Japan. At the urgent request of the emperor, Li Ju-Sung accepted the task of carrying on the war against the Japanese in Korea. Li, at the head of a large army, proceeded to Manchuria, where Sung Ying-Chang was stationed and was preparing for war with Japan. After an interview, Sung showed great willingness to coöperate with Li.

In December, 1592, when Li and his army were advancing toward the Korean border, Shen Wei-Ching was on his way to Peking, returning from his second visit to Yukinaga at Pyeng Yang. When Li learned of Shen's peace movement, he became greatly angered, and ordered that Shen should be arrested and put to death. Li Ying-Shih, the chief of the military staff, strongly opposed the murder of Shen, asserting that Shen might be useful for military purposes provided his whereabouts was kept absolutely secret from both the Chinese and the Japanese. While Yukinaga and his men were waiting for prospects of peace, Li's army might attack them unexpectedly and take Pyeng Yang with but little bloodshed. Acting upon this advice, Li Ju-Sung ordered that Shen be held as a secret war prisoner in his army.[77] On December 24, Li's entire army crossed the river Yalu and came to the northern border of Korea. On December 25, the advance guard of his army reached within fifty miles of Pyeng Yang. Having explicit faith in Shen, Yukinaga fully expected the coming of a peace envoy from the Ming, and knew nothing at all of the large Chinese army that was approaching under Li Ju-Sung. On January 6, 1593, Cha Ta-Shou, the commanding general of the second division of Li's army, came within a half-mile of Pyeng Yang. He sent a party of men to Yukinaga to notify him of the approach of the imperial envoy and his party that had been sent by the Ming emperor to negotiate peace in accordance with the terms of the agreement made with Shen.[78] Yukinaga, completely deceived, began preparations for their reception. In the midst of these preparations for peace negotiations, Cha and his army, closely followed by the main body of the army under the command of Li Ju-Sung, made a sudden attack upon Pyeng Yang. In the battle that followed, Yukinaga and his army, though taken by surprise, fought bravely and well. The battle lasted for three days. Finally, on the night of June 8, 1593, Yukinaga and his army, finding the place untenable, abandoned Pyeng Yang and retreated to Keijo, the national capital of Korea. It is generally

stated that the army under the command of Li Ju-Sung consisted of from 100,000 to 200,000 men. Its actual fighting
strength was between 45,000 and 60,000 and that of Yukinaga's
army was only 15,000. The Japanese had faced a Chinese force
of three or four times its own strength.[79]

After their defeat at Pyeng Yang, the Japanese military leaders concentrated their entire fighting strength at Keijo. This
meant that all the thirteen strongholds that the Japanese had
occupied between Pyeng Yang and Keijo were abandoned, one
after another.[80] The Japanese Sixth Division, which was noted
for its bravery and fighting power and which was under the
command of Takakage, assisted by Muneshige, marched out
from a place called Piti Kuan (Hekitei Kan), which is a few
miles north of Keijo, determined to give battle to the victorious Ming army. The Ming army under Li Ju-Sung was not
able to follow the retreating Japanese immediately, because of
lack of transportation facilities in Korea and because of the
unexpected resistance of Yukinaga's army.

On January 13, 1593, Li began his southward military advance. His hope of military success was greatly increased when
he discovered that all the military strongholds along the line
of march had been abandoned by the Japanese. On January 18,
Li's army reached Kai-Cheng, midway between Pyeng Yang
and Keijo, and the largest and strongest of all the fortifications.
When Li found that it, too, had been abandoned by the Japanese, he concluded that a great military success would be his at
Keijo. He therefore decided to reach Keijo by a forced march
of but three days, hoping to arrive there before the Japanese
would have time to abandon the city, gain a decisive victory,[81]
and take occupation of the Korean capital. On January 26, Li's
army approached Piti Kuan, where the Sixth Division of the
Japanese army under the command of Takakage and Muneshige was encamped. There Li's army was obliged to engage
in the decisive battle of Piti Kuan. The battle reached its climax after five hours of fierce and bloody struggle in which the

large army of the Ming was almost completely destroyed. Li Ju-Sung was miraculously saved through the voluntary sacrifice of one of his military aides, who gave his own life to rescue him. With the remnant of his troops, Li Ju-Sung made a hasty retreat to Pyeng Yang, the northernmost stronghold in Korea and the nearest point of approach to Manchuria.[82]

The destruction of the main body of the Ming army at Piti Kuan was not only a great military disaster, but also a severe moral blow to the military forces of the Chinese armies in both Korea and Manchuria. After this defeat, Li Ju-Sung, who had gone to Korea with the definite purpose of first destroying the Japanese army in Korea and then of carrying a punitive expedition into Japan, was in despair. In fact, he lost all hope and no longer had either military spirit or energy. He realized that the Ming army of China could not cope with the fighting power and the military spirit of the Japanese, and was convinced that China had no fighting chance against Japan. Li therefore reached the conclusion that a treaty of peace on the best terms possible would be the sanest step and would bring the war to a close. In this situation he found it necessary to depend upon the prisoner, Shen Wei-Ching, whom he had previously decided to kill because of Shen's peace movement and whose life had been saved on the advice of the chief of the Chinese military staff.

In the early part of March, 1593, Shen, in compliance with the request of Li Ju-Sung, went to Keijo, the national capital of Korea, and approached Yukinaga with respect to the renewal of peace negotiations. At that time, the war had lasted more than a year. Most of the Koreans had deserted their homes, agricultural work had been virtually abandoned, and there was a nation-wide famine. The line of Japanese communication was frequently threatened and at times cut off by reason of the Korean uprisings, so that the Japanese were feeling the shortage of food more and more. Most of the Japanese troops in Korea were from Kyushu, Shikoku, and the southwestern part of Honshu, the warm belt of Japan. They therefore suffered much from the severe cold of the Korean winter, and sickness and death became increasingly prevalent among them. Everyone, both high and low, was weary of war. In Japan, Hideyoshi was confronted unceasingly by difficulties in sending additional troops and food supplies. He became convinced that, because of the total lack of naval support, his original plan for the conquest of China could not be carried out, and that therefore the war in Korea was one of meaningless bloodshed.[83] He greatly desired to end the war if such an outcome were possible without the sacrifice of his prestige and dignity. In the winter of 1593, everybody—Hideyoshi and his associates in Japan as well as the Japanese military leaders and their men in Korea—longed for peace just as fervently as did Li Ju-Sung, Sung Ying-Chang, and the other Chinese military leaders in Korea and in Manchuria.[84] When Shen Wei-Ching again came to Yukinaga with peace proposals, the latter was highly pleased. He made up his mind, however, that the Japanese should not again be deceived as they had been at Pyeng Yang. So Yukinaga told Shen that Japan would not enter upon peace negotiations until China should give evidence of the sincerity of her desire to end the war. After further discussion, Shen left Keijo, having promised Yukinaga that he would return to ask for renewal of peace negotiations and would bring with him the national hostages of the Ming.

The Chinese generals, Li and Sung, having heard Shen's report, decided to send two military leaders, Hsu I-Huan and Hsieh Yung-Tsu, under the guise of national representatives, to Keijo. In the early part of April, Shen again arrived at Keijo accompanied by Hsu and Hsieh, whom he introduced to Yukinaga as imperial envoys sent by the Ming emperor, Shen-Tsung, as his representatives. Shen said that he had made his pledge good by bringing these national hostages (referring to the envoys) and that therefore Yukinaga should renew peace negotiations. Hsu and Hsieh at the same time expressed their willingness to cross the waters to Japan, there to have an interview with Hideyoshi with respect to preliminary peace terms.[85]

The Ming emperor having sent envoys in evidence of his sincerity, the Japanese generals in Korea concluded that they should likewise give evidence of the sincerity of their desire for peace. They accordingly proposed to Hideyoshi that they should withdraw from Keijo, the national capital of Korea, and, after obtaining his consent, the entire Japanese military force, on April 18, 1593, left Keijo and went to southern Korea.[86] Ostensibly the Japanese troops abandoned Keijo to facilitate the peace negotiations, but their real aim was to establish themselves in southern Korea where the weather was warmer and better food supplies were obtainable. After withdrawing from Keijo, the Japanese built a chain of sixteen strongholds in various parts of southern Korea, especially in the Keisho-Do district. With the coöperation of friendly Koreans, the Japanese military men then engaged in agricultural work, cultivating the districts in the vicinity of their military stations, their purpose being the establishment of military settlements in southern Korea.

Hsu I-Huan and Hsieh Yung-Tsu, the representatives of the Ming emperor, left Keijo about the time that the Japanese troops withdrew. They went to Fusan and then crossed the water to Kyushu, Japan. In May, 1593, they arrived at Nagoya, the military headquarters of Hideyoshi, where they were received in grand style and with the courtesy due to envoys from a great nation.[87] They were introduced to Hideyoshi as imperial envoys sent to Japan by the Ming emperor to express his regret and to apologize for the military action taken in Korea; they were also to inquire about terms of peace. Hideyoshi appointed as his representatives four of his most trusted officers—Masuda, Ishida, Otani, and Konishi, and had them convey to the Ming envoys, for purposes of discussion, peace terms consisting of seven articles. The most important of these peace terms were these: (1) the Ming emperor should recognize the transfer by

Korea to Japan of the ruling authority of the kingdom of Korea; (2) the Ming emperor should grant Japan trade privileges in China; (3) the Ming emperor should send one of his daughters to Japan to be married to the Japanese emperor; and (4) Korea should send to Japan, as hostages,[88] one of her royal princes and one of her statesmen of the rank of state minister.

The peace negotiations were conducted most irregularly. In the first place, neither China nor Japan had appointed men of responsibility as their national representatives; they were, in fact, only underlings. The entire matter was conducted by Yukinaga and Shen Wei-Ching, both of whom were officers of comparatively low rank in their respective governments. Neither of them bore a letter of credence. Shen and Yukinaga not only deceived each other, they even misrepresented matters to their respective governments.[89] On one occasion, Yukinaga sent one of his personal friends, named Fujiwara Joan, to the Ming court at Peking to discuss peace terms with the state minister of the Ming, in the presence of the Ming emperor. Fujiwara Joan presented peace terms that were entirely unknown to Hideyoshi and wholly contrary to Hideyoshi's original plan. Shen and Yukinaga went so far, indeed, as to coöperate in a joint forgery, by writing a letter purported to have been written by Hideyoshi, which they addressed to the Ming throne.[90] In this letter, they stated that Hideyoshi was ready to surrender the entire matter, without reservation, to the Ming emperor. They grossly deceived Hideyoshi as well. Finally, the Ming Emperor Shen-Tsung and Hideyoshi were both so completely deceived and misled by them that each believed he could dictate terms of peace to the other as if he were the victor in the war.[91] The peace negotiations occupied more than three years. Meanwhile, most of the Ming troops had returned either to Manchuria or to China, and Hideyoshi had recalled all the Japanese troops, with the exception of an army a few thousand strong stationed at Fusan. Before recalling his troops, Hideyoshi desired to demonstrate the fighting power of

Japan. He accordingly ordered his military leaders to attack and destroy Chin-Chou [Shin-Shu] Castle, the strongest fortification in Korea. The battle of Chin-Chou was the greatest and bloodiest in the entire campaign;[92] it is said that more than 60,000 Koreans lost their lives. Because of the repeated delays in the conclusion of peace, Hideyoshi announced time and again his plans to renew the war. At that particular time, however, he had apparently abandoned his plan of continental conquest, and in his peace terms he was satisfied to annex to Japan only the southern half of Korea. He still planned to extend the authority of Japan by annexing many of the islands lying south of the chain of Japanese islands. With this in view, in November, 1593, Hideyoshi wrote a letter to the ruler of Formosa, demanding his acknowledgment of submission by sending a tribute-bearing envoy in order to show due reverence to the imperial throne of Japan.[93]

In August, 1596, three years and two months after Hideyoshi had handed his seven-articled peace terms to the Ming representatives, the Ming Emperor Shen-Tsung sent Yang Fang-Heng and Shen Wei-Ching as peace envoys to Japan. Yang and Shen brought with them two state papers entitled the "Imperial Edict" and the "Imperial Command" of the Ming emperor to Hideyoshi. In September, 1596, Hideyoshi granted an audience to the Ming envoys, Yang and Shen, who handed the two state papers of the Ming to him. The Ming Emperor Shen-Tsung entirely disregarded Hideyoshi's seven-articled peace terms; the imperial princess of the Ming emperor did not come to Japan to marry the Japanese emperor; the southern half of Korea was not ceded to Japan.

Korea, likewise disregarding Hideyoshi's demand, sent neither a royal prince nor a prominent statesman to Japan as national hostages. Korea sent, as envoys to Japan, officials of low rank, to whom Hideyoshi therefore refused to grant audience. The Ming emperor in his imperial edict invested Hideyoshi as "King of Japan" and considered Japan as a dependent state of China. He instructed Hideyoshi how to rule his kingdom and how to maintain peaceable and friendly relations with neighboring nations. In his "Imperial Command" the Ming emperor ordered Hideyoshi to end the war in Korea and strictly to observe three terms, namely: (1) to withdraw his entire forces stationed at Fusan, and not to permit a single Japanese to remain there; (2) not to seek trade privileges from China, such as were sometimes granted to tributary states; (3) not again to invade Korea.[94]

When Hideyoshi became acquainted with the content of these state papers, in which he found no reference whatever to his seven-articled peace terms, but, quite to the contrary, most unexpected instructions to him, in addition to degrading him to be the king of a dependent state of China, he was greatly angered. He ordered his government to drive the Ming envoys and the Korean envoys from Japan forthwith. At the same time, he prepared for a second invasion of Korea, which was started three months after the envoys left Japan. As for the Ming Emperor Shen-Tsung, he was likewise angered because of the failure of the peace negotiations with Japan. He considered it a great national disgrace that Hideyoshi should refuse investiture as "King of Japan"—the first instance of rejection of the imperial investiture by China since the founding of the empire. The emperor ordered that Shen Wei-Ching be arrested and put to death on the ground that he had both deceived and disgraced the throne in negotiating peace with Japan. The supreme state minister, Shih Hsing, who had entrusted Shen with the work of negotiating peace with Japan and in accordance with whose advice the emperor had sent two state papers to Hideyoshi, was remanded to the Department of Justice and a group of state ministers for trial.[95] The department and the state ministers reported to the throne that Shih Hsing should be exiled and disgraced. The emperor refused to accede to this recommendation and issued to its proponents an edict in which he demanded sterner judgment (the text follows).

"During the entire period of peace negotiations with the outside barbarian nation Japan, Shih Hsing deceived his lord and disgraced his state. You, State Ministers, in the trial of his case, must adhere strictly to your duty and enforce the laws of the nation. In fact, Shih has committed high treason against both the nation and the throne. . . . We should consider it disloyal to the throne if you should have sympathy for your former comrade and friend."[96]

Finally, the death sentence was announced, but Shih Hsing died in prison before the sentence was carried out. His entire family and all his relatives were exiled to a far-off border state.

Hideyoshi's second invasion was begun on January 14, 1597, when Kiyomasa and his troops effected a landing in Korea and established military connections with the small body of troops of the first invasion that had remained at Fusan in Korea. On February 1, Yukinaga and his troops, a part of the second division, landed at Fusan, but the organization of the army of the second invasion was not completed until February 21, 1597. It was composed of seven divisions. The total strength of the army, 141,500 men, was approximately half the fighting strength of the army of the first invasion.[97] The entire army of the second invasion completed its landing in Korea in March, 1597.

When the Ming Emperor Shen-Tsung was appealed to by the king of Korea for military aid, he immediately undertook to raise the largest possible army and to save Korea from destruction by the island invaders. But the Ming government encountered great difficulty in organizing an army of the necessary strength. The nation was financially exhausted as a result of the previous campaign. The renewal of the war with Japan was exceedingly unpopular in China, and the people were both unwilling and slow to enlist. The government was therefore forced to get recruits from the wild tribes in the far-off border provinces, and the army was recruited at various times. The total fighting strength of the Ming army thus raised was

142,700. Because of the slowness of its organization, the Ming army did not enter Korea until May 18, 1597.

In this second invasion, the Japanese and Chinese armies in Korea were of almost the same numerical strength.[98] Hideyoshi still declared that it was possible for him to lead his army in person and to invade China with the purpose of occupying Peking, but his real plan was to invade Korea and to occupy the southern half of that kingdom. The second invasion was neither a continental nor a Chinese campaign,[99] but simply a Korean campaign. After landing, the second Japanese army did not advance so rapidly as had the army of the first invasion. First, a strong military base was established at Fusan, then gradually the coast districts were occupied, and a chain of strong fortresses built along the coast and in strategic mountainous districts. The marked difference between the first and second invasions was in the navy: in the second invasion, the Japanese had a strong and well-organized navy. On July 15, 1597, a great naval battle was fought. The Korean navy was almost completely destroyed, only twelve of their war vessels escaping. Hsien-Shan (Kanzan) Island, the naval base of Korea, was occupied by the Japanese naval force. Having thus gained command of the sea, the Japanese military and naval forces were in a position to coöperate and carry on military undertakings in accordance with Hideyoshi's original plan. Keisho-Do, Zenra-Do, and most of the rest of southern Korea having been occupied, Japan virtually controlled the southern half of the peninsula.[100]

No bloody or decisive battles were fought until after the coming of the Ming army. Those at Nanyuan, Chishan, Chin-Chou, Urusan, and Ssuchuan all ended in decisive victories for Japan. The battle at Ssuchuan lasted for nearly a week. In the very last engagement, which was fought on October 1, 1598, the Ming army was completely routed, and 38,700 slain Chinese were left on the field.[101] The Ming Emperor Shen-Tsung was greatly shocked and disappointed when the news of this great military disaster at Ssuchuan reached him. He immediately issued the following imperial instructions, in which he also upbraided all the military leaders in that battle:

"In our army, some of our military leaders, being self-conceited, have disregarded the fighting strength and skill of the enemy [the Japanese]. Others of our military leaders, being cowardly and effeminate, feared the enemy. The commanding general could not crush or shatter those self-satisfied and vainglorious men. Nor could he stimulate and inspire the humiliated and downcast military men in our army. Therefore, the military divisions of our army were not distributed or handled in accordance with military laws and regulations. Military commands and orders were neither enforced nor obeyed. Consequently, when a division of our army was forced to retreat, all the other divisions hastily followed, thus bringing great military disaster to our entire army. Our military men have thus disgraced and dishonored our nation and have lowered our military prestige and standing. They have thus caused us great remorse and sorrow. They must therefore be severely punished. We hereby issue our imperial command that Ho San-Ping and Ma Cheng-Wen be summoned to the front of the imperial army in Korea and be beheaded there. Their heads shall then be exposed to public view. Peng Hsin-Kou should be summoned and the death sentence pronounced upon him. However, his execution should be temporarily suspended so that opportunity may be afforded him to expiate his military crime by rendering distinguished service in future. Tang I-Yuan shall be degraded one rank, with instructions to render some distinguished service. Hsing Chen is hereby specially instructed to lead our military force with great caution and to see that his men engage bravely in battle. He and his men should always stand on the field of battle, firm and steady as a mountain. In the field, all military movements shall be carried out in strict accordance with the military laws and strategies. At the same time, changing conditions in the field shall be keenly observed and every opportunity grasped in order that a complete and glorious victory may be ours."[102]

This imperial command was ineffective. After the disastrous defeat at Ssuchuan, the Ming forces in Korea were completely demoralized. They lost all their fighting spirit and courage, and did not dare to engage again in battle with the Japanese. Two weeks after the battle at Ssuchuan, Mao Kuo-Ki, the supreme military leader of the Ming army, sent his brother, Mao Kuo-Ko, as hostage to Shimazu, the commanding general of the Japanese army at Ssuchuan, to ask for a truce, his ultimate purpose being the negotiation of peace with Japan.[103] The sincerity of the Ming general was doubtful; nevertheless, the Ming army in Korea did make an attempt to settle the war with Japan either through peace negotiations or by some other means that would do away with further fighting.

On August 18, 1598, about six weeks before the great Ssuchuan battle, Hideyoshi had suddenly died after a brief illness. It had been his opinion that after his death there would remain no military leader in Japan ambitious enough to carry on the Korean campaign, and therefore, on his deathbed, he had instructed Iyeyasu, Toshiiye, and others of his military leaders to recall the entire army from Korea.[104] Because they had been victorious, the Japanese forces in Korea withdrew successfully without any serious difficulties, although the Chinese and the Korean military and naval forces made desperate attempts to attack the Japanese on their way home and thus avenge themselves for the seven years of suffering that they had gone through. The last Japanese army left Fusan, Korea, in the latter part of November, 1598, and arrived at Hakata in Kyushu, Japan, in the early part of December. Thus the cruel "Seven Years' War" came to an end.[105]

In Japan, this Seven Years' War is called *Ryo-to Ja-bi* ("The Dragon-head and Snake-tail Campaign"),[106] a name which was given it because it began with the grand plan of conquering the Asiatic continent and ended with accomplishing barely anything. The Seven Years' War (the actual duration of the fighting periods was only about three years, although the war was not terminated until the end of seven years) was most destructive. China and Korea suffered greatly from it. Historians are agreed that toward the close of the war both China and Korea were militarily and financially exhausted and that they had no fighting chance against the Japanese.[107] Only the death of Hideyoshi saved them from inevitable military calamity. Had Hideyoshi lived but a few years longer and continued with the war, though Korea and China might not have been conquered by Japan, their national existence would have come to an end in one way or another through the total exhaustion of their resources. In fact, only a few years after the close of the Seven Years' War, Nurhachi, of the Aisin Gioro family (he was the Emperor Tai-Tsu of the Ching dynasty and founder of the Manchu dynasty in China) rose in the southeastern part of Manchuria, a district near the northern border of Korea. In 1616, he became a recognized power in Manchuria. In 1621, he defeated the Ming army in Manchuria and occupied Mukden. In 1625, he completed the founding of the Manchurian empire, making Mukden its capital.[108] In 1627, the Manchu army invaded Korea, the Ming emperor was not able to render any assistance to the dependent state, and the king of Korea therefore sued for peace, doing reverence to the Manchu emperor as his elder brother. In 1632, as a result of a second invasion, Korea was completely conquered and reduced to a tributary state of Manchuria. This took place only thirty-four years after the termination of the Seven Years' War.

As for the Ming, while its army was continuously losing battles in Manchuria, it had to confront a series of rebellions in different parts of China. The Ming government was, nevertheless, able to continue in power until 1631, when Li Tsu-Cheng rebelled against the Ming emperor. While the victorious Manchu army was steadily approaching the Great Wall, the rebel army under the command of Li Tsu-Cheng made a victorious advance toward Peking, and finally, in 1644, stormed and occupied that city. The Ming emperor thereupon put an end to his life by hanging himself in the imperial palace. The military leaders of the Ming, finding themselves powerless to avenge the death of their emperor, invited the Manchu emperor, against whom they had been fighting up to that time, to come to Peking and restore order there. In the same year, the Manchu emperor responded to this request, and he defeated Li Tsu-Cheng, who was killed in the following year. In 1645, with the founding of his government at Peking, the Manchu emperor, Shih-Tsu, promulgated a law by which the Chinese were ordered to adopt the Manchu custom of arranging the hair in a queue. Thus did China again come under the rule of a foreign dynasty. This took place forty-seven years after the Seven Years' War. Although that war may not have been the sole cause of the downfall of the Ming dynasty in China, nor of the reduction of Korea to a tributary state of Manchuria, yet none can deny that it was the chief cause of these great national disasters.

The Seven Years' War was one of the most cruel and unprovoked wars that the world has ever witnessed. Korean civilization was completely destroyed. The Korean people suffered to such a degree that even the graves of their kings were molested and rifled. At the close of the war Korea was a land of ruins, so great had been the devastation. The Koreans have ever since fostered great enmity toward the Japanese. Even today, Korea is filled with monuments, traditions, and literature describing the horrors of the Seven Years' War. Thus does Korea keep alive the memory of Japanese atrocities, generation after generation. The difficulties that Japan has experienced in her administration of Korea since 1910 are generally accounted for by this lasting memory of an old war.[109]

As for Japan, the Seven Years' War on the one hand not only failed to bring her any territorial or financial gain, but it also engendered toward her the everlasting hatred of the

Koreans. On the other hand, by reason of this war, Japan profited both intellectually and industrially. At the time of Hideyoshi's invasion, the civilization of Korea had reached its peak. She had metallic movable type of her own invention; in fact, Korea had movable type several years before its invention in the Occident. The Japanese gathered up most of this type and took it to Japan; it was only after her invasion of Korea that Japan learned to print books with any facility. From Korea, Japan also learned the art of weaving various kinds of goods. The most noteworthy industrial knowledge that Japan gained from Korea was the manufacture of porcelain ware. Such famous wares as those of Satsuma, Hirado, Rakuzan, Agano, Takatori, and Hagi, which are famous today as special products of Japan, were originated by skilled laborers in Korea whom various Japanese feudal lords took prisoners and settled permanently in the various provinces.[110] It is said that the process is now a lost art in Korea. World history contains no parallel to this wholesale uprooting of the civilization of one nation and its transplantation in another.

Japan also greatly benefited morally because of the Seven Years' War. She had suffered for nearly one hundred and fifty years from the continuous internecine warfare of the Dark Age, and had undertaken the Seven Years' War in a foreign country immediately following the national unification and the restoration of peace. Because this foreign war ended without any of the territorial or material gains that had been expected, after the Korean campaign the Japanese military men were completely disgusted with taking the lives of others and risking their own. This new national attitude toward warfare contributed to the bringing about of a period of peace. It may be said, indeed, that the period of prosperity and tranquillity which Japan enjoyed for about three hundred years beginning in the seventeenth century, was a by-product of the war.

Moreover, during the Seven Years' War, Japanese military men had fully convinced the Chinese and the Koreans that the Japanese were militarily superior and that Japan was invincible. This reputation spread among the Asiatic nations and assured the safety of Japan from invasion by continental nations. In the middle of the nineteenth century, when a reopened Japan emerged from her peaceful seclusion of more than two hundred years, she encountered an outside world at the very time when the leading nations in Europe and America were engaging in extensive national expansion. Russia was carrying on a successful expansion in northeastern Asia. Germany had just completed her unification. The kingdom of Italy had risen by extending her rule over all the minor states in the peninsula. The United States had forced Mexico to surrender a vast territory. Japan therefore naturally asked herself if there was any possibility of her national expansion. Hideyoshi's seven years' campaign on the continent became a source of great inspiration to the young Japanese. Because of the brilliant victories of Hideyoshi, the Japanese concluded that battles with either Chinese or Koreans meant victory. Imbued with this conviction, Japan entered upon a new period of national expansion.[111] The Sino-Japanese War (1894–95), which was a onesided struggle ending in complete victory for Japan without the loss of a single battle either on land or on the sea, encouraged the young Japanese to believe that they were destined to finish the uncompleted work of Hideyoshi. The Seven Years' War of the sixteenth century has therefore been of great significance in the formation of the national ideals of New Japan. It may even be said that the Seven Years' War was the first chapter in the national expansion of Japan that began toward the close of the nineteenth century.[112]

Hideyoshi left an only son, five years of age. He earnestly desired that his son should be carefully reared and fitted to be his successor. He therefore made all the prominent military men, taking the gods and goddesses as witnesses, pledge their loyalty to his son, Hideyori.[113] Before his death, Hideyoshi organized a "Board of National Trustees," the duty of which was to be the administration of both civil and military affairs during the minority of Hideyori. Five of the most powerful feudal lords, including Iyeyasu, who was their head, constituted the Board.[114] However, immediately after the death of Hideyoshi, great difficulties arose with respect to the birth of Hideyori and because of the underhanded intrigues of Iyeyasu. Hideyori's mother was not the legal wife of Hideyoshi. She was a woman of great ambition and surrounded herself with men of power and influence. Hideyoshi's wife was a woman of high attainments and splendid personality and had the sympathy of many prominent military leaders who had served under her husband. This state of affairs divided both the military and the civil officials, who had close connections with the Toyotomi family, into two factions.[115]

Iyeyasu, already a man of advanced age, firmly believed that he, one of the great men with whose coöperation the national unification had been effected, had a right to become the founder of a military government, as Nobunaga and Hideyoshi had done. He very cleverly made himself a third disturbing element. The military men who championed the cause of Hideyori united under a leader named Ishida Mitsunari; the others gathered under the leadership of Iyeyasu.[116] This situation brought on the battle of Sekigahara, which was fought in 1600. This battle lasted but a single day, and nearly 200,000 men were on the field. It was one of the greatest and most decisive battles in the history of Japan. Iyeyasu won a complete victory and became the supreme leader in both military and civil affairs. All the national disputes in Japan being thus settled, three years later, in 1603, the emperor appointed Iyeyasu to be shogun.[117] He became the founder of the fifth military government, which was also known as the third shogunate government and as the Tokugawa shogunate, after the name of the family of Iyeyasu. With the founding of the Tokugawa shogunate, Japan entered upon a period of peace and prosperity that lasted for nearly three hundred years.

NOTES TO CHAPTER I

1 Kume, *Nippon Kodai-Shi* (History of the Ancient Period in Japan), vol. 1, pp. 422–23, 426. Yoshida, *Tojo Nippon-Shi* (History of Japan in Reverse Order), vol. 10, pp. 245–47.

2 Mitsukuni (Tokugawa), *Dai-Nihon Shi* (History of Great Japan), vol. 2, pp. 17–18. Hagino, *Dai-Nippon Tsushi* (A Comprehensive History of Great Japan), pp. 65–66.

3 Kume, *op. cit.*, pp. 441–42.

4 Mitsukuni, *op. cit.*, vol. 164, p. 720. Ariga, *Dai Nippon-Rekishi* (Unabridged History of Japan), vol. 1, pp. 131–32.

5 Appendix 1, below, p. 193.

6 Kume, *op. cit.*, pp. 368, 395.

7 Mitsukuni, *op. cit.*, vol. 3, pp. 32–33.

8 *Ibid.*, pp. 34–37.

9 The names of the three kingdoms in Korea are each written with two Chinese characters. In Chinese, they are pronounced, respectively, Hsinlo, Paichi, and Kaoli. In the Korean language, they are pronounced Silla, Pakche, and Koryu. In the Japanese language, they are pronounced Shinra or Shiragi, Kudara or Hyakusai, and Korai or Koma. In the text of the present work, the names Shinra, Kudara, and Korai are used throughout because they are the names that are generally accepted today in the study of Korean history.

10 App. 2, below, p. 195.

11 Kume, *op. cit.*, vol. 2, pp. 81–82.

12 Omachi, *Nippon Bunmei-Shi* (History of Japanese Civilization), p. 49.

13 App. 3, below, p. 198.

14 App. 4, below, p. 214.

15 App. 5, below, p. 221.

16 App. 6, below, p. 224.

17 Ariga, *op. cit.*, pp. 238–39. Sanyo. (Rai, Jo), *Nippon-Gaishi Rombun* (Historical Essays on Japanese National Subjects), pp. 4–5, 11–12, 21.

18 Mitsukuni, *op. cit.*, vol. 154, p. 540.

19 Hagino, *Dai-Nippon Tsushi*, p. 163. Kuroita, *Kokushi no Kenkyu*, pp. 60–61.

20 Yoshida. *Tojo Nippon-Shi*, vol. 10, p. 373: *Chingting Erh-Shih-Ssu Shih* (Imperial Authorized Edition of the History of the Twenty-four Dynasties in China).

21 Mitsukuni, *op. cit.*, vol. 162, pp. 687, 689, 709. Hagino, *Nippon-Shi Kowa* (Lectures on Japanese History), pp. 56, 153.

22 Kume, *op. cit.*, vol. 2, p. 219.

23 Hagino, *Nippon-Shi Kowa*, p. 71.

24 *Ibid.*, p. 75.

25 *Ibid.*, p. 76.

26 App. 7, below, p. 227.

27 Kume, *op. cit.*, vol. 2, p. 297.

28 *Ibid.*, pp. 279, 285–86.

29 Yoshida, *Tojo Nippon-Shi*, vol. 10, p. 452.

30 Kume, *op. cit.*, vol. 2, pp. 346–48.

31 App. 8, below, p. 228.

32 Yoshida, *op. cit.*, vol. 10, pp. 452–54.

33 App. 9, below, p. 229.

34 Yoshida, *op. cit.*, vol. 10, p. 452.

35 Kume, *op. cit.*, vol. 2, pp. 415–16. Kuroita, *op. cit.*, p. 98.

36 Yoshida, *op. cit.*, vol. 10, pp. 457–58.

37 Hagino, *op. cit.*, pp. 256–57.

38 App. 10, below, p. 231.

39 Kume, *op. cit.*, vol. 2, pp. 424–25.

40 Yoshida, *op. cit.*, vol. 10, pp. 462–64.

41 Ito, *Dai-Nippon Minzoku-Shi* (History of the Race of Great Japan), p. 238.

42 Apps. 11, 12, below, pp. 231, 232.

43 App. 13, below, p. 234.

44 App. 14, below, p. 235.

NOTES TO CHAPTER II

1 Kume, *Nippon Kodai-Shi*, vol. 2, pp. 414–16.

2 Tsuji, *Kaigai Kotsu Shiwa* (Historical Account of Communications of Japan with Nations Beyond the Seas), p. 57.

3 Hagino, *Dai-Nippon Tsushi*, p. 50.

4 Mitsukuni, *Dai-Nihon Shi*, vol. 2, pp. 29–30.

5 Hagino, *Nippon-Shi Kowa*, pp. 47–48.

6 *Ibid.*, pp. 49–50.

7 Kuroita, *Kokushi no Kenkyu*, pp. 98–99. Toneri, *Nihon Shoki* (Chronicle of Japan), vol. 27, pp. 475–76.

8 Kuroita, *op. cit.*, p. 100.

9 *Ibid.*, pp. 100–01. Mitsukuni, *op. cit.*, vol. 10, p. 130. Tsuji, *op. cit.*, pp. 68–69. Hagino, *Nippon-Shi Kowa*, p. 155.

10 Kume, *op. cit.*, vol. 2, p. 424.

11 Hagino, *Nippon-Shi Kowa*, pp. 156–57.

12 *Ibid.*, pp. 180–86. Kuroita, *op. cit.*, pp. 106–07.

13 Ariga, *Dai Nippon-Rekishi*, vol. 1, pp. 537–86.

14 Omachi, *Nippon Bunmei-Shi*, pp. 67–68.

15 The traditional usage in the Orient was to employ the title "Emperor" exclusively with respect to the ruler of a nation with suzerain power and to use the title "King" with respect to the ruler of a tributary nation, that is, a nation paying tribute to a foreign power.

16 Kimiya, *Nisshi Kotsu-Shi* (History of Communications Between China and Japan), vol. 1, pp. 178–80.

17 Kuroita, *op. cit.*, p. 101. Hagino, *Nippon-Shi Kowa*, p. 156.

18 Omachi, *op. cit.*, pp. 94–95.

19 *Ibid.*, pp. 63–72.

20 Hagino, *Nippon-Shi Kowa*, pp. 254–57. Kuroita, *op. cit.*, pp. 161, 193, 198.

21 Hagino, *Dai Nippon Tsushi*, pp. 375–77. Sanyo, *Nippon Gaishi Rombun*, pp. 44.

22 Kuroita, *op. cit.*, pp. 218–23.

23 Hagino, *Nippon-Shi Kowa*, pp. 256–58.

24 Kuroita, *op. cit.*, pp. 206–08. Hagino, *op. cit.*, pp. 254, 261–62.

25 Sanyo, *op. cit.*, pp. 50–51. Hagino, *op. cit.*, pp. 228–29.

26 Kuroita, *op. cit.*, p. 196.

27 *Ibid.*, p. 211.

28 Hagino, *Dai-Nippon Tsushi*, p. 523.

29 *Idem*, *Nippon-Shi Kowa*, pp. 245–46.

30 *Ibid.*, pp. 241–43.

31 Sanyo, *op. cit.*, pp. 66–67. Kuroita, *op. cit.*, p. 223. Hagino, *op. cit.*, pp. 234–35.

32 Sanyo, *op. cit.*, p. 67. Hagino, *op. cit.*, pp. 269–71. Kuroita, *op cit.*, pp. 255–58.

33 Kuroita, *op. cit.*, pp. 244–46.

34 *Ibid.*, pp. 257–58.

35 *Ibid.*, pp. 259–60.

36 Sanyo, *op. cit.*, p. 51. Kuroita, *op. cit.*, pp. 273–76. Hagino, *Dai-Nippon Tsushi*, pp. 270–72, 886.

37 Kuroita, *op. cit.*, p. 275. Ikeda, *Heian-Cho Jidai-Shi* (History of the Heian Imperial Period), pp. 554–55.

38 Kuroita, *op. cit.*, pp. 271–72.

39 *Ibid.*, pp. 281–82, 299.

40 App. 15, below, p. 245.

41 Sanyo, *op. cit.*, pp. 26, 77.

42 Hagino, *Nippon-Shi Kowa*, pp. 316–18.

43 Kuroita, *op. cit.*, pp. 191–92. Ariga, *Dai Nippon-Rekishi*, vol. 1, pp. 869–70.

44 Kimiya, *op. cit.*, vol. 1, pp. 400–06.

45 Origin of the name "Korea": The name of this peninsular kingdom is written with two Chinese characters which are pronounced Korai in Japanese, Koryu in Korean, and Kaoli in Chinese. The name "Korea" is probably a Latinized corruption of one or another of these three names.

[46] *Chinting Yuan-Shih* (Imperial Authorized Edition of the History of the Yuan [Mongol] Dynasty), vol. 208, pp. 1–20. Yoshida, *Tojo Nippon-Shi*, vol. 8, p. 175.

[47] Kimiya, *op. cit.*, pp. 101–02.

[48] *Chinting Yuan-Shih*, vol. 208, p. 4. Kimiya, *op. cit.*, p. 102.

[49] *Chinting Yuan-Shih*, vol. 208, p. 6.

[50] Kimiya, *op. cit.*, vol. 2, pp. 102–03. Ko, S. M., *Hsin Yuan-Shih* (New History of the Mongols), vol. 250, pp. 1a–b.

[51] Ko, *op. cit.*, pp. 2b–3a.

[52] *Ibid.*, p. 2a.

[53] *Chinting Yuan-Shih*, vol. 208, pp. 3–7. Ko, *op. cit.*, pp. 2–4. Jo, Kyo-Sei, *Togoku Tsugan* (History of the Eastern Nation [Korea]), chapter on "The Fifteenth Year of Junso, the Korean King." Kimiya, *op. cit.*, pp. 102–04. App. 16, below, p. 245.

[54] *Chinting Yuan-Shih*, vol. 208, p. 9a. Ko, *op. cit.*, p. 3b.

[55] Kimiya, *op. cit.*, pp. 105–06. Ko, *op. cit.*, pp. 4a–b. *Chinting Yuan-Shih*, vol. 208, p. 9. App. 17, below, p. 248.

[56] Ko, *op. cit.*, p. 4b. Kimiya, *op. cit.*, p. 107.

[57] Ko, *op. cit.*, p. 5a.

[58] Kimiya, *op. cit.*, pp. 113–14. Tsuji, *Kaigai Kotsu Shiwa*, pp. 211–13. Ko, *op. cit.*, pp. 5a–6b. *Chinting Yuan-Shih*, vol. 208, p. 9b. App. 18, below, p. 251.

[59] *Chinting Yuan-Shih*, vol. 208, p. 9. Ko, *op. cit.*, pp. 5–6.

[60] Kimiya, *op. cit.*, p. 114.

[61] Kimiya, *op. cit.*, vol. 2, pp. 114–15. Ko, *op. cit.*, p. 6a.

[62] Kimiya, *op. cit.*, p. 117. Ko, *op. cit.*, pp. 6a–b.

[63] Ariga, *op. cit.*, vol. 2, p. 169.

[64] *Chinting Yuan-Shih*, vol. 208, p. 9b. Kimiya, *op. cit.*, p. 116.

[65] Ko, *op. cit.*, pp. 6–7.

[66] Yoshida, *Tojo Nippon-Shi*, vol. 8, p. 180.

[67] *Ibid.*, pp. 181–83, 187.

[68] Tsuji, *op. cit.*, pp. 213–18. Ko, *op. cit.*, p. 9b. Kuroita, *op. cit.*, pp. 356–57. Hagino, *Nippon-Shi Kowa*, p. 369.

[69] Tsuji, *op. cit.*, pp. 229–30. Ko, *op. cit.*, pp. 8–10. Ariga, *op. cit.*, pp. 169–74. Kimiya, *op. cit.*, pp. 118–21. Hayashi, *Chosen Tsushi* (Comprehensive History of Korea), pp. 84–85.

[70] *Chinting Yuan-Shih*, vol. 208, p. 10b. Tsuji, *op. cit.*, p. 231. Yoshida, *op. cit.*, vol. 8, p. 185.

[71] *Chinting Yuan-Shih*, vol. 208, pp. 9b–10.

[72] The birth of the New Japan may be traced directly to the annihilation of the armadas of Kublai Khan in 1274 and in 1281, respectively, and since that time, *Shinkoku* (The Divine Nation), *Tenyu* (The Grace of Heaven), and *Shinpu* (The Wind Sent by God) have become sacred words in Japan. These notable historical events in the thirteenth century are inseparably connected with the national expansion of Japan. Prior to that time, Japan believed that her country was *Shinkoku* and that she had *Tenyu;* but the idea of ever conquering China had never occurred to her. A knowledge of Kublai Khan's armada, of its destruction, and of the effects of that destruction upon the national consciousness is essential to an understanding of the later national undertakings of New Japan. This is why so lengthy a description of Kublai Khan's invasions is given in this text.

[73] *Chinting Yuan-Shih*, vol. 12, p. 3a. Kimiya, *op. cit.*, vol. 2, p. 123.

[74] *Chinting Yuan-Shih*, vol. 12, pp. 4–6. Jo, Kyo-Sei, *Togoku Tsugan*, chapter on "The Ninth Year of the Rule of Churetsu, the King of Korea."

[75] *Chinting Yuan-Shih*, vol. 13, p. 16. Kimiya, *op. cit.*, vol. 2, p. 124.

[76] Kimiya, *op. cit.*, vol. 2, pp. 124–25.

[77] *Chinting Yuan-Shih,* vol. 13, pp. 7–9. Ko, *op. cit.,* vol. 11, p. 11.

[78] Kimiya, *op. cit.,* vol. 2, p. 126.

[79] *Chinting Yuan-Shih,* vol. 168, pp. 6a–b. Kimiya, *op. cit.,* vol. 2, p. 127.

[80] *Chinting Yuan-Shih,* vol. 14, p. 1a.

[81] Kimiya, *op. cit.,* vol. 2, p. 128.

[82] *Chinting Yuan-Shih,* vol. 15, pp. 2, 7. Jo, Kyo-Sei, *op. cit.,* chapter on "The Fourteenth and the Eighteenth Years of the Rule of Churetsu, the King of Korea."

[83] Tei, Rin-Shi. *Korai-Shi* (History of the Kingdom of Korai), chapter on "The Tenth Month in the Eighteenth Year of the Rule of Churetsu, the King of Korea." Kimiya, *op. cit.,* vol. 2, p. 129.

[84] *Chinting Yuan-Shih,* vol. 208, p. 10b. Kimiya, *op. cit.,* vol. 2, pp. 129–30. Jo, Kyo-Sei, *op. cit.,* chapter on "The First Month in the Twentieth Year of the Rule of Churetsu, the King of Korea."

[85] Ko, *op. cit.,* vol. 12, p. 13.

[86] *Chinting Yuan-Shih,* vol. 208, p. 10b. Kimiya, *op. cit.,* vol. 2, p. 130.

[87] Ko, *op. cit.,* vol. 250, pp. 10–11. Kimiya, *op. cit.,* vol. 2, pp. 130–31.

[88] Ko, *op. cit.,* vol. 250, p. 11a. Kimiya, *op. cit.,* vol. 2, p. 131.

[89] Tanaka, *Ashikaga Jidai-Shi* (History of the Ashikaga Period), pp. 117–18, 122–23.

[90] Kuroita, *op. cit.,* pp. 361–63. Yoshida, *op. cit.,* vol. 8, pp. 190–94. Yokoi and Hirade. "Shodo no Tokusei," *Shigaku Zasshi,* vol. 6, p. 290. "The First Law of Repudiation in Japan," *Magazine of Historical Science,* vol. 6, pp. 290–98.

[91] Kuroita, *op. cit.,* p. 360.

NOTES TO CHAPTER III

[1] Kuroita, *Kokushi no Kenkyu*, p. 421.

[2] Hagino, *Nippon-Shi Kowa*, pp. 403, 405.

[3] Kuroita, *op. cit.*, pp. 385–86.

[4] Yoshida, *Tojo Nippon-Shi*, vol. 7, p. 221. Tanaka, *Nanboku-Cho Jidai-Shi*, pp. 91–93. Kuroita, *op. cit.*, p. 422.

[5] Hagino, *op. cit.*, p. 403.

[6] Waseda University, *Dai-Nippon Jidai-Shi* (History of Great Japan, Period by Period), vol. 6, pp. 300–07. Kuroita, *op. cit.*, pp. 427–28.

[7] Hagino, *op. cit.*, pp. 405–08.

[8] Yoshida, *op. cit.*, vol. 7, pp. 240–42. Ariga, *Dai Nippon-Rekishi* (Unabridged History of Japan). vol. 2, pp. 263–64.

[9] App. 19, below, p. 253.

[10] Hagino, *op. cit.*, pp. 429–30.

[11] Waseda University, *Dai-Nippon Jidai-Shi*, vol. 6, pp. 449, 465–66. Kuroita, *op. cit.*, pp. 438–39. Hagino, *op. cit.*, pp. 417–18.

[12] Tanaka, *op. cit.*, pp. 11–12.

[13] Hagino, *op. cit.*, pp. 431–33, 447, 473. Aoki, *Dai-Nippon Rekishi Shusei* (Comprehensive History of Great Japan), vol. 2, p. 668.

[14] Tanaka, *op. cit.*, p. 10. Kuroita, *op. cit.*, p. 463. Hagino, *op. cit.*, pp. 480–81. Aoki, *op. cit.*, vol. 2, p. 669.

[15] Aoki, *op. cit.*, p. 579.

[16] Yoshida, *op. cit.*, vol. 7, p. 29.

[17] Tanaka, *op. cit.*, pp. 117–18. Ariga, *op. cit.*, vol. 2, pp. 365–66. Kuroita, *op. cit.*, p. 476.

[18] Tsuji, *Kaigai Kotsu Shiwa*, pp. 81, 87, 89.

[19] Shuho, *Zenrin Kokuho-Ki* (Records of State Papers and Communications [National Treasures] Exchanged with Neighboring Nations), vol. 1, p. 22.

[20] Kimiya, *Nisshi Kotsu-Shi*, vol. 2, p. 2. *Chinting Sung-Shih* (Imperial Authorized Edition of the History of the Sung), vol. 491, p. 5.

[21] *Chinting Sung-Shi*, vol. 320, pp. 4, 6. Kuroita, *op. cit.*, p. 360. Hagino, *op. cit.*, pp. 561–62. Yoshida, *op. cit.*, vol. 7, pp. 132–33.

[22] Historical Research Association, *Zoku Shiteki Kenkyu* (Historical Research, second series), pp. 12–13.

[23] *Ibid.*, pp. 3–4.

[24] Aoki, *op. cit.*, vol. 2, pp. 968–69. Ariga, *op. cit.*, vol. 2, pp. 365–66.

[25] Tsuji, *op. cit.*, p. 239. Hayashi, *Chosen Tsushi*, pp. 112–13.

[26] Tanaka, *op. cit.*, p. 119. Hayashi, *op. cit.*, pp. 114–15.

[27] Korean Historical Association, *Chosen-Shi Taikei* (A Series of Fundamental Histories of Korea), vol. 3, p. 41. Hayashi, *op. cit.*, pp. 116–17. Tanaka, *op. cit.*, p. 122.

[28] Korean Government-General, *Korai-Shi Setsuyo* (Essence of the History of Korai; edited), vol. 32, pp. 5–7, 10, 12–14, 18–19, 31–32. Hayashi, *op. cit.*, pp. 137–40.

[29] Tanaka, *op. cit.*, pp. 120–21. Aoki, *op. cit.*, vol. 2, p. 969. Historical Research Association, *Zoku Shiteki Kenkyu*, p. 20. Hayashi, *op. cit.*, pp. 98, 108–12, 115–16, 127–28, 137–41, 174. Kuroita, *op. cit.*, p. 480. Tsuji, *op. cit.*, p. 240.

[30] Yoshida, *op. cit.*, vol. 7, p. 376. Tsuji, *op. cit.*, p. 240. Hayashi, *op. cit.*, p. 221.

[31] Waseda University, *op. cit.*, vol. 7, pp. 49–50.

[32] Tanaka, *Nanboku-Cho Jidai-Shi*, pp. 238–45. Kuroita, *op. cit.*, pp. 468–69. Waseda University, *op. cit.*, vol. 7, pp. 74, 77–79.

[33] Tanaka, *Nanboku-Cho Jidai-Shi*, pp. 279–84. Waseda University, *op. cit.*, vol. 7, pp. 97–98. Kuroita, *op. cit.*, pp. 466–67. App. 19, below, pp. 253–54.

[34] Yoshida, *op. cit.*, vol. 7, p. 376.

[35] Hayashi, *op. cit.*, p. 300.

[36] Waseda University, *op. cit.*, vol. 7, pp. 249–52. Hayashi, *op. cit.*, pp. 221–26. Historical Research Association, *op. cit.*, pp. 7–8, 14. Kuroita, *op. cit.*, pp. 481–82.

[37] Shuho, *Zenrin Kokuho-Ki*, vol. 2, p. 32. Yoshida, *op. cit.*, vol. 7, p. 376.

[38] Shuho, *op. cit.*, vol. 2, pp. 32–33.

[39] National History Research Association, *Ashikaga Jugodai-Shi*, pp. 400–01. Waseda University, *op. cit.*, vol. 7, pp. 249–50. Hayashi, *op. cit.*, pp. 221–23. Tanaka, *op. cit.*, p. 121. Shuho, *op. cit.*, vol. 2, p. 33. Kuroita, *op. cit.*, p. 481.

[40] Waseda University, *op. cit.*, vol. 7, pp. 248, 622–23. Aoki, *op. cit.*, vol. 2, pp. 971–75. Yoshida, *op. cit.*, vol. 7, pp. 133–34, 379–80. Historical Research Association, *op. cit.*, pp. 11, 15, 17.

[41] Yoshida, *op. cit.*, vol. 7, pp. 377–78. Higasa, *Nissen Kankei no Shiteki Kosatsu to Kenkyu* (Study and Research from a Historical Viewpoint Concerning Relations Between Japan and Korea), pp. 87–88.

[42] Chosen-Shi Gakkai, *Chosen-Shi Taikei*, vol. 3, p. 28. Hayashi, *op. cit.*, pp. 221, 225–26, 300. Historical Research Association, *op. cit.*, pp. 7–8. Aoyagi, *Richo-Shi Daizen* (Complete History of Korea in the Period of the Yi Dynasty), pp. 190, 192.

[43] *Chinting Ming-Shih*, vol. 1, pp. 506; vol. 2, p. 1. Waseda University, *op. cit.*, vol. 7, p. 232.

[44] Kimiya, *op. cit.*, vol. 2, pp. 271–72. Aoki, *op. cit.*, vol. 2, p. 976. App. 20, below, p. 253.

[45] Kimiya, *op. cit.*, vol. 2, p. 272.

[46] *Chinting Ming-Shih*, vol. 322, p. 1a. Kimiya, *op. cit.*, vol. 2, p. 273.

[47] *Chinting Ming-Shih*, vol. 322, pp. 1a–b.

[48] Kimiya, *op. cit.*, vol. 2, p. 273.

[49] *Chinting Ming-Shih*, vol. 322, p. 1b. Kimiya, *op. cit.*, vol. 2, p. 274.

[50] *Chinting Ming-Shih*, vol. 2, p. 4a. Kimiya, *op. cit.*, vol. 2, pp. 274–75.

[51] *Chinting Ming-Shih*, vol. 322, p. 1b. Tsuji, *op. cit.*, p. 301. Hasegawa, *Wako* (Invasions Along the Chinese and Korean Coasts by Pirates from Japan), pp. 41–42.

[52] Yoshida, *op. cit.*, vol. 7, p. 369.

[53] Tsuji, *op. cit.*, pp. 302–03. *Chinting Ming-Shih*, vol. 322, p. 2a. Hasegawa, *op. cit.*, pp. 43–44. Kimiya, *op. cit.*, vol. 2, pp. 280–81. App. 21, below, p. 256.

[54] Tsuji, *op. cit.*, p. 303, Hasegawa, *op. cit.*, pp. 42–43.

[55] National History Research Association, *op. cit.*, p. 391. Hasegawa, *op. cit.*, p. 63. *Chinting Ming-Shih*, vol. 322, p. 2b.

[56] Higasa, *op. cit.*, pp. 83–86, 92–93. Hasegawa, *op. cit.*, pp. 55–58. Waseda University, *op. cit.*, vol. 7, pp. 623–24, 637.

[57] Yoshida, *op. cit.*, vol. 7, p. 366. Historical Research Association, *op. cit.*, pp. 9–10.

[58] *Chinting Ming-Shih*, vol. 322, pp. 6a–b.

[59] Kimiya, *op. cit.*, vol. 2, p. 283.

[60] Tanaka, *op. cit.*, pp. 45–46. Shuho, *op. cit.*, vol. 2, pp. 32–33. Hasegawa, *op. cit.*, p. 42. App. 22, below, p. 258.

[61] Tanaka, *op. cit.*, pp. 37–38, 41–43.

[62] *Ibid.*, pp. 49–50. Kimiya, *op. cit.*, pp. 299, 321. *Chinting Ming-Shih*, vol. 322, pp. 2b–3a.

[63] Tsuji, *op. cit.*, pp. 305–06. Kuroita, *op. cit.*, pp. 477–79. Shuho, *op. cit.*, pp. 34–35.

[64] Association of Japanese History-Geography, *Nippon Kaijo Shiron* (History of Japan on the Sea), pp. 210–11. Tanaka, *op. cit.*, pp. 51–52. Hasegawa, *op. cit.*, p. 62. Ito, *Dai-Nippon Minzoku-Shi*, pp. 52–53. App. 23, below, p. 266.

[65] Shuho, *op. cit.*, vol. 2, pp. 34–35. Aoki, *op. cit.*, vol. 2, p. 980.

[66] Tsuji, *op. cit.*, pp. 306–07. Tanaka, *op. cit.*, pp. 47–48. Kimiya, *op. cit.*, vol. 2, pp. 289–91.

[67] Tsuji, *op. cit.*, p. 307.

[68] Shuho, *op. cit.*, vol. 2, p. 37.

[69] Tsuji, *op. cit.*, p. 308. *Chinting Ming-Shih*, vol. 322, p. 3a. Shuho, *op. cit.*, vol. 2, pp. 37–38. Aoki, *op. cit.*, vol. 2, p. 982.

[70] Shuho, *op. cit.*, vol. 2, pp. 38–39.

[71] Tanaka, *op. cit.*, pp. 49–50.

[72] Kimiya, *op. cit.*, vol. 2, pp. 293–95. Waseda University, *op. cit.*, vol. 7, pp. 624, 627. *Chinting Ming-Shih*, vol. 322, p. 3a.

[73] Kimiya, *op. cit.*, vol. 2, pp. 229–301. Yoshida, *op. cit.*, vol. 7, pp. 378–79. Waseda University, *op. cit.*, vol. 7, pp. 635–36.

[74] Tanaka, *op. cit.*, p. 149. Tsuji, *op. cit.*, pp. 308–13; App. 24, below, p. 273.

[75] Kuroita, *op. cit.*, p. 477.

[76] Yoshida, *op. cit.*, vol. 7, pp. 378–79. Waseda University, *op. cit.*, vol. 7, p. 236.

[77] *Ibid.*, vol. 7, p. 237.

[78] Ito, *op. cit.*, pp. 532–33. Tsuji, *op. cit.*, p. 313.

[79] Tanaka, *op. cit.*, p. 50. Ariga, *op. cit.*, vol. 2, p. 311. Kimiya, *op. cit.*, vol. 2, p. 305.

[80] Shuho, *op. cit.*, vol. 2, p. 40. *Chinting Ming-Shih*, vol. 322, p. 3a. App. 25, below, p. 275.

[81] National History Research Association, *op. cit.*, p. 393. Tanaka, *op. cit.*, p. 91. Shuho, *op. cit.*, vol. 2, p. 42. Kimiya, *op. cit.*, vol. 2, p. 302.

[82] Kimiya, *op. cit.*, vol. 2, pp. 305–06. *Chinting Ming-Shih*, vol. 6, pp. 3b, 4b; vol. 322, pp. 3a, 4b.

[83] Yoshida, *op. cit.*, vol. 7, p. 347. Tanaka, *op. cit.*, pp. 91–92. Shuho, *op. cit.*, vol. 2, pp. 42–43. Tsuji, *op. cit.*, p. 315.

[84] Shuho, *op. cit.*, vol. 2, pp. 43–44. Waseda University, *op. cit.*, vol. 7, pp. 238–39. Kimiya, *op. cit.*, vol. 2, pp. 306–07. App. 26, below, p. 277.

[85] Kimiya, *op. cit.*, vol. 2, p. 309.

[86] *Chinting Ming-Shih*, vol. 322, p. 3a.

[87] Kimiya, *op. cit.*, vol. 2, p. 319. *Chinting Ming-Shih*, vol. 322, p. 3a. Aoki, *op. cit.*, vol. 2, p. 988.

[88] Shuho, *Zenrin Kokuho-Ki*, vol. 2, p. 47.

[89] *Ibid.*, vol. 2, pp. 47–49; vol. 3, pp. 66–68. App. 27, below, p. 282.

[90] Kimiya, *op. cit.*, vol. 2, pp. 320–21.

[91] Tanaka, *op. cit.*, p. 221. Ito, *op. cit.*, p. 534. Tokutomi, *Kinsei Nippon Kokumin-Shi* (A History of the Japanese People in Modern Times), vol. 1, p. 52. Tsuji, *op. cit.*, p. 317. National History Research Association, *op. cit.*, p. 394.

[92] Hasegawa, *op. cit.*, p. 74.

[93] *Chinting Ming-Shih*, vol. 322, p. 3b. Kimiya, *op. cit.*, vol. 2, p. 294. National History Research Association, *op. cit.*, pp. 394–95.

[94] Tsuji, *op. cit.*, p. 318. Ito, *op. cit.*, pp. 534–55.

[95] Kimiya, *op. cit.*, vol. 2, pp. 293–94.

[96] *Ibid.*, vol. 2, p. 395.

[97] *Chinting Ming-Shih*, vol. 322, pp. 3a–b, 5b. Tsuji, *op. cit.*, p. 329.

[98] *Chinting Ming-Shih*, vol. 322, pp. 4a–b.

[99] Kimiya, *op. cit.*, vol. 2, p. 295.

[100] Waseda University, *op. cit.*, vol. 7, p. 74.

[101] Kuroita, *op. cit.*, pp. 498–99. Waseda University, *op. cit.*, vol. 7, pp. 168–70. Tanaka, *op. cit.*, pp. 177–78.

[102] Kuroita, *op. cit.*, pp. 491–92. Hagino, *op. cit.*, pp. 473–75. Tanaka, *op. cit.*, pp. 192–98.

[103] Kuroita, *loc. cit.* Hagino, *loc. cit.* Tanaka, *loc. cit.*

[104] Tokutomi, *op. cit.*, vol. 1, pp. 12–13. National History Research Association, *op. cit.*, pp. 224–25. Waseda University, *op. cit.*, vol. 7, pp. 269–72.

[105] Tanaka, *op. cit.*, p. 222. Shuho, *op. cit.*, vol. 2, pp. 62–64.

[106] National History Research Association, *op. cit.*, pp. 226–75.

[107] *Chinting Ming-Shih*, vol. 322, p. 4a. Shuho, *op. cit.*, vol. 3, pp. 75–77. Kimiya, *op. cit.*, vol. 2, pp. 381–82. Ito,

op. cit., p. 534. Hasegawa, *op. cit.,* pp. 76–77. Tokutomi, *op. cit.,* vol. 1, pp. 53, 56–57. Waseda University, *op. cit.,* vol. 7, pp. 625–26. App. 28, below, p. 286.

[108] Hagino, *op. cit.,* pp. 498–99. Waseda University, *op. cit.,* p. 42. Tokutomi, *op. cit.,* vol. 1, p. 37.

[109] Kuroita, *op. cit.,* p. 562. Tanaka, *op. cit.,* pp. 333–34.

[110] Tokutomi, *op. cit.,* vol. 1, p. 36. Tanaka, *op. cit.,* pp. 330–31. Waseda University, *op. cit.,* vol. 7, p. 434.

[111] National History Research Association, *op. cit.,* p. 316. Ariga, *op. cit.,* vol. 2, pp. 397–400. Hagino, *op. cit.,* pp. 506–07. Aoki, *op. cit.,* vol. 2, pp. 843, 849, 855–56.

[112] Kuroita, *op. cit.,* p. 565. National History Research Association, *op. cit.,* p. 317. Aoki, *op. cit.,* vol. 2, pp. 854–56. Tokutomi, *op. cit.,* vol. 2, pp. 37–38.

[113] Tanaka, *op. cit.,* pp. 270, 273–74.

[114] Kuroita, *op. cit.,* p. 559. National History Research Association, *op. cit.,* pp. 325–27.

[115] Tokutomi, *op. cit.,* vol. 1, pp. 311–12. National History Research Association, *op. cit.,* pp. 356–59.

[116] Tokutomi, *op. cit.,* vol. 1, pp. 531–32, 538. Hagino, *op. cit.,* p. 535.

[117] Zuikei, *Zenrin Kokuho-Ki,* second series, pp. 21–22. *Chinting Ming-Shih,* vol. 322, p. 4a. Hasegawa, *op. cit.,* pp. 77, 80.

[118] Zuikei, *op. cit.,* pp. 25–26.

[119] Kimiya, *op. cit.,* vol. 2, p. 326. App. 29, below, p. 291.

[120] *Chinting Ming-Shih,* vol. 10, pp. 5a–b; vol. 11, p. 1a–b.

[121] *Chinting Ming-Shih,* vol. 322, pp. 6a–7b. Kimiya, *op. cit.,* vol. 2, pp. 322–25, 445–50. Hasegawa, *op. cit.,* p. 84. National History Research Association, *op. cit.,* pp. 395–96.

[122] *Chinting Ming-Shih,* vol. 322, p. 7.

[123] Tsuji, *op. cit.,* pp. 262–63. *Shigaku Zasshi,* vol. 5, pp. 28–37. App. 30, below, p. 295.

[124] Tsiang, *Sino-Japanese Diplomatic Relations, 1870–1894,* pp. 4–7. Wang, *Liu-Shih-Nien Lai Chung-Kuo yu Jih-Pen* (Relations Between China and Japan During the Past Sixty Years), vol. 1, pp. 33, 36–38. Ku-Kung Powu-Yuan (editor), *Chou-pien I-wu Shih-mo* (China's Dealings and Transactions with Foreign Nations in Her Diplomatic and International Affairs During the Thirteen Years of the Tung-Chih Era Ending in 1874), vol. 79, pp. 7–8, 47–48; vol. 80, pp. 10–11.

NOTES TO CHAPTER IV

[1] Kuroita, *Kokushi no Kenkyu*, p. 551. Hagino, *Nippon-Shi Kowa*, p. 507.

[2] Kuroita, *op. cit.*, p. 597.

[3] Ariga, *Dai Nippon-Rekishi*, pp. 393–94. Hagino, *op. cit.*, p. 525.

[4] Tokutomi, *Kinsei Nippon-Kokumin Shi*, vol. 1, pp. 106–09.

[5] Hagino, *op. cit.*, p. 527.

[6] Aoki, *Dai-Nippon Rekishi Shusei*, vol. 2, pp. 1096–1101.

[7] Tanaka, *Oda Jidai-Shi* (History of the Oda Period), pp. 17–18. Tokutomi, *op. cit.*, vol. 1, pp. 147–48.

[8] Ariga, *op. cit.*, vol. 2, pp. 451–52. Kuroita, *op. cit.*, pp. 552–53. Tokutomi, *op. cit.*, vol. 3, pp. 85–86.

[9] Hagino, *op. cit.*, p. 530. Kuroita, *op. cit.*, p. 584.

[10] Tokutomi, *op. cit.*, vol. 1, pp. 106–07, 279. Tanaka, *op. cit.*, pp. 21, 239, 243–45.

[11] Waseda University, *Dai-Nippon Jidai-Shi*, vol. 8, pp. 228–31. Tanaka, *op. cit.*, pp. 216, 219–20.

[12] Tokutomi, *op. cit.*, vol. 2, pp. 114–18. Tanaka, *op. cit.*, pp. 131, 143.

[13] Kuroita, *op. cit.*, pp. 605–09. Tanaka, *op. cit.*, pp. 163, 165–67. Waseda University, *op. cit.*, vol. 8, pp. 146–47, 150.

[14] Tokutomi, *op. cit.*, vol. 3, pp. 36–52. Waseda University, *op. cit.*, vol. 8, pp. 156–62.

[15] Tanaka, *op. cit.*, pp. 202–03. Kuroita, *op. cit.*, pp. 613–14.

[16] Tokutomi, *op. cit.*, vol. 4, pp. 504–05. Waseda University, *op. cit.*, vol. 8, pp. 478–79.

[17] Yoshida, *Tojo Nippon-Shi*, vol. 6, pp. 323, 327. Waseda University, *op. cit.*, vol. 8, p. 257.

[18] Hagino, *op. cit.*, pp. 546–47. Kuroita, *op. cit.*, p. 625.

[19] Yoshida, *op. cit.*, vol. 6, pp. 321–22. Tanaka, *Toyotomi Jidai-Shi* (History of the Toyotomi Period), pp. 23–26.

[20] Hagino, *op. cit.*, p. 548. Tokutomi, *op. cit.*, vol. 4, pp. 79, 83.

[21] Tokutomi, *op. cit.*, vol. 4, pp. 234–35.

[22] Hagino, *op. cit.*, p. 551.

[23] Tanaka, *Toyotomi Jidai-Shi*, pp. 103–11.

[24] Kuroita, *op. cit.*, p. 641. Hagino, *op. cit.*, p. 560.

[25] Yoshida, *op. cit.*, pp. 330–31. Tanaka, *Toyotomi Jidai-Shi*, pp. 41–44.

[26] Tanaka, *Toyotomi Jidai-Shi*, p. 47. Kuroita, *op. cit.*, p. 633.

[27] Tokutomi, *op. cit.*, vol. 5, pp. 490–93. Waseda University, *op. cit.*, vol. 8, pp. 353–54. Tanaka, *Toyotomi Jidai-Shi*, pp. 133–34.

[28] App. 31, below, p. 299.

[29] Kuroita, *op. cit.*, pp. 622–23. Tokutomi, *op. cit.*, vol. 5, pp. 3–5. Waseda University, *op. cit.*, vol. 8, p. 478.

[30] Tanaka, *Toyotomi Jidai-Shi*, pp. 127–28. Tokutomi, *op. cit.*, vol. 6, pp. 35–40. Waseda University, *op. cit.*, vol. 8, p. 349.

[31] Kuroita, *op. cit.*, pp. 648–49. Yoshida, *op. cit.*, vol. 6, pp. 360–63.

[32] Tokutomi, *op. cit.*, vol. 6, pp. 499–508. Waseda University, *op. cit.*, vol. 8, pp. 359–62. Yoshida, *op. cit.*, vol. 8, pp. 347–52.

[33] Aoki, *op. cit.*, vol. 2, pp. 1177, 1182. Kuroita, *op. cit.*, p. 630. Yoshida, *op. cit.*, vol. 6, pp. 325, 370. Tanaka, *Toyotomi Jidai-Shi*, pp. 283–84. Tokutomi, *op. cit.*, p. 131.

[34] Hagino, *op. cit.*, p. 576. Waseda University, *op. cit.*, vol. 8, pp. 403, 405. Tsuji, *op. cit.*, pp. 423–26, 429.

[35] Tokutomi, *op. cit.*, vol. 7, pp. 139–40.

[36] *Ibid.*, vol. 10, pp. 4–9. Hagino, *op. cit.*, p. 577. Apps. 33, 34, 35, below, pp. 305–14. *Chinting Ming-Shih*, vol. 322, p. 8a.

[37] Yoshida, *op. cit.*, vol. 6, pp. 373–75. Hagino, *op. cit.*, p. 576. Tsuji, *op. cit.*, pp. 387, 397–98.

[38] App. 32, below, p. 300. Aoki, *op. cit.*, vol. 2, p. 1178.

[39] *Ibid.*, vol. 2, p. 1179. Tokutomi, *op. cit.*, vol. 7, pp. 235–36.

[40] Aoki, *op. cit.*, vol. 2, pp. 1188, 1194. Waseda University, *op. cit.*, vol. 8, pp. 408–10. Tokutomi, *op. cit.*, vol. 7, pp. 247–49, 278, 281–85.

[41] Aoki, *op. cit.*, vol. 2, pp. 1189, 1201. Waseda University, *op. cit.*, vol. 8, pp. 247–249, 278, 281–85.

[42] Tokutomi, *op. cit.*, vol. 7, pp. 341–43. Waseda University, *op. cit.*, vol. 8, pp. 412–13. Aoki, *op. cit.*, vol. 2, p. 1198.

[43] Tokutomi, *op. cit.*, vol. 7, pp. 390–92.

[44] Waseda University, *op. cit.*, vol. 8, pp. 414–15. Yoshida, *op. cit.*, vol. 6, p. 376. Hayashi, *Chosen Tsushi*, pp. 324–25. Tokutomi, *op. cit.*, vol. 7, pp. 392, 394–95.

[45] Tokutomi, *op. cit.*, vol. 7, pp. 430–33. Waseda University, *op. cit.*, vol. 8, p. 421. Kuroita, *op. cit.*, p. 663.

[46] Tokutomi, *op. cit.*, vol. 7, pp. 451–52. Aoki, *op. cit.*, vol. 2, pp. 1186–87. Apps. 36, 37, below, pp. 314–20.

[47] Aoki, *op. cit.*, vol. 2, p. 1194.

[48] Tokutomi, *op. cit.*, vol. 7, pp. 469–76.

[49] *Ibid.*, vol. 7, pp. 588–89. Waseda University, *op. cit.*, vol. 8, pp. 422–23.

[50] *Ibid.*, vol. 8, pp. 421–22. Aoki, *op. cit.*, vol. 2, pp. 1194–95. Yoshida, *op. cit.*, vol. 6, pp. 377–78. Kuroita, *op. cit.*, p. 663.

[51] App. 39, below, p. 327.

[52] Tokutomi, *op. cit.*, vol. 7, pp. 515–21. Waseda University, *op. cit.*, vol. 8, p. 418.

[53] Hayashi, *op. cit.*, pp. 334–35. Tokutomi, *op. cit.*, vol. 7, p. 673.

[54] Aoki, *op. cit.*, vol. 2, pp. 1199–1200. Yoshida, *op. cit.*, vol. 6, p. 376. Kuroita, *op. cit.*, pp. 662–63. Hayashi, *op. cit.*, pp. 327–28, 330. Tokutomi, *op. cit.*, vol. 7, pp. 530, 536–43. *Chinting Ming-Shih*, vol. 20, p. 5b.

[55] Hayashi, *op. cit.*, p. 331. Tokutomi, *op. cit.*, vol. 7, pp. 550–52.

[56] *Ibid.*, vol. 7, pp. 29–91, 606–69.

[57] *Ibid.*, vol. 7, pp. 612, 618–19, 649, 664, 667–68. Waseda University, *op. cit.*, vol. 8, pp. 420–21.

[58] Tokutomi, *op. cit.*, vol. 7, pp. 338, 340.

[59] Hayashi, *op. cit.*, pp. 332–34.

[60] Tokutomi, *op. cit.*, vol. 7, pp. 624, 630, 641, 652–54, 656, 661–62.

[61] *Ibid.*, vol. 7, pp. 663, 666.

[62] *Ibid.*, vol. 7, pp. 661, 673–77. Kuroita, *op. cit.*, p. 663.

[63] Tokutomi, *op. cit.*, vol. 8, pp. 16–17, 19, 30. Ryu Sei-Ryo, *Chohi Roku* (Records of the National Sufferings for the Purpose of Giving Warning to the Koreans of Future Generations).

[64] Tokutomi, *op. cit.*, vol. 8, pp. 21, 23–24. Shin Kei, *Saizo Hanpo-Shi* (Records of the Rehabitation and Reorganization of Our Honored Dependent State After the Japanese Invasion).

[65] Tokutomi, *op. cit.*, vol. 8, pp. 26–27.

[66] *Ibid.*, vol. 8, pp. 27–28. Shin Kei, *op. cit.*

[67] The possible movements of the Japanese army thus outlined by Shih Hsing coincide exactly with the military proceedings of the Japanese movement in Manchurian affairs that ended in the summer of 1933, when the Japanese army was within striking distance of Peking and when China asked for a truce.

[68] Tokutomi, *op. cit.*, vol. 8, pp. 64–65.

[69] *Ibid.*, vol. 8, pp. 73–74.

[70] *Ibid.*, vol. 8, p. 30. Ryu Sei-Ryo, *op. cit.*

[71] Tokutomi, *op. cit.*, vol. 8, pp. 19, 30.

[72] *Ibid.*, vol. 8, pp. 36, 114. Waseda University, *Dai-Nippon Jidai-Shi*, vol. 8, p. 427.

[73] Hayashi, *op. cit.*, p. 337. Hagino, *op. cit.*, p. 579. Aoki, *op. cit.*, vol. 2, p. 1205. Tokutomi, *op. cit.*, vol. 8, pp. 36–39.

[74] Tokutomi, *op. cit.*, vol. 8, pp. 48–50. Aoki, *op. cit.*, vol. 2, p. 664.

[75] Tokutomi, *op. cit.*, vol. 8, pp. 52–60, 454. Yoshida, *op. cit.*, vol. 6, p. 91. *Chinting Ming-Shih*, vol. 320, p. 6b.

[76] Hayashi, *op. cit.*, pp. 338, 339.

[77] Tokutomi, *op. cit.*, vol. 8, pp. 86–90.

[78] *Ibid.*, vol. 8, pp. 130–32, 134. Ryu Sei-Ryo, *op. cit.*

[79] Tokutomi, *op. cit.*, vol. 8, pp. 140–41, 143–44, 157–58, 168. Hayashi, *op. cit.*, pp. 339–40. Ki Ji-ken, *Senso Jitsuroku.*

[80] Hayashi, *op. cit.*, p. 340. Tokutomi, *op. cit.*, vol. 8, p. 175.

[81] Tokutomi, *op. cit.*, vol. 8, pp. 198–99.

[82] *Ibid.*, vol. 8, pp. 210, 219, 236, 255–58. Aoki, *op. cit.*, vol. 2, p. 1206. Hayashi, *op. cit.*, p. 340. Shin Kei, *op. cit. Chinting Ming-Shih*, vol. 20, p. 6a.

[83] Tokutomi, *op. cit.*, vol. 8, p. 242, 268–70, 292–99, 314–15, 319, 320–21, 327–30, 330. *Chinting Ming-Shih*, vol. 320, p. 7a. Ri Tan, *Senbyo Hokan* (The Treasured Mirror Which Reflected the Rule of Senso, the King of Korea). Shin Kei, *op. cit.* Ki Ji-Ken, *op. cit.*

[84] Tokutomi, *op. cit.*, vol. 8, pp. 317, 325, 331, 333–37; vol. 9, pp. 3–4. Kuroita, *op. cit.*, p. 664.

[85] Tokutomi, *op. cit.*, vol. 8, pp. 366–67, 482–84. Shin Kei, *op. cit.*

[86] Tokutomi, *op. cit.*, vol. 8, pp. 365, 371–72.

[87] *Ibid.*, vol. 8, pp. 479, 484–86, 488, 515.

[88] Zuikei, *Zenrin Kokuho-Ki*, second series, pp. 14–15. Waseda University, *op. cit.*, vol. 8, pp. 429–30. Hayashi, *op. cit.*, p. 342. Tokutomi, *op. cit.*, vol. 8, pp. 467–69, 519–24; vol. 9, pp. 147–49. *Chinting Ming-Shih*, vol. 320, p. 7a. Hagino, *op. cit.*, pp. 580–81. App. 39, below, p. 327.

[89] Tokutomi, *op. cit.*, vol. 8, pp. iv, 101, 103, 558, 675–81.

[90] *Ibid.*, vol. 8, pp. 567–74.

[91] *Ibid.*, vol. 8, pp. 449–50, 473–74.

[92] *Ibid.*, vol. 8, pp. 430–48. Aoyagi, *Richo-Shi Daizen*, pp. 323–26.

[93] Tsuji, *Kaigai Kotsu Shiwa*, pp. 441–43.

[94] Tokutomi, *op. cit.*, vol. 8, pp. 731–38. Hayashi, *op. cit.*, pp. 346–47. Waseda University, *op. cit.*, vol. 8, pp. 433–35. Aoyagi, *op. cit.*, pp. 326–27. App. 40, below, p. 332.

[95] Tokutomi, *op. cit.*, vol. 9, pp. 503–04, 508.

[96] *Ibid.*, vol. 9, pp. 509–12. *Chinting Ming-Shih*, vol. 320, p. 8a. Ryu Sei-Ryo, *op. cit. Chinting Ming-Shih*, vol. 21, p. 1a.

[97] Tokutomi, *op. cit.*, vol. 9, pp. 406–10. Aoyagi, *op. cit.*, pp. 228–30.

[98] Shin Kei, *op. cit.* Tokutomi, *op. cit.*, vol. 9, pp. 418, 428–29.

[99] *Ibid.*, vol. 9, pp. 353, 355, 405, 453.

[100] *Ibid.*, vol. 9, pp. 441–46. Kuroita, *op. cit.*, pp. 664–65. Ryu Sei-Ryo, *Chohi Roku.* Korean Historical Association, *Chosen Shi Taikei*, vol. 3, pp. 157–58.

[101] Tokutomi, *op. cit.*, vol. 9, pp. 623–25, 641–42. Aoyagi, *op. cit.*, p. 361.

[102] Tokutomi, *op. cit.*, vol. 9, pp. 580–81, 645–47.

[103] Tokutomi, *op. cit.*, vol. 9, pp. 660–63, 668. Hayashi, *op. cit.*, pp. 354–55.

[104] Hagino, *op. cit.*, p. 583. Waseda University, *op. cit.*, vol. 8, p. 474. Kuroita, *op. cit.*, p. 665. Tokutomi, *op. cit.*, vol. 9, pp. 649–53, 707. Korean Historical Association, *op. cit.*, vol. 3, p. 162.

[105] Waseda University, *op. cit.*, vol. 8, p. 474. Tokutomi, *op. cit.*, vol. 9, p. 729.

[106] Tokutomi, *op. cit.*, vol. 9, pp. 423–708. Waseda University, *op. cit.*, vol. 8, p. 448.

[107] *Chinting Ming-Shih*, vol. 320, p. 9b; vol. 322, p. 8b. Tokutomi, *op. cit.*, vol. 9, pp. 731–32.

[108] Tokutomi, *op. cit.*, vol. 9, pp. 421–23.

[109] *Ibid.*, vol. 9, pp. 733–34.

[110] *Ibid.*, vol. 9, pp. 734–35. Korean Historical Association, *op. cit.*, vol. 3, p. 167. Aoki, *op. cit.*, vol. 2, pp. 1225–37. Kuroita, *op. cit.*, pp. 665–68. Hagino, *op. cit.*, p. 584.

[111] Tokutomi, *op. cit.*, vol. 9, p. 736; vol. 10, p. xiv. Omori, *Dai-Nippon Zenshi* (Complete History of Great Japan), vol. 2, pp. 882–83.

[112] App. 41, below, p. 340.

[113] Tokutomi, *op. cit.*, vol. 10, pp. 60, 68–69, 71–72. Waseda University, *op. cit.*, vol. 8, pp. 469–71.

[114] Tokutomi, *op. cit.*, vol. 10, pp. 88–89, 94–95. Kuroita, *op. cit.*, p. 671. Hagino, *op. cit.*, pp. 585–86.

[115] Tokutomi, *op. cit.*, vol. 11, pp. 35–36, 40–44, 511. Kuroita, *op. cit.*, pp. 669–70. Omori, *op. cit.*, vol. 3, pp. 10–11.

[116] Kuroita, *op. cit.*, pp. 674–77. Hagino, *op. cit.*, pp. 588–90, 593. Tokutomi, *op. cit.*, vol. 11, pp. 336, 482.

[117] Kuroita, *op. cit.*, pp. 677–78, 704. Hagino, *op. cit.*, pp. 593–94, 595–96. Omori, *op. cit.*, vol. 3, p. 20. Waseda University, *op. cit.*, vol. 9, p. 30.

DOCUMENTS

CHAPTER I

APPENDIX 1

Mimana in Korea, and the Date of Its Founding

THE POWER OF JAPAN to rule in Korea began with the creation of the State of Mimana as her protectorate so that Shinra could not invade it. Japan's power in Korea began to decline with the destruction of her government-general in Mimana by Shinra, and finally, when the allied armies of China and Shinra, in 663, annihilated her military force in Korea, Japan was forced to abandon all her claims there. She did not regain authority in Korea until after the Russo-Japanese War.

The date of the founding of Mimana is therefore essential to a determination of the period of suzerainty that Japan exercised over Korea prior to 1905. This date is not only a much mooted question but also a puzzling one. According to the historical records of Japan, Tsunuga Arashito, the ruler of Kaya, whose kingdom was continuously threatened by a powerful neighboring state, learned of the rise of a great emperor in Japan and decided to place his kingdom under the suzerainty of Japan in order to maintain its safe existence. Accordingly, in 33 B.C., King Arashito sent his trusted subject, Sonakashichi, to Japan as a tribute-bearing envoy to present the petition to the emperor of Japan. Because of the long, hazardous water route and his unfamiliarity with the geography of Japan, the envoy spent four years wandering from place to place. It was not until 29 B.C., when the Emperor Sujin died and his son, Suinin, ascended the throne as the eleventh emperor of Japan, that the envoy finally reached the Japanese imperial court and succeeded in the mission entrusted to him by King Arashito. In the following year, when the envoy was returning to Korea, the Emperor Suinin sent his imperial instructions to Arashito by him. The emperor said, in part:

"Had your envoy been more successful in his traveling, and had he reached our empire sooner, he would have been able to present your petition to our Father Emperor in person and to have gained his gracious sanction. We now hereby instruct you, in commem-

[193]

oration of our deceased emperor, to adopt his personal name, Mimana, as the new name of your kingdom."[1]*

At the same time, the Emperor Suinin sent the able statesman, Shihotare Hiko, to Mimana with a strong military force, to remain there as the imperial representative of Japan in Korea. Thus did 28 B.C. prove to be an important year in the history of Japan. In that year, through the establishment of a protectorate over Mimana in Korea, Japan extended her authority as a nation beyond the waters to the Asiatic continent. Nevertheless, it is a most mysterious and unaccountable fact that during the more than two hundred years following this momentous national event, there is no entry whatever in the history of Japan concerning affairs in Mimana or the international relations of Japan with Korea, China, or any other Asiatic nation. In the Chinese histories, such as the *Hou-Han Shu* and the *Wei Shu,* and in other standard annals of later generations, there is, again, no mention of Mimana[2] until the beginning of the fourth century, when Chinese histories began to record affairs in Mimana and her relations with Japan.

Turning to Korean histories, we find that although in the *Togoku Tsugan* (an ancient Korean history) the name "Mimana" is used incidentally, none of the standard histories of Korea makes any mention whatever of Mimana as a separate kingdom;[3] its existence was either entirely unknown to Korean historians in the ancient period, or was disregarded by them. In the latter part of the nineteenth century, the successful excavation of the *Kotai-O Hi* (a large stone monument) in northern Korea, shed new light upon the international relations between Japan and Korea in ancient times. This old Korean monument was erected in 414 A.D. in honor of the great king, Kokaido, of Korai, by his son who succeeded him. King Kokaido was one of the most powerful kings of the fifth century. He ruled almost all of northern Korea for twenty years, his reign ending in 412 A.D. This monument is an immense natural stone, on the four sides of which is recorded the life work of King Kokaido, especially his military enterprises. The inscription makes incidental mention of the fact that in the latter part of the fourth century Mimana was a leading military station of Japan in Korea.[4]

Turning again to Chinese sources, we find that several standard

* Superior figures refer to notes which will be found on pp. 343–46.

Chinese histories covering the fifth and sixth centuries contain accounts of Mimana with respect to its relations with Japan. Especially during the three-quarters of a century beginning in 420, the Japanese sent envoys to China on several occasions in an endeavor to gain China's recognition of Japan's ruling power in Mimana as well as in several other states in Korea.[5] Strange to say, at this time Japan was rapidly losing the very authority for which she was seeking recognition. Taking into consideration the foregoing facts, historians of the modern school have concluded that the state of Mimana lasted 150 years or more, probably 200 years at most, beginning at some time in the middle of the fourth century and ending in the year 562. This length of time may likewise be taken as the approximate duration of the ruling power exercised by Japan in southern Korea, if she really had ruling power in Korea prior to 1905.

The facts may be stated briefly as follows: (1) the ancient Korean monument (the *Kotai-O Hi*) bears an inscription showing that certain events concerning Mimana took place in 400 A.D.; (2) although, according to the *Nihon Shoki,* the state of Mimana was founded in 29 B.C., this event is generally considered mythological—Japanese histories contain no entries of any historical value about Mimana prior to the second half of the fourth century; (3) it was in the early part of the fifth century that Japan began to approach the imperial court of China with respect to the control of Mimana by Japan; and (4) in 562, the Japanese government-general at Mimana was destroyed by Shinra, and Mimana was annexed to Shinra.

APPENDIX 2

The Conquest of Korea by the Empress Jingo

THE KOREAN CONQUEST by the Empress Jingo is a noteworthy event in the history of Japan because it was Japan's first foreign conquest and because it was accomplished by a woman leader. However, the glorious national event has no reliable source of evidence other than accounts found in the *Kojiki* (compiled in 712 A.D.) and in the *Nihon Shoki* (compiled in 720 A.D.), and these descriptions are of the nature of myths or fairy tales. The account given on the following pages is translated from the *Kojiki.*

"Her Imperial Majesty the Empress Okinaga-Tarashi was divinely possessed by a great heavenly god. At that time, His Imperial Majesty the Emperor, with his Empress, dwelt at the palace of Kashihi in Tsukushi. He was planning to invade the land of Kumaso [Kyushu]. The Emperor was playing his lute. The Prime Minister, Takenouchi-no-Sukune, who kept himself pure in order to be able to approach the Divine Being, requested divine instructions. The divinely possessed Empress thereupon, being divinely inspired, said:

" 'There is a land west of this place wherein the Emperor will find innumerable treasures that dazzle the eyes. These include gold, silver, and many other precious things. We shall now bestow this land upon the Emperor.'

"His Majesty the Emperor then replied: 'When we ascend a high plateau and look westward we shall not find any land, but we shall view a vast expanse of water.'

"The Emperor believed that the god was telling an untruth. He stopped playing his lute and pushed it from him. Thereupon, the god, through the person of the Empress, expressed his anger and said to the Emperor: 'That great empire under Heaven! It is not the land over which you rule. You are destined to go to Hades.'

"The Prime Minister, Takenouchi-no-Sukune, thereupon said: 'I tremble at the consequences of this divine anger upon the person of Your Majesty. I plead that Your Majesty may start to play on your lute.'

"His Majesty the Emperor thereupon slowly drew the lute to him and languidly began to play it, but almost immediately the sound of the lute became inaudible. When they turned the light on him, they found that His Majesty the Emperor was dead. Astonished and alarmed, they removed the Emperor's dead body to a mortuary. Takenouchi-no-Sukune presented to the spirits the nation's great offerings, which included clothes made in Kyushu. Moreover, he entered and stayed in the sanctified court and there awaited the commands of the gods. He did this after he had sought out and eliminated crime of all sorts, such as flaying alive, the breaking down of the divisions between the rice fields, the filling up of ditches, the excavating of excrement and urine, the having of intercourse with horses, with cattle, with dogs, and with fowl.

He thus completely purified the land. After he had accomplished this, the instructions of the gods were given to him. These divine instructions were an exact counterpart of those that he had previously received. They read as follows:

" 'That great empire under Heaven! It is the land to be ruled by the imperial child in the womb of the Empress.'

"To this, Takenouchi-no-Sukune replied: 'I am filled with awe, my great gods! What sort of child is this imperial babe?'

"The gods replied, saying, 'It is a male child.'

"Takenouchi requested further information, saying: 'May I learn the names of the gods who have just instructed us?'

"The gods replied thus: 'All these things have been done by the Great Sacred Heaven-shining Deity, and by the Three Great Deities also, which are the Bottom-controlling Male, the Middle-controlling Male, and the Surface-controlling Male. If the Ruler of the Nation [Japan] desires to control the land beyond the water, he must first present offerings of white and blue cloths to every one of the heavenly deities and to every one of the earthly deities, as well as to the deities of the mountains, of the rivers, and of the seas. Then he must set up the divine souls of all these sacred deities in the war vessels that sail to the lands beyond the sea. Moreover, he must fill gourds with the ashes of the *Podocarpus macrophylla* trees. Likewise, he must make a great quantity of chop sticks and of broad but shallow food plates. He must then scatter all these on the waters of the Great Sea which the war vessels of the nation are to cross to lands beyond the waters.'

"Thereupon, Her Majesty the Empress promptly and faithfully fulfilled all these instructions given by the gods to Takenouchi. She mustered and equipped an army, gathered her war vessels, and crossed the sea to the land of her destination. During the cruise, all kinds of fish both large and small came up from the bottom of the sea. They all aided the Empress by bearing her war vessels on their backs. With the rise of favorable winds, the war vessels crossed the billows. The waves bore the vessels to the land of Shiragi in Korea.

"The King of Shiragi was both surprised and frightened by the sudden appearance of the war vessels of the Empress of Japan. He petitioned the Empress with trembling.

" 'Henceforth [he said] I will obey the commands of the Great Heavenly Ruler of Japan [the Empress]. I shall gladly and humbly serve her horses, and I shall send vessels annually with tribute to the throne of Japan. I shall never permit the oars and keels of our vessels to get dry, as I shall send the vessels to Japan continuously. I shall reverently and loyally serve the throne of Japan while Heaven and earth shall endure.' "[6]

In this way, the land of Shiragi in Korea became a tributary state of Japan, the King of Shiragi himself showing a willingness to perform so humble a service as that of attending the horses of the Empress. The land of Kudara in Korea likewise became a tributary state. Before returning home to Japan, the Empress set up her imperial emblem at the gate of the palace of the King of Shiragi, thus showing him that he was a subject of Japan. The Empress then instructed the violent soul of the great god of the water of Sumi to become the guardian god of the newly acquired land in Korea. She then started back to Tsukushi [Kyushu]. However, as it was the desire of the Empress that this great imperial work (the conquest of Korea) should be completed prior to the birth of her imperial son, she bound a heavy stone around her waist in order to restrain her womb. Therefore, her imperial son was born after she returned to the land of Tsukushi. The place where the imperial son was born was called Umi, which means "the land of birth." This imperial son became Ojin, the fifteenth emperor of Japan. He was the posthumous son of the fourteenth emperor, Chuai. He was born fourteen months after his conception.

APPENDIX 3

A Corrected Chronological Table of the Ancient Historical Period of Japan

IN THE EARLY PART of the eighth century, when the first national history was compiled, the date of the founding of the empire of Japan was arbitrarily decided upon as 660 B.C. Both real and imaginary events were then distributed over a period of about a thousand years beginning with 660 B.C. The ancient history of Japan is therefore replete with error, and no reliance can be placed in either the dates or the happenings recorded therein. How to correct these errors is a great problem. In the past half-century, several noted Japanese historians of modern training have prepared chronological tables of happenings in Japan's ancient period and have made known the results of their historcal research. The table prepared by Dr. Kunitake Kume is considered the most reliable. The following is a translation of that table, together with the gist of an introduction prepared by Inamura, of Waseda University, who based his findings upon the research of Dr. Kume.[7]

"Dr. Kume says that histories of China generally begin with a description of the Tien-Kuang and of the Ti-Kuang ruling families, in each of which there were twelve brothers all of whom enjoyed a longevity of eighteen thousand years. Histories of Japan contain similar exaggerations. The *Kojiki,* which was compiled in 712 A.D., states that Hikohohodemi lived in the palace of Takachiho and ruled the nation [Japan] for a period of 580 years. Men of intelligence have always regarded these fantastic statements as absurd, and historians place but little credence in these traditions. So far as factual history is concerned, it is entirely useless to make a study of them. But if errors occur and become widely accepted, these errors should be corrected for the sake of historical accuracy. In Oriental history, it frequently happens that important national events unrecorded in the history of one nation are mentioned in the histories of neighboring nations. Whenever historians come upon occurrences of this kind, they must make a careful comparative study of the histories of contemporary nations in order to complement the history of the nation about which they are writing. Because there are numerous errors in the narratives of the international relationships and dealings between Japan and continental nations, such as China and Korea, statements made in the various histories of those nations must be carefully compared in order to eliminate error, and to discover actual facts. Furthermore, the same historical events are sometimes recorded in Japanese histories and in Chinese and Korean histories in very different ways, either because different dates are given or because different proper names are used. For example, a certain historical event that is recorded in Japanese history as having occurred fifteen hundred years ago, is mentioned in the history of Korea as having taken place a thousand years earlier. Sometimes, again, the name 'Satsuma' which is used in Japanese history is found in Chinese history written as 'Touma'. Moreover, it often happens that the same historical event is described in the histories of the three nations in so exaggerated a fashion that the truth is wholly obliterated and modern historians are unable to sift out the facts even after a careful comparison of records. Japanese historians are still unable to identify so momentous an event as the conquest of Korea by the Empress Jingo with any of the events described in Korean histories. This difficulty is mainly accounted for by the fact that the accounts of Japanese happenings in the ancient period have been in such large part obscured by erroneous or fictitious dates assigned to these ancient historical descriptions, as, for example, the fictitious date of the founding of the empire of Japan. It was only after Dr. Kume had completed his historical research and made known his chronological table that the Empress Jingo's conquest of Korea was identified with certain historical events in the history of Shinra. In fact, the making of a reliable chronological table of the ancient period of Japanese history constitutes the first step in a real research into the early history of Japan.

"The Kotai-O monument [see Appendix 5], which was erected about fifteen hundred years ago in commemoration of King Koangkai-Tho (392–412 A.D.) of Korai, Korea, has been discovered recently in a district near the Yalu River and has been completely excavated. This monument consists of a large natural stone about eighteen feet in height. On its four sides, the life work of King Koangkai-Tho [Kokaido] in connection with international relations between China and Korea is minutely described. The description on this Kotai-O monument is now used as the key to long-disputed historical problems concerning the ancient periods of China, Japan, and Korea. Modern historians, taking the description on this monument as a basis, have discovered that the Japanese invasion of Korea, which is recorded in the ancient history of Japan as having taken place in 271 A.D. in the reign of the Emperor Ojin, took place in fact in the year 'Shin-Bo' (391 A.D.). This shows a historical error of 120 years.

"Historians are agreed that the death of the Emperor Kinmei (the twenty-ninth ruler of Japan) is correctly recorded in the

Nihon Shoki as occurring in 571 A.D. and that, beginning with this record of the death of the Emperor Kinmei, the historical dates in the *Nihon Shoki* are, in general, trustworthy. The Japanese invasion of Korea in the year Shin-Bo, in the reign of the Emperor Ojin (the fifteenth ruler of Japan), took place 299 years before the death of the Emperor Kinmei. In this comparatively short period of 299 years, there is an error of 120 years in the history of Japan, the Korean invasion which took place in 391 having been recorded in the *Nihon Shoki* as an event of 271. Therefore, the unreliability and the numerous errors in the ancient history of Japan are recognized and undisputed facts.

"According to the record in the *Nihon Shoki,* the first thirteen emperors, beginning with the Emperor Jimmu, the founder of the empire, ruled Japan for the following numbers of years, respectively: Jimmu, 76 years; Suizei, 33; Annei, 38; Itoku, 35; Kosho, 83; Koan, 102; Korei, 76; Kogen, 57; Kaika, 60; Sujin, 68; Suinin, 99; Keiko, 60; Seimu, 60. The total length of the period during which these thirteen emperors reigned is therefore 851 years and the average length of an emperor's reign is 65 years.

"Historical research shows that when a ruling line in an Oriental nation was carried on by succession from father to son, the total number of years of the reigns of the emperors is entirely independent of the ages of the emperors, as it is the sum total of the years that cover a period beginning with the birth of each emperor and ending at the time when an emperor became a father. For example, if thirteen ruling emperors who had succeeded their respective fathers should become fathers by the age of 30, the total length of the years of rule of these thirteen emperors would be 390 years. If the length of the reigns of the emperors in the ancient period as recorded in the *Nihon Shoki* be accepted as true, the first thirteen emperors must each have become a father at an average age of 65 years. This is contrary to the law of nature; therefore, the statements in the *Nihon Shoki* are both fictitious and absurd.

"Dr. Kume found that, in the authentic historical period, which covers 1274 years, beginning with the accession of the Empress Suiko in 592 A.D. and ending with the death of the Emperor Komei in 1866, there were forty-six generations by succession from father to son. From this datum Dr. Kume calculated that the length of the average reign was about 28 years. Dr. Naka selected the period of 1360 years beginning with the birth of the Emperor Keitai and ending with the birth of the Emperor Meiji in 1852 as the authentic historical period of Japan. He divided this period into forty-nine generations of father-to-son succession, thus obtaining an average reign of 28 years, the same as that obtained by Dr. Kume.

"Taking this average of 28 years to a reign as a basis, we find the length of the combined reigns of the first thirteen emperors (Jimmu to Seimu) to be 364 years instead of 851 years, as recorded in the *Nihon Shoki*. However, because some of these emperors married at an early age and others did not marry until they were much older, and further, because some of these emperors were succeeded by their eldest sons and others were succeeded by their youngest sons, the length of their reigns cannot be estimated by taking the average of 28 years as a basis.

"In addition to taking the average reign of 28 years as a basis, Dr. Kume took into consideration many special customs of the ancient period. He estimated the length of the combined reigns of the first thirteen emperors to be 371 years. There is seven years' difference between his estimate and the estimate made by taking 28 years as the sole basis. Dr. Kume stated that historians should be satisfied with the work in the historical research of ancient Japan even though it inevitably lacks accuracy to the degree that one might make an error of a mile in the survey of a wilderness a hundred miles in extent, or that he might make an error of ten miles in the measurement on the sea of a water route of a thousand miles, if he has not been provided with accurate instruments. The statement of Dr. Kume is both sensible and justifiable. Table 1, on pages 203–06, is a chronology of the ancient historical period of Japan prepared by Dr. Kume. This table covers the period beginning with the founding of Japan as a nation and ending in 571 A.D., when the history of Japan began to be historically authentic."

Thus, beginning in 571 A.D., the traditional dates given in the *Nihon Shoki* agree exactly with the dates of contemporary historical events, as recorded in the histories of China and of Korea. From the second half of the sixth century on, therefore, Japanese dates and events as given in Japanese histories are trustworthy.

"However, the errors in traditional historical dates given in the

TABLE 1

A CHRONOLOGICAL TABLE OF THE ANCIENT HISTORICAL PERIOD OF
JAPAN, PREPARED BY TAKING CONTEMPORARY EVENTS IN CHINA, JAPAN,
AND KOREA INTO CONSIDERATION, THUS CORRECTING THE OLD TRADI-
TIONAL AND ERRONEOUS JAPANESE DATES

(1) Japanese historical event	(2) Contemporary historical event in China and in Korea	(3) Corrected historical date as estimated by Kume	(4) Historical date recorded in the *Nihon Shoki*	(5) Actual difference between dates
Birth of Izanami and Izanagi	Kaotsu (emperor) of the Han dynasty	200 B.C.		
Birth of Ninigi (grandson of the Sun Goddess)	Wu Ti (emperor) of the Han dynasty	140 B.C.		
Birth of the Emperor Jimmu	Hsuan Ti (emperor) of the Han dynasty, in the third year of the Yuan-Kang era	63 B.C.		
Accession of Jimmu		25 B.C.	660 B.C.	635 years
Death of Jimmu	Ai Ti of the Han dynasty, in the second year of the Yuan-shou era	1 B.C.	584 B.C.	583 years
Accession of Suizei	Ping Ti of the Han dynasty, in the first year of the Yuan-shih era. Shinra, Korea, in the third year after its founding.	1 A.D.	581 B.C.	582 years
Accession of Annei	Kwang-Wu Ti of the Later Han dynasty, in the fifth year of the Chien-wu era	29 A.D.	548 B.C.	577 years
Accession of Itoku	Kwang-Wu Ti of the Later Han dynasty, in the twenty-ninth year of the Chien-wu era	54 A.D.	510 B.C.	564 years
Accession of Kosho	Chang Ti of the Later Han dynasty	81 A.D.	475 B.C.	556 years
Accession of Koan	An Ti of the Later Han dynasty, in the third year of the Yung-Chu era	109 A.D.	393 B.C.	502 years
Accession of Korei	Shun Ti of the Later Han dynasty, in the second year of the Yang-Chia era	133 A.D.	290 B.C.	423 years

TABLE 1—(*Continued*)

(1) Japanese historical event	(2) Contemporary historical event in China and in Korea	(3) Corrected historical date as estimated by Kume	(4) Historical date recorded in the *Nihon Shoki*	(5) Actual difference between dates
Accession of Kogen	Hwan Ti of the Later Han dynasty, in the third year of the Yuang-Shou era	157 A.D.	214 B.C.	371 years
Death of Kogen	Ling Ti of the Later Han dynasty in the fifth year of the Chung-Ping era	188 A.D.	158 B.C.	346 years
Death of Kaika	Hsien Ti of the Later Han dynasty in the twenty-third year of the Chien-an era	218 A.D.	98 B.C.	316 years
Death of Sujin	Fei Ti of the Wei dynasty, in the first year of the Chia-Ping era	249 A.D.	30 B.C.	279 years
Death of Suinin	Wu Ti of the Chin dynasty, in the fourth year of the Tai-Kang era	282 A.D.	70 A.D.	212 years
Death of Keiko	Hwai Ti of the Chin dynasty, in the fourth year of the Chien-Hsing era	316 A.D.	130 A.D.	186 years
Death of Seimu	Cheng Ti of the Eastern Chin dynasty, in the eighth year of the Hsien-Kang era	342 A.D.	190 A.D.	152 years
The Emperor Chuai's military expedition in the year Otsu-Ki	In the year Otsu-Ki, Japan sent an envoy to Shinra and terminated international relations	345 A.D.	199 A.D.	146 years
Death of Chuai in the year Heigo	Mu Ti of the Eastern Chin dynasty, in the second year (Heigo) of the Yung-Ho era. King Syokheur-Hai of Shinra, in the thirty-seventh year of his reign	346 A.D.	200 A.D.	146 years
Invasion of Korea by the Empress Jingo in the year Heigo	In the year Heigo, Japanese came, unexpected, and surrounded the capital of Shinra	346 A.D.	200 A.D.	146 years
In the year Shin-Bo, the Emperor Ojin sent four generals to invade Kudara	In the year Shin-Bo, Japan conquered Kudara and reduced ——— and Shinra to vassal states (Kotai-O monument)	391 A.D.	271 A.D.	119 years

TABLE 1—(*Continued*)

(1) Japanese historical event	(2) Contemporary historical event in China and in Korea	(3) Corrected historical date as estimated by Kume	(4) Historical date recorded in the *Nihon Shoki*	(5) Actual difference between dates
In the year Jin-Shin, the four generals made Aka the king of Kudara and returned to Japan	In the year Jin-Shin, Aka ascended the throne (History of Kudara)	392 A.D.	272 A.D.	120 years
Takenouchi ruled Tsukushi	————	398 A.D.	278 A.D.	120 years
In the year Ki-gai, Japanese generals invaded Shinra	In the year Ki-gai, Kudara violated a national pledge and made peace with Japan (Kotai-O monument)	399 A.D.	......	....
In the year Ko-Shin, Achiki, a Korean scholar, made his home in Japan	Japan unjustifiably invaded Taiho in Korai (Kotai-O monument)	404 A.D.	284 A.D.	120 years
In the year Otsu-Ki, Wani, a Korean scholar, made his home in Japan	An Ti of the Eastern Chin dynasty, in the first year of the I-Hsi era	405 A.D.	285 A.D.	120 years
In the year Ki-Yu, the accession of Nintoku	An Ti of the Eastern Chin dynasty, in the fifth year of the I-Hsi era	409 A.D.	313 A.D.	96 years
The reigns of the emperors Richu, Hansei, and Inkyo	....	......	......	....
In the year Ki-gai, the death of Inkyo	Hsiao-Wu Ti of the Sung dynasty, in the third year of the Ta-Ming era	459 A.D.	453 A.D.	6 years
Assassination of Anko in the year Koshi	Hsiao-Wu Ti of the Sung dynasty, in the sixth year of the Ta-Ming era	462 A.D.	456 A.D.	6 years
Accession of Yuryaku in the year of Kibo	Hsiao-Wu Ti of the Sung dynasty, in the seventh year of the Ta-Ming era	463 A.D.	457 A.D.	6 years
Death of Yuryaku in the year of Jingo	Wu Ti of the Liang dynasty, in the first year of the Tien-Chien era	502 A.D.	479 A.D.	23 years
Death of Seinei in the year of Teigai	Wu Ti of the Liang dynasty, in the sixth year of the Tien-Chien era	507 A.D.	484 A.D.	23 years
Reigns of the emperors Kenso, Ninken, Buretsu, Keitai, and Ankan	....	Approximately 25 years	......	....

TABLE 1—(*Concluded*)

(1) Japanese historical event	(2) Contemporary historical event in China and in Korea	(3) Corrected historical date as estimated by Kume	(4) Historical date recorded in the *Nihon Shoki*	(5) Actual difference between dates
Death of Senka in the year of Shingai	Wu Ti of the Liang dynasty, in the third year of the Chung-Ta-Tung era	531 A.D.	539 A.D.	8 years
Accession of Kinmei in the year of Jinshi	Wu Ti of the Liang dynasty, in the fourth year of the Chung-Ta-Tung era	532 A.D.	532 A.D.	0 years
In the year Bogo, the king of Kudara sent an image of Buddha and sutras to Japan	Wu Ti of the Liang dyansty, in the fourth year of the Chung-Ta-Tung era	538 A.D.	552 A.D.	14 years
Death of Kinmei in the year Shin-Bo	....	571 A.D.	571 A.D.	0 years

Nihon Shoki become greater and greater as the record goes backward, beginning from 571 A.D., when the Emperor Kinmei died, and following back to the date of founding. In fact, in the *Nihon Shoki*, the accession of Jimmu, the 'Founder Emperor,' is recorded as having taken place about 635 years earlier than it actually occurred. In this way, the length of the national life has been extended by more than six hundred years."

It is the consensus among leading historians, such as Kume, Naka, and Yoshida, that there is an error of more than six hundred years in the records of the national life of Japan. The accession of the Emperor Jimmu must have taken place sometime near the beginning of the Christian era, and the founding of the empire may be assumed to have taken place about the same time as the founding of the Roman empire rather than in 660 B.C., the traditional date given in Japanese history. Yet, even today, all the national documents and state papers bear the dates of the national calendar, which counts 660 B.C. as the date of the national foundation.

In the early part of the eighth century, when the first history of Japan was compiled, historians had no material whatever to facilitate determination of the date of the founding of the empire.

It is now believed on the basis of the extensive research of Dr. Michiyo Naka, that the historians, in determining this date, too superstitiously trusted and revered the statements in the *Wei-Shu,* an ancient Chinese astrological work of reputed divine origin. According to the philosophy of evolution expounded therein, the fate and destiny of each individual and nation, as well as of all material substances in the world, is definitely fixed. Each year has a cycle symbol of its own, formed by the combinations of one of the ten heavenly stems with one of the twelve symbolic animals, which somewhat correspond to those in the Occidental zodiac. Thus the years have come to have such cycle symbols as Ko-Shi (the rat of the heavenly Ko stem), Hei-In (the tiger of the heavenly Hei stem), Shin-Yu (the fowl of the heavenly Shin stem), and Ko-Shin (the dragon of the heavenly Ko stem).

Sixty years form the prime period of the cycle of evolution; that is, the "cycle element." Seven cycle elements, or 420 years, form the primary period of the cycle of evolution, and three primary periods, or twenty-one cycle elements, complete one grand division of the cycle of evolution. The grand division of the cycle, with the following cycle element (the transition period of sixty years), which together make 1320 years, complete one grand cycle period of evolution. When the first year in the first cycle element begins with certain cycle symbols, such as Ko-Shi, Hei-In, or Shin-Yu, this year will be repeated in every sixty-year cycle period; that is, all the cycle elements will begin with the year of the same cycle symbol. One grand division of the cycle evolution will contain twenty-one years which have the same cycle symbol (namely, the symbol of the first year of the first cycle element—the first sixty-year period).

According to the *Wei-Shu,* the fate of an individual, a nation, or anything else is always fixed by the nature of the cycle symbol of the year with which the first cycle element of the grand division of the cycle of evolution has begun. For example, the cycle symbol Shin-Yu signifies revolution and change. A nation founded in the year that has Shin-Yu as its cycle symbol is destined to encounter twenty-one national changes of various kinds at intervals of sixty years in the first period of its national existence of 1321 years. Finally, in the beginning of the twenty-second cycle element, the nation would undergo the second national reformation and, at the same time, it would enter upon the period of its second grand division of the cycle of evolution.

When, in the eighth century A.D., the Japanese historians compiled the first national history of Japan, they recognized the historical fact that in the period of sixty years beginning in 601 A.D., which was the Shin-Yu year, and ending in 661 A.D., which was also the Shin-Yu year, Japan experienced a series of great national events; for example:

(1) From Korea the calendar was introduced, the adoption of which made it possible for the Japanese to keep a systematic record of events with the dates attached.

(2) The first written law was framed and promulgated. By its provisions, social and national affairs were regulated.

(3) The patriarchal form of government was abolished, and an absolute monarchy of the continental type was set up.

(4) The national ambition of conquering foreign nations was abandoned, and the work of domestic improvement was begun.

(5) Laws and codes, as well as manners and customs of continental nations, were introduced and adopted, thereby effecting revolutionary changes in the national and social life of Japan.

(6) In the year of Shin-Yu of 661 A.D., the Emperor Tenchi, upon the completion of this great national reformation, came to rule the empire as the second founder of Japan.

Japanese historians in the eighth century studied and defined all these great national events, as well as the reformation of the seventh century, guided solely by the astrological theory of the *Wei-Shu*. They decided that the sixty years beginning in 601 A.D. was the transition period (cycle element) between the first grand division of the cycle of evolution and the second grand division of the cycle of evolution. They thereby assumed that by 601 A.D. (the Shin-Yu year) the first grand division of the cycle of evolution came to an end, and that in 661 A.D. (the Shin-Yu year) Japan had entered upon the second grand division of the cycle of evolution. In pursuance of this conclusion, they counted back twenty-one cycle elements, beginning with 601 A.D., and selected 660 B.C., the Shin-Yu year which dated back 1320 years from 661 A.D., as the first cycle element in the first grand division in the cycle of evolution of Japan. In this way, without taking into consideration any national traditions or any historical material or evidence, and simply through superstitious reverence for an ancient Chinese astrological work, the historians selected February 11, 660 B.C., as the date of the founding of the empire of Japan. The ancient history of Japan, thus compiled, is today not only the most unreliable history in the

TABLE 2

COMPARATIVE AGES OF THE FIRST FIFTEEN JAPANESE EMPERORS

Emperor	Age as given in the Kojiki	Age as given in the Nihon Shoki	Length of reign	Emperor	Age as given in the Kojiki	Age as given in the Nihon Shoki	Length of reign
	Years	Years	Years		Years	Years	Years
Jimmu.........	137	127	76	Kaika..........	63*	115	60
Suizei..........	45	84	33	Sujin..........	168*	120	68
Annei...........	49	57	38	Suinin.........	153*	140	99
Itoku...........	45*	77	34	Keiko..........	137*	143	60
Kosho..........	93*	114	83	Seimu..........	95*	107	61
Koan...........	123*	137	102	Chuai..........	52*	52	9
Korei..........	106*	128	76	Ojin...........	130*	110	41
Kogen..........	57*	116	57				

* Estimated.

world, but also so muddled as to make it exceedingly difficult for modern historians to sift out fact from myth.[8]

In compliance with imperial commands, two national histories were compiled. In 712, the *Kojiki* (Chronicles of Ancient Matters) was completed, and in 720, the *Nihon Shoki*. Although these two standard national works were written at an interval of only eight years, they differ widely in their statement of facts. The same historical events are described in wholly different ways in these two works, and they even differ with respect to the ages of ruling emperors (see table 2).

By taking the length of life of these emperors and the length of their respective reigns into consideration, it is possible to make a rather close estimate of the dates when they became fathers of the heirs-apparent to the throne. By this method of estimating, we might conclude that Suizei was born to the Emperor Jimmu when

the latter was about 80 years of age. In turn, Suizei became the
father of Annei at the age of 66. Koan became the father of Korei
at the age of 86, and Korei became the father of Kogen at the age
of 70. Sujin became the father of Suinin at the age of 80, and Suinin
of Keiko at the age of 95. The Emperor Keiko became father of his

TABLE 3

A COMPARATIVE STUDY OF THE NUMBER OF RULERS OF SEVERAL
COUNTRIES

Nation	400-year period (A.D.)	Number of rulers	Nation	400-year period (A.D.)	Number of rulers
Japan........	1–400	7	China........	1462–1862	17
Shinra........	1–400	16	France........	1000–1400	16
Kudara........	1–400	16	France........	1400–1800	15
China........	1–400	38	England........	1087–1487	15
Japan........	400–800	33	England........	1487–1887	21
Shinra........	400–800	32	Scotland........	1167–1567	19
China........	662–1062	36	Wales........	840–1240	17
China........	1062–1462	35			

firstborn at the age of 96; according to the *Nihon Shoki,* he became
the father of eighty sons and daughters in all.

Most of these emperors are said to have lived about twice as long
as do people of the present time. Primitive people, perhaps, do have
greater longevity than people now have, yet to become the father
of a first-born at the age of 86 or 95 is, generally speaking, contrary
both to the law of nature and to historical fact.[9]

Dr. W. G. Aston, the noted English scholar who translated the
Nihon Shoki into English, prepared a table (table 3) in which he
compared the numbers of those who actually ruled for certain periods of four hundred years in both Occidental and Oriental nations, including Japan, with the numbers of rulers as mentioned
in the *Nihon Shoki.*[10] He thus rather strikingly proved how abnormal and untrustworthy are the statements made in the first histories
of ancient Japan.

As table 3 shows, because of national conditions the number of
rulers approximated either thirty or seventeen. However, according to the *Nihon Shoki,* in the period of four hundred years begin-

ning in 1 A.D. only seven rulers occupied the throne. These seven emperors are reputed to have enjoyed an average life span of 102 years. A history presenting this sort of record, which is not duplicated in the annals of any other nation, obviously has but little historical value.

TABLE 4

A COMPARATIVE STUDY OF LENGTH OF GENERATION

Nation	Period	Number of rulers	Number of generations in direct succession from father to son	Average length of the generations in years
Japan............	660 B.C.– ———	25	17	68
	506 A.D.– ———	—	—	—
Japan............	506 A.D.–1868 A.D.	95	50	28
China............	1320 B.C.– 813 B.C.	30	17	38
China............	796 B.C.– 256 B.C.	35	32	27
China............	618 A.D.– 906 A.D.	20	14	25
China............	960 A.D.–1278 A.D.	18	13	29
China............	1368 A.D.–1644 A.D.	17	12	26
Kudara..........	166 A.D.– 663 A.D.	19	14	24
Shinra..........	356 A.D.– 935 A.D.	39	21	29
Korai............	936 A.D.–1351 A.D.	30	16	31
Korea............	1392 A.D.–1890 A.D.	26	20	27

Dr. Naka, too, has prepared a table of generations based on the standard reference histories of China and Korea as well as of Japan, including the *Nihon Shoki*. This table (table 4) shows up the average length of the generations as given in the *Nihon Shoki* as so abnormal and absurd that, historically, the record is quite unacceptable.

The average length of generations on the Asiatic continent, according to table 4, has ranged from 24 to 31 years, and the average length of generations in Japan prior to the beginning of the sixth century A.D., based on the *Nihon Shoki*, has been 68 years. No other nation is credited with such lengthy generations, nor can this longevity be attributed to exceptionally favorable racial and climatic conditions in Japan. This record is found in the *Nihon Shoki* alone. The actual average length of generations in Japan

TABLE 5

A COMPARATIVE STUDY OF DATES OF EVENTS

Records in the *Nihon Shoki*	Records in the *Togoku Tsugan*	Difference in years
In the year Otsugai (the fifty-fifth year of the reign of the Empress Jingo, 255 A.D.) King Shoko of Kudara died	In the year Otsugai (the third year of the Ning-Kang era of the Chin of China, 375 A.D.) King Shoko of Kudara died	120
In the year Koshin (the sixty-fourth year of the reign of the Empress Jingo, 264 A.D.) King Kishu (Kyushu) of Kudara died. Prince Shinryu succeeded him and became king	In the year Koshin (the ninth year of the Tai-Yuan era of the Chin of China, 384 A.D.) King Kyushu of Kudara died. His eldest son, Shinryu, succeeded him	120
In the year Otsuyu (the sixty-fifth year of the reign of the Empress Jingo, 265 A.D.) King Shinryu of Kudara died. His son, Aka, being young, Shinshi, an uncle of Aka, usurped the throne and declared himself king of Kudara	In the year Otsuyu (the tenth year of the Tai-Yuan era of the Chin of China, 385 A.D.) King Shinshi of Kudara died. The crown prince, Aka, a younger brother of the deceased king made himself king of Kudara	120
In the year Jinshin (the third year of the reign of the Emperor Ojin, 272 A.D.) the king of Kudara failed to pay due reverence to the throne of Japan. Japan then sent Ki-no-Tsuno and three other generals, with a large army, for punitive purposes. The Kudara people thereupon killed their king in order to express their national regret to Japan. These four Japanese generals made Prince Aka king of Kudara, and returned home	In the year Jinshin (the seventeenth year of the Tai-Yuan era of the Chin of China, 392 A.D.) the king of Kudara died suddenly at his separate palace at Kugen. Prince Aka, a son of the former king, Shinryu, thereupon ascended the throne	120
In the year Teiyu (the eighth year of the reign of the Emperor Ojin, 277 A.D.) King Aka of Kudara failed to pay due reverence to Japan. The emperor of Japan therefore deprived Kudara of her ruling power in eastern Korea. King Aka made apologies and sent his son to the imperial court of Japan as a hostage for the good behavior of Kudara	In the year Teiyu (the first year of the Luang-An era of the Chin of China, 397 A.D.) Kudara concluded peace with Japan and sent her crown prince, Tenshi, to Japan and stationed him there as a hostage for her good behavior	120
In the year Otsu-Shi (the sixteenth year of the reign of the Emperor Ojin, 285 A.D.) King Aka of Kudara died. The Emperor Ojin called before him the Korean prince, Tenshi, who was stationed in Japan as a hostage, and instructed him to return to Korea to succeed his father as king of Kudara. The emperor granted him ruling power over eastern Korea. Prince Tenshi was sent to Korea under a Japanese military escort	In the year Otsushi (the first year of the I-Hsi era of the Chin of China, 405 A.D.) King Aka of Kudara died. Because Crown Prince Tenshi was away in Japan as hostage, his brother, Kunkai, acted as regent while awaiting the return of crown prince from Japan. Setsurei, a brother of the deceased king, killed the regent Kunkai and usurped the throne. The ruler of Japan sent Tenshi to Kudara with armed men. The people of Kudara thereupon killed the usurper, reverently received Tenshi and recognized him as their king	120

from the sixth century A.D. until the middle of the nineteenth century was 28 years, which is virtually the same as that of continental Asia. The unreliability of the records in the *Nihon Shoki* would seem established beyond any doubt.[11]

Dr. Naka made a further careful study of the *Nihon Shoki* in comparison with the *Togoku Tsugan*, a standard national history of Korea. He found that several important international events were entered in both of these histories for the same year according to the cycle symbols, but that in the calendar years there was a difference of 120 years between the records in Japanese histories and those in Korean histories. He compiled a table (table 5).

The content of table 5 bears witness that the national histories of both Korea and Japan contain correct records of their international affairs, and that the events are assigned to years of the same cycle symbols. Nevertheless, there is uniformly a difference of 120 years in the dates.

This discrepancy may be accounted for as follows: In the reigns of the Empress Jingo and the Emperor Ojin, the Japanese, like the Chinese and the Koreans, learned to keep records of events by attaching cycle symbols to the happenings of each year. (The Koreans had already introduced the Chinese imperial calendar into their country, and were therefore able to add dates to the cycle symbols.) Japan had no calendar, native or foreign, until the seventh century, when the Chinese calendar was introduced into Japan from Korea. In compiling the first history of Japan, the Japanese historians found it necessary to assign time values to the cycle symbols used in the reigns of Jingo and of Ojin, in order to ascertain to which cycles those symbols belonged. Either by mistake or on purpose, these historians estimated the years that had cycle symbols to have been two complete cycle periods, that is, covering 120 years. Historians of modern times are in virtual agreement that this was done on purpose, because the Japanese historians of the eighth century placed the date of the nation's beginning more than 600 years earlier than it really was. In order to spread this long stretch of time, many years were added to the different reigns, 120 years being added to the reigns of the Empress Jingo and the Emperor Ojin. It is the consensus of modern historians that there is an error of 635 years in the date of the nation's founding, and of

120 years at the time of the Emperor Ojin. The statement in the ancient Japanese histories that the works of Confucius were introduced into Japan in 285 A.D., in the reign of the Emperor Ojin, is now changed in modern histories to read 405 A.D.

The chronological tables prepared by Kume, Naka, and Yoshida virtually agree with respect to the difference between the real historical date and the fictitious date given in the ancient Japanese histories. As a further result of historical research and of the comparative studies of the histories of China, Korea, and Japan, modern historians have established two important facts, namely:

(1) Toward the close of the fourth century A.D. the Japanese began to record national happenings in a more reliable manner, by using Chinese characters.

(2) In the fourth and fifth centuries, at which time the ruling authority of the imperial government not only failed to extend over Yezo and Kyushu, but even the northeastern part of Honshu was outside of its control, the imperial armies crossed the water to Korea several times and established the authority of Japan in southern Korea. Thus the conquest of the Asiatic continent was begun long before the national unification of Japan was undertaken; in fact, the national expansion to the continent by way of Korea has always been an inherent ambition of the Japanese.[12]

APPENDIX 4

Korean Records of Dates and Events of Japanese Invasions of Shinra, Mostly Unmentioned in Japanese History

"IN THE YEAR 14 B.C., the Japanese invaded our coasts with more than a hundred war vessels. They finally besieged Kinjo, our capital. In the course of this military campaign, a large meteor fell into the Japanese camp, causing the terror-stricken Japanese to withdraw.

"In 59 A.D., we concluded peace with Japan.

"In 73, the Japanese invaded our island, Mokushutsu, and effected a landing. Our king sent troops under the command of Ucho, who was defeated and killed.

"In 121, in April, the Japanese ravaged our eastern coast.

"In 123, we made peace with Japan.

"In 173, the Japanese queen, Himeko, sent an envoy to express good will.

"In 193, Japan suffered from a great famine. In June of that year, thousands of Japanese came to our coasts and begged food.

"In 208, the Japanese invaded our coast. Our king sent Ibatsurion with troops and successfully defended the coast.

"In 232, the Japanese made a sudden inroad into our country and besieged our capital, Kinjo. Our king headed a large army and killed a thousand Japanese in a successful military engagement.

"In 233, in the summer, we suffered from a great storm which did tremendous damage, destroying thousands of houses. In May, the Japanese invaded our eastern coast.

"In 249, the Japanese invaded our coast, and killed Uro, one of our prominent officers.

"In 287, in the summer, the Japanese suddenly invaded our coast and started fires in various places. They took many prisoners.

"In 289, having been informed of the approach of the Japanese invaders, we made military preparation.

"In 292, in June, the Japanese army stormed and occupied the 'Shadow castle.' We sent an able general with a large army to re-occupy the castle.

"In 294, in the summer, the Japanese army made an unsuccessful attack on the Choho castle.

"In 295, the king promulgated an edict to the effect that the Japanese had frequently ravaged our castles and villages, thus making it impossible for our subjects to exist in safety. We therefore planned to form an alliance with Kudara and then to cross the water to Japan in order to inflict severe punishment upon them and upon their nation. However, on the ground that we were not accustomed to naval engagements, and that it would therefore be a great risk to send such an expedition beyond the waters to Japan, and on the ground that Kudara was a very unreliable nation, the king's plan was not followed.

"In 300, in January, we exchanged communications with Japan and entered into friendly relations.

"In 312, in March, the king of Japan sent an envoy and requested one of our royal princesses to be the wife of his son. In compliance with this request, we sent Princess Asokuri to Japan.

"In 344, in February, the king of Japan sent an envoy asking that our king permit his marriage to one of our royal princesses. We declined on the ground that all our princesses of marriageable age had already been married.

"In 345, Japan sent a state paper notifying us of the termination of international friendship between Japan and Shinra.

"In 346, the Japanese army made a sudden invasion of our Futo district, and then proceeded to and besieged Kinjo, our capital. Our king decided to take all available troops and give battle to the Japanese. Our enemy came from a great distance, yet his troops were full of hope and courage; therefore we thought it would be best for us to let them surround our castle and thus wear out their fighting spirit. The king gave approval. He then ordered that all the gates of the castle be closed and that his soldiers be kept inside. Finally, because of lack of provisions, the enemy was preparing to retreat. Thereupon our king sent against them and won a victory.

"In 364, in April, a large Japanese army landed on our coast. Our king feared that the Shinra army had no fighting chance, so he commanded that several thousand straw images be made and dressed in uniform, and he placed a thousand brave soldiers behind these straw images. While the Japanese were mowing down the straw images, our brave soldiers sprang up and made an unexpected attack upon the enemy. They won a great victory, most of the Japanese being killed.

"In 393, in May, a Japanese army came and besieged Kinjo, our capital. The battle lasted five days. Our troops asked the king to go out and give battle to the enemy, but the king refused and ordered that all the castle gates be closed and that we engage in defensive operations. Finally, the Japanese withdrew, as they had no chance to storm the castle. Thereupon, our king made a quick onrush and won a victory.

"In 402, in March, we made peace with Japan and sent Mishikin, a son of our king, as hostage to Japan.

"In 405, in April, the Japanese army landed on our coast and made an unsuccessful attack on our Meikatsu castle.

"In 407, in March, the Japanese invaded our eastern coast. In June, they again came and invaded our southern coast. They carried away about one hundred of our people as prisoners.

"In 408, in February, our king was informed that Japan had stationed an army of great strength on Tsushima [Tsu island] in the Korean Channel, and had stored great quantities of food and military weapons on the island, with a view to invading our kingdom. Our king therefore planned to attack the Japanese on the island by sending our well-trained soldiers before Japan should start military activities against us. One of our trusted statesmen warned the king, saying: 'According to my understanding, weapons are murderous implements; war is a risky undertaking. Moreover, it would be hazardous to cross the water to attack well-prepared fighting men on foreign soil. If we should fail to win, our regret would be no compensation for our loss. Therefore, it would be better for us to have our coasts well fortified, and to give battle to our enemies when they come. It should be our policy to defend our honor and national existence.' The king gave his approval.

"In 415, in August, we engaged in a successful battle with the Japanese in our Futo district.

"In 418, Mishikin, a younger brother of our king, who had been held in Japan as a hostage, escaped and returned to our kingdom.

"In 431, in April, the Japanese invaded our eastern coast and besieged the Meikatsu castle. They finally withdrew without having gained anything.

"In 440, the Japanese invaded our southern coast and carried away a great number of our people as prisoners.

"In June of the same year, they again invaded our eastern coast.

"In 444, in April, a large Japanese army besieged Kinjo, our capital. In October, because of lack of provisions, they abandoned their military camp and began their homeward retreat. Thereupon, our king, disregarding the advice of his officers, attacked the retreating enemy. They gave battle desperately at the eastern side of Mount Doku. The king was defeated and lost half of his army of several thousand men.

"In 459, in April, Japan sent more than one hundred war vessels and attacked our eastern coast. Finally, they effected a landing and besieged the Getsu castle, but our troops were successful in defending the castle. This forced the enemy to retreat. Thereupon, we chased them to the coast, where more than half of their men were drowned.

"In 462, the Japanese stormed and occupied our Kakkai castle and carried away our men, to the number of about one thousand, as prisoners.

"In 463, in February, the Japanese made an unsuccessful attack on our Kanryo castle. Because of repeated attacks by the Japanese on our coasts, our king ordered that two strong fortifications should be built on our coasts.

"In 476, in June, the Japanese invaded our eastern coast. The king sent an army under the command of General Tokuchi, who defeated the enemy. More than two hundred of the enemy's men were either killed or taken prisoners by our forces.

"In 477, in May, the Japanese invaded our kingdom at five different points at once. We forced them to retreat.

"In 481, Korai, assisted by Makkatsu troops, invaded our northern district, and stormed and occupied the Komen and six other castles. Our army received military assistance from Kudara and from Kaya. A battle was then waged against Korai, and a great victory gained. More than a thousand of the enemy were decapitated.

"In 482, a great storm visited our country and caused much damage. It destroyed houses and uprooted many trees. The south gate of Kinjo, the capital city, was destroyed by fire. In May, the Japanese invaded our coasts.

"In 486, in April, the Japanese invaded our coasts.

"In 497, in April, the Japanese invaded our coasts.

"In 500, in March, the Japanese stormed and occupied the Choho castle.

"In 523, in September, our king made a local inspection tour of the southern boundary line of our kingdom, especially of the newly developed district. The king of Kaya came to the border line and showed due respect to our king.

"In 531, the ruler of the State of Kinkan, accompanied by his wife and three children, surrendered and brought all his national coffers and treasures. Our king received him and his family with due royal dignity.

"In 554, in September, we repaired and strengthened our Meikatsu castle. Meirei, the king of Kudara, at the head of both his own army and that of Kaya, invaded and attacked the Kanzan castle. Kankan Toku and Iso Chinchi, our military commanders, took our army and gave battle to the enemy, but our troops suffered great defeat. Having learned of our great national disaster, Kin Buriki mustered all the fighting men in his state, which was called Shinshu, and proceeded to and joined our king's army. Our combined forces made an onrush upon the bodyguard of the king of Kudara and killed the king. Then, in carrying on the victory, our army attacked the main body of the army of Kudara and won a decisive victory, killing the four leading military men and 29,600 soldiers.

"In 562, in July, Kudara invaded our borders. Our king headed our army in person and defeated the invaders, killing more than one thousand men."[13]

This history of Shinra, as recorded in *San Goku Shi* (The History of the Three Kingdoms), contains the account of a series of invasions at short intervals by the Japanese from 50 B.C. to 500 A.D., none of which has been recorded in the history of Japan.

Japanese historians believe that the invasions which took place prior to the fourth century A.D. were most probably not from Japan Proper, but from the island of Kyushu. Up to the middle of the fourth century, Kyushu had been an independent state. In it were many military rulers. Their military chiefs, as a rule, pledged loyalty to China rather than to Japan. The Chinese *History of the Later Han Dynasty* states that a small island to the south of Korea (Kyushu) was divided into more than a hundred separate states, that the rulers of thirty of these states sent tribute to the imperial court of the Han, and that each of the rulers styled himself "king" in his state papers. To these historical matters, also, no reference whatever is to be found in the history of Japan, but accounts are given of the disorderly conditions in Kyushu prior to the fourth century. Both Korean and Chinese records reveal that the authority of Japan did not extend to the island of Kyushu. It was only in the second half of the fourth century that Kyushu became an integral part of the empire of Japan. This fact is incidentally verified in the *T'ang Shu* (Chinese *History of the T'ang Dynasty*), which says that Nihon (Japan) was originally a small state but that it had conquered and annexed the entire State of Wa (Kyushu) and had thus attained its present standing.

According to Korean records, the Japanese invasions of the kingdom of Shinra were conducted on a larger scale than those of the preceding century. This attack must have been directly from Japan, and not from Kyushu. Korean history gives contradictory accounts of these battles. According to the accounts, in the beginning Shinra was defeated every time and her capital besieged, but at the end of each battle she won a brilliant victory and chased the Japanese away. When peace was concluded, Shinra sent a royal prince to Japan as a hostage for good faith. This would indicate that Shinra was a defeated nation. If these Korean records are ever studied in connection with the records of these wars as found in the inscription on the Kotai-O monument (appendix 5) and the Japanese historical records, some light may be shed on the much-mooted historical problem of the early international relations between Japan and Korea.

The date of the very last of the innumerable Japanese invasions of Shinra is 500 A.D. After that date, not a single attack by the Japanese on Shinra is recorded. This new state of affairs in Shinra may be interestingly studied in the records contained in the *Sung Shu* (appendix 6), and further in connection with the rebellion of Ouiwa, the Japanese governor-general at Mimana, against the home government in Japan, which took place in 487 A.D.

The entry in this Korean *History,* under date of 554, of the invasion of Shinra by Kudara which ended in the death of the king of Kudara and the total destruction of his army, agrees in every detail with the record in the *History of Japan,* even with respect to the number of Kudara men who were killed; both state the number to be 29,600. The Japanese record was most probably based upon the official report of the kingdom of Kudara, a faithful tributary state of Japan. This agreement exemplifies the reliability of this Korean *History.*

The title of this historical work is *San Goku Shi* (The History of the Three Kingdoms). It consists of fifty volumes. The famous Korean historian Kin Fushiki wrote it in compliance with the royal request of King Jinso, who ruled Korea from 1123 to 1146. The work was completed in December, 1145; that is, this work was written about 450 years after the destruction of the three kingdoms in Korea. (In fact, the three kingdoms were unified through the conquest of the other two by one of the three kingdoms.) This *History* naturally contains many traditional accounts, as well as historical facts. It is the oldest of the ancient historical works in Korea, and is therefore a very valuable piece of work.

APPENDIX 5

The Kotai-O Hi in the Kingdom of Korai

THE KOTAI-O HI was a monument erected in 414 A.D. by King Choju in honor of his father, King Kokaido, who ruled in the kingdom of Korai from 392 to 412. It is a large natural stone 18 feet high, about 5½ feet wide, and about 4½ feet thick. This monument was set up originally at a place near the left bank of the river Yalu, just outside of the ancient capital of Korai. Because of a change in the course of the Yalu, and because of changing conditions in the soil, this 1500-year-old monument lay buried for several hundred years. Some three hundred years ago, after a great storm, the upper point of the monument became exposed, but because of their superstitions, the people covered it again with earth. However, with every storm, the part of the monument exposed became larger and larger, and finally the attention of archaeologists was attracted to it. Later, the Chinese government began to take an interest in the monument. Excavations were made at irregular intervals and, in 1882, Mr. Tso Sheng Ching, a military viceroy, completed the work of excavation down as far as the base of the monument, which is still so deeply buried in the earth that the exact height of the monolith is unknown.

On the four faces of the monument, the life of King Kokaido, together with a brief historical account of the kingdom of Korai, had been engraved in the Chinese classical language. Disintegration caused by the weather and careless handling at the time of the excavation have obliterated here and there some of the Chinese characters. The writing is arranged in forty-four lines, each line consisting of forty-one Chinese characters, the total number being approximately eighteen hundred characters. In spite of the scattered obliterations, after years of painstaking study the meaning of the inscription has been made clear, and is considered a most valuable historical source.

International affairs between Korea and Japan had long been

regarded by historians as a subject impossible of investigation. In the first place, there is a series of errors in historical dates in Japan, whereby a history of approximately seven hundred years was written as if it were thirteen hundred years, and all events were artificially distributed through them. (See appendix 3.) In the second place, the dates in Korean histories are, on the whole, more reliable than those in the Japanese histories; but the Korean historians, for the sake of national glorification, twisted their historical events, sometimes stating that certain wars ended in victory for them when in fact they had suffered defeat. This is especially marked in the annals of the kingdom of Shinra, a state that was almost continuously at war with Japan.[14]

The monument erected in honor of King Kokaido bears a record of historical events written by historians of Korai, who had no special leaning for any one state. It therefore contains many historical events not mentioned elsewhere, on the one hand, and, on the other, it sheds light on several much mooted historical events. For example, in the ninth line on the front of the monument it is stated that in the year of Shin-Bo (391 A.D.) the Japanese crossed the waters and reduced Kudara and Shinra to vassal states of Japan, making the people their subjects.

According to the record of the kingdoms, in 393 Kinjo, the capital of Shinra, was besieged by the Japanese army, but the besieged finally succeeded in driving the Japanese away. (See appendix 4.) Another Korean history, *Togoku Tsugan*, states that this military event took place in 392. Turning to the record in Japanese history, we find that in the third year of the Emperor Ojin (271 A.D.) the emperor sent a punitive military expedition to Kudara. The people of Kudara killed their king, Shinshi, and readily submitted to Japan. (The kingdom of Shinra had been conquered by Japan some time before that, so Kudara alone is mentioned in this record.) The *History of Kudara* states that the death of King Shinshi took place in the seventeenth year of the Taiyun era of China (392). If we compare the records in the three Korean histories with that given in the Japanese history, with special reference to this particular military event, we shall see that there is approximately one hundred and twenty years' difference in the dates given in the respective national records. We shall also note that Korean history asserts that the Koreans succeeded in driving the Japanese away even though they were victorious in the beginning. All the histories in Japan and in Korea were written from five hundred to six hundred years after the termination of the existence of the three kingdoms, but the Kotai-O monument was erected in their middle period, that is, about two hundred and fifty years before the termination of their existence. The inscription on the monument, a record made at the time of the three kingdoms, is naturally more trustworthy. In many ways the inscription on this monument serves as a key to disputed historical events. Korean dates are, on the whole, more nearly correct than Japanese dates. Although Japanese history frequently omits records of events in Korea, still, those that are noted are generally more reliably described than those given in Korean history. At any rate, the inscription on the Kotai-O monument evidences the fact that there is a discrepancy of about one hundred and twenty years in the dates given in Japanese history toward the end of the fourth century.

In the sixth line on the left face of the monument, it is stated that, in the ninth year of the king (Kokaido), 399 A.D., Kudara violated her pledge and made peace with Japan. Although nothing is said of this in Japanese history, most probably Korai gave military assistance to Kudara and caused her to rise against Japan, her suzerain. Because of the invincible military power of Japan, Kudara was forced again to recognize the suzerainty of Japan in her suit for peace. The following description on the monument gives evidence of this: In the eighth and ninth lines on the left face of the monument, it is stated that in the ninth year of the king (400 A.D.) [which was the same year in which Kudara made peace with Japan], the king of Shinra sent an envoy to the king of Korai and complained, saying, "The Japanese have invaded our kingdom and occupied all the border districts, destroying cities and strongholds," and asked for military protection. The inscription further states that in the tenth year of the king (401 A.D.), Korai, in response to the request of Shinra, sent an army fifty thousand strong to rescue Shinra from Japan. This military expedition of Korai most probably failed to attain its end, and therefore Shinra was forced to make peace with Japan. The *History of the Three Kingdoms* states that in March, 402, Shinra concluded peace with Japan and sent Mishikin, one of the king's sons, as a hostage to the imperial court of Japan.

In the third, fourth, fifth, and sixth lines on the rear face of the monument, it is stated that in the fourteenth year of the king (405), the Japanese invaded Taiho, the southern border district of the kingdom of Korai. The army of Korai won a series of battles fought along the Han-Kiang and the Tai-Tung rivers. In the seventeenth year of the king, he sent an army fifty thousand strong and made a successful attack on the Japanese military base in Korea. (Many of the characters in these four lines are obliterated so that the lines cannot be fully read; yet, from the context, the foregoing translation has been made.)

None of the military expeditions in Korea that are recorded on this monument are mentioned in the history of Japan, but if one takes the descriptions on the monument and compares them with statements in Korean history, and then studies Japanese history, making allowance for the great discrepancies in historical dates, he will see that, about the close of the fourth or at the beginning of the fifth century, Japan had established her authority in Korea over such states as Kudara, Shinra, and Mimana and that she even had a military force in Korea of sufficient strength to enable her to invade Korai, the northernmost state. (It is stated in Japanese history that this conquest in southern Korea took place in 200 A.D.)

The Kotai-O monument was erected in honor of the king of Korai. Its inscription was, naturally, written to represent Korai as the supreme state, and it exaggerated statements with respect to the affairs of that kingdom. Nevertheless, historians agree in general that the statements in the inscription are reliable.[15]

Appendix 6

Japan's Request to China for Recognition of Her Ruling Power in Southern Korea

SEVERAL IMPERIAL AUTHORIZED EDITIONS of Chinese histories, among which are Sung-Shu, Nanchi-Shu, Liang-Shu, and Nan-Shih, record the fact that Japan had requested the recognition by China of Japan's ruling authority in southern Korea. The Sung-Shu, in addition to giving a detailed account of this international matter, contains a copy of the text of the memorial presented by the ruler of Japan to the Sung emperor of China, of which the translation below has been made (*Sung-Shu,* vol. 97, pp. 8a-b).

In the reign of the Sung dynasty of China (420–478 A.D.), Japan sent envoys a number of times, especially in the years 421, 425, 443, 451, 462, and 478. In those days, Japan recognized China as her suzerain power and requested the Sung imperial government to recognize the ruling power of Japan in the five states in Korea, namely, Kudara, Shinra, Mimana, Shinkan, and Bakan, as well as in the kingdom of Wo [Japan]. In the second year of the Sheng-Ming era of the Emperor Shun of the Sung dynasty (478 A.D.), King Wu of Japan presented the following memorial to the imperial throne of China.

"From the times of our forefathers, we have armed ourselves, crossed mountains and rivers and have continuously waged war against wild tribes. We have thereby subjugated fifty-five districts in the east and sixty-six districts in the west. Finally, we have crossed the waters and reached the land to the north of our country [i.e., Korea]. We have made it possible for the people in that country to enjoy peace and prosperity under our rule. . . . Nevertheless, the King of Kuli [Korai] has stood in our way and has interfered with our reaching the imperial court of Your Majesty in order to pay due respect to the throne. My father and my brother, who preceded me in ruling our country, completed military preparations for punishing the King of Kuli, but both of them died without accomplishing that work. Now, as it is the season of national mourning, we cannot undertake this military work. . . . We hope to carry out this punitive expedition under the imperial cognizance of Your Majesty. We shall then succeed in crushing Kuli, our powerful enemy nation."

In response to this request of Japan, the Emperor Shun of the Sung dynasty of China recognized Wu, the "King of Japan" (Yuryaku, the twenty-first emperor of Japan), as ruler of both Japan and Korea, and conferred upon him the official title of "Military Viceroy Who Will Command the Army for the Pacification of the East, Including Wo [Japan], Shinra, Mimana, Kaya, Shinkan, and Bakan."

The bearing of the foregoing memorial and the action taken

by China in response to it upon the relative standing, as nations, of China and Japan is obvious. The attitude taken by Japan on this point may be stated as follows:

(1) Although all the standard Chinese histories contain these seven official communications between Japan and China, none of these communications is recorded in any history of Japan.

(2) Japanese historians of the present time are fully convinced that all these communications are genuine. Nevertheless, they do not believe that these communications were sent directly by the imperial court of Japan.

(3) According to Japanese historical records, direct international relations between the imperial courts of China and Japan were first entered into in 607 A.D. In the state papers exchanged in the seventh century, the title "Emperor" was used for both the Chinese and the Japanese rulers, Japan in this way maintaining, in her own eyes at least, her claim to equal standing with China. However, all state papers sent from Japan to China in the fifth century were written as though China were a suzerain power and Japan were a tributary state.

(4) Japanese historians have concluded that these state papers of the fifth century were sent by the Japanese governor-general of Mimana in Korea under the name of the "Ruler of Japan" without the knowledge of the Japanese imperial court.

(5) The Japanese governor-general in Korea probably took this course in order to strengthen his authority over the Koreans, reasoning, no doubt, that if the authority of Japan in Korea should be recognized by the Chinese emperor, Korea would readily submit to Japan.

(6) For these reasons, the Japanese state papers and memorials of the fifth century that were addressed to the Chinese throne, of necessity took the form of documents exchanged between suzerain and tributary states.

APPENDIX 7

Source Materials on Japan's Difficulties with Kingdoms in Korea

THE RISE AND FALL of the power of Japan in Korea may be identified with the creation and the destruction of the state of Mimana. As stated in appendix 1, none of the Korean histories mentions anything about Mimana. Chinese history mentions Mimana casually but says nothing of historical value. Japanese sources alone must perforce be depended upon in describing the difficulties in Mimana which ended in the destruction of the Japanese government-general at Mimana by Shinra and Mimana's annexation to Shinra. Even the records in Japanese history often conflict, so that careful, comparative studies of the statements in standard Japanese historical works have been made for the purpose of eliminating possible errors.

Among the standard histories are the following:

(1) Ariga, *Dai Nippon Rekishi* (Unabridged History of Japan), vol. 1, pp. 176–211, 371–89.

(2) Hagino, *Nippon-Shi Kowa* (Lectures on Japanese History), pp. 72–82.

(3) *Ito, Dai Nippon Minzoku-Shi* (History of the Race of Great Japan), pp. 168–69.

(4) Kuroita, *Kokushi-no-Kenkyu* (Research in National History), pp. 60–61.

(5) Ota, *Nikan Kodai-Shi Shiryo* (Historical Materials on the Ancient Periods of Japan and Korea), p. 183.

(6) Shidehara, *Chosen Shiwa* (Historical Account of Korea), pp. 13–22.

(7) Waseda University, *Dai-Nippon Jidai-Shi* (History of Great Japan Period by Period), vol. 1, pp. 96–113, 213–62.

(8) Yoshida, *Tojo Nippon-Shi* (History of Japan in Reverse Order), vol. 10, pp. 409–17.

APPENDIX 8

Japan Prior to the Adoption of the Chinese Calendar

JAPANESE AND CHINESE HISTORIES give a general idea of how the Japanese lived before the adoption of the calendar. The following is a translation of the main content of a description of conditions in Japan prior to the seventh century, as given in Japanese histories.

"It was only in the twelfth year of the reign of the Empress Suiko [604 A.D.] that Japan adopted the Chinese calendar system, which was introduced by way of Korea, and that accounts of affairs in Japan came to be concisely and reliably recorded. However, even after that date, people living in the suburbs of the capital city, as well as those living in country districts, still reckoned time by the old methods of their forefathers. They generally divided the year into four seasons, taking the heat and the cold as well as the sprouting of new shoots and the falling of the leaves as bases. Each season was divided into three parts, the increase and the decrease of heat and cold, besides the condition of the trees, being taken into consideration. Each of these three divisions was governed by the cycle of the moon, the same marking the length of the month. The cycle of the moon was also divided into three parts, taking the phases of the moon as reference. The first part was from the new moon to the egg-shaped moon; the second from the egg-shaped to the second egg-shaped moon through the full moon; and the third cycle from the second egg-shaped moon to the new moon. The first part was called the growing moon, the second part was called the moon hope, and the third part was called the hiding moon. Each part was counted by ten, taking the fingers and thumbs of one's two hands as reference. (The Japanese of those days could count no higher than ten. Even today, there is no method of counting higher than ten in the Japanese language, and in counting higher than ten, the Japanese use Chinese numerals.")[16]

Chinese history also contains the following statement with respect to the way the Japanese calculated their dates in the pre-calendar period:

"The Japanese do not know how to record the years correctly, neither can they make right divisions of the four seasons. They are merely able to reckon their dates and years by taking their spring sowing and autumn harvest (together with other natural phenomena) into consideration."[17]

APPENDIX 9

The First Direct International Intercourse Between China and Japan

ACCORDING TO THE RECORDS in Chinese histories, as early as the beginning of the Christian era Japan was sending envoys, time after time, to China, in recognition of their international relationship. In early Japanese history, on the contrary, there is not the slightest reference or hint that any international relationship existed. It is generally believed that the envoys to China in the early period were sent either by military chieftains or by Japanese governors-general stationed at Mimana in Korea, who approached the imperial court of China in the name of Japan on their own responsibility. Moreover, all the state papers exchanged between China and Japan prior to the seventeenth century used the terms "Emperor of China" and "King of Japan." It was time-honored international usage in China and in other Asiatic nations that the title *Huang-Ti* ("Emperor") should be used exclusively for the ruler of a suzerain nation, and the title *Wang* ("King") for the ruler of a tributary nation. In strict conformity with this traditional usage, the Japanese officials and the military chiefs recognized China as a suzerain power, but they did so without the sanction of the imperial court of Japan. For this and other reasons, no Japanese historian recognizes the international relationship thus maintained between China and Japan prior to the seventh century as being a relationship existing between the two nations.

According to the records in Japanese histories, Japan first entered into international relations with China in the year 607 A.D. This was the fifteenth year of the Suiko era in Japan, and the third year of the Taiyeh era in China. The envoy that Japan sent to China in that year bore state papers in which the title of "Emperor" was used to designate both the ruler of Japan and the ruler of China, a clear indication that Japan was of the same national status as China.

The state paper sent by Japan to China in the year 607 begins: "The Emperor of the Nation of the Rising Sun respectfully addresses the Emperor of the Nation of the Setting Sun, inquiring after the imperial health. . . ." The Sui emperor of China was greatly displeased when this state paper was presented to him. He said to his state minister, "A state paper from a barbarian nation that has failed to observe traditional usages and that has thereby shown lack of due reverence to us should not be presented to our throne." Nevertheless, in the following year (608) the Sui emperor sent a trusted court officer, Fei Ching, as envoy to Japan.[18] In the state paper that Fei Ching carried to Japan, the title "King" was used in addressing the ruler of Japan, and the title "Emperor" when the Chinese ruler was referred to. The state paper reads as follows:

"The Emperor herewith addresses the King of Japan. Your envoy has arrived at our court and has informed us with respect to your condition and that of your nation.

"Since our succession to the throne in response to the command of Heaven, we have always desired to extend our protection and blessing over all the world so as to enable the people both near and far to enjoy happiness and prosperity. We are highly pleased to be informed that you, who live in a far-off island nation, know how to protect your people and make it possible for them to maintain a happy, prosperous, harmonious existence."

When the Chinese envoy, Fei Ching, returned to China, the ruler of Japan sent with him a second envoy, bearing the following state paper:

"The Emperor of the East respectfully addresses the Emperor of the West. Your envoy, Fei Ching, arrived at our court and informed us of your condition and that of your country, concerning which I had long desired to hear. The season being the latter part of autumn, cool weather is approaching. I hope your Majesty will enjoy peace and good health. Here, we are spending our days as usual without any noticeable events."

In this state paper, the ruler of Japan continued to use the imperial title for both herself and the ruler of China, thus making it clear that she considered the Japanese nation as of equal standing with China. However, having been informed that the Chinese emperor had been especially displeased with the expression, "Nation of the Setting Sun," in this second state paper she substituted the terms "East" and "West" to designate, respectively, Japan and China.[19]

APPENDIX 10

Source Materials on the Battle at Hakko (Hakuson-ko) in 663 A.D.

THE FOLLOWING Chinese and Japanese histories contain records of the battle at Hakko (Hakuson-ko) which was fought in 663 A.D. The descriptions agree in every detail.

(1) *T'ang-Shu* (History of the T'ang, imperial authorized edition), vol. 220, pp. 7–8.

(2) Yoshida, *Tojo Nihon-Shi* (History of Japan in Reverse Order), vol. 10, pp. 459–61.

APPENDIX 11

Source Materials on the National Strength of Kudara and Korai When Destroyed

IN 663, THE KINGDOM OF KUDARA was destroyed, with no possibility remaining for its restoration. This kingdom came to so sad an end after having maintained its existence for 678 years, during which time 30 kings had ruled. According to historical records, Kudara consisted of 5 states, divided into 37 districts, which were again subdivided into 350 counties, with a population of 1,200,000, there being 240,000 families.

During the last sixteen months of its existence, Kudara was a kingdom in name only. In fact, in those days, Kudara was breathing her last under the military protection of Japan, and with her destruction (which involved also the destruction of the kingdom of Korea) Japan's power in Korea completely disappeared.[20]

Five years after the destruction of Kudara, that is, in 668, the kingdom of Korai came to an end, after an existence of 705 years under the rule of 28 kings. At the time of its destruction, Korai consisted of 5 states, having 178 cities and towns, and approximately 697,000 families.[21]

At the time that Japan withdrew from Korea and entirely abandoned her claims in the peninsula, her authority extended only
over Kyushu, Shikoku, and the southwestern half of Honshu, together with numerous small adjacent islands. The total area of
Japan in the seventh century was between 80,000 and 90,000 square
miles, and its population between 6,000,000 and 7,000,000.

APPENDIX 12

Historical Memorials of Kudara and Korai
in Japan Today

WHEN KUDARA was destroyed in 663, and when Korai was destroyed in 668, several thousand Koreans from those destroyed
kingdoms fled to Japan. These Koreans established settlements in
various parts of Japan under the protection of the Japanese government. In commemoration of the kingdoms of their forefathers,
these Koreans gave geographical names to their new settlements;
such as County of Kudara, County of Korai, Kudara Mountain,
Korai village, and Kudara River. A number of these names still
persist—landmarks in Japan of the once prosperous kingdoms
in Korea.

The following translations from standard Japanese histories
afford some idea of the dependence of the Koreans upon Japan
after the destruction of their kingdoms and the use they made of
her protection and hospitality.

"In the autumn of 663, when the military situation of Japan
in Korea became hopeless and desperate after the crushing defeat
in the battle at Hakko, the Japanese generals gathered the rem-
nants of their troops and returned home. At that time, several
thousand Koreans, including the members of the royal family and
Koreans of the ruling class of Kudara as well as the common
people, fled to Japan. Upon their arrival, they were kindly received. The Emperor Tenchi assigned them to various provinces
and allotted to them extensive tracts of arable land. Four hundred
people from Kudara were settled in the Province of Omi, and two
thousand in eastern Japan."[22]

The title *Kudara-O* (king of Kudara) was conferred upon Prince
Zenko, younger brother of the former king of Kudara, and exten-

sive estates in Naniwa, now known as Osaka, were granted him. This district was known as the "County of Kudara." Seven hundred men and women of Kudara were settled in the County of Gamo. They were allowed to reclaim the wilderness on liberal terms.[23]

The following statement, which has similarities with those of Hagino and of Kume, is found in the *Nihon Shoki* compiled by imperial order in 720, that is, about half a century after the destruction of the kingdom of Kudara.

"In 665, four hundred Kudara men and women were instructed to establish their homes in the Province of Omi. In the winter of 666, more than two thousand Kudara men and women were instructed to establish their homes in eastern Japan. To them, the government provided the food necessary for three years."[24]

In 668, the kingdom of Korai was destroyed by the joint armies of the T'ang and of Shinra. Like the people of the kingdom of Kudara, several thousands of Koreans from Korai fled to Japan. Yoshida, in his geographical encyclopedia, gives some account of what became of these people from Korai:

"In the second year of the Reiki era, 716 A.D., the government set aside the entire southwestern section of the County of Iruma for the home of the Kudara refugees. The name *Koma Gun* ("County of Korai") was given to this section. Then all the Korai people who were scattered in the seven provinces of Suruga, Kai, Sagami, Kazusa, Shimosa, Hidachi, and Kozuke, the total number of whom was 1799, were invited to establish permanent homes in the newly established County of Korai. In the same year, the Korai people to the number of 990, who were living in various parts of the Province of Tamba, were invited to join their countrymen in the County of Korai. This County of Korai existed for nearly 1200 years. In 1896, just one year after the Sino-Japanese war, this county was consolidated with the County of Iruma. It is at present under the administration of the Tokyo prefecture."[25]

APPENDIX 13

Occidental Misconceptions of the International Status of Japan and Korea

ALL STANDARD JAPANESE HISTORIES record that for a period of at least two hundred years, ending in the seventh century, Japan had held suzerain power in Korea. The *Twenty-four Histories of China* record that the imperial government of China recognized the authority of Japan in Kudara, Shinra, Mimana, and the other states in southern Korea. Although there are grounds for dispute, it is a widely accepted historical fact that prior to the seventh century a sort of suzerain and tributary relationship existed between Japan and the kingdoms and states in southern Korea. However, Japanese and other Oriental historians are agreed that after the destruction of the kingdom of Kudara in 663, and of the kingdom of Korai in 668, Japan abandoned her claims in Korea, her authority having been completely overthrown. None of the Chinese, Japanese, or Korean histories states that during the period of approximately thirteen hundred years beginning in the latter part of the seventh century Japan ever claimed suzerainty over Korea; nor do they state that Korea ever sent tribute to Japan. In fact, up to 1876, when Japan forced Korea to conclude a treaty containing the provision that Korea was an independent nation, having equal rights with Japan, Korea had been recognized by Japan as a tributary kingdom of China. Notwithstanding this fact, Occidental historians have confused the suzerain power that Japan exercised in Korea prior to the seventh century with Hideyoshi's Korean campaign and its outcome, and these historians have therefore made erroneous statements saying that Japan had suzerain power over Korea prior to 1894. This historical error is comparable with one that might be made by historians writing European history who, confusing the Norman Conquest and the desire of Napoleon to conquer England, should state that prior to the twentieth century England was a country subjugated by France. In spite of the striking absurdity in view of the actual facts, quite a number of Occidental historians persist in making erroneous statements of this sort in their publications.[26]

APPENDIX 14

Japanese Conceptions of the National Status of Korea in the Late Seventh Century

ALL JAPANESE HISTORIANS of note are agreed: (1) that in the reign of the Emperor Tenchi, the thirty-eighth sovereign of Japan, upon the destruction of the Japanese military forces in Korea and with the subsequent abandonment of authority in Korea, Japan's suzerainty in Korea was terminated; and (2) that since the termination of the relationship of suzerain and tributary states between Japan and Korea in the seventh century, this relationship has never been reëstablished.

Dr. Shidehara, president of the Imperial University in Formosa, and a recognized authority on Korean history, states in his work:

"The Emperor Tenchi thereupon determined to reëstablish the kingdom of Kudara. This caused Japan to go to war with the T'ang [China]. This military campaign unfortunately terminated in a disastrous battle at Hakuson-ko [Hakko]. Subsequently, Japan lost her authority in Korea completely.

"After abandoning Korea [in the seventh century], Japan on many occasions planned to regain power in that country. She sometimes invoked various gods, asking their assistance, and she had her young men learn the language of Shinra so that they would be prepared to serve as military interpreters. She strongly fortified her own coasts in order to defend herself from a possible attack by Korea; and having thus safeguarded her own country, she carried her military work farther with the purpose of again invading Korea and regaining her suzerainty there. However, owing to the steady rise of the intellectual and military power of a Korea united under the rule of Shinra, Japan had no opportunity to start a military campaign, and her ambitious plans to reëstablish her power in Korea were gradually abandoned. [In the latter part of the sixteenth century, Hideyoshi's invasion of Korea, which lasted seven years, was finally abandoned in 1598 because of his death from old age. After the abandonment of this military campaign, Japan proposed to Korea that peace be concluded, but Korea promptly refused, citing as her reason for doing so the cruelties and acts of vandalism committed by some of Hideyoshi's soldiers. Consequently, Japan decided to buy the good will of Korea. In pursuance of this policy, she returned all the prisoners taken in war, and she sent to Korea all the Japanese soldiers who had committed crimes while participating in Hideyoshi's campaign, so that they might be punished in accordance with the laws of Korea. She also met all other demands made by Korea. Finally, in 1609, a treaty of peace was concluded between Japan and Korea.] By the terms of this treaty, Korea permitted Japan to engage in trade with her on a limited scale.

"At the same time, Korea and Japan agreed to observe a new usage, according to which each nation should send an envoy bearing congratulations at the time of the great national event of the other: Korea should send an envoy to Japan when a new shogun came into power; Japan should send an envoy to Korea when a new king ascended the throne. [Korea, in order to impress Japan with the strength and dignity of her people, sent her envoy and his party in a most elaborate way. The party usually consisted of approximately 400 men. When the envoy from Korea came to Japan in 1711, his party numbered 491. This party first landed on Tsushima, a small Japanese island in the Korean Channel. There they received the first grand reception. They then proceeded to the main island and traveled approximately nine hundred miles before reaching Yedo, the military capital of the shogun. These parties usually spent three months in Japan. The shogunate and the local governments had to entertain them in every city and town in which they lodged. During the Tokugawa shogunate, the receiving and entertaining of the Korean envoy and his party constituted one of the greatest financial burdens of the nation.] In 1811, when Korea sent her envoy and party to Japan at the time that the eleventh shogun, Iyenari, succeeded to power, because of financial depression Japan could not entertain the envoy and his party in the customary way. The shogun therefore sent his representative to the Korean Channel to meet the envoy and his party in Tsushima, an island in the Channel, and the envoy and his party returned home from Tsushima without proceeding to Yedo."[27]

Korea was undoubtedly offended by this shabby reception, and the envoy of 1811 was the last one sent by Korea to Japan. When

THE EMPEROR TENCHI (662–671)
Thirty-eighth emperor of Japan and second founder of the empire

the twelfth, thirteenth, fourteenth, and fifteenth shoguns succeeded to power, Korea sent no envoys. Altogether, Korea sent
envoys to Japan eleven times in the period of rule of the Tokugawa
shogunate (1603–1867).

The historical fact that Korea sent envoys to Japan eleven
times in the 264 years that Japan was under the rule of the Tokugawa shogunate has been misstated by the American authors of a
European history, as follows: "Korea had paid a yearly tribute to
the Shoguns of Japan until the time Japan began adopting the
western civilization (1868)."[28]

Dr. Kida, a noted historian, gives the following information in
his book, *The Annexation of Korea to Japan and the National
History*. In the reign of the Emperor Tenchi, the kingdom of Kudara was completely destroyed by reason of the disastrous defeat
of the Japanese troops at Hakuson-ko in 663. The kingdom of
Korai was destroyed in 668. The unification of Korea was subsequently effected under the rule of Shinra, and the relations between Japan and Korea were completely terminated.[29]

Dr. Hagino, Professor of History in Tokyo Imperial University,
states that in the seventh century, with the gradual increase of the
power and influence of the T'ang in Korea, the authority of Japan
steadily declined. In the second half of the seventh century, Japan
lost all her power in Korea, no trace remaining of her former
glorious rule in the peninsula. After withdrawing from Korea,
Japan strongly fortified Tsushima and the island of Iki in the Korean Channel. The coasts of Kyushu and of Yamato were likewise
fortified.

Japan then made it a national policy to prepare herself against
possible invasion from Korea, on the one hand, and, on the other,
to approach China in the most friendly way possible, so that she
might benefit by the introduction of Chinese civilization, together
with the Chinese methods of national organization and administration, thereby advancing her national standing.[30]

Dr. Ariga, a noted historian and a scholar of international reputation, says that, in the second year and in the seventh year of the
reign of the Emperor Tenchi (663 and 668), the kingdoms of Kudara and of Korai were destroyed by the joint armies of the T'ang
and of Shinra. However, neither China nor Shinra showed any

intention of carrying its victories beyond the water to Japan. On the one hand, Japan completely abandoned her claims in Korea; on the other, she strongly fortified her islands in the Korean Channel and along the coasts of Kyushu, Shikoku, and Honshu in order to defend herself against possible attack from the continent. Entering on a passive stage of national existence, she began to devote her energy to domestic uplift instead of to ambitious plans in foreign countries.[31]

Gingetsu Ito says that, with the destruction of Kudara, Japan lost everything she had in Korea. In the seventh century, Japan no longer had an inch of land in Korea under her control, nor was there a single Korean who looked to Japan for protection.[32]

Dr. Kuroita, who is noted for his critical study of Japanese history, states that in the twenty-third year of the reign of the Emperor Kinmei (562) Shinra destroyed the Japanese government-general at Mimana and annexed that state. This marked the beginning of the downfall of Japan's power in Korea. From the time of the rule of her King Taiso, Shinra was a rising power there. In 660, when the kingdom of Kudara was destroyed by Shinra, assisted by the army of the T'ang, Japan realized the seriousness of her situation in Korea. She therefore first sent the royal prince of Kudara, who was then a hostage in Japan, back to Korea with a strong military force and had him reëstablish the kingdom. The aged empress of Japan, accompanied by her crown prince, proceeded to Kyushu at the head of a large army and supervised the military campaign. This campaign of Japan in Korea ended in a disastrous defeat at Hakko and Japan thereupon decided to abandon Korea. The remnant of the Japanese army, accompanied by thousands of Korean military men and civil officers as well as people of Kudara of the common classes, returned to Japan. The Kingdom of Korai was likewise destroyed in 668. Then a united Korea was ruled by Shinra.

The kingdoms in Korea had for a time been Japan's main source of national wealth. Besides the rich tribute received by Japan from these kingdoms, she had depended entirely upon Korea for both her intellectual and her industrial development. After the seventh century, that is, in the reign of the Empress Suiko, when Japan entered into direct international intercourse with China, the intellectual usefulness of Korea to Japan ceased. Moreover, because of their internal disturbances, the kingdoms in Korea had become heavy military and financial burdens to Japan: because of the traditional suzerain and tributary relations, Japan was obliged to undertake dangerous and expensive military expeditions in behalf of Mimana, of the kingdom of Kudara, and even of the kingdom of Korai. In this connection, Japan not only fought against Shinra, the newly risen power in Korea, but she also had to fight against the T'ang, the greatest political and intellectual power in Asia.

At this time, the middle of the seventh century, Japan undertook a great national reformation under the dominating influence of Chinese civilization. In the midst of this national reform, she suffered the great military disaster at Hakko while fighting against the allied armies of the T'ang and of Shinra. As a result of this defeat, the kingdom of Kudara, her faithful tributary state, was destroyed. Japan had nothing left to fight for in Korea. Had she continued to carry on this hopeless war and to fight against China, not only would her national existence have been threatened, but also her work of national reform, which had been so auspiciously begun, would have been seriously handicapped by reason of the impossibility of further importation of the elements of Chinese civilization. The Emperor Tenchi carefully studied the delicate and serious position of Japan in both domestic and foreign affairs, and came to the wisest and soundest decision; namely, to withdraw from Korea completely, maintain friendly relations with China, and devote the national energy of Japan to the completion of the national reformation and reorganization.[33]

In 1910, when Korea was annexed to Japan, the Japanese magazine *History and Geography,* in which are published the results of research by prominent scholars in the fields named in its title, issued a special edition, the Korean Number. In the preface to this edition, the chief editor made the following statement:

"The Emperor Tenchi abandoned entirely Japan's claims in Korea because of Japan's military disaster in that peninsula in 663, and because Japan might have suffered injury by remaining unfriendly with China. Since the time of the reign of the Emperor Tenchi, the relations between Japan and Korea have undergone radical change. Following the seventh century, Korea showed neither fear of Japan nor respect to her. She made it her national policy to depend upon the greatest of her neighbor nations. This state of affairs persisted for centuries. In Korea there were many changes in the ruling dynasties. Japan's national life was stormy at intervals. Finally, however, in 1868, the work of the imperial restoration was completed and New Japan emerged. With the restoration of the imperial rule, the empire adopted the policy of extending a helping hand to Korea. However, it was only through the Sino-Japanese and the Russo-Japanese wars that the work of Japan in Korea was completed. This great accomplishment may be regarded by some as the restoration of Japan's ruling power in Korea that she had lost in the seventh century. However, we must not look upon this great national event as the mere regaining of Japan's ruling power in Korea of the ancient period, but we should consider it as the natural outcome of the glorious life of our empire for two thousand years."

Dr. Shidehara contributed a valuable article to this magazine in which he reviewed the relations between Japan and Korea, the substance of which has already been translated (see pp. 235–36).[35]

Dr. Hoshino states that for centuries Korea made *Jidai* (i.e., dependence upon the greatest neighboring nation in order to maintain existence) her national policy and readily recognized the suzerainty of China. Because for generation after generation the Koreans maintained so spiritless and self-degrading a national life, it became second nature to them to be servile and to enjoy ease at any cost. In 1876, Korea was forced by Japan to conclude a treaty, in one of the provisions of which she declared herself an independent nation. In this way Korea on the one hand took a step merely to satisfy the demand of Japan, and on the other, continued her tributary obligation to China, which nation exercised suzerain power over her. It was only after the Sino-Japanese war in 1894–95 that Korea finally became free from the overlordship of China.[36]

Dr. Otokichi Omori, in an article in this same magazine, wrote to the following effect:

More than twelve hundred years have passed since the Emperor Tenchi (662–71) abandoned Japan's claims in Korea because it was more vital that Japan should complete her domestic reformation than to maintain the semblance of national power abroad.

During this long period, many dynasties in Korea rose and fell. All those dynasties, however, followed and made traditional the policy of maintaining suzerain and tributary relations with China.

Geographically, Korea adjoins the Chinese empire on the north. Japan is Korea's southern neighbor, separated from her only by a narrow strip of water. Therefore, whenever these two great powers came into conflict, Korea was always the battle ground. In 1868, when the work of the imperial restoration had been completed in Japan, the imperial government sent an envoy to Korea in the name of the emperor of Japan and requested that friendly relations be established. Korea refused on the ground that she knew of the kingdom of Japan but never had heard of the existence of the empire of Japan. She even refused to acknowledge the state paper presented by the envoy from Japan on the ground that terms used in the document violated international usage.

After years of international discord between the two nations, in 1876 Korea was forced to conclude a treaty with Japan, according to one of the provisions of which she was forced to declare herself an independent nation having equal rights with Japan. With this declaration by Korea, Japan introduced her to the world as an independent country and, at the same time, made Korea pledge to discontinue all her traditional obligations to China, thus putting an end to the time-honored suzerain and tributary relationship with China.[37]

CHAPTER II

APPENDIX 15

The Shogun and His Official Functions

"SHOGUN" is the abbreviation of *Sei-i Tai-shogun*. *Sei-i* means "Barbarian-subjugating" ("barbarian" refers to the Ainu; *Tai-shogun* means "Great General"; hence, *Sei-i Tai-shogun* means the great general who was commissioned to subjugate the Ainu). This was an official title created temporarily in 801 A.D., when the Ainu tribes had their greatest uprising and repeatedly defeated the imperial army. Tamuramaro, the outstanding military genius of the time, was appointed by the emperor as commander of the imperial army, and the special title was conferred on him. After the Ainu had been completely subjugated, in the middle of the ninth century, the title "Sei-i Tai-shogun" fell into disuse. In 1192, when Japan entered upon the Feudal Period, this ancient title was revived. Yoritomo of the Minamoto, the founder of the feudal military government, was appointed Sei-i Tai-shogun by the emperor. At that time there were neither Ainus nor any other barbarian tribes strong enough to warrant the revival of this official title. Therefore, although the title had lost its official significance, the emperor was nevertheless obliged to delegate completely his civil, military, diplomatic, judicial, and all other imperial authority to the title-holder. Consequently, throughout the Feudal Period, the shogun was the actual ruler of the empire. However, members of the Minamoto family and the princes of imperial blood were alone qualified to be appointed Sei-i Tai-shogun by the emperor.

APPENDIX 16

State Papers: Kublai Khan to the Ruler of Japan and to the King of Korea; the King of Korea to the Ruler of Japan

(1) THE FOLLOWING is a translation of the state paper which Kublai Khan sent to the ruler of Japan. It bore the date of "August, in the third year of the Chih-Yuan era [1266]." Kublai Khan's envoy while on his way to Japan encountered a great storm and was forced back

to Korea. Therefore this state paper did not reach Japan until January, 1268. In that year, the envoy of the king of Korea carried to Japan both this state paper of Kublai Khan and the state paper of the king of Korea.

The state paper of Kublai Khan dated August, 1266, reads:

"The Emperor of the Great Mongols being commissioned by Heaven hereby addresses the King of Japan. From time immemorial, rulers of small states the borders of which closely adjoined have always endeavored to maintain friendly relations with each other and have manifested mutual respect and trust. On our part, we, from the time of our forefathers, have received the heavenly command and have ruled the universe. Innumerable rulers from far-off strange lands have learned to fear our power and dignity and have longed for our virtuous rule and protection. They have come to pay homage to us of their own accord.

"When we ascended the throne, the innocent and helpless people of Korea had suffered long because of military struggles. We, therefore, ordered them to give up their arms, and to settle their border disputes amicably. Korea has become united under our suzerainty. Both the ruler and the people cheerfully present themselves at our court and pay due reverence to us. Although the legal relation between ourselves and the Korean ruler is that of sovereign and subject, yet in feeling we are as father and son. Korea is our eastern tributary state. It is geographically near to Japan. The state of affairs in our empire, as well as our relations with Korea, is already known to you and to your government. History records that from remote antiquity your kingdom has time and again established relations with the Middle Kingdom. However, since our accession, you have not yet sent an envoy to our court; neither have you indicated a desire to establish due relations with us. This apparent negligence on your part is probably to be accounted for by the fact that you have not yet been properly informed of the rise of our great empire. Therefore, we now send a special envoy bearing our state papers to inform you of our desire. We hope that henceforth you will enter into due relations with us, and that both our people and yours will enjoy peace and harmony.

"It is a teaching of the sages that the entire universe should be one home. Therefore, if Japan should remain aloof and should not establish due relations with us, thus staying outside of the home, it would be contrary to the doctrine of the sages. Neither we nor you would desire to appeal to arms to settle this question. I hereby leave the entire matter to your conscientious consideration."[1]

(2) In 1266, when Kublai Khan sent his envoy to Japan, China had not yet been completely conquered. Kublai Khan's envoy could approach Japan, therefore, only by going through Korea and then crossing the water. Consequently, Kublai Khan sent a personal letter to the king of Korea advising him to provide his envoy with a guide so that he might reach Japan safely. Kublai Khan's letter reads as follows:

"Chao Fun, a man from your kingdom, has recently come to our court and has informed us that Japan and your kingdom are in close proximity, being separated only by a narrow strip of water; and that Japan is a country that has admirable laws and methods of administration, and that during the reigns of the Han, of the T'ang, and of the succeeding dynasties sent envoys to the Middle Kingdom time and again, thus showing due respect. Therefore, we are now sending Hu Ti as our envoy to Japan with instructions to cause that kingdom to establish due relations with us. You are hereby advised to provide Hu Ti, our envoy, with a safe guide who will be able to let Japan know how to revere us. The entire responsibility in this important affair is thus entrusted to you. You should not seek excuse because of storms and other dangers of the water route in reaching Japan. Neither should you try to escape this responsibility because Japan is a country unknown to you. Your loyalty and sincerity are greatly depended upon. Consequently, you should exert yourself in assisting our envoy to succeed in his mission."[2]

Hu Ti, Kublai Khan's envoy, and Sung, the envoy of the king of Korea, who accompanied Hu Ti, failed to reach Japan because of a great storm. When Kublai Khan was informed of their failure, he was angered and accused the king of Korea of lack of sincerity and loyalty. He issued instructions time and again to the king of Korea urging him to put forth his best efforts to make Kublai Khan's desire known to Japan.

Finally, in September, 1267, the king of Korea sent Pan Fu as envoy to Japan and had him carry the original state paper of Ku-

blai Khan together with a personal letter from the king himself
addressed to the ruler of Japan. It read as follows:

"For many years, our country has served the Great Mongol Empire as a subject state and has used the calendar era of the Mongol
Emperor as the calendar of our kingdom in evidence of the fact
that our kingdom is a faithful tributary state of the Mongol empire. The Emperor, being a most brilliant and benevolent ruler,
has always regarded the entire universe as one home. All the people
who live in places where the sun and the moon shine have come
to admire the imperial virtue and to seek protection from the Emperor. Now, our Emperor desires to establish relations with your
country and he has entrusted me with this important work saying
that I should not make any excuse because of storms and dangers
of the sea. Thus, his imperial instructions are both urgent and imperative. Therefore, I am impelled to send our subject Pan Fu
and am having him carry to you the personal letter of our great
Emperor. According to historical records, your country has in the
past sent envoys to the Middle Kingdom, generation after generation. Will you not respect this traditional usage of your own country? What our great Emperor desires is not to seek tribute of value
from your country, but he desires that there shall not be any nation
in the universe where his fame and dignity are not respected. Also
he desires to make the people of every nation happy under his rule.
If you should send an envoy to his imperial court, the envoy would
be kindly received. Therefore, are you not willing to send an envoy
to the Mongol imperial court so that he may see how splendid a
reception is awaiting him? I sincerely leave the entire matter to
your kind consideration."[3]

APPENDIX 17

The Second State Paper Sent by Kublai Khan to the
Ruler of Japan

KUBLAI KHAN'S first state paper was not acknowledged by the ruler
of Japan. Because Kublai Khan could get no reply from Japan,
despite the fact that he demanded a reply time and again, he decided to send a second state paper. This time, he appointed one
of the most eminent statesmen of his time, Chao Liang-Pi. Stand-

ard histories give accounts of his departure under various dates. The *Imperial Authorized Edition of the History of the Mongols* states that Kublai Khan sent his envoy in December, 1269; the *New History of the Mongols* states that the envoy was sent in December, 1270. The histories written by Kimiya and by Yoshida both give the date of the arrival of the envoy in Japan as September, 1271. Nagao states in his history that the envoy left Peking in February, 1270, and arrived in Japan accompanied by the envoy from Korea in September, 1271. Miura says in his *History of the Kamakura Period* that the envoy did not arrive in Japan until 1273. Nevertheless, all these historians are in agreement with the following account:

Upon his arrival in Japan, the envoy Chao Liang-Pi persistently demanded that he be allowed to proceed to the national capital of Japan and in person hand the state paper of Kublai Khan to the ruler of Japan so that he might get a reply. His demand was not acceded to. Finally, as a sort of compromise, a copy of the state paper was handed to a Japanese official. This copy was sent to Kamakura, the military capital, and then to Kyoto, the imperial capital. Like the first state paper, it contained threatening military terms; therefore the original of the state paper was not requested of Chao, but rather he and his party were requested to depart from Japan.

When leaving Japan, Chao compelled twelve Japanese to accompany him. Upon his return to China, he sent these Japanese to the imperial court of Kublai Khan at Peking to bear witness that he had been in Japan. In 1273, Chao again went to Dazai-fu, Japan, but, as formerly, he did not succeed in proceeding to the national capital. He was finally driven from Japan in disgrace. In June, 1273, Chao went to Peking, and presented the entire matter to Kublai Khan in person. To sum up: In December, 1269, Chao Liang-Pi was appointed envoy to Japan by Kublai Khan, and provided with the second state paper. But Chao failed in his mission. This caused Kublai Khan to appeal to arms, and resulted in the invasion of Japan by the first armada in 1274.

The second state paper of Kublai Khan read as follows:

"The Great Ruler of the World will have no nation in the universe where his fame and dignity are not respected. Korea and our empire have long been one home. Your kingdom has thus become our neighbor nation. Therefore, we sent an envoy some years ago, provided with our personal letter, and instructed him to establish due relations with your country. The men at your frontier ignorantly and stubbornly stood in his way and made it impossible for our envoy to carry out the mission entrusted to him. He and his party therefore returned to us, bringing with them two of your countrymen by force. We instructed our officials to treat them kindly and allow them to return to their homes in Japan. At the same time, we sent an official note to you with respect to the establishment of relations with our empire. Since that time, we have heard nothing from you.

"On our part, in Korea, a man named Lin Yen took advantage of the undeserved trust and overconfidence of his king. He controlled the affairs of the kingdom in an arbitrary way, thus bringing about a great national disturbance. This state of affairs in Korea prevented our sending another envoy to you. Perhaps it was because of this rebellion in Korea that you could not send an envoy to our court. Possibly, however, you sent an envoy to our empire, and he failed to reach us because the road was blockaded by the Lin Yen rebellion. Otherwise, Japan, which has long been recognized as a nation of great courtesy and propriety, would certainly not have committed this unaccountable impropriety of remaining out of communication with us.

"The Lin Yen rebellion in Korea has now been suppressed; the royal throne has been restored to the king; the ruler of Korea and his subjects are enjoying peace and prosperity. We, therefore, are sending Chao Liang-Pi as our envoy, bearing our state papers addressed to you. Will you not appoint an envoy to us and have him come to our court in company with our envoy when he returns home? If so, the harmonious and excellent work due to a neighbor nation will be admirably performed by you. Neither we nor you nor anybody else would be happy if we should be forced to appeal to arms because of your further delay in settling this pending problem between our nation and yours. We leave the entire matter to your conscientious consideration."[4]

Appendix 18

Source Material on Kublai Khan's Armadas

THE HISTORICAL RECORDS in China, Japan, and Korea are all agreed with respect to the size of Kublai Khan's first armada, which consisted of 900 war vessels. Widely varying statements are made, however, concerning its fighting strength. The *Imperial Authorized Edition of the History of the Mongols* (vol. 208, p. 9) states that the fighting strength was 15,000 men. Shao-Min Ko in the *New History of the Mongols* (vol. 250, p. 5) states that the combined number of Mongols and Chinese was 15,000. The king of Korea, however, was instructed by Kublai Khan to send an additional 1600 Korean fighting men to aid the armada. Of his own accord, the Korean king sent 8000 instead of the required 1600, thus making a total of 23,000. Yoshida, in his *History of Japan* (vol. 8, p. 179), states that the men in Kublai Khan's first armada of 1274 consisted of 25,000 Chinese and Mongols, 8000 Koreans, and 7000 helpers and members of the crews, the total number being 40,000 men. This statement of Yoshida's is verified in volume 125—page 3—of the *Imperial Authorized Edition of the History of the Mongols,* thus contradicting the statement made in volume 208 of the same work.

In volume 125 it is stated that in the tenth year of the Chih Yuan era, Liu Fu-Heng was appointed assistant commanding general. At the head of 40,000 men, on 900 war vessels, he invaded Japan and defeated Japanese troops, 100,000 strong, in every engagement. Miura says, in his *History of the Kamakura Period* (p. 477), "Kublai Khan's fighting men consisted of 25,000 Mongolians and Chinese together with 8000 Koreans, the total number being 33,000." A Korean history, *Kaoli-Shi,* verifies Miura's statement that the fighting force of Kublai Khan was 25,000 Mongolians and Chinese in addition to the Korean troops. Hayashi's *History of Korea* (p. 83) states that the men in the armada of 1274 consisted of 25,000 Chinese and Mongolians and 8000 Koreans.

On the whole, it is generally believed that the total numerical strength of Kublai Khan's fighting men was appreciably more than 30,000. Kublai Khan's army was incomparably better trained and equipped than was the Japanese army; it was even provided with firearms. In the brief war of but two weeks, Kublai Khan's army defeated the Japanese in every engagement and took great numbers of prisoners. Consequently, even though the armada had to depart suddenly from Japan because half its vessels were destroyed and 13,000 men were drowned in a single night by reason of the great storm, the Mongols were nevertheless able to carry hundreds of Japanese prisoners to the continent.

Historical records in China, Japan, and Korea concerning the second armada, which came to Japanese waters in 1281, are agreed in almost every detail. The armada consisted of 45,000 war vessels with a force of fighting men of about 150,000. This time Japan was better prepared in a military way. She also had great confidence in divine protection. So she fought successfully for two months, thus preventing the landing of Kublai Khan's men. Then a great storm, that lasted two days and two nights, destroyed the armada and drowned most of the men. Chinese and Korean histories give exaggerated accounts of this catastrophe. Some Chinese histories state that only three of Kublai Khan's fighting men were able to return to China. Japanese historians, after careful research and investigation, have found that the disaster was not so complete as has been recorded. It is now generally conceded that out of the original 45,000 war vessels, approximately 200 made a safe return to either China or to Korea; and that out of 150,000 fighting men, at least one-fifth, that is, 30,000 men, survived.[5]

CHAPTER III

APPENDIX 19

The Three Sacred Imperial Insignia and the Throne of Japan

IN JAPAN, no coronation celebration is observed in connection with the accession to the throne, as in other kingdoms and empires, but an enthronement celebration is held, and it is regarded as most sacred. The imperial crown has no connection with the throne, but the three sacred imperial insignia are so inseparably connected with the throne that they are held in as high regard as is the "throne" itself. These three sacred imperial insignia consist of the sacred mirror, the sacred sword, and the sacred jewel. According to the national tradition, when the Sun Goddess sent her grandson, Ninigi, from Heaven to Japan to rule that nation, she presented to him a mirror, a sword, and a jewel, saying: "These three sacred objects constitute the habitation of my divine soul. Keep them with you always, whether waking or sleeping. Revere them and obtain my divine instructions through them whenever you are confronted with serious problems. The nation so founded and conducted will be able to maintain its existence as long as Heaven and Earth endure." This divine behest had been faithfully obeyed until the time of the tenth emperor, Sujin. In his time human beings were sinful, and moral standards had changed. Sujin concluded that human habitations were no longer suitable for the residence of the divine soul of the Sun Goddess. He therefore built a separate edifice and placed therein the sacred mirror and the sacred sword. The eleventh emperor, Suinin, in accordance with divine instructions, selected a place called Ise and there he built a permanent national temple wherein the divine soul of the Sun Goddess might dwell. He also placed the sacred mirror within the temple as an object of worship. The twelfth emperor, Keiko, built a second national temple at Atsuta into which he put the sacred sword as an object of worship. The sacred jewel was kept in the imperial palace. Thus the three original sacred objects were distributed in three different places, in which they remain to this day. Prior to the removal of the sacred mirror and the sacred sword from the imperial palace, the tenth emperor, Sujin, had ordered replicas made of the mirror and the sword. The original sacred jewel and these two replicas have since been known as the "Three Sacred Imperial Insignia," and have become inseparably associated with the imperial throne. Since the time of the tenth emperor, Sujin, it has been a national tradition as well as a provision of the "Imperial House Law" that the ruling emperor, before his accession, must qualify (1) as a prince of the imperial blood and heir apparent to the throne and (2) as the possessor of the three sacred imperial insignia. At those times at which Japan had two emperors each of whom claimed to be the rightful ruler, the one who had possession of the three sacred insignia was recognized as the emperor and the other was considered a pretender. The situation of the Emperor Gokomatsu in the four-teenth century, while Japan was under the rule of the Northern and Southern dynasties, clearly illustrates this regulation. The Em-peror Gokomatsu ruled Japan for twenty-nine years (1383–1412), although he is only credited with a rule of twenty years, having been regarded during the first nine years of his reign as being only a pretender. The Emperor Gokameyama, who was the emperor of the Southern dynasty during those nine years, was considered the rightful emperor because of his possession of the three sacred im-perial insignia. In 1392, when the Northern and Southern imperial governments were united, the Emperor Gokameyama transferred the three sacred imperial insignia to the Emperor Gokomatsu, who was then recognized as the ninety-ninth emperor, successor to Gokameyama, the ninety-eighth emperor. Throughout the entire twenty-nine years of his reign (nine years as so-called pretender and twenty years as emperor), he made Kyoto his imperial capital and occupied the same imperial throne. Japan thus has no actual throne; the seat occupied by the emperor who possesses the three sacred imperial insignia is known as the throne, no matter in what part of Japan it may be.[1]

APPENDIX 20

*The Imperial Edict of 1368 Issued by the Emperor Tai-Tsu,
Founder of the Ming Dynasty, to the Rulers of Annam,
Cochin China, Korea, and Japan*

"OF YORE, when our sovereigns ruled our nation, all countries, near and far, where the sun and the moon shone, enjoyed their benevolent rule. Our Middle Nation was thus the center of peace and prosperity as well as of admiration and devotion. All the barbarian nations, north, south, east, and west, paid reverence and made ready submission and obeisance. However, the Yuan [Mongols] intruded upon and debased our nation. Subsequently, they lost their fighting power, and our nation entered upon a period of military struggle and chaos. Especially in the past seventeen years, national undertakings and procedures have been completely disrupted, and intercourse and relations with outside nations have been discontinued. Prompted by the suffering of the people, we have started the work of national reorganization at Kiang-Tso. We have conquered and subjugated all the unruly and disorderly military chiefs and their followers, and our nation has thereby been pacified and united. We have responded to the earnest appeals and entreaties of our subjects and people and have made ourselves masters of the nation. 'Tai-Ming' has been adopted as the name of our empire, and 'Hung-Wu' as the name of our era. Having conquered the Yuan and having completely occupied their national capital, the domain of our empire now includes the entire Middle Kingdom and we are recognized by Heaven as successors to the sovereigns of the former dynasty. All nations, both far and near, have gained tranquillity and their people are enjoying prosperity and happiness under our benevolent administration. You, the chiefs of the four barbarian nations [Annam, Cochin China, Korea, and Japan], because of your geographical distance from us, have perhaps not heard of our heavenly mission. Therefore, we are issuing this imperial edict in order to let you know that reverence is due from you to our throne."[2]

The Emperor Tai-Tsu, the founder of the Ming dynasty, believed that the founding of his empire in China would automatically establish suzerain and tributary relationships with the smaller nations. He, therefore, in the first year of his reign (1368), issued imperial edicts to the rulers of the four so-called "barbarian nations," demanding that they recognize his suzerainty. Annam, Cochin China, and Korea promptly responded to the demand of the Ming and in the following year (1369) they sent tribute-bearing envoys to the Ming throne. Japan not only ignored the demand of the Ming, but also, in January, 1369, Japanese pirates made an inroad into Shantung province. In May and June, 1370, they invaded Shantung, Chekiang, and Fukien provinces, plundering and ravaging as they went. In March, 1369, the Ming emperor sent an envoy to Japan bearing state papers saying that, unless Japan should send a tribute-bearing envoy to the imperial court of the Ming without delay, she might as well make preparations for the defense of her country. If she should continue to permit her subjects to ravage the coast of China, the imperial government of the Ming would send a strong military force to Japan and inflict due punishment upon both the ruler and the people. One year later, in March, 1370, the Ming emperor again sent a state paper to Japan saying that she would have to suffer the consequences of her accumulated wickedness. In accordance with his heavenly mission the Ming emperor was about to send a punitive expedition, and because of years of unsatisfactory diplomatic negotiations the Ming emperor threatened Japan with the more determination. Therefore, in 1382, the imperial prince Kanenaga, who was the military governor-general of Kyushu under the Southern imperial government of Japan, replied to the state paper of the Ming emperor, expressing his readiness to accept the Ming's challenge of war.

APPENDIX 21

State Paper from Prince Kanenaga, of the Southern Imperial Dynasty of Japan, to the Ming Emperor, 1382

"IN CHINA of yore, the Three Sovereigns established human relationships and national organizations. The Five Emperors laid down the traditional rule of the dynastic succession. This does not imply that China alone had great sovereigns and that other nations had none. Heaven and earth are vast and extensive and cannot be placed under the sovereignty of a single master. The universe is great and wide. Many states exist therein and pursue their respective heavenly missions. By the grace of Heaven, the world belongs to all and no individual may claim it as his own. We live in Japan, a country small in size and far from the continent. Our cities and fortresses scarcely number sixty; our domain barely extends three thousand miles. Nevertheless, we are well satisfied with our share and with our destiny. You, as the sovereign of China, have ten thousand chariots of war at your command. Your cities and fortresses exceed several thousands in number. Your domain extends a million miles. But you are not satisfied with this vast gift of Heaven. You yield to the desire to conquer other nations. . . . We understand that you have a plan for war. We have a plan for defense. We are informed that you have selected trusted generals and instructed them to take the best of your troops to invade our country. Besides our military preparation, we have a geographical advantage: our country has the natural defenses of sea and mountains. We shall certainly not kneel down by the roadside and permit your troops to trample over our country. Ready submission might not insure to us our safety and our lives; stubborn opposition might not terminate in our destruction and death. We are ready to repeat the famous war game of Mount Garan. We have no fear of the outcome. Should you win and we lose, it would satisfy you. Should we win and you lose, it would bring neither satisfaction nor glory to our country, because we seek reverently to adhere to the instructions of our forefathers; namely, 'To maintain peace is the highest aim and to refrain from war is the strongest policy of our nation. To keep people free from the suffering consequent upon war and to rescue them from hardship and misery are the duties of the Ruler.'

"Peace or war is at your command. I hereby send an envoy bearing this state paper, and thus submit the entire matter to you for your consideration."[3]

The Emperor Tai-Tsu, the founder of the Ming dynasty, conducted international affairs with Japan almost exclusively through the *Seisei-Fu* ("Kyushu Military Government-General") of the Southern imperial government of Japan. Prince Kanenaga, the head of the Seisei-Fu, ignored entirely the demand of the Ming for suzerainty over Japan, and in transacting national affairs with China, he treated her as a nation of equal standing. When the Emperor Tai-Tsu repeatedly threatened Japan with war, Prince Kanenaga replied that, although it was the national policy of Japan to maintain peace with foreign nations, at the same time Japan was always ready to engage in war when war was forced upon her. Upon receipt of this state paper, the Emperor Tai-Tsu was deeply offended. Yet, because he feared a possible repetition of the great disaster that befell the armada and the armies of Kublai Khan in Japanese waters in the thirteenth century, he abandoned his plan of invading Japan. Thereafter he classed Japan among the fifteen nations that were beyond the control of China, and broke off all relations with her. At the same time, the Emperor Tai-Tsu instructed his government to complete works of defense along the entire coast of China in order to protect her from the ravages of the Japanese pirates.

This condition obtained until the beginning of the fifteenth century, when the third Ashikaga shogun, Yoshimitsu, gained complete control of Japan, in consequence of the unification of the Northern and Southern imperial governments. At that time, Yoshimitsu bartered away the dignity and honor of Japan for mere economic gain and established relations with China on terms that were satisfactory to the Ming court.

APPENDIX 22

Relations Between Japan and Korea and the National Standing of Each with Respect to China

IN THE MIDDLE of the seventh century, after the annihilation of her military and naval forces in Korea, Japan abandoned her claims in that peninsula. In the second half of the thirteenth century, Kublai Khan conquered Korea. Although Korea was permitted to maintain her existence as a tributary state of China, in actual fact she was an integral part of the Mongol empire. Throughout the quarter-century that Kublai Khan was conducting a military campaign against Japan, Korea placed both her military forces and provisions at his disposal. On many occasions, his military head-quarters for the invasion of Japan were established within the confines of the Korean kingdom. After the annihilation of Kublai Khan's armada in 1281, and the subsequent abandonment of his plan to conquer Japan, neither China nor Korea made peace with Japan. On the contrary, a state of war existed. Hence, in the fourteenth and fifteenth centuries, when the attacks and ravages of Japanese pirates upon the Korean coast became increasingly serious, there was no diplomatic channel by which Korea might approach Japan concerning this outrage. Finally, the Buddhist church and its priests were employed as a medium of negotiations, and the Korean government sent a state paper to Japan by a Buddhist priest.

The Ashikaga shogunate government had a Japanese Buddhist priest write the reply to this Korean state paper on behalf of the shogun. Later, the shogun issued an official written statement to a prominent officer of his government whenever a Korean envoy bearing a state paper came to Japan. The shogun ordered this officer to transact the nation's affairs with Korea in accordance with his written instructions. In and after the fifteenth century, when international relations between Japan and Korea had been fully established and official communication had come to be conducted directly between the two governments, all the state papers of Korea were addressed to the shogun as "His Royal Highness the King of Japan." The ruler of Korea, in signing these papers, used the title, "King of Korea." The state papers of Japan were always addressed to the ruler of Korea as "His Royal Highness the King of Korea." These papers were signed by the shogun, who sometimes used his family and his given name, and at other times the title, "King of Japan."

When the state papers exchanged between Korea and Japan mentioned the Ming emperor of China and his Court, the rulers of both Japan and Korea, respectively, always employed the terms, "His Majesty the Emperor of the Great Ming," and "Imperial Court of Heavenly Authority." In the state papers that were sent from either Japan or Korea to China, the shogun of Japan and the ruler of Korea used an identical form, namely, "His Majesty the Emperor of the Great Ming." These papers were signed, respectively, "The King of Japan, a subject of the Ming Emperor," and "The King of Korea, a subject of the Ming Emperor."

These Japanese and Korean state papers were always dated according to the Chinese national calendar, that is, by referring to the year on the throne of the ruling Ming emperor. Neither Japan nor Korea ever used its own national calendar. In all the imperial edicts and state papers issued by the Ming emperor of China to the ruler of Japan and to the ruler of Korea, the terms, "You, the King of Japan," and "You, the King of Korea," were used, respectively. All these historical documents are still extant today. They evidence the facts that, for a period of nearly two hundred years, terminating in the latter part of the sixteenth century: (a) Japan and Korea looked upon China, under the Ming dynasty, as their suzerain power; (b) the Ming emperors of China always regarded Japan and Korea as their tributary states; and (c) Japan and Korea recognized each other as nations of equal standing.

DOCUMENT 1

De Facto State Paper Written by a Japanese Buddhist Priest and Sent to Korea under Date of December 27, 1392

"I, the head priest of Shokoku Joten Monastery, Japan, respectfully reply to the state ministers, their excellencies of the government of Korea. In the early winter of this year, Kakutai, a Buddhist priest of your country, came to Japan in accordance with your instructions and presented the state papers of your country to our shogunate government. The shogun was informed thereby that, because of the continuous invasions and plunderings of the Japanese pirates along the Korean coast, Japan and Korea were steadily approaching a breaking point. The shogun deeply regrets this situation. For several years past, our subjects in distant places along the coast have violated national and humane laws, and have committed great violence. The rulers and the subjects in our country have felt greatly ashamed of this situation. The shogun has already instructed the governor-general of Kyushu strictly to prohibit piracy and to confiscate all pirate ships. The shogun has also ordered that he seek out in various parts of Japan all the

Koreans who have been taken prisoners by the pirates, and return them to their native land. Our government is in this way sincerely preparing to establish friendly relations with Korea with the hope that both nations may enjoy permanent peace. However, we in Japan have no established usage whereby the shogun and his officers may exchange communications with the rulers and officers of nations beyond the water. Therefore, the shogun cannot reply personally to the state paper sent us from your country. Consequently, I, a Buddhist priest, have been instructed by the shogun to write you on his behalf and to pay due respect to your government and your nation. We hope that the step thus taken will not be looked upon by you as a breach of courtesy. A Buddhist priest, Juin, is being sent to you with instructions to deliver orally further details in this matter."[4]

DOCUMENT 2

In August, 1398, Yoshimitsu, the third Ashikaga shogun, issued the following written instructions to Lord Ouchi, the governor-general of Kyushu, directing him how he should deal with the Korean envoy who was returning to Korea.

"This instruction is hereby given to you, Ouchi Sakyo-no-Tayu. The Korean envoy, in compliance with the command of his government, came to our country, crossing waters of vast expanse. He brought us a gift of great value from his nation, thus showing us great courtesy. We have highly appreciated this. Now that this envoy is returning to his country, we should send products of our land in recognition of this gift and as a token of our good will. You are also instructed to inform the Korean envoy that all the pirates and persons of the unruly class in Kyushu have been arrested and punished in accordance with the provisions of our laws, and that we are sending troops under the convoy of our fleet to various far-off islands with the purpose of annihilating all the remaining pirate bands. Therefore, from this time on, all ships coming from and returning to Korea will be safeguarded. Thus will the friendship of the two nations be maintained.

"For several years past, we have made many earnest attempts to publish the *Daizo-Kyo*, a standard Buddhistic sutra, but have not yet succeeded. According to our understanding, Korea has an excellent edition of this sutra. We would therefore ask that Korea meet our long-felt need by sending us a complete set of this edition. If Korea should grant this request, the propagation of Buddhism toward the East would be materially advanced. We also desire to have a large Buddhistic church bell made of copper, and we also wish to secure good medicinal herbs from Korea. The Buddhistic sutras and accessories are needed in our country in order to save our people from suffering in a future existence. The medicinal herbs will enable our people to enjoy health and longevity in this present world. Korea possesses them in great abundance. You are imperatively instructed to convey these desires to the Korean envoy and to impress him with our great need of and desire for them, in order that we may not fail to obtain them."[5]

DOCUMENT 3

The three following papers are of no special historical value, because no serious international problems are dealt with therein; but they do reveal certain interesting facts, namely: (1) in the beginning of the fifteenth century, the Japanese and the Korean governments began to conduct their international intercourse directly, thus opening diplomatic channels; (2) in the beginning of the fifteenth century, also, for the first time in their history, the terms, "His Royal Highness the King of Japan," and "His Royal Highness the King of Korea," were used in all state papers and official communications exchanged between these two nations. Each thereby recognized the other's country as of equal standing with his own; (3) the contents of these documents show that, in the fifteenth century, the Buddhistic sutras had great national value. They also reveal that, throughout this century, Korea was a nation far superior to Japan, both intellectually and industrially.

(1) In May, 1422, Yoshimochi, the fourth Ashikaga shogun, wrote to the king of Korea saying:

"I, Yoshimochi of Japan, respectfully reply to His Royal Highness, the King of Korea. Owing to the great distance by water, I have delayed replying to your communication. As it is the wet season, we have no clear days. Heavy storms ravage the land. Nevertheless, we are impressed with the great sublimity of the heavenly power. I am happy to congratulate you upon your good health and your increasing prosperity. We hereby express our sincere gratitude for and appreciation of the Buddhistic sutras which you have presented to us in compliance with our request.

"We must now again request you to make us another gift, even though it may seem that we are making endless demands. We must have sutras so that our people may prepare themselves for the blessings of Buddha, during their existence in this present world. Therefore, I am asking that you generously supply us with a complete set of the seven thousand volumes of the standard Buddhistic sutras. . . ."[6]

In the following year, when the Korean envoy was about to return home, the Japanese government sought out a number of Korean prisoners and sent them back to Korea with the envoy and his party. By this Korean envoy, Yoshimochi again sent a communication to the king of Korea saying that, instead of a set of the standard Buddhistic sutras, he really wanted the original engraved printing blocks, so that Japan might print great numbers of copies. He also said that, according to his understanding, Korea had more than one set of these blocks. Therefore, he sincerely hoped that the king would be good enough to send one set of them to Japan. In August, 1424, Yoshimochi wrote again to the king of Korea asking for the original blocks of the seven thousand volumes of the Buddhistic sutras. The complete work covered several hundred thousand of these heavy blocks. They were objects of great intrinsic value and were regarded as one of the greatest national treasures of Korea. Therefore, in May, 1425, the king of Korea wrote to Yoshimochi, saying:

"The King of Korea respectfully replies to His Royal Highness the King of Japan. Your envoy has arrived with your communication, through which we have learned of your present activities as well as of your prosperity and health. We have also received the excellent gift sent by you, for which we would express our gratitude. As for the original printing blocks of the standard Buddhistic sutras that you requested, we should like to say that we have but one set of the printing blocks. They are a sacred national bequest from our forefathers, having been handed down for generations. Consequently, though we regret it, we are unable to comply with your request. We hope that you will understand our situation."[7]

(2) Very probably, after the receipt of the Korean king's letter of May, 1425, Japan gave up her idea of obtaining the original printing blocks of the standard Buddhistic sutras and apparently compromised with Korea to her own satisfaction by receiving, instead, a set of the volumes. In a state paper of Korea dated March 28, 1460, the king of Korea stated that, in October, 1459, the Korean government had sent to Japan a shipload of gifts, including a set of the volumes of the standard Buddhistic sutras, together with fourteen sets of other Buddhistic works, including treatises and comments of distinguished Buddhist scholars, as well as great quantities of various kinds of medicinal herbs, along with several pieces of tiger, leopard, and other skins. Unfortunately, the ship had encountered a great storm and had gone to the bottom of the sea.

On August 4, 1476, the eighth shogun, Yoshimasa, wrote a letter to the king of Korea, saying:

"I respectfully present this writing to His Royal Highness the King of Korea. To inquire concerning each other's welfare, thereby maintaining international friendship, has been a practice of Korea and Japan for many generations. However, owing to the great distance, we have sometimes failed to live up to this national courtesy. This should not be construed as negligence. Now, with respect to the seven thousand volumes of the standard Buddhistic sutras, our country has still been unable to engrave printing blocks for them. Therefore, whenever we desire to have a complete set of these sutras, we always look to you to provide us with them, out of your generosity. . . . The Ankokuji monastery in Echizen Province in our country, which has long been the Buddhist center in the northern part of Japan, is now in urgent need of this set. Therefore, I appeal to your generosity in this matter."[8]

On May 12, 1482, the king of Korea sent to Japan a complete set of the sutras, as requested, together with quantities of medicinal herbs. In 1485, Japan made another request for another set. In the following year, 1486, the king of Korea wrote a letter addressed to "His Royal Highness the King of Japan" (the ninth Ashikaga shogun, Yoshihisa). In this letter, the king of Korea first mentioned the great civil war that was raging in Japan. He also complained incidentally of the activity of Japanese pirates along the coast of his own land. He concluded his letter with another request for sutras, as follows:

"With respect to the seven thousand volumes of the Buddhistic sutras for which you have made a request, we have made every effort to obtain a complete set, but have found one nowhere. We shall continue our search, and if we find a set we will send it to you without delay."[9]

Japan repeated this demand in 1487, 1488, and in 1489. So, in September, 1489, the king of Korea wrote a letter to Japan, as follows:

"The King of Korea respectfully replies to His Royal Highness the King of Japan. Your special envoy bearing a state paper has come to us. Through him, we have been informed of your good health and prosperity. We have also received your thoughtful gift. Permit us to express our happiness at your condition, together with our gratitude for your gift. Concerning the seven thousand volumes of the standard Buddhistic sutras: In the past we have had a number of sets of this work, but at present our stock is exhausted. In our letter of 1486 we made a statement to this effect. At the same time, we sent such odd numbers as were obtainable. We now again regret our inability to meet your request. However, we will send men to all the Buddhist monasteries in our country with the hope of gathering odd copies here and there so that we may thus obtain a complete set."[10]

Two years later, in October, 1491, the king of Korea finally succeeded in assembling a complete set of the seven thousand volumes of the Buddhistic sutras and sent it to Japan.[11]

(3) In the sixteenth century, how to obtain from Korea copies of the seven thousand volumes of the standard Buddhistic sutras was still a national problem in Japan. In 1499 and in 1503, Yoshizumi, the eleventh Ashikaga shogun, wrote letters to the king of Korea in which he styled himself "King of Japan." In the letter of 1499, Yoshizumi said:

"This letter is respectfully addressed to His Royal Highness, the King of Korea. The year is steadily approaching its end. I hope that you are enjoying prosperity and good health. Whenever we send an envoy for the purpose of cultivating international friendship, we always make a request for the set of the seven thousand volumes of the standard Buddhistic sutras. Why do we so continuously make this request? It is because all the leading Buddhist monasteries in our country have made it their ambition to possess complete copies of the *Daizo* [the seven thousand volumes of the standard Buddhistic sutras]. These Buddhist monasteries strive by means of this great work to save the people and to promote the national welfare under the blessing of Buddha. By reason of this, in former times, our forefathers requested your country to supply us with the original printing blocks of the *Daizo,* but your government refused to comply with our request and said: 'We have but one set of the printing blocks of the 7000 volumes of the standard Buddhistic sutras. They are a sacred national bequest from our forefathers, having been handed down for generations. Consequently, to our regret, we are unable to comply with your request.' From the time that you definitely refused to send us the original printing blocks, it has been our practice to content ourselves with getting from you, from time to time, complete sets of the *Daizo,* as gifts. However, in the Eleven-Year Great Civil War [which started in 1467] most of our Buddhist monasteries lost their sets of the *Daizo.* The people in our nation are now spiritually destitute because of the loss of these standard sacred books of Buddha. We are therefore sending Seiryu as our special envoy with instructions to obtain at least one complete set of the *Daizo* as a gift from your country. Upon his arrival he will give orally further details in this very urgent matter.... The products of our land, as listed on a separate sheet, are respectfully sent for your kind acceptance. We are confronting a snowy winter. Hoping that you are well and able to withstand this threatening weather, I am,   Yoshizumi."[12]

Appendix 23

International Relations Between Japan and China in the Ashikaga Period

IT IS A RECOGNIZED historical fact that throughout the greater part of the Ashikaga period China was, diplomatically, the suzerain power over Japan. How and why Yoshimitsu, as the ruler of Japan, approached the Ming throne and served the Ming emperor, styling himself the emperor's subject, is a much mooted problem. The following translations are of selections from the works of Japanese scholars noted for their historical research.

(1) TSUJI, ZENNOSUKE. *Kaigai Kotsu-Shiwa* (Historical Account of Communications of Japan with Nations Beyond the Seas; Tokyo, 1930), pp. 313–16.

"In the state paper sent by the Ming emperor to Yoshimitsu in 1402, the term, 'You, the King of Japan,' was used. At the same time, the *Taito-Reki* (the Ming national calendar) was sent to Yoshimitsu with instructions to use dates determined by reference to the ruling year of the Ming throne. In this way, the Ming emperor indicated his conception of Yoshimitsu as his subject and of Japan as a tributary state. He also recognized Yoshimitsu as the ruler of Japan and addressed him as the 'King of Japan.' For his part, Yoshimitsu acted in strict compliance with the will of the Ming emperor. In all the state papers and memorials that he sent to the Ming throne, he styled himself the 'King of Japan, a subject [of the Ming Emperor].' He also used the dates of the Ming national calendar, instead of the dates of the calendar of Japan. By thus styling himself 'King of Japan' and by using the dates of the Ming calendar, Yoshimitsu showed his loyalty to the Ming throne; indeed, he accepted the Ming investiture as 'King of Japan.' Even in the time of Yoshimitsu, such noted scholars as Shuho and Zuikei criticized these acts and said: 'To style himself "King" in the memorial that Yoshimitsu sent to the Ming throne is tantamount to accepting the Ming investiture. To use the word "subject" in the memorial is absolutely wrong.' Shurin Keijo described what happened in his day in his work entitled *Kanrin Koroshu:* 'In August, in the ninth year of the Oyei era [1402], Japan welcomed the ships sent by the Great Ming. On September 5, Tenrin Zenshi, the envoy of the Great Ming, was received in grand style at *Kitayama Betsu-gyo* [Yoshimitsu's mansion]. The aged emperor of the Great Ming invested Yoshimitsu with the kingship. A tremendous quantity of rare and wonderful treasures, silk brocades, and other valuable woven goods was brought by the Ming envoy.' Statements of this sort establish that, at the time of Yoshimitsu, it was fully recognized that state papers from the Ming emperor contained an account of the investiture of Yoshimitsu as king of Japan, and that Yoshimitsu accepted the investiture.

"In the state papers that the Ming emperor, Cheng-Tsu, sent to Yoshimitsu, the statement, 'The Seal is conferred upon you', appears in two different papers. Moreover, in his written statement, Yoshimochi, the son of Yoshimitsu, gave the following reasons for his desire to terminate the national relationship with the Ming. 'When my father, Yoshimitsu, was taken seriously ill, by means of divination we learned that his sickness was a divine punishment. We therefore urgently prayed to the various gods and begged their forgiveness. Then the god of supreme power made a revelation through an oracle. It was as follows: "From the time of the nation's founding, none ever degraded himself so far as to style himself a subject of a foreign nation. Yoshimitsu ignored the national traditions and violated the laws of our sacred sovereigns of former days. Both the calendar and the seal of a foreign nation were given him. Instead of sending them back, as he should have done, he accepted and used them. This wrong committed by Yoshimitsu has brought his present illness upon him." ' An explanation of the nature of the seal given by a foreign ruler to Yoshimitsu is to be found in the diary of Mansai Junko, a prominent statesman of the Ashikaga period. It reads as follows: 'By an understanding with successive Chinese emperors, all the Ashikaga shoguns, beginning with Rokuyen-In [Yoshimitsu], have become kings of Japan. In fact, the seal presented by the Chinese emperor has engraved upon it the words, "King of Japan." '

"The imperial gift of the seal, as described in state papers, was a gift of the official seal to the king of Japan. Consequently, the imperial gift of the seal to Yoshimitsu was, in fact, his investiture as king of Japan by the Ming emperor. According to the *Taimin Kaiten* (National Code of the Ming Empire), the rulers of Korea, of Liu Chiu, of Cochin China, and of Annam are entitled to receive seals of solid gold from the Ming throne. Only gilded seals are given to the rulers of other tributary states of China. Whether a seal of solid gold or a gilded seal is to be given to the ruler of Japan is not definitely stated in the National Code of the Ming Empire. However, since the state paper of the Ming emperor sent to Yoshimitsu reads, 'We hereby confer the Seal upon you', Yoshimitsu must have received the investiture of kingship from the Ming emperor, the same as did the ruler of Korea. Yoshimitsu certainly must have known that he violated the national tradition, acted disloyally to the imperial throne of Japan, and brought great disgrace and shame upon Japan by thus receiving investiture as king of Japan at the hands of the Ming emperor.

"Yoshimitsu willingly accepted this investiture and styled himself 'A subject of the Ming Emperor'. He did this in order to gain trade concessions with their attendant profits from the Ming. This act of Yoshimitsu in thus degrading Japan and sacrificing the national dignity and honor to any degree required of him, provided only that he might gain money and economic advantage, is so outrageous that we have no fit words by which to describe it."

(2) KUROITA, KATSUMI. *Kokushi-no-Kenkyu* (Research in the National History of Japan; Tokyo, 1918), pp. 478–79.

"In 1402, the Ming emperor sent a state paper to Yoshimitsu in which he addressed him, 'You, the King of Japan'. In his reply to the Ming emperor, Yoshimitsu styled himself as 'the King of Japan, a subject of the Ming Emperor'. Yoshimitsu also employed dates in accordance with the Ming national calendar. He thus degraded the national standing of Japan and brought disgrace and injury upon his nation. [One of the original documents exchanged between Yoshimitsu and the Ming emperor is to be found in the archives of the Shokokuji monastery at Kyoto.] Yoshimitsu thus doubtless sacrificed the national dignity and honor merely for the sake of economic advantage and other profits to be obtained by trade concessions from the Ming. In fact, he made bold thus to dishonor Japan in order to satisfy his selfish personal desires and his vanity. His policy was outrageous. All the state papers and memorials sent by Yoshimitsu to the Ming throne bore dates in accordance with the Ming calendar, in entire disregard of the national calendar of Japan.

"Yoshimitsu reverently used the Ming national calendar in connection with all diplomatic affairs. This act of his shows that he made himself subject to the Ming emperor and pledged loyalty to the Ming throne. Moreover, he led an arrogant life of self-aggrandizement, even going so far as to ignore the existence of the emperor of Japan. He frequently put on the official robes of the Ming and, thus dressed, presented himself in the imperial court before the emperor of Japan. He also raised the rank of his wife to one similar to that of the empress of Japan, and had her assume the title 'Mother of the Nation'. All these things with regard to Yoshimitsu give the impression that Yoshimitsu was 'King of Japan' in fact as well as in name."

(3) ITO, GINGETSU. *Dai-Nihon Minzoku-Shi* (History of the Race of Great Japan; Tokyo, 1913), pp. 532–33.

"In October, in the third year of the Meitoku era [1392], the emperor of the Southern dynasty, by way of compromise, handed over the sacred imperial insignias to the emperor of the Northern dynasty, thus uniting the Northern and Southern imperial governments. This national unification was brought about through national desire: it was not the work of a single leader. Nevertheless, Yoshimitsu arrogantly claimed it as his own. On December 25, in the first year of Oyei [1394], he gained from the emperor his appointment as *Dajodaijin* ("Grand Supreme State Minister"); subsequently, his rank was raised to one similar to that of the empress. Yoshimitsu led a most extravagant and luxurious life, even surpassing that of the emperor. He built the Shokokuji monastery, the Hanagosho palace, and the Golden Hall villa. He was always eager for self-aggrandizement. It was therefore quite natural that his finances became exhausted and that he found it imperative to seek out all possible sources of revenue. He availed himself of the opportunity to get much-needed money at the time when the Ming emperor was urgently demanding that Japanese pirate bands, which were continuously ravaging the Chinese coast, should be suppressed. Yoshimitsu asked for money to finance this undertaking. Finally, for the sake of economic gain, he degraded both himself and his nation by bowing before the copper coins of the Ming. He styled himself 'a subject of the Ming Emperor'. In compliance with the request of the Ming emperor, he attacked the pirates and captured their chiefs, whom he sent to the Ming court. He even ignored the existence of the emperor of Japan by receiving investiture from the Ming emperor and by reverently using the Ming national calendar. Thus did Yoshimitsu place a great stain on the glorious history of Japan."

(4) TANAKA, YOSHINARI. *Ashikaga Jidai-Shi* (History of the Ashikaga Period; Tokyo, 1922), pp. 47–52.

"On August 1, in the ninth year of the Oyei era, Ming ships

arrived at Hyogo [Kobe]. Yoshimitsu went to Hyogo and welcomed them. The Ming envoy and his party were subsequently received at Kyoto. The Hojuji monastery was assigned to them as their official residence during their stay in Japan. From that time on, the international dealings between the Ming and Japan became increasingly frequent. In the tenth year of Oyei [1403], the Ming emperor [Cheng-Tsu] sent Chao Chu-Jen as his envoy, provided with a state paper, to Yoshimitsu. The Ming emperor used the term 'You, the King of Japan' in addressing Yoshimitsu, and conferred 'the Seal' upon him. Internationally speaking, these two events are most significant. The standard Chinese *History of the Ming* and *Tushu Chicheng* (a standard work compiled under the auspices of the imperial Manchu government) contain records to the effect that the Ming emperor [Cheng-Tsu] sent the coronet and the official robes to Yoshimitsu at the same time. All these facts bear witness that Yoshimitsu received investiture as 'King of Japan' from the Ming emperor, and that the seal sent by the Ming emperor was the official seal of the 'King of Japan'.

"Under date of June 30, in the sixth year of the Yeikyo era (1434), Mansai Junko made the following entry in his diary: 'All the shoguns since Rokuyen Inden [Yoshimitsu] may be rightfully called kings of Japan. The seal sent to our country from the Chinese imperial court bears the engraving, "The Seal of the King of Japan." '

"Inryoken made the following entry in his diary, under date of June 13, in the sixth year of the Kansei era (1465): 'The turtle-shaped golden seal shines brilliantly and fairly dazzles our eyes. As it is very heavy, both hands are necessary in order to use it. Indeed, this seal is a national bequest of immeasurable value'.

"The golden seal mentioned in these diaries was undoubtedly the one that the Ming emperor sent to Yoshimitsu. Because Yoshimitsu accepted from the Ming emperor the title of 'King of Japan' as well as the official seal and the coronet, together with the official robes, it is an undeniable historical fact that Yoshimitsu received investiture as the 'King of Japan' from the Ming throne.

"In July, 1404, when the Ming envoy, Chao, was returning home to China, Yoshimitsu sent Meishitsu with him as his envoy to the Ming court. In 1405, when Meishitsu returned home to Japan, the Ming emperor sent with him Panyang and Wang Chin as envoys to Japan. This time, the Ming emperor sent to Yoshimitsu the official robes of the Kyusho rank. In July, 1407, an envoy came from the Ming. This time, the Ming emperor sent gifts of enormous value to Yoshimitsu, including 1000 *ryo* of silver, 15,000 *kan* of copper coin, and several hundred rolls of silk brocade and of other valuable woven goods. In the imperial edict that the Ming emperor sent to Yoshimitsu with these gifts, he expressed appreciation of and high praise for Yoshimitsu's great service to the Ming throne in his attack upon and capture of pirate chiefs, thus freeing the Chinese coast from their ravages. After establishing national relations with the Ming in 1401, throughout the remainder of his life Yoshimitsu sent his tribute-bearing envoy almost every year to the Ming court. He always styled himself 'a subject of the Ming Emperor'; he reverently used the Ming national calendar, thus showing submission and loyalty to the Ming court; and he made every effort to gain the good will of the Ming emperor. It is generally believed that Yoshimitsu pursued this course in order to obtain economic advantages and trade with the Ming. Judging from the financial condition of his government, however, one cannot think that Yoshimitsu was so hard pressed as to make it necessary thus to humble himself and degrade his nation. He must have had some other object.

"During the Ashikaga Period, a number of prominent statesmen and scholars, among whom were Yoshimasa, Shuho, and Yoshimochi, the son of Yoshimitsu, were fully convinced that Yoshimitsu had disgraced both himself and the nation, as well as broken his pledge to the imperial throne of Japan. For this reason, Yoshimochi temporarily terminated relations with the Ming after the death of his father. In the face of strong opposition, Yoshimitsu had dared to commit this great wrong. He did so because he was planning to usurp the imperial throne of Japan. He accepted investiture as 'King of Japan' from a foreign emperor with the purpose of first gaining recognition by foreign nations of his sovereign power in Japan and of later compelling the emperor to surrender to him the imperial authority."

Appendix 24

The Financial Benefit Which Yoshimitsu Obtained from the Ming Throne

Yoshimitsu recognized the suzerain power of the Ming over Japan, with the following results:

(1) He sent products of Japan to the Ming throne under the name of tribute, in return for which he received liberal compensation under the name of "Gifts from the Ming emperor." Thus was trade conducted in favor of Japan under the guise of gifts and tribute.

(2) Yoshimitsu attacked the Japanese pirate bands and captured the pirate chiefs. He sent the latter to the Ming and thus kept the Chinese coast free from pirate ravages. He always received very liberal rewards for this service.

(3) Yoshimitsu monopolized the trade between Japan and China.

Yoshimitsu was always very faithful in the sending of tribute-bearing envoys to the Ming throne. In fulfillment of the duty of a subject to his sovereign, he busied himself in attacking pirate bands and capturing their chiefs, thus keeping the coast of China clear of piracy. The Ming emperor, Cheng-Tsu, was greatly pleased with the loyalty and faithful service of Yoshimitsu, and sent an envoy almost every year with gifts as an expression of his appreciation. On November 17, in the first year of the Yung-Lo era (1403), the Emperor Cheng-Tsu sent an envoy bearing an imperial edict which read, in part:

"You, the King of Japan, know the doctrine of Heaven and you reverence human law. Immediately after my accession to the throne, you sent a tribute-bearing envoy. Your promptness in thus showing loyalty to us is to be highly commended."[13]

The Emperor Cheng-Tsu sent imperial edicts to Yoshimitsu in 1404, 1406, 1407, and 1408. On May 26, in the fifth year of the Yunglo era (1407), in addition to sending the regular imperial edict, the Emperor Cheng-Tsu issued a special edict to Yoshimitsu, together with a gift of great value. This edict read as follows:

"The Emperor hereby issues this imperial edict to Yuan Tao-i [Yoshimitsu], King of Japan. You, the King, have always been loyal, wise, and faithful. You have continuously rendered brilliant service to us. You reverently respect our throne. You have performed for us a great and effective service in attacking and exterminating the inhuman marauders. You now send us the pirate chiefs whom you have taken prisoners. Now, the people who dwell along the coast of our empire may henceforth be able to enjoy a peaceful and carefree existence. All this benefit is owing to the brilliant work that you have accomplished. You have rendered most outstanding service to us, of which there is no parallel in either ancient or modern history. We hereby confer upon you, King of Japan, a reward in order to show our pleasure. This edict is issued especially to command you to accept the following articles: (1) Hua-ing silver, 1000 *ryo* in 40 ingots; (2) 15,000 *kan* of copper coin; (3) 10 rolls of silk brocade; (4) 50 bales of fancy hemp thread of various colors; (5) 30 rolls of thin *la*-silk; (6) 20 rolls of light *sha*-silk; (7) 300 rolls of fine silk of various colors [there were twenty-two different kinds in all]."[14]—Document in the archives of the family of the Marquis Tokugawa, lord of Owari during the Feudal Period.

Keimitsu and Churitsu, whom Yoshimitsu sent as envoys to the Ming court, also received rewards when they were leaving Peking for Japan. The following imperial edict was issued to them under date of May 25, in the fifth year of the Yung-Lo era (1407):

"The Emperor hereby issues an edict to the envoy Keimitsu and to the assistant envoy Churitsu, from Japan. Yuan Tao-i [Yoshimitsu], 'King of Japan', has always been both wise and loyal. He has been happy in performing meritorious service to us. He has reverently followed the heavenly doctrine and has sincerely served our throne. He has successfully attacked and destroyed rovers and pirate bands, thus clearing our entire coast. The sincerity and loyalty of the King are commended by Heaven as well as by our throne. We ascended the imperial throne as the lord of various nations. It is our aim to enjoy things in this world peaceably and harmoniously with others. Your King well knows our heart and desires. You, his two envoys, have traveled a great distance by water and have come to our capital to convey the salutations and messages of your King. You have fulfilled the mission thus entrusted to you. As we highly approve of your faithfulness and sincerity, we hereby issue this edict commanding that you accept four articles of Shih-Kuo as a gift."[15]—Document in the archives of the Shokoku-Ji monastery, Kyoto.

APPENDIX 25

The Last Imperial Edict of the Ming Emperor, Cheng-Tsu, Addressed to the Departed Soul of Yoshimitsu

THE EMPEROR CHENG-TSU, from the year 1404 on, issued an imperial edict almost annually to Yoshimitsu in which he praised him and expressed appreciation of his service in the matter of suppressing the pirates.

In the edict of December 2, 1404, he said: "You have reverently obeyed our imperial commands and have prohibited and suppressed pirate bands in Iki, Tsushima, and in other islands, thereby clearing the coast of our empire. We recognize and highly praise your sincerity and faithfulness."[16]

In the edict of January 16, 1406, the emperor said: "We instructed you, the King of Japan, to destroy the pirate bands. You promptly sent troops which annihilated them, destroyed their ships, and captured their chiefs. You thus revered and obeyed our imperial commands."[17]

In the edict of May 26, 1407, the emperor said: "Your troops chased and attacked the pirates in the north, the east, the west, and the south, searching them out in all directions. By the employment of various and numerous tactics, you captured most of the leading pirate chiefs. In sending these chiefs to us, you have also sent a memorial to our throne. . . . Your remarkable work fully meets our expectations and gives us great satisfaction. Henceforth the coast of our empire will be safe and clear, and our people will no longer fear the raising of the fire signal [used to warn them of pirate attacks]. Even the dogs, pigs, chickens, and other domestic animals will now be able to maintain a safe existence. All this is owing to your meritorious service."[18]

In the edict of December, 1408, the emperor said: "You reverently complied with our instructions and applied yourself without delay, using your wisdom and power. Now you have completely destroyed the marauders and the pirate bands even in the far-off islands of the sea. Your sincerity and loyalty shine brilliantly like the sun and the stars. This loyalty is of such strength as to pierce rock and steel."

Yoshimitsu died in 1408. When the Ming emperor, Cheng-Tsu, learned of his demise, he mourned greatly and immediately sent an eminent officer of the imperial household department, named Chou Chuan-Yi, to worship the departed soul of Yoshimitsu and to read the imperial edict before his tomb. In this last edict, the Emperor Cheng-Tsu summarized the service of Yoshimitsu to the Ming throne and eulogized his personality and attainments. The edict read as follows:

"On this day, December 21, in the sixth year of the Yung-Lo era, the Emperor sent Chou Chuan-Yi, an officer of his household, to worship the departed soul of Yuan Tao-i [Yoshimitsu], the former King of Japan. We are deeply impressed by the fact that the King was a person of merciful and sympathetic nature as well as of brilliant and high attainments. He always conducted himself in accordance with the rites and with propriety, and attended to all affairs with righteousness and justice. His heart turned toward goodness and the right. He abhorred wrong and injustice. He revered Heaven and served the Highest above. His public and private life were alike sincere. He showed magnanimous consideration and judgment and possessed eminent genius and ability. His benevolences and kindness influenced all his subjects, causing harmony and unity to obtain. His wisdom and uprightness shine far and near.

"From the time that we ascended the throne, his heart was always turned toward us. He complied with all the duties and obligations owed by a tributary state. He promptly and reverently obeyed our imperial command. He exerted himself in attending to our imperial commands and instructions with awe and fear, striving to leave nothing undone. Therefore, he was able to annihilate pirate bands and marauders in all the islands, even including those in far-off waters. Because of this, multitudes of people dwelling along our coasts now enjoy a safe and happy existence. Even the chickens, dogs, and pigs exist in safety. All this is owing to his notable and meritorious service to us. His loyalty and sincerity shone brightly like the sun and the stars. This loyalty was of such strength as to pierce both rock and steel. His greatness was recognized in both Heaven and earth and gained the admiration of both gods and departed souls. Since the founding of the nation, Japan has never before produced a man whose virtue was so high and brilliant as his. We had always hoped that he would enjoy long and lasting prosperity. His sudden departure from this world is a most unexpected and regretful event. When this sad information reached us, we were overcome with grief and with regret for so great a loss. At the same time, we recollected and admired his brilliancy and eminent virtue. However, it is a law of nature that all things have the Yang and the Yin sides, just as the day is divided into light and darkness. All who have life must meet death. Now, Yuan Tao-i has departed from this world after having lived a brilliant, natural life. His outstanding work will permanently influence our eastern tributary state [Japan] and make a lasting impression on our imperial court. His work will be recorded in history and his name will go down through the generations. His brilliant service to our imperial court will be remembered as long as Heaven and earth exist. You, the King, will certainly neither lament nor regret the departure of your soul from this world. We hereby send our trusted officer to observe solemn rites in honor of your soul. Your soul in Chiu-Yuan [Hades] is instructed to accept this imperial offer."[19]

APPENDIX 26

The Termination of Japan's Relations with China by the Fourth Shogun, Yoshimochi

IN MAY, of the fifteenth year of the Oyei era (1408), Yoshimitsu died. The Emperor Cheng-Tsu was greatly grieved because of his demise. He sent a special envoy and conferred upon Yoshimitsu the posthumous title, *Kyoken-O*, which means "the King of Reverent Virtue who rendered distinguished service to the Ming Throne." At the same time, the Emperor Cheng-Tsu sent a state paper to Yoshimochi in which he expressed condolence. He also sent a gift of five hundred rolls of silk and five hundred rolls of fine linen. Yoshimochi always regretted the fact that his father had disgraced the nation by recognizing China as a suzerain power and by

attacking and destroying the Japanese pirates in compliance with
the command of the Ming emperor. Even when Yoshimitsu lay ill,
Yoshimochi discontinued military undertakings against the pirates.
Consequently, almost immediately after the death of Yoshimitsu
the coast of China again began to suffer from pirate inroads. The
Ming emperor, Cheng-Tsu, therefore invested Yoshimochi as "King
of Japan" and, at the same time, issued an imperial edict under
date of December 26, in the sixth year of the Yung-Lo era (1408).
The edict read: "The Emperor hereby issues an edict to Minamoto-
no-Yoshimochi, King of Japan. The coast of the empire is now ravaged by pirates from the far-off sea [Japanese waters]. They have
acted with great violence, thus causing our people to suffer loss of
both property and crops. In former days, your father, King Kyoken
[Yoshimitsu] cheerfully and promptly obeyed our instructions; he
sent troops and exterminated the pirate bands, thus clearing and
pacifying our coast. Our subjects therefore enjoyed peace and prosperity. As his meritorious work has been recorded in our annals,
his reputation will be handed down to future generations and his
name revered. You, King of Japan, are hereby instructed to follow in the footsteps of your father. You should organize an army to
attack the pirates, and you should frame and enforce a law prohibiting piracy. If you should thus terminate the outrageous marauding of the pirates, your service to our throne will be brilliantly
recorded in our annals, thus becoming known to and revered by
posterity. We hereby issue this edict to you with instructions to
obey our commands reverently without delay and to perform
promptly and effectively this work which is hereby entrusted to
you by your Emperor."[20]—Document in the archives of the family
of Marquis Asano, lord of the province of Aki during the Feudal
Period.

Yoshimochi ignored both the investiture as king and the imperial edict. He allowed the pirates to pursue their own course.
In the eighteenth year of the Oyei era (1411), the Emperor Cheng-
Tsu again sent an envoy to Japan with instructions that Yoshimochi suppress the pirates. This time, the envoy and his party were
driven away from Hyogo (Kobe) without even being permitted
to land in Japan. In this unsuccessful diplomatic interval, the
ravages of the Japanese pirates along the coast of China became

increasingly frequent and serious. In 1418, the Emperor Cheng-Tsu sent Lu-Yen as envoy to Japan. He bore state papers demanding that Yoshimochi reëstablish international relations between China and Japan. Although Yoshimochi again refused to grant an interview, he appointed Kodo Choro as his personal representative and had him explain to the envoy of the Ming why Japan had terminated relations with the Ming empire in China.

In 1419, another envoy came from the Ming. This time, Yoshimochi issued a written statement under date of July 20, in the twenty-sixth year of the Oyei era (1419) to his trusted officer, Genyo Seido, instructing him to explain to the Ming envoy why Japan had closed the nation against China. This instruction read as follows:

"I, the Shogun, hereby issue this written statement to you, Genyo Seido. Envoys from the Ming have come time and again, insisting that we should maintain international relations with the Ming empire on the ground that Japan would thereby obtain great benefit. However, I have strong grounds for rejecting this proposal. Since the national founding of Japan, it has been our sacred tradition and practice that national affairs should be conducted only after being brought before our native gods and approved by them. Even though the matter be a minor one, we have never dared to carry it out without first obtaining divine consent. In former days, my father, Yoshimitsu, was misled by his officials and, without investigation, trusted their erroneous reports. He entered into international relationships with a foreign nation without first laying the matter before our gods. From that time on, our divine and human affairs were greatly disturbed. We suffered thereby from many catastrophes of nature. Subsequently, my father, at the time of his death, pledged to the native gods that Japan would terminate relations with the foreign nation. We should certainly not disregard this sacred pledge. Last year, when the envoy came from the Ming, I instructed Kodo Choro to explain our national policy to the envoy. Now the Ming has again sent an envoy. This causes us to suspect that our explanation to the Ming envoy last year has not been properly conveyed to the Ming court.... You, Genyo Seido, are hereby instructed carefully to attend to this matter and to make the present envoy fully understand our national policy."[21]

In the winter of that same year, the Emperor Cheng-Tsu again sent an envoy to induce Yoshimochi to renew the former relations with the Ming empire. Yoshimochi again issued a written statement to Genyo Seido in which he repeated his former instructions and gave fuller details. This second instruction read, in part:

"We have been repeatedly approached by the envoy from the Ming with respect to the matter of trade. The envoy has asked us whether it would not be a policy both wise and desirable for Japan to establish relations with her neighboring nation, and to engage in trade, thereby enabling her people to enjoy profit. However, I have strong grounds for refusing an interview with the Ming envoy and for rejecting the proposal made by the Ming. When my father, Yoshimitsu, was taken seriously ill, we learned by means of divination that his sickness was a divine punishment. We therefore urgently prayed to the various gods and begged their forgiveness. Then the gods of supreme power made a revelation through an oracle. They stated that, from the time of the nation's founding, no person had ever degraded himself and his nation so far as to style himself 'a subject of a foreign nation.' Yoshimitsu ignored national traditions and violated the laws of our sacred sovereigns of former days. Both the calendar and the seal of a foreign nation were given him. Instead of sending them back as he should have done, he accepted and used them. This wrong committed by Yoshimitsu brought illness upon him. My father, Yoshimitsu, greatly feared the divine curse. He pledged to the gods that he would thenceforth never receive any command from a foreign nation, and that he would instruct his offspring to adhere strictly to this pledge. Later, a Buddhist priest by the name of Kenchu came to our country with a Ming envoy. I did not desire to see this envoy.... When he was about to return to his country, we instructed Kenchu to explain our new national policy to him. Probably he failed to convey our message to his government. Last year, another envoy came from the Ming. We appointed a trusted man to explain our policy to him, also. We are at a loss to know why this envoy did not report to his ruler what he had been told in our country. The Ming has since sent envoys again and again. We have neither granted interviews to these envoys nor sent our envoys to the Ming. This is not because we depend upon the geographical advantage of our country's being surrounded by vast waters, but because we desire to obey the instructions of our gods."[22]

As a last resort, the Emperor Cheng-Tsu sent a state paper containing a military threat, which read, in part: "Our heavenly commissioned troops will soon swoop down upon your country and make a thunder-like attack upon your forces. Your small country has neither natural precipices nor impregnable defenses. You should therefore build high your castle walls and dig deep your castle moats in order to prepare to protect yourselves from our heavenly troops. Soon the time will come when your repentance will be too late to save your country."[23]

Yoshimochi's reply to the Ming emperor read, in part: "In former generations, great armadas of the Mongols came twice to our country. Their ships and soldiers numbered thousands upon thousands, but they went down to the bottom of the sea without having accomplished anything. The fate thus suffered by the Mongols was not owing to our man power but mainly to the divine power which always guards and protects our nation. The peoples of distant countries who hear about these great national events in our country may be tempted to regard them as mythological. But these facts are recorded in the history of our nation as well as in our annals. Now, because your envoys to our country have failed to accomplish their missions, you have decided to appeal to arms and you advise us to make due military preparation. It will not be necessary for us either to dig deep castle moats or to build high walls for defense. We are ready to receive your troops and to welcome them."[24]

Upon receipt of this reply from Yoshimochi, just as the Emperor Tai-Tsu, the founder of the Ming dynasty had done, the Emperor Cheng-Tsu feared that his troops might meet the same sort of disaster in Japanese waters as the great Mongol armada of Kublai Khan had encountered. He therefore abandoned his plan to invade Japan.

APPENDIX 27

The Reëstablishment of the Suzerain and Tributary Relationships Between China and Japan

AFTER THE DEATH of Yoshimitsu, his son Yoshimochi completely severed all relations with China. This condition obtained for approximately a quarter-century. In 1432, the Emperor Hsuan-Tsung again sought to reëstablish relations with Japan. With this in view, he sent an imperial edict to Japan through the offices of the king of Liu Chiu. He took this step because he feared that Japan would decline to accept his edict if it were sent directly by his envoy. Contrary to the record in Japanese history certain Chinese texts state that Yoshimochi continued international relations with the Ming, just as in the time of Yoshimitsu.[25] Most of the standard histories of China, as well as international documents, fully verify the fact that Yoshimochi terminated Japanese relationships with China. Huang-Ming Shih-Lu (Historical Facts of the Imperial Ming Dynasty) contains the following entry under date of the seventh year of the Hsuan-Te era (1432). The Emperor Hsuan-Tsung announced that since his accession barbarian nations in all parts of the world had been sending tribute to the Ming throne.[26] Japan alone had not sent a tribute-bearing envoy. The emperor therefore sent an officer of his imperial household, by the name of Chai Shan, to the kingdom of Liu Chiu with instructions to its king to persuade Japan to send an envoy and to pay due reverence to the Ming throne. Chai Shan brought with him an imperial edict of the Ming emperor addressed to the "King of Japan" and requested the king of Liu Chiu to forward it to Japan. This edict of the Ming emperor read as follows:

"Of yore, our imperial grandfather the Emperor Tai-Tsung Wen ruled our empire. At that time, your father Tao-i [Yoshimitsu], the King of Japan, revered the heavenly doctrine and served our imperial court. Our Emperor Tai-Tsung conferred upon him honor and dignity. Now we have succeeded to the imperial throne and are carrying out the imperial policy and desire of our grandfather. We plan to protect all the people both far and near and to make it possible for them to live peaceably and harmoniously under the protection of our imperial throne. We especially issue this edict and instruct the King of Japan to revere and obey the heavenly will, thus following and respecting the course of his father, by sending an envoy to our imperial court. We shall then regard you, the King of Japan, with kindness, as our grandfather the Emperor Tai-Tsung regarded your father, Yoshimitsu, the King of Japan. Our empire and your kingdom will then enjoy a harmonious union as one nation and one family. The people along the coasts of our empire will then be blessed with peace and prosperity. You, the King of Japan, are hereby instructed to revere this imperial edict."[27]

Yoshinori was a man of great ambition. Unlike his brother, Yoshimochi, he planned to revive the diplomatic policy of Yoshimitsu in order to obtain trade and economic concessions from the Ming. Upon receipt of the imperial edict of the Emperor Hsuan-Tsung, he promptly sent Doyen as his tribute-bearing envoy to the Ming throne. As evidence of his recognition of China as the suzerain power over Japan, he signed his memorial to the Ming throne, "Yoshinori, King of Japan: a subject of the Ming Emperor."[28] The Emperor Hsuan-Tsung was highly pleased by Yoshinori's attitude and sincerity. On June 11, 1433, he sent envoys bearing an imperial edict, together with valuable gifts to Yoshinori.

The *Huang-Ming Shih-Lu* contains the following entry under date of June of the eighth year of the Hsuan-Te era (1433):

"Pan-Ssu, Kao-Chien, Lei-Chun, and other officers were sent to Japan as envoys. They bore the imperial edict dated June 11, 1433, together with gifts of silver and various sorts of woven goods as a gift from the Ming throne to Yoshinori, King of Japan. In former times, in the reign of the Emperor Tai-Tsung, the King of Japan, Yuan Tao-i [Yoshimitsu], reverently served our imperial court and showed great loyalty to the Ming throne. After his death, tribute-bearing envoys ceased entirely to come to our imperial court. Therefore, His Majesty the present Emperor has issued an imperial edict to the King of Japan containing suitable instructions. Upon receipt of this edict, Yoshinori succeeded to the rank and title of his father and sent Doyen as his tribute-bearing envoy, thus showing due reverence to the Ming throne. In recognition of this act of the King of Japan, His Majesty the present Emperor sent envoys bearing gifts from the throne to Yoshinori."[29]

The imperial edict which the Emperor Hsuan-Tsung sent to Yoshinori in June, 1433, read as follows:

"The Emperor issues this imperial edict to Minamoto-no-Yoshinori, King of Japan. We, in accordance with the heavenly command, have succeeded to the great imperial throne of our ancestors, and have thus come to rule myriads of people. Since our accession, we have respected and obeyed the heavenly will and the desires of our ancestors by giving uniformly the same love and benevolence to all peoples. Therefore, the nations both within and without the sea, as well as everywhere that the sun and the moon shine, long for our righteousness and place themselves under our imperial influence. All peoples have pledged loyalty to our throne.

"Now you, the King of Japan, have sent your envoy, Doyen, bearing a memorial together with products of your land as tribute to the throne. You have thus shown your reverence of Heaven and your service to the supreme power [China]. Your sincerity and faithfulness are highly approved. . . . When your father King Tao-i [Yoshimitsu] ruled Japan, he reverently served our imperial grandfather Tai-Tsung Wen Huang-ti (the Emperor Cheng-Tsu). The loyalty and sincerity of your father were of a strength such as to pierce both rock and steel. Therefore, our grandfather conferred upon him honor and dignity exceeding that of other barbarian chiefs. As all these facts are recorded in our national annals, your father's name will shine brilliantly in the far-off future. After his death, envoys ceased to come to us from your country. This state of affairs has obtained for many, many years. Now you, the King, have come to rule Japan and have distinguished yourself by your loyalty to our throne and by your filial piety to your deceased father, in thus reviving the suzerain and tributary relation. Your course is both wise and noteworthy. Even the kings of great wisdom in the ancient times could not have done better. . . .

"We hereby send Lei-Chun as envoy, and Pei-Kuan, Pan-Ssu, and Kao-Chien as assistant envoys. They carry our edict, together with silver and woven goods as gifts from our throne. We are sending them to express our pleasure and approval of the course taken by you. You, King, should serve our throne with diligence and with reverence, thus meeting our expectations.

"This edict is issued to you especially for this purpose. [Dated] June 11, of the eighth year of the Hsuan-Te era [1433]."[30]

The Emperor Hsuan-Tsung died in 1435. His son Ying-Tsung ascended the throne in 1436. He named his era "Cheng-Tung." Yoshinori, signing himself "King of Japan, a subject of the Ming Emperor," sent a memorial to the Emperor Ying-Tsung, renewing his pledge of loyalty to the throne. Ying-Tsung thereupon issued the following edict:

"The Emperor issues this imperial edict to Minamoto-no-Yoshinori, King of Japan. Our imperial dynasty, in accordance with a heavenly command, rules all nations. Our imperial authority extends over the nations both within and without the sea. In the entire universe there does not exist a single individual who would not pledge loyalty to our throne. Since the founding of our empire, sage emperors have succeeded each other in ascending our throne. They have ruled both far and near and have given uniformly benevolent and merciful administrations. Japan has long been our eastern tributary state. She has sent tribute regularly and has faithfully served our throne with increasing loyalty and sincerity. In the reign of our father the Emperor Hsuan-Tsung, your country was granted special favors. Now you, King, have sent Chusei and others as envoys, bearing a memorial as well as products of your land as tribute to our throne. Thus you have shown great sincerity and have observed due ceremonial rites. We have ascended our great imperial throne, succeeding our forefathers. We aim to enjoy peace and happiness along with multitudes of people throughout the world. Therefore we are especially pleased to have you thus sending envoys in token of your desire to serve the supreme power. Now your envoys are returning home. By them we are sending to you and to your Queen silver and woven goods as gifts from the throne. We do this in recognition of your sincerity and loyalty. You, King, should always revere and obey the heavenly will and protect and love your people so that Japan may long remain a tributary state of our empire.

"This edict is issued specially in order that you may follow our instructions and rule your country well. [Dated] February 4, of the first year of the Cheng-Tung era [1436]."[31]

The articles received by Yoshinori in 1433 from the Ming throne

were given him by the Emperor Hsuan-Tsung. They consisted of
200 *ryo* of silver, 4 rolls of silk brocade, 20 rolls of fancy linens of
various colors, 20 rolls of light *la*-silk, 20 rolls of thin *sha*-silk, and
20 rolls of fine silk of various colors.

Yoshinori's wife, as the "Queen of Japan," received, at the same
time, 100 *ryo* of silver, 4 rolls of silk brocade, 10 rolls of fine linen
of various colors, 8 rolls of light *la*-silk, 8 rolls of thin *sha*-silk, and
10 rolls of fine silk of various colors.

Besides these gifts from the Ming throne to the "King and the
Queen of Japan" (Yoshinori and his wife), in the same year (1433)
the Ming emperor, Hsuan-Tsung, made the following gifts to the
"King and the Queen of Japan" jointly: a golden-lacquered sedan
chair, together with two umbrellas, cushions, curtains, a footstool,
and other accessories, totaling 34 articles in all; 10 rolls of golden
la-silk; 10 rolls of golden *sha*-silk; 300 rolls of fine silk of various
colors; 20 pieces of silverware; 20 pieces of art work made of silk
thread; 900 pieces of writing materials including stationery, writing brushes, etc.; 10 boxes of *Chin Hsiang* (incense wood), weigh-
ing 500 pounds; 110 fine rugs; 280 skins of animals, including those
of 50 tigers, of 30 bears, of 30 panthers, and of 100 monkeys.

When sending the imperial edict in the first year of the Cheng-
Tung era (1436), the Emperor Ying-Tsung made the following
throne gift to the "King and the Queen of Japan" (Yoshinori and
his wife): to Yoshinori, 200 *ryo* of silver, 5 rolls of silk brocade, 20
rolls of fine linen of various colors, 20 rolls of thin *sha*-silk, and
40 rolls of light *la*-silk; to the "queen," the wife of Yoshinori, 100
ryo of silver, 3 rolls of silk brocade, 10 rolls of fine linen, 8 rolls of
thin *sha*-silk, and 8 rolls of light *la*-silk.[32]

APPENDIX 28

Yoshimasa's Request to the Ming Throne for Additional Copper Coins

IN THE BEGINNING of the fifteenth century, Yoshimitsu recognized
China as his suzerain power and concluded a treaty with the Ming
on the subject of suppressing the pirate bands. He attacked and
destroyed the pirates from 1403 to 1408, for which service he received due reward from the Ming throne.

Yoshinori recognized the Ming empire (China) as his suzerain power and concluded a treaty with the Ming on the subject of suppressing the Japanese pirates. From 1433 to 1441, Yoshinori received a regular throne allowance from the Ming court. However, he failed to accomplish anything in the way of suppressing the pirates.

In 1444, the eighth shogun, Yoshimasa, began to rule Japan. As this was the beginning of Japan's Dark Age, Yoshimasa was not in a position even to promise the Ming that he would attempt to suppress the pirates. However, he was in urgent need of money. So he stressed the fact that China was Japan's suzerain power, thus impressing upon the Ming emperor the idea that the Ming throne should give financial assistance to Japan, its tributary state. On this account, Yoshimasa not only styled himself "a subject of the Ming Emperor," but also ended his memorials, "This memorial is presented by Yoshimasa, a subject of the Ming Emperor, with awe and reverence, bowing low once and then again to the imperial throne of the Ming."

This humble way of signing, which was original with Yoshimasa, his successors adhered to for generations, whenever they presented memorials to the Ming throne.

Under date of August 28, of the eleventh year of the Cheng-Hua era (1475), Yoshimasa sent a memorial to the Ming throne which read as follows:

"Minamoto-no-Yoshimasa, a subject of the Ming emperor, respectfully presents this memorial to His Majesty the Emperor of the Great Ming. Just as Heaven looks down with affection and sympathy and just as the sun shines with great brilliancy, the Great Ming rules myriads of nations and makes them revere the throne. The imperial influence, vast and magnanimous as the sea and as tender and productive as the spring season, reaches in all directions, north, south, east, and west. Hua-Hsia [China], as well as all the barbarian nations, turns toward the imperial benevolence and blessing. Even the weeds, trees, insects, and fishes likewise maintain and develop their respective instincts.

"His Majesty the Emperor of the Great Ming, as mighty as gods and sages both in times of peace and in times of war, by his wisdom, mercy, and sympathy, makes it possible for the imperial dynasty and the nation to maintain harmony and unity. As for my humble state, it suffers continuously from military disturbances, the sound of drums and of trumpet shells not ceasing for even a moment. Although your humble subject lives in a district in the eastern extremity, far beyond the mountains and rivers in Yu-Kung [China], yet he fortunately maintains his existence between Heaven and earth, and he has learned how to turn his heart to the Ming throne. I hereby send Myomo as envoy and Keiyu Shuza as assistant envoy reverently to present this memorial, together with products of our land as tribute to the throne. May your imperial favor be conferred upon them, and may my faithful and sincere motive gain your imperial approval and consideration."[33]

As a sort of supplement to this memorial, Yoshimasa sent a petition to the throne, asking copper coins as an additional throne allowance. It read in part as follows:

"The imperial favor and blessing are so great and magnanimous that both my hands and my feet are thrilled. But the imperial gift was seized by marauders on the way, my envoy and his party, however, being so fortunate as to return home alive. . . . Because of long-continued warfare in my humble state, all of the copper coins have been scattered and lost. The state coffers are completely empty. The land is laid waste. The people suffer from extreme poverty. We have absolutely neither means nor ways of protecting and saving them. The books have also been destroyed by the weapons of the soldiers. It has long been our custom to have copper coins and books provided for us by the supreme nation. As the records show, in the Yung-Lo era, the imperial throne made abundant gifts of copper coins to our state. Recently no gifts of this sort have been sent. Nothing is now so urgently needed in our humble state as are books and copper coins. This state of affairs is hereby reverently laid before the throne, with urgent hope for imperial consideration and grants."[34]

In reply to the pitiful petition and the memorial presented by Yoshimasa, the Ming Emperor Hsien-Tsung issued two imperial edicts and granted 50,000 *kan* of copper coins to Yoshimasa, in addition to the regular throne allowance. One of the imperial edicts read as follows:

"The Emperor issues this edict to Minamoto-no-Yoshimasa,

King of Japan. You, King, have presented a memorial to our throne stating that because of long-continued national disturbance in your country your state coffers are entirely empty. On the basis of events that took place in the Yung-Lo era, you have petitioned for a gift of copper coin from our throne so that you may save your people from distress. We have referred the matter to the Imperial Board of Rites for investigation. That Board has reported to the throne stating that there is no record that copper coins were ever given to the King of Japan by the throne. However, because your envoy, Myomo, has repeatedly appealed to our throne for a grant, therefore, lest we should disappoint you, we hereby specially grant copper coins to you, amounting to fifty thousand *kan*. These are being sent to you by your envoy, Myomo. You are hereby instructed to accept them.

"This edict is issued to you for this purpose.

"[Dated] February 9, of the fourteenth year of the Cheng-Hua era [1478]."[35]

The other imperial edict issued to Yoshimasa under the same date read as follows:

"The Emperor issues this imperial edict to Minamoto-no-Yoshimasa, King of Japan. We, in accordance with the heavenly command, have succeeded to the throne and have come to control and to rule Hua-I [China and the Barbarian States]. You, King, having wisdom and attainments, know how to revere Heaven and to serve the supreme power. You have now sent your envoy, Myomo, and his party to present a memorial, together with horses and products of your land as tribute to our throne. Your loyalty and sincerity are hereby approved and recognized. By your envoy, who is now returning to your state, we are sending this imperial edict, together with silver and woven goods to you and your Queen as a gift from our throne. You, King, are hereby instructed to comply with our desires and to meet our expectations.

"This edict is issued to you for this purpose.

"[Dated] February 9, of the fourteenth year of the Cheng-Hua era [1478]."[36]

The throne gift to the "King of Japan" consisted of 200 *ryo* of silver, 4 rolls of silk brocade, 35 rolls of fine linen, 20 rolls of fine silk of various colors, 20 rolls of thin *sha*-silk, and 20 rolls of light *la*-silk. The throne gift to the "Queen of Japan" consisted of 100 *ryo* of silver, 2 rolls of silk brocade, 14 rolls of fine linen, 10 rolls of fine silk of various colors, 8 rolls of thin *sha*-silk, and 8 rolls of light *la*-silk.[37]

Yoshimasa was greatly pleased and encouraged by the receipt of the 50,000 *kan* of copper coins. Therefore, in the nineteenth year of the Cheng-Hua era, when he sent an envoy to the Ming, he presented a special memorial to the throne, besides the regular memorial, petitioning for another throne allowance of copper coins to the amount of 100,000 *kan*. This special memorial read as follows:

"This memorial is respectfully presented to the throne through the Imperial Board of Rites. All the state papers and the throne gifts which have been sent to us have reached us. We have carefully handled and stored those gifts, article by article, turning our worship toward the throne each time. The magnanimity expressed by these gracious gifts thrilled my body and my soul and impressed me deeply. Now, I have a serious matter to present to the throne. As our humble state has long suffered from national disturbances and military onslaughts, our copper coins are exhausted. Nowhere in our land can a single copper coin be found. Our state coffers are all empty. We have nothing with which to protect and look after the interests and welfare of the people. We are now sending an envoy to the throne. Our sole purpose in sending him is to find some way of saving our people from their suffering. We would appeal to the sympathy and mercy of our sage Emperor for a grant of one hundred thousand *kan* of copper coins so that our urgent need may be met. Should such a gift be granted, it would be esteemed as the greatest happening of our lives. This memorial is reverently presented for imperial consideration with an earnest hope that an imperial grant will be made.

"[Dated] March, the spring in the nineteenth year of the Cheng-Hua era [1483]."[38]

Under the same date, Yoshimasa sent a regular memorial which read, in part:

"Yoshimasa, King of Japan, a subject of the Ming Emperor, reverently addresses the throne. The highest Heaven and Mother Earth praise the life and the thought of Chung-Hua [China]. . . . His Majesty the Emperor is a sage as well as a divinity. He, being mighty and wise in war and in peace, brilliantly approaches Yao and Shun of yore, and he far surpasses the founders of the Han and of the T'ang. As to our humble state, although it continuously enjoys the imperial favor and blessing, yet, because of continued domestic suffering and struggles, we sometimes have been obliged to delay the sending of our tribute-bearing envoys to the throne. ... Now, we are sending our special envoys, Shui Choro and others, bearing products of our land as tribute to the throne. ... Minamoto-no-Yoshimasa, a subject of His Majesty the Ming Emperor, reverently presents this memorial to the throne with awe and fear, bowing low once, and then again.

"[Dated] March, the spring in the nineteenth year of the Cheng-Hua era [1483].

"Yoshimasa, King of Japan, a subject of the Ming Emperor [SEAL]."³⁹

APPENDIX 29

International Relationships and Conditions Obtaining in the Fifteenth and Sixteenth Centuries Between China, a Suzerain Power Under the Ming Dynasty, and Japan and Other Nations

FROM ITS BEGINNING, the Ming dynasty, as did other imperial dynasties in China, demanded suzerainty over the small nations in Asia. During its rule, the suzerain and tributary relationships existed between China, on the one hand, and, on the other, Japan, Korea, Siam, Annam, and other small Asiatic nations. The suzerainty over these nations, however, had not been gained through military conquests, nor did the Ming attempt to exercise ruling power over them. It is true that such tributary states as Japan, Korea, Siam, and Annam sent tribute-bearing envoys, who addressed the Ming throne with great reverence, loyalty, and sincerity. But all this was done as a mere formality. As a matter of fact, these tributary states sent tribute in full expectation of liberal remuneration from the Ming throne. This was especially true of Japan.

From the middle of the fifteenth century on, when an envoy and his party came to China from Japan, they usually brought with them, under the name of tribute, quite superfluous things, over the value of which they often disputed seriously with the officials of the Ming government. Sometimes the envoy's party acted with great violence, attacking and destroying cities and towns and killing many innocent people, in much the same way as did the pirate bands. Nevertheless, the Ming throne did not take any definite steps against them, for fear that Japan might then establish relations with the pirate bands.

An imperial edict issued by the Emperor Hsien-Tsung, under date of February 15 of the twenty-first year of the Cheng-Hua era [1485], gives some idea of conditions in those days. The edict reads as follows:

"The Emperor issues this edict to Minamoto-no-Yoshimasa, King of Japan. In preceding years, when Siam and other states sent their tribute-bearing envoys, the interpreters and other men in the parties of these envoys frequently failed to observe our rites, regulations, and laws, and acted in most disorderly ways. When they were homeward bound, their vessels were accompanied by ships in which there were secret guard rooms. In those guard rooms they confined our subjects, male and female, whom they had purchased. They sometimes dishonored the women. Sometimes they quarreled and fought in public places with our men, wounding them seriously. Each time, after the men in the envoy's party had thus acted wildly, officials of our local government presented the entire matter to the throne, with a request that all the offenders be arrested and severe punishment inflicted. We, however, always took into consideration the fact that the men in the envoy's party had traveled a great distance to come to us and therefore dealt with them generously. We merely issued imperial edicts to their respective kings, advising them to punish the offenders according to their own laws.

"The envoy and his party whom you, King, sent us this time behaved well and observed our rites and regulations. We have given them a reception, and are sending them home to you with our commendation. We felt, however, that we must tell you of the events previously described with respect to the trouble we have had with men from tributary states. Henceforth, whenever you, King, send us an envoy accompanied by interpreters and other assistants, you should select them from among persons who have general cultural attainments, and who also know how to observe our rites and regulations. Moreover, you should strictly instruct the envoy and his party to attend to all matters with great caution and modesty, both when coming to and returning from our imperial court, and to refrain from all improper conduct, no matter how inconsequential the affair may seem. They should always strive to observe our rites and ceremonials, thereby enabling themselves to present tribute to the throne, and thus fulfill their mission.

"Concerning the tribute and other things to be presented to the throne, the Imperial Board of Rites has presented a memorial to the throne petitioning that henceforth the envoy from Japan should not be permitted to bring superfluous articles. All transactions should be conducted in strict accordance with the provisions of the Hsuan-Te agreement. The various kinds of swords brought from Japan should not exceed thirty pieces each. The Board of Rites has presented this petition to the throne with the hope that both our empire and Japan might, by observing the provisions of this memorial, reduce both labor and expense. Our throne has approved and granted the petition of the Board. We hereby inform you, King, of this plan of the Board of Rites, the same now being in effect.

"There is a wise saying of old that one who visits another should come heavily laden but should return home with a light load. There is another wise saying that the things presented to others may be light, materially, but that they should be profound and weighty sentimentally. This saying should be observed by small and weak states when they are serving the great and supreme nation. One cannot express one's sincerity and loyalty [merely] through the quantity and quality of things presented to another. You, King, are hereby instructed to comply with our desire.

"This edict is issued for this special purpose.

"[Dated] February 15, of the twenty-first year of the Cheng-Hua era [1485]."[40]

The foregoing edict did not have the desired effect. The "King of Japan" sent a memorial eulogizing the Ming emperor in the most extravagant terms but he continued to present, as "tribute to the throne," superfluous articles and insignificant local products. The Japanese envoys still persisted in frequent and serious controversies over the value of the things that they brought with them, thus causing great trouble to the Ming.

Two months after this edict had been issued by the Ming emperor to the "King of Japan," that is, on March 19 of the same year, when the envoy of the "King of Japan" [Yoshimasa] was returning home, the Ming Emperor Hsien-Tsung sent the regular throne allowance to the "King of Japan" and his "queen," but he also issued an edict which read thus:

"The Emperor issues this edict to Minamoto-no-Yoshimasa, King of Japan. You, King, are known to us as a person of wisdom and attainments. You reverently obey the heavenly will and faithfully serve our imperial court. You have sent your envoy, Shusho, and his party bearing a memorial, and horses, together with products of your land, as tribute to our throne. Your envoy is now returning to Japan. We are specially instructing him to carry this edict to you, King, together with silver and some woven goods, as a gift to you and to your Queen from our throne.

"You, King, are hereby instructed to comply with our desire.

"This edict is issued for this special purpose.

"[Dated] March 19, of the twenty-first year of the Cheng-Hua era [1485]."[41]

The throne gift to the "King of Japan" consisted of 200 *ryo* of silver and several tens of rolls of silk brocade, of fine linen, fine silk, thin *sha*-silk, and light *la*-silk.

The throne gift to the "Queen of Japan" consisted of 100 *ryo* of silver, 2 rolls of silk brocade, 14 rolls of fine linen, and other such goods.

In the middle of the fifteenth century, when Yoshinori renewed the suzerain and tributary relations with China, and from that time on, the Ming throne made the fixed amount of the throne gift to the "King and Queen of Japan" (the Ashikaga shogun and his wife) 200 *ryo* of silver together with several tens of rolls of woven goods to the "king," and 100 *ryo* of silver together with various sorts of woven goods to the "queen." In the early part of the fifteenth century, when the "King of Japan" (Yoshimitsu) was performing faithful service to the Ming throne by destroying Japanese pirate ships and by sending the captured pirate chiefs to the Ming, the throne gifts from the Ming were far greater. For example, the throne gift in 1406 consisted of 1000 *ryo* of silver, many pieces of silverware, and many hundreds of rolls of various kinds of woven goods. The throne gift in the following year [1407] consisted of 1000 *ryo* of silver, 15,000 *kan* of copper coins, many pieces of bronze art goods, and nearly 1000 rolls of various sorts of woven goods.[42]

APPENDIX 30

The Law for Control and Punishment of Japanese Pirates, Promulgated by Hideyoshi in 1588

FROM THE EARLY PART until the middle of the fifteenth century, when Yoshinori died, the Ming confidently depended upon Japan to control and suppress the pirate bands. They believed that the "King of Japan" would be able to keep the coast of China free from the inroads of Japanese pirates. In the second half of the fifteenth century, when Yoshimasa was the eighth shogun ("King of Japan"), the Ming became well acquainted with the chaotic condition of Japan. Nevertheless, the Ming emperors still hoped that the "King of Japan" might do something toward controlling the pirates. The Ming court believed that the maintenance of suzerain and tributary relationships with Japan would at least reduce the number of pirate attacks on the coast of China. Believing thus, the Ming emperors still continued to send the throne allowance to the "King of Japan." In the middle of the sixteenth century, with the steady increase of national chaos in Japan, the Ming almost entirely gave up hope of getting any aid from Japan in suppressing the pirates, and decided that China would have to protect her coast with her own military forces. With this in view, the Ming government built extensive works of defense along the Chinese coast, organized and maintained large armies in the several provinces that faced the water, and stationed several fleets here and there along the coast.

Chinese historians assert that these military undertakings of the Ming against the Japanese pirates brought about the desired results. In the sixteenth and seventeenth years of the Wan-Li era (1573–1619) the Ming quite cleared the coast of China of the pirate bands. Nevertheless, the suppression of the pirates was only partly owing to this military success of the Ming. It is mainly to be accounted for by the national unification and the establishment of a strong central government in Japan. In the fifteenth year of the Tensho era (1587), Hideyoshi (the "Napoleon of Japan") conquered the entire island of Kyushu. He placed all the feudal lords under his own control and inflicted severe punishment upon all unruly lords. In particular, he dealt severely with the pirates and those military leaders who had any connection with piracy. In the following year (1588), Hideyoshi determined upon a fixed policy for the extermination of the pirates. He took this step of his own accord, his sole purpose being to maintain the national dignity and honor; as a matter of fact, he was not approached by the Ming government with respect to this matter. Hideyoshi issued several ordinances and regulations for the control and suppression of piracy. Finally, under date of July 8, in the sixteenth year of the Tensho era (1588), Hideyoshi framed and promulgated a law with respect to the pirates. It consisted of three Articles, which are as follows:

"Article I

"To maintain ships for the purpose of piracy and to engage in piracy has been strictly prohibited. Therefore, nowhere in the waters round about our nation should there be found any pirate ships. However, our government has recently been informed that certain pirate ships are still operating in the waters near the provinces of Bingo and Iyo, as well as on Izu and on other small islands. These offenders are hereby declared to be outlaws. Prompt and severe punishment is to be inflicted upon them.

"Article II

"Officials of local governments and their deputies shall summon immediately all the seafaring men who are engaged in trade, fishing, or other work in ships. They shall carefully inquire into their daily life and work. If their explanations prove satisfactory, they may be permitted to continue their work. But they should be required to make sworn statements before the gods that they will never engage in piracy. All these sworn statements should be forwarded to the governments of the respective feudal lords.

"ARTICLE III

"Henceforth, when, owing to the negligence or wrongdoing of *Kyujin* or of *Ryoshu* [local magistrates or owners of estates along the coast], pirates shall be discovered operating in the waters under their control, the Kyujin or the Ryoshu will be held responsible and will be severely punished. Their estates as well as their personal property will be confiscated.

"All the provisions in this law are to be put in force immediately. Any offenders will be punished to the full extent of this law.

"[Dated] July 8, of the sixteenth year of the Tensho era [1588].
"Hideyoshi [SEAL]"

This document is in the possession of the Honpo-Ji monastery, Kyoto, and a copy of it is in the possession of the Kobayakawa family.[43]

CHAPTER IV

APPENDIX 31

The Shogunate Government and Its Functioning

IN THE FEUDAL PERIOD, which began in July, 1192, when Minamoto-no-Yoritomo was appointed as shogun (Sei-i Tai-shogun), and ended in October, 1867 (675 years), when Yoshinobu, the last shogun of the Tokugawa, surrendered his ruling authority to the throne, there were what are known as the Five Military Governments. For thirty years of this period, beginning in July, 1573, when Yoshiaki, the last shogun of the Ashikaga, was permanently exiled from Kyoto, thus putting an end to the Ashikaga rule, and ending in March, 1603, when Iyeyasu was appointed shogun, thus founding the Tokugawa shogunate, no man held the office of shogun. In these thirty years, the third and the fourth military governments were founded by Nobunaga and Hideyoshi, respectively. However, because neither of these men held the office of shogun, these two particular military governments were not known either as "Bakufu" or as "Shogunate." Nobunaga and Hideyoshi founded their respective military governments at Azuchi and at Osaka, but they also held official positions in the imperial court and, as civil officials, ruled the empire on behalf of the emperor. Both Nobunaga and Hideyoshi were undisputed military leaders who had absolute power, yet they were not appointed shoguns, as were all the other founders of the military governments. This peculiarity is to be traced to national traditions. In 1192, Yoritomo, of the Minamoto family, founded the first military government and was appointed shogun. In 1638, Takauji, of the Ashikaga family (a branch of the Minamoto), founded the second military government and was appointed shogun. During the period of nearly four hundred years, ending in 1573, that Japan was under the rule of the first and second military governments, the descendants of Yoritomo and Takauji who succeeded them as heads of the military governments were always appointed shogun by the emperor. Thus, for hundreds of years, only men of the Minamoto blood held the title of shogun and it became a national tradition that, just as none but a prince

[299]

of the imperial blood might ascend the throne, likewise none but persons of Minamoto blood were eligible for appointment as shoguns. This tradition was strictly adhered to throughout the Feudal Period; not even the emperor might appoint as shogun a man who was not of Minamoto blood. No matter how powerful a person might be, he could not aspire to an appointment as shogun. Nobunaga and Hideyoshi ruled Japan on behalf of the emperor and occupied high civil positions in the imperial court, but they were not appointed as shoguns because they were not men of the Minamoto blood.

In 1603, Iyeyasu completed the organization of the fifth military government, and because he was the head of the Tokugawa family, which was a branch of the Minamoto family, the emperor promptly appointed him as shogun. Most Occidental historians, owing to their unfamiliarity with this Japanese tradition with respect to the appointment of the shogun, labor under the impression that the head of the military government was always a shogun and identify the military governments with the shogunate governments. In consequence, they make erroneous statements in their works, as, for example, the statement that Japan had five shogunate governments during the Feudal Period.[1]

APPENDIX 32

Diplomatic Dealings and Letters Between Japan and Korea

EVEN BEFORE THE COMPLETION of national unification, Hideyoshi had planned to invade and conquer China. In 1587, when he subjugated Kyushu, he revealed his plan to his officials and his intention to send his army to China through Korea. At that time, Hideyoshi did not understand the time-honored relations between China and Korea. He believed that the king of Korea would readily recognize his authority and would open his kingdom to him, thus making it possible for his army to march upon Peking by way of Manchuria. Accordingly he instructed Yoshitomo, the lord of Tsushima, an island in the Korean Channel, to proceed to Korea and advise the Korean king to come to Japan to make due reverence to the imperial throne. The lord of Tsushima, who was well informed with respect to conditions in Korea, hesitated to undertake this task, feeling that it was next to impossible. Yielding to the strong persuasion of Hideyoshi, the lord of Tsushima sent his trusted official to Korea in 1588, to inform the king of Korea that Hideyoshi, having completed the conquest of all the islands of Japan, had united the sixty-six provinces under his rule. He further informed the king of Korea that Hideyoshi was planning a foreign invasion. In the past, he said, the Tsushima government had sent envoys in the name of Japan a number of times. Korea had sent none in response. Therefore, he urged Korea to send immediately an envoy bearing a letter to Japan. The king of Korea did not comply with this request. Hideyoshi then decided to deal with Korea in one of two ways: should the king of Korea decide to come to Japan in person in order to show due reverence to the throne, the question would be automatically settled; otherwise, there would be an appeal to arms. The lord of Tsushima, who had extensive interests in Korea as well as in Japan, feared that diplomatic negotiations between Japan and Korea were about to take a serious turn. In 1589, accompanied by several prominent followers, he went to Korea in person. Taking advantage of this visit, the king of Korea sent a personal letter to Hideyoshi, under date of March, of the eighteenth year of the Wan-Li era of the Ming emperor (1590). The letter of the Korean king read as follows:

"Yi Yen, King of Korea, respectfully addresses His Royal Highness the King of Japan [Hideyoshi]. We are happy to be informed that you are enjoying good health these warm and calm spring days. According to our understanding, you, the Great King, have unified more than sixty provinces and have placed the entire nation under your rule. Upon receipt of this pleasing news, we were eager to send immediately to you an envoy of good will and to cultivate friendly relations with your nation. To our deep regret, because of the great distance and the dangers of the water route, we have failed to carry out this long-cherished desire. Now, we have instructed our envoys, Ko In-Kitsu, Kin Sei-Ichi, and Kyo Sei-Shi, to proceed to your country in company with your envoy who is returning thither, in order to present this letter of congratulation to you. May we hope that henceforth we shall maintain the most happy and cordial relations with our great neighboring nation. We are sending herewith some local products, which are detailed on a separate sheet. May we ask that you kindly accept this gift."[2]

The present of the king of Korea to Hideyoshi contained, among other things, one hundred tiger skins, several packages of medicinal herbs, fruit, and rice.

This letter from the king of Korea did not satisfy Hideyoshi. Under date of November, of the eighteenth year of the Tensho era of the Japanese emperor (1590), he wrote to the Korean king as follows:

"Hideyoshi, the Supreme Imperial Advisor of the Emperor of Japan, hereby addresses His Excellency the King of Korea. We have received your letter and have read it with pleasure a number of times. Throughout the past century, all our sixty-six provinces were split into small, inefficient units. The rites and laws of our nation were not observed, and unruly military chieftains entirely ignored the imperial authority. Moved by deep regret because of the chaotic condition of our nation, I waged war upon the rebellious subjects of the throne and overcame all of them within the space of a few years. Every district, whether near or far, including even small and distant islands, is now under complete control. Although I was born to a family of low rank, my mother conceived me immediately after she had dreamed that the Sun had entered into her bosom. A physiognomist interpreted this dream and predicted that I was destined to extend my authority to all parts of the world wherever the sun shines. When I came to manhood, my benevolent rule would be admired by nations in every direction. People within the four seas would all come under my influence and power. Because I was born with so great a destiny, which was revealed by this omen, those who have fostered feelings of enmity and opposition have been crushed and destroyed. Whenever and against whomever I have waged war, the victory has always been mine. The lands and districts invaded by me have always been conquered. Now our empire has entered upon a period of peace and prosperity, and the people are enjoying a benevolent rule. Lonely old men and forlorn widows and orphans are all well provided for. Both the national wealth and that of individuals have been so greatly augmented that it is unparalleled in our history. Since the nation's founding, our empire has never before witnessed such glory as that of our imperial court and such splendor as that of our imperial capital.

"However, human life in this world is brief. Even those who have enjoyed rare longevity have barely attained the age of a hundred years. I am not willing to spend the remaining years of my life in the land of my birth. According to my idea, the nation that I would create should not be separated by mountains and seas, but should include them all. In starting my conquest, I planned that our forces should proceed to Tai-Min Koku [China] and compel the people there to adopt our customs and manners. Then that vast country, consisting of more than four hundred provinces, would enjoy our imperial protection and benevolence for millions of years to come. I have in mind a plan of conquest which will certainly be carried to a successful ending. Your kingdom has taken the lead among the continental nations by sending an envoy to our court, thus showing reverence to our throne. You have acted in accordance with the wise saying of the ancients that one who has foresight and is humble and cautious will always be free from grief and worry. Even those nations that are distant from us and even the islands in far-off seas cannot expect mercy if they delay in joining our glorious military campaign. You, King of Korea, are hereby instructed to join us when we proceed to Tai-Min [China], at the head of all your fighting men. You may thereby further renew your pledge of service due to us as a neighboring nation. Our sole desire is to have our glorious name revered in the three nations [China, Korea, and Japan]. We are hereby presenting you some of our local products, as described on a separate sheet. You are requested to accept them.

"[Dated]: The days in the midst of winter, in the eighteenth year of the Tensho era.

"Hideyoshi, the Supreme Imperial Advisor
of the Emperor of Japan."[3]

In the spring of 1591, King Syong-Cho of Korea replied to the letter of Hideyoshi. The king's letter read, in part:

"You stated in your letter that you were planning to invade the supreme nation [China] and requested that our kingdom [Korea] join in your military undertaking. This demand was most unexpected. We cannot even understand how you have dared to plan such an undertaking and to make such a request of us.... For thousands of years, from the time of yore when Chi-Tsu, the founder of the kingdom of Korea, received the investiture from the Chow dynasty [of China], up to our own time, our kingdom has always been known as a nation of righteousness.... The relation of ruler and subject has been strictly observed between the supreme nation [China] and our kingdom. In former generations, your nation likewise sent tribute-bearing envoys time and again to the imperial capital [of China]. As for our kingdom, generation after generation, we have reverently adhered and attended to all duties and obligations due from a tributary state of Chung-Chao [China]. In fact, Chung-Chao has always regarded our kingdom as a part of its own nation. Our two nations have always kept each other informed of all national events and affairs. Each has given ready assistance when the other has suffered calamity or has been in trouble. Our two nations have acted as a single family, maintaining the relationship of father and son as well as that of ruler and subject. This inseparable and amiable relationship between Chung-Chao and our kingdom is well known throughout the world. Your kingdom should be acquainted with this fact.... We shall certainly not desert 'our lord and father nation' [China] and join with a neighboring nation in her unjust and unwise military undertaking. Moreover, to invade another nation is an act of which men of culture and intellectual attainments should feel ashamed. We shall certainly not take up arms against the supreme nation. As all the members of our nation are just and righteous persons, as well as cultured and intellectual in their attainments, [they] know how to revere 'our lord and father nation'.... We urgently hope that you will reflect on these things and will come to understand your own situation as well as ours. We would conclude this letter by saying that your proposed undertaking is the most reckless, imprudent, and daring of any of which we have ever heard."[4]

APPENDIX 33

A Letter to Hideyoshi from the King of Liu Chiu and Hideyoshi's Reply

THE KINGDOM of Liu Chiu is a very small archipelago situated between China and Japan. It maintained its independent existence by pledging allegiance to both China and Japan. Liu Chiu always sent tribute-bearing envoys to both China and Japan; yet, with the knowledge of Japan, the Liu Chiu kings always received investiture by the emperor of China. Consequently, after the death of the ruling king, the crown prince could not succeed to the throne, with the title of king, without the consent of the emperor of China. Although Japan considered Liu Chiu as her tributary state, the ruling authority in Liu Chiu was entrusted to the lord of Shimazu, most powerful feudal lord in Kyushu. Consequently, the kingdom of Liu Chiu was, during the Feudal Period, regarded as a dependency of the lord of Shimazu. When Hideyoshi completed the national unification of Japan, King Shonei of Liu Chiu sent the following letter to Hideyoshi.

"According to our understanding, more than sixty provinces having been completely subjugated, all the people in Japan now pay due reverence to you and pledge their loyalty to the throne. Moreover, we have heard that your authority has been extended to Korea, to the Philippines, and to other islands in the south. Now, under your rule, all the peoples dwelling within the bounds of the four seas are enjoying peace and prosperity. Permit me to congratulate you upon the fact that you have put into actual practice the ancient admonition, 'Put aside bows and arrows and protect and bless the barbarians in all four directions.' Our small and humble island kingdom, because of its great distance and because of lack of funds, has not rendered due reverence to you. However, now, in compliance with the instructions that our great lord, Shimazu Yoshihisa, has sent us by his envoy, Daijiji Seiin-Osho, we have caused Joten Ryotoan-Osho to proceed to your country, carrying with him a humble gift that consists of lacquer ware of the Ming dynasty, together with some of our local products, as described on a separate sheet. These articles are sent to you with the sole desire to show our sincerity and courtesy, and not because we think them of any great value.

"[Dated] May 17, of the seventeenth year of the Wan-Li era of the Ming Emperor [1589].

"To His Royal Highness the Supreme Imperial Advisor of the Emperor of Japan."[5]

Hideyoshi replied to this letter of the king of Liu Chiu as follows:

"Hideyoshi, the Supreme Imperial Advisor of the Emperor of Japan, hereby addresses His Excellency the King of Liu Chiu. We have received your letter and have read it repeatedly with an impression that we were in the same hall, and that you were there to address us in person. As you stated in your letter, our nation, which consists of more than sixty provinces, having been subjugated without leaving a single foot of land unconquered, our people are now under a benevolent rule and are enjoying peace and prosperity. Our only regret is that we have not yet established our desired relations with nations of the outside world. We have now received products of your country, and these are of great interest to us. We have therefore become increasingly desirous of extending our observations beyond our boundaries, and thereby increasing our knowledge. In fact, it has long been our cherished desire to place foreign lands under our rule and to have the people therein enjoy our benevolent rule and protection. Of all the nations, yours is the first to send an envoy, together with rare and unusual things. This has pleased us greatly. It is human nature to be interested in things that come from distant lands, and also to be attracted by things that are rarely seen. For this reason we are particularly impressed with the gifts that you have sent. From this time on, although our countries are separated by thousands of miles, we may nevertheless maintain friendly relations with the feeling that your country, together with the other nations that are within the four seas, constitute but a single family. We are hereby sending you some of the local products of our country, which are described on a separate sheet. Further details will be given orally by Tenryuji Toan Todo, whom Shimazu Yoshihisa will send to you as his representative.

"[Dated] February 28, of the 18th year of the Tensho era [1590].

"The Supreme Imperial Advisor of the Emperor of Japan.

"To the King of Liu Chiu."[6]

In 1591, when Hideyoshi decided to invade Korea, he ordered the king of Liu Chiu to come to Japan at the head of a large army, bringing with him the necessary provisions, and to participate in the pending campaign. He threatened that if the king of Liu Chiu failed to comply with this demand, his kingdom would suffer invasion. Liu Chiu consists of 55 small islands, the total area of which is 935 square miles. At that time, its total population was approximately 350,000. The king of Liu Chiu found that both in respect of man power and of financial strength, it would be impossible for him to comply with the demand of Hideyoshi. He sent Hideyoshi's letter to the viceroy of Fukien and asked that he forward it to the Ming throne, so that the kingdom of Liu Chiu might be rescued from its critical situation. No assistance was given him by the Ming throne, but a sort of compromise was arrived at. Taking into consideration the great distance of Liu Chiu from Japan, and Liu Chiu's lack of man power, Hideyoshi exempted the kingdom of Liu Chiu from giving military service, but at the same time he stipulated that Liu Chiu should meet annual military requisitions consisting of set amounts of gold, silver, foodstuffs, and forage. Throughout the seven years of Hideyoshi's military campaign in Korea, Liu Chiu was obliged to meet these demands. She was thus greatly impoverished.

Liu Chiu is one of the smallest and most insignificant countries in the Orient, yet she constitutes a landmark in modern Oriental history. The annexation of Liu Chiu by Japan in 1879 marks the beginning of Japan's aggression and national expansion in the Orient. Prior to that time, the kingdom of Liu Chiu had maintained its national existence by pledging allegiance to both China and Japan. In 1879, however, Japan annexed Liu Chiu in spite of the strong opposition of China. This marked the beginning of the ill-feeling between China and Japan.[7]

APPENDIX 34

Letters Sent by Hideyoshi to the Rulers of the Philippines and of Formosa

THE MILITARY CAMPAIGNS of Hideyoshi in the sixteenth century had as their goal the conquest of Korea and of China, thus to bring

Japan, Korea, and China under a single rule; and then to proceed to India and to Persia with the purpose of creating a single great Asiatic empire. At the same time, he planned to extend his power over Liu Chiu, Formosa, the Philippines, Borneo, and the other South Sea islands. His ultimate aim was to extend the power of Japan over Asia on both land and sea. In dealing with the nations on the continent, Hideyoshi employed military power; he sought to gain the suzerainty over the islands through diplomacy. While the campaign was being waged on the continent, he sent threatening letters to the rulers of the respective islands.

In 1591, only a few months before his army set sail for the continent, Hideyoshi sent a personal letter to the Spanish governor of the Philippines. The letter read as follows:

"For more than a hundred years, military leaders in all the provinces had fought with one another and had been continuously engaged in warfare. Our country had thereby lost its national unity, having been split into innumerable separate units. It had also lost communication and traffic facilities. My birth was accompanied by miraculous omens, which were interpreted by physiognomists to mean that I was destined to rule nations. This prediction has been fulfilled. Even in my youth, to control national affairs became my duty. Within less than ten years the unification of the nation was effected, not even an inch of land being left unconquered. Our national authority has been extended far beyond our borders. Korea, Liu Chiu, and other nations that are far away have sent their tribute-bearing envoys and paid homage to us. We are now undertaking the conquest of Tai-Min [China]. This step, however, is not actuated by our own inclination, but is taken in pursuance of a heavenly command. As for your country, we have not yet received either homage or tribute. Accordingly, we have decided to send our military forces to your country to mete out due punishment. Our war vessels are ready to sail to your shores. However, Harada Magoshichiro, who has visited your country a number of times in connection with his trade undertakings, and who is therefore well informed concerning your national affairs, has approached us through one of our trusted officials and has stated that, if he should be permitted to proceed to your country [the Philippines] and explain to you how and why our war vessels have been made ready for a punitive expedition to the Philippines, he would be able to convince you that great danger to your country was pending, and thus to persuade you to meet our demand. Impressed by the ancient saying that a man of genius may sometimes remain in his military headquarters and yet win a brilliant victory over a country a thousand miles away, we have decided that Harada, notwithstanding his lowly origin, should be permitted to act in accordance with his own plans. Therefore, at the present time, no command will be issued to our military leaders to proceed to the Philippines. In the coming spring [1592], we shall establish our military headquarters [for the conquest of China] at Hizen in Kyushu. You are hereby instructed to proceed to Hizen without delay and to make submission to us. If you hesitate to act promptly, your country shall surely suffer from our punitive expedition. You are advised to refrain from placing yourself in such a position that regret will not save you.

"[Dated] September 15, of the nineteenth year of the Tensho era [1591]."[8]

In the early spring of 1592, a ship from Japan arrived at Manila. It brought word that a Japanese army of great fighting strength would shortly come to the Philippines. Upon investigation, it was found that a man named Gaspar Faranda, who had lived in the Philippines for some years, had gone to Japan and had informed Hideyoshi that the Philippines might be readily conquered because of the total lack of defensive works in the islands. Hideyoshi thereupon decided first to send an envoy to the Philippines with the demand that the Philippine government should recognize his authority and send tribute. Gómez Pérez das Mariñas, who was then the Spanish governor of the Philippines, was greatly astonished by this news. He immediately ordered that the coast defenses of the Philippines be strengthened. At the same time, the governor of the Philippines wrote to his home government in Spain as well as to the governor of New Spain (Mexico) in North America, asking that they send the necessary military supplies. While the governor was thus making military preparation against possible invasion by Japan, Harada arrived from Japan bearing the letter of Hideyoshi, dated September 15, 1591. The governor, desiring to avoid military trouble, received Harada in grand style. Later, the governor sent Captain Lope de Llano and a Dominican priest by the name of Juan Cobos as his envoys to Japan. Upon their arrival at Nagoya, Hizen, in Kyushu, where Hideyoshi maintained military headquarters, these envoys presented to him the reply of the governor of the Philippines. It was dated May 1, 1592. In this reply, the governor first explained the national conditions and standing of Spain. Since the founding of the Spanish empire, he stated, Spain had conquered nations both large and small in all parts of the world. Thus extending her domain in the east, west, north, and south, Spain had become the greatest and most powerful nation in the world. He then said that a tradesman named Harada had brought the letter of Hideyoshi to him. The governor eulogized Hideyoshi and remarked that he was well informed with respect to the genius and ability of Hideyoshi and of his great accomplishments in the Orient. Because he was a great admirer of Hideyoshi, he was happy to receive a letter from him, but it was both a surprise and a disappointment to him to find that Hideyoshi had entrusted a state paper to an ordinary tradesman and had empowered such a person to transact affairs of international moment between the two great empires. Because of his surprise and disappointment, the governor continued, he had begun to suspect the genuineness of the letter purporting to come from Hideyoshi. If so great a man as Hideyoshi should send a letter to the Philippine government, he surely would send a trusted statesman as his envoy. The governor therefore feared that a certain unscrupulous person was pretending to be an envoy sent by Hideyoshi and had come with the sole purpose of exacting things of value. In order to discover the exact situation, the governor decided to send two envoys to Japan to ascertain whether Hideyoshi had really sent Harada as his envoy and whether the letter that Harada had brought was a genuine state paper. The governor concluded his letter by saying:

"We, however, have already sent to the King of Spain the letter that Harada brought to us, and have requested instructions from our King concerning how we should deal with this matter. Because it is the policy of our King to maintain friendly relations with all the nations in the world, whether near or far, we believe that our King will direct us to deal with courtesy with your country. Therefore, before long, we may be able to enter into amicable relations. At any rate, your country and our nation are two of the great powers in the world. Consequently, both should strive to maintain friendly relations and a prosperous existence. We hereby send Lope de Llano and Juan Cobos as our envoys, bearing some of our local products, in order to show due recognition to you and also as a sort of recognition of the letter brought to us by Harada."[9]

THE LETTER SENT BY HIDEYOSHI TO FORMOSA

In November, 1593, when the invading army of Hideyoshi had won a series of brilliant victories, thus making the positions of both China and Korea hopeless, and when, upon Chinese initiative, negotiations for peace were in progress, Hideyoshi sent an envoy to Formosa carrying the following letter:

"The sun is the source of power and energy. All things upon which the sun shines, including the land and the water, the mountains and the rivers, trees and plants, birds and insects, enjoy its blessings. When my mother conceived me, she was given a miraculous omen with respect to the sun, and on the very night that I was born the room was suddenly aglow with sunlight, thus changing night to day. All persons present were astounded. Physiognomists gathered and debated upon this wonderful happening. They finally divined that the child whose birth was attended by these miracles was destined to become a man of unusual attainments. His benevolent virtues would shine brilliantly in every land within the four seas. His dignity and authority would extend in all directions. This prediction is fulfilled in me. Within less than ten years, I have conquered and overcome all people of the unruly classes, thus unifying and pacifying the whole of the Nation Within the Sea. Even distant nations in the outside world have learned to admire our benevolent rule and to express their urgent desire to become our dependencies. Envoys have sailed from their respective countries and have rivaled each other in speed, hoping to be first in making obeisance to our throne.

"However, Korea, a land that was long our tributary state, has failed to live up to her pledge of loyalty. At the very time that our troops started out to conquer Tai-Min [China], Korea rebelled. I therefore sent a punitive expedition under the command of prominent military leaders. Having lost all hope, the Korean king abandoned his national capital, setting fire to it and reducing it to ashes. Upon hearing of the national crisis in Korea, Tai-Min sent several hundreds of thousands of troops with the hope of saving that kingdom. In spite of the fact that those Chinese armies engaged in a number of desperate battles with our troops, they always suffered defeat. Tai-Min therefore sent an envoy to sue for peace. We thereupon built a number of fortresses in Keishodo in Korea, and ordered our troops to cease fighting and gather in these fortresses, there to remain until the sincerity of the peace proposal of Tai-Min might be ascertained.

"The Philippines and Liu Chiu have sent tribute-bearing envoys to our country, thus showing due reverence. These nations have learned to establish relations with us by utilizing both water and land facilities. Your country, however, has not yet sent any envoy to our military headquarters. This lack of loyalty will certainly bring the curse of Heaven upon you. Because of geographical disadvantage, however, your country has not been kept informed of conditions in the outside world, and has therefore unintentionally disregarded our authority. We hereby send Harada as our envoy, bearing this letter. He will soon sail to your country. If you should fail to pay due reverence to us after having received our instructions, we shall immediately instruct our military leaders to invade your country and to inflict severe punishment. We wish to remind you that it is the sun that makes all things in the universe to grow, and it is the sun that makes all things to dry up and perish. We leave the entire matter to your conscientious consideration.

"[Dated] November 5, of the second year of the Bunroku era [1593]."[10]

When Hideyoshi's envoy, Harada, reached Formosa, he found there neither a central government nor a ruling authority. Consequently, he returned to Japan bringing back Hideyoshi's letter with him. At the present time, this document is to be found in the archives of the family of the Marquis Mayeda (the lord of Kaga during the Feudal Period).

Appendix 35

The Letter of Hideyoshi to the Ruler of India

In 1591, when Hideyoshi was completing his preparations for the sending of his army to China, the Portuguese viceroy at Goa sent an envoy named Valignano to Japan, in the name of India. In January, 1591, Valignano, having been granted an interview, presented to Hideyoshi the letter entrusted to him by the Portuguese viceroy. Under date of July 25, in the nineteenth year of the Tensho era (1591), Hideyoshi wrote the following letter to the viceroy:

"You have sent us a letter from a great distance. I have read it and have been so impressed that I feel as though I could see the mountains and rivers of your country thousands of miles away. As you stated in your letter, our country, which consists of more than sixty provinces, had long suffered from continuous warfare, the people having been deprived almost completely of days of peace and tranquillity. Disorderly people rivaled each other in wrongdoing. All the military leaders formed factions of their own and quite ignored the imperial authority. I, having been born and raised under the special favor of the Sun, possess cultural attainments together with all essential knowledge for ruling the people. When I reached manhood, I had learned how to conduct all the national affairs with great far-sightedness and caution. I have always been guided by benevolence, fairness, and courage. I have trained all our fighting men in this spirit, and have ruled the masses with great sympathy and kindness. The affairs of the nation are being conducted by prompt and strict enforcement of our national laws, both in matters of reward and in matters of punishment. By reason of this, within only a few years I have completed the national unification, and our empire has been placed on the strongest foundation in its history. Our authority has now been extended near and far to many nations in the outside world. These nations have manifested a sincere desire to maintain their existence under our benevolent rule. Rulers in the east, west, south, and north have made ready obeisance to us. The imperial commands of our sage Emperor may soon be transmitted to all corners of the world. Our military leaders, who are noted for their genius and ability, are able to extend our national dignity and authority far beyond our borders.

"Facilities for transportation and communication in our country having been completed, the land and the sea having been cleared of disorderly people, and our national life and existence having been entirely reformed, our nation is now an outstanding world power. It is our desire to extend our ruling power over Tai-Min Koku [China]. A plan has been completed for sending our war vessels and fighting men to Chuka [China]. It will be carried out before many days. After completing our heavenly mission of conquering China, we shall readily find a road by which to reach your country [India]. Our war vessels and fighting men will accomplish the work entrusted to them regardless both of distance and the sort of warriors they may conquer. . . ."[11]

In this letter, Hideyoshi indicated that he stood ready to invade India after completing his campaign in China. The letter was dated July 25, in the nineteenth year of the Tensho era (1591). This letter, translated into English, and somewhat modified, is to be found in Hildreth's *Japan As It Was and Is* (1855 ed.; pp. 110–11). The original draft is now in the possession of the Tomioka (Kenzo) family, Kyoto.

APPENDIX 36

Hideyoshi's Plan of Continental Conquest, Sent to Kampaku Hidetsugu

ON APRIL 12, 1592, the invading army of Hideyoshi effected a landing at Fusan, Korea, and on May 2 the national capital of Korea was occupied. On the sixteenth day of the same month, the news of this great military success in Korea was received by Hideyoshi at his military headquarters in Nagoya, Hizen, Kyushu. Two days later (i.e., on May 18) Hideyoshi framed an outline of his intended continental conquest. He sent it to Kyoto addressed to Hidetsugu, his nephew, whom he had adopted as his son, resigning in his favor the official position of *Kampaku* ("Supreme Advisor of the Emperor"). The document consisted of twenty-four articles. In them Hideyoshi first instructed Hidetsugu to prepare to join the military campaign, and then explained how China, Japan, and Korea should be organized into the first unit of his empire. The document is to be found in the archives of the family of the Marquis Mayeda, and is therefore sometimes called "the Mayeda document." It says:

"1. Your Excellency [Hidetsugu] is hereby advised to make preparations for the military campaign so that you may be ready to march from Kyoto in January or February of the coming year.

"2. The national capital of Korea was occupied on the second day of this month. I myself will cross the sea to the continent. Before long, the whole of Tai-Min Koku [China] will be under our rule. Your Excellency will then be expected to proceed to China in the official capacity of Kampaku of that great nation.

"3. Your Excellency is to sail from Hyogo [Kobe] with thirty thousand fighting men under your personal command.

"4. Although we do not believe that there is any military organization in China, Korea, or Japan strong enough to oppose us, yet, for the sake of caution as well as to impress the people with the military strength and efficiency of our fighting men, we should provide our forces with every sort of military equipment, as well as with abundant provisions. All the men in our forces, of both high and low rank, shall be strictly instructed with respect to these points."

In Articles 5, 6, 7, and 8, Hideyoshi gave minute instructions with respect to the provisions and rations as well as the types, qualities, and quantities of weapons with which Hidetsugu should supply his army.

"9. In case of necessity, Your Excellency may first transfer silver bullion to the amount of ten thousand *mai* from the treasure house at the Juraku palace to the Osaka castle. You may also use gold bullion from the Osaka castle to the amount of one thousand *mai*. The rate of exchange of gold and silver should be taken as one to ten.

"10. If there is need of damask silk, gold silk brocade, and other textiles, Your Excellency may order them in any quantities from the traders."

In Articles 11, 12, 13, 14, and 15, instructions are given concerning armor and chests, and concerning the horses to be distributed to the various districts as well as the coolies to be employed by Hidetsugu along the route of march.

"16. After our military campaign in China is begun, we shall request Miyabe Keijun to take entire charge of the national capital of Korea. He will be summoned to Korea in due time. Your Excellency is hereby instructed to advise Miyabe to prepare for this important post.

"17. As soon as we have conquered Korea, His Majesty our Emperor will be requested to remove the imperial capital from Kyoto to Peking, where he will be enthroned as the Ruler of the Great Empire. Your Excellency must be prepared for this great national undertaking. It is to be hoped that this will be effected the year after next [1594]. . . .

"18. After the enthronement of His Majesty our Emperor, at Peking, he will appoint Your Excellency [Hidetsugu] Kampaku of the new empire. Then, either Hashiba Hidetoshi or Ukida Hideiye will be appointed Kampaku of the empire of Japan.

"19. The imperial throne of Japan will most likely be occupied by His Royal Highness Prince Hachijo.

"20. The rule over the kingdom of Korea shall be entrusted to either Hashiba Hidekatsu or to Ukida Hideiye, and Shibata Hideaki shall be appointed governor of Kyushu.

"21. When His Majesty our Emperor is enthroned at Peking, it will be necessary for him to take the long journey from Japan to China. All the rites, regulations, and ceremonials connected with this imperial journey, as well as the selection of the route to be taken, should be carefully planned. The route of the imperial journey from Japan to Shintan Koku [China] should be along the route of our military march. . . .

"22. Korea and Tai-Min [China] will soon be conquered. We should therefore arrange matters so that the people dwelling along our route of march shall not suffer by reason of our coming. The magistrates whom we have dispatched to various parts of these two nations to inform the people that there is no reason to fear our coming because both their lives and property will be secure, will soon return to us. When they come back, we shall assign them to some military service.

"23. As for the persons who are to take charge of Heian-Jo [Kyoto] and of the Juraku palace in our absence, their names will be announced later.

"24. Miyabe Keijun, Ishikawa Sadamasa, and other persons should begin immediately to prepare for the work to be assigned them. I hereby request Your Excellency to advise them to present themselves at our military headquarters as soon as they can.

"Nishio Bungo-no-Kami is hereby instructed to carry these articles to Your Excellency. Further details will be delivered by him orally.

"[Dated] May 18, in the twentieth year of the Tensho era [1592].

"Hideyoshi [SEAL]"

"To His Excellency, Kampaku."[12]

In this plan for continental conquest, Hideyoshi, instead of outlining the way in which China was to be invaded and conquered, gave details with respect to the manner in which the new empire embracing China, Japan, and Korea was to be ruled. Evidently, upon receipt of the news of the occupation of the national capital of Korea, Hideyoshi took it for granted that China, as well as Korea, would be conquered without any appreciable military opposition. This hasty conclusion was undoubtedly one of the principal causes of the failure of Hideyoshi's continental campaign. However, events of the fifteenth and sixteenth centuries in China and Korea, together with the actual conditions of his time, led Hideyoshi to ignore the existence of both China and Korea as military powers. For nearly two hundred years, down even to Hideyoshi's boyhood, all the provinces along the coasts of China and Korea had been at the mercy of Japanese pirate bands. Cities and towns and even fortified military strongholds had crumbled under the attacks of the pirates, and the organized Chinese army of several thousand men had been dispersed by a pirate band of Japanese approximately one hundred strong. In his own time, the Japanese army had either destroyed or routed all the Korean armies that had offered battle, and had stormed and occupied all the strongholds along the route of march. Within less than three weeks, the Japanese conquered and occupied districts and provinces that it took travelers two weeks to pass through. The national capital of Korea was occupied by Hideyoshi's army. When the news of the fall of the capital reached Hideyoshi, he decided to cross the water to Korea and take charge of his army in person with the view of immediately starting to invade China.

All these events led Hideyoshi to conclude that his military march into China would surely bring about the conquest and occupation of that country, and they explain why, in his document to Hidetsugu, Hideyoshi outlined how the new empire was to be ruled instead of telling him how it should be established.

APPENDIX 37

The Kumiya Document, Detailing Hideyoshi's Continental Campaign

ON MAY 18, 1592, the date on which Hideyoshi prepared and sent his plan for the conquest of the continent to Hidetsugu, Yamanaka Kichinai (Yamakichi), private secretary to Hideyoshi, wrote a long letter to Mesdames Higashi and Kyakushin, ladies in waiting to Kita-no-Mandokoro, wife of Hideyoshi. It is generally believed that Yamakichi wrote this letter at Hideyoshi's instruction and addressed it to the two ladies in waiting with the hope that they would inform Hideyoshi's wife of the contents. This letter is now in the possession of Kumiya Rokurozayemon, a resident of the city of Kohama in the Province of Wakasa, and it is therefore known as "the Kumiya document." The content of this document as a whole duplicates that of the Mayeda document. However, besides giving more details, Yamakichi gave information on subjects not mentioned in the Mayeda document. The Mayeda and the Kumiya documents are therefore taken as authentic material with respect to Hideyoshi's ambitions and plans for continental conquest.

The content of the Kumiya document is as follows:

"On the second day of this month [May 2, 1592], the national capital of Korea was occupied by our army. His Excellency our Lord [Hideyoshi] is now busily occupied making preparations to cross the water to Korea. All the transports and other vessels that are now in Korean waters have been called back to Japan. Upon their arrival, our Lord will sail to Korea taking with him all the units of fighting men. According to present plans, our Lord expects to be in the national capital of Korea by the end of this month [May, 1592]. However, the length of time it will take to reach Korea depends entirely upon the condition of the waters. The date of his arrival in the Korean capital is therefore uncertain. . . .

"According to the news from the war front, when the army of our Lord had advanced halfway on the road to the capital, and had crossed the river, the King of Korea set fire to his palace and fled to an unknown destination. Our forces are now searching in various directions for this fleeing king. Our Lord deeply regrets this incident because he has time and again given instructions to his military leaders in Korea to see that the King should not be harmed in any way. [The next ten words in the document cannot be deciphered because the manuscript is worm-eaten.] The King may die of starvation. Therefore, our Lord has ordered his men in Korea to do all in their power to find the King. At any rate, it should be understood that the King will be treated with due courtesy. According to the latest reports, the King has fled to a place called Keian-Do near the border of Taito [China]. Because our troops are now pursuing the King in the right direction, he will surely be taken ere long. Magistrates have been sent to various districts in Korea to assure the people that their lives and property will be safeguarded. Those who have fled from cities and villages because of the fighting will be advised to return to their homes, as all places, including the national capital and the leading cities, have remained in perfect condition. If the people will but return to their homes, they will enjoy a happy and peaceful existence and will not be molested in any way. Because all the agricultural land in Korea has been thoroughly cultivated, the standing crops and other farm products are growing well and give the appearance of fields in Japan during the month of June. As for rice, it has been stored in abundance, not only in the national capital and in the leading cities, but also in great quantities in every district and village. Our officers and soldiers have been both surprised and pleased to find these unexpected supplies. It has been reported that many warehouses, one *cho* square, filled with hulled rice, have been found in various districts.

"According to our understanding, our Lord will first cross the water to Korea, taking with him as many fighting men as he can. All the transports and other vessels will be sent back to Japan immediately so that more troops may embark for Korea. Then the entire fighting force in Korea under the personal command of our Lord will invade Taito [China]. It is planned that Peking, the national capital of Taito, will be occupied by our Lord before the end of this year. In the absence of our Lord, Miyabe Keijun and Hashiba Hideaki will be entrusted with the entire charge of the Korean capital and the Nagoya military headquarters, respectively. They have already been instructed to present themselves at the military headquarters of our Lord by August of this year. Upon the conquest of Taito, the authority over that empire will be entrusted to His Excellency our Kampaku [Hidetsugu]. Therefore, our Lord has already advised the Kampaku to prepare for this important office by June of next year [1593]. His Majesty our Emperor has consented to take up his residence in the national capital of Taito [Peking]. Therefore, after Taito has been conquered, our Emperor will undertake a long journey from Kyoto to Peking. Our Lord has given instructions that due preparations be made for this great national event. About ten of the large provinces surrounding the city of Peking will be set aside and their revenues will be used exclusively for the expenses of the imperial court and of the imperial household. . . . Either Hashiba Hidekatsu or Ukida Hideiye will be entrusted with power in Korea. As for our Lord, he will at first reside in Peking, whence he will control the national affairs of China, Japan, and Korea. After the founding of the new empire is completed, he will appoint some man of worth as his deputy at Peking, and will establish his own permanent residence at Ningpo [a seaport in South China, nearest to Japan].

"All military leaders who shall render successful vanguard service in the coming campaign in Taito will be liberally rewarded with grants of extensive states near India, with the privilege of conquering India and extending their domains in that vast empire. . . . According to our understanding, Her Excellency Kita-no-Mando-koro [Hideyoshi's wife] will be requested by our Lord to join him in due time. Further detail concerning this matter will be entered into at the time when our Lord sails for Korea. I shall then write you again. Hoping that you will have opportunity to approach Her Excellency Kita-no-Mandokoro, and make known to her the content of this letter, I remain,

"Yamakichi

"[Dated] May 18 [1592].

"To Mesdames Higashi Sama and Kiyakushin Sama."[13]

APPENDIX 38

Hideyoshi's First Plan of Crossing the Waters to Korea and Its Abandonment

IT HAD BEEN the practice of Hideyoshi to plan each campaign himself and to lead his army to the field of battle. Under no circumstances did he trust others to take command; hence all the battles that he fought, both great and small, were under his direction. In 1592, when he began the campaign of continental conquest, he first sent his army, 160,000 strong, to Korea, keeping about 250,000 as a reserve force in Japan. He remained at Nagoya in Kyushu, which was the nearest way of approach to Korea. It was his plan first to establish a military base at Nagoya and then to cross the water to Korea, there to take entire charge of the army and lead it in the conquest of China. The vanguard of the first division of the army effected a landing in Korea on April 12, and the vanguard of the second division landed on April 17. On May 2, the national capital of Korea was taken, and on May 18, 1592, just two days after the news of the fall of the Korean capital had reached him at his military headquarters in Nagoya, Hideyoshi announced that he would sail at once to Korea, in accordance with his statement in the Mayeda document. Yamanaka, Hideyoshi's private secretary, stated in the Kumiya document that Hideyoshi had planned to reach the Korean capital by the end of May, 1592.

In a personal letter dated May 6, 1592, and addressed to his wife at Osaka, Hideyoshi briefly outlined his intended campaign on the continent. This letter read, in part:

"The national capital of Korea will soon be taken. I shall join our army there. The summer clothes that you so thoughtfully sent to me will be gladly worn by me there in Korea. I fully expect to celebrate the coming September Sekku [a national holiday which falls on September 9] at the capital of Taito [China], Peking.

"Our invading armies have stormed and occupied numerous cities and strongholds in Korea and are now rapidly advancing toward the Korean capital, which is about sixty miles distant from the waters in which our ships are anchored. . . . China, as well as Korea, will soon be conquered. Hoping that the happy days will soon come when I shall be able to request you to join me in the conquered lands, I remain,

"Taiko [Hideyoshi]

"[Dated] May 6, 1592."[14]

The content of this letter of Hideyoshi's to his wife, as also the content of the Kumiya document, bears witness to the fact that in the early part of May, 1592, he fully planned to make a triumphant entry into the Korean capital by the end of May, and to take Peking, the national capital of China, by the middle of September, 1592. This military schedule could not be carried out. In May, 1592, when all preparations had been made for the sailing of Hideyoshi to Korea, Iyeyasu and Toshiiye, the two most powerful leaders and statesmen in Japan, strongly urged Hideyoshi not to attempt so serious and hazardous an undertaking. This matter is described in the letter of Joda, a personal friend of Hideyoshi, to the chief priest of the Tojiu monastery at Kyoto, under the date of June 10, 1592.

The main content of this letter is as follows:

"Our Lord Taiko [Hideyoshi] has fully determined to cross the water to Korea. He has completed all preparations for so doing. However, Iyeyasu and Toshiiye have come forward and earnestly appealed to Hideyoshi not to risk his life. They have stated that, as May and June mark the beginning of the stormy season, it would be a most hazardous undertaking to attempt to cross the water. They have said further that if Hideyoshi should be overcome in this venturesome voyage, the very existence of the nation would be jeopardized. Because Hideyoshi's life is too precious to be risked in so reckless an undertaking, if it should be necessary for some man of great military experience to go, either Iyeyasu or Toshiiye or both should be sent. . . . Under the strong pressure of these two great military leaders, Hideyoshi has been obliged to reconsider."[15]

Iyeyasu and Toshiiye had been colleagues of Hideyoshi's during the rule of Nobunaga, and after Nobunaga's death both had cooperated with Hideyoshi in successfully effecting national unification. These two men later became very powerful in both military and national matters, and Hideyoshi therefore could not entirely ignore their advice. Iyeyasu and Toshiiye not only objected to Hideyoshi's plan of crossing the water; they also even opposed the whole idea of a continental campaign in view of Hideyoshi's advanced age. They began by objecting to his crossing the water to Korea. Their hope was that he would ultimately abandon the idea of going in person to Korea to take command of the army; that, then, the scale of the campaign would be gradually reduced; and that, soon, when Hideyoshi's ambitions had been partly satisfied, the whole matter might come to an end. While Hideyoshi's plan to cross the water was gradually developing into a serious national problem, in the summer of 1592 the Emperor Goyozei wrote a personal letter to him, requesting that he abandon so serious and desperate an undertaking. The emperor's letter read as follows:

"Your plan to proceed to Korea, braving great storms and dangerous seas, is both too serious and too desperate to be considered. You should realize how precious is your life and how necessary you are to the national welfare. A man of your genius and attainments may direct an army thousands of miles distant and be able to win a brilliant victory, as great military leaders of yore have done. Moreover, the military men whom you have already sent to the continent, together with those whom you are about to send, will be capable of conducting the military work satisfactorily. For the sake of the throne and for the sake of the empire, we urgently request that you abandon your plan to go in person. If you will but concur in our conclusion, you will relieve us of worry and make us happy. Our imperial envoy, to whom we are entrusting this letter, has been instructed to make known our desires orally and in detail."[16]

This was the first time in the history of Japan that the emperor had ever addressed a subject with the purpose of expressing confidence and trust in him. Hideyoshi was greatly impressed by the words of the emperor. Furthermore, Iyeyasu and Toshiiye urged Hideyoshi at least to change his original plan; that is, first to send his reserve forces to the continent, and then, a few months later, when the stormy season should be over, to proceed to Korea in person. If he should persist in going immediately to Korea, even though he might reach that country in safety, the armies that he would leave behind would rival each other in their desire to join their commander. They might embark regardless of the weather, thus placing their lives at the mercy of the sea, and possibly meeting a fate similar to that of Kublai Khan's armada in the thirteenth century, which went to the bottom.

Finally, Hideyoshi consented to postpone his date of sailing to Korea until March of the next year (1593). He sent the following letter in the autumn of 1592 to the military leaders in Korea:

"All preparations for crossing the waters having been completed, I made ready to sail. However, Iyeyasu, Toshiiye, and several other prominent military men came forward and begged that I change the plans, saying that the hurricane season was approaching, and that the transportation of our troops to Korea would require several months, extending to even August or September, after which water traffic would be closed because of the stormy weather. The transportation of troops in these seasons would cause great loss of life and possibly end in disaster. Therefore, we decided to postpone sailing to Korea until next March when the sea should be open and the sailing safe.

"Taking the God of War and other deities as witnesses, we pledge that this decision to delay is wholly contrary to our desire, but was necessary because of conditions. As it is a settled national question that Tai-Min [China] is to be conquered, my plan of sailing to the continent and assuming personal charge of our entire army in the coming spring will certainly be carried out. . . ."[17]

On June 3, of the twentieth year of the Tensho era (1592), Hideyoshi sent Ishida, Masuda, and Otami, his three most trusted men, to Korea as his personal representatives, entrusting them with all the work of administration in the conquered land. Hideyoshi divided the main army in Korea, which numbered 130,000, into three divisions and gave instructions that the invasion of China by way of Manchuria should be undertaken without delay. At the same time, under date of June 3, 1592, Hideyoshi wrote a letter of instruction addressed to Kato and Nabeshima, the two leading military leaders in Korea. The letter read as follows:

"It has long been presumed by leading men in our imperial capital that our punitive expedition in Korea would be carried out as easily as dust is swept up with a broom. Hashiba Tsushima and Konishi Settsu, whom we have sent in the vanguard of our army, have now virtually subjugated the whole of that nation. There is no reason why Tai-Min [China] should not meet the same fate at the hands of our army as has Korea. As explained in a separate paper of instructions, we have divided our fighting men into three divisions, each of which should take turns in vanguard service in our army when we invade Tai-Min. Our fighting strength in Korea will be greatly increased by reason of our sending troops continuously from Japan to the war front in Korea. We earnestly request that, in addition to winning victories, you will always promote, by observing strict military discipline and stratagem, the interests and welfare of the people in the lands conquered.

"Throughout my service, beginning with the time when I was a man of low military rank, I have always taken part in battles, heading but a small force of from five hundred to one thousand fighting men against armies of several tens of thousands, and I have uniformly gained the victory. Finally, all the military families, both large and small, having been either subjugated or conquered, our nation was unified, and I became the undisputed master of the empire. Now, as for yourselves, you, as commanding generals of many hundreds of thousands of men, are to wage war against the armies of Tai-Min, who resemble helpless women in their military spirit and fighting ability. Therefore, you and your men of tested military experience and courage will be able to overcome the army of Tai-Min as easily as great mountain rocks roll upon and crush eggs. It is not Tai-Min alone that is destined to be subjugated by us, but India, the Philippines, and many islands in the South Sea will share a like fate. We are now occupying the most conspicuous and enviable position in the world.

"It was my original plan to cross the water in person before additional forces should be sent to Korea, and to take charge of the army on the continent. Later, however, it was feared that the military men left behind in Japan might rival each other in attempting to cross the water, without taking weather conditions into consideration, in order that they might join us sooner. As it is the stormy season, they might meet disaster, thus bringing great loss both to themselves and to our nation. Therefore, we have decided first to send troops under cautious direction and guidance; then, after transporting the remainder of our troops, I shall cross the water accompanied by military staffs and other attendants. Although instructions with respect to the conduct of the campaign have been sent to you, necessary changes in the military maneuvers will have to be made in accordance with the movements of the enemy. You are, therefore, instructed to use your best judgment in directing your troops to meet the ever changing situations.

"[Dated] June 3, in the twentieth year of the Tensho era [1592].
"Taiko [SEAL]
"To Kato Kazuye-no-Kami; Nabeshima Kaga-no-Kami."[18]

The change in Hideyoshi's plan of crossing the water had a far-reaching effect upon his military undertaking. This change proved to be the death blow to his continental campaign. After he had once changed his plan, he met with one difficulty after another, thus entailing successive delays. Finally, he was obliged to abandon entirely his plan to cross the water and assume personal charge of his army on the continent. Within only a few months after Hideyoshi had approved the plans of Iyeyasu and Toshiiye, involving his agreement to postpone the date of his sailing to Korea from May, 1592, until March, 1593, he fully realized the seriousness of the error he had made. Under date of November 10, 1592, in a letter addressed to Kobayakawa Takakage, the most trusted military leader of the Japanese forces in Korea, Hideyoshi said:

"In the middle of last summer [May, 1592] I made all arrangements to cross the water to Korea, there to take entire charge of our army. Because of the earnest requests of some of the leaders, I postponed the time of my sailing. This decision has placed both myself and my army in Korea in a most deplorable situation, for which I feel a thousand regrets."[19]

Had Hideyoshi, in accordance with the original plans, crossed the water to Korea in the summer of 1592, and invaded China before the latter had realized the seriousness of the situation and made military preparation to meet it, even though he might not have been able to occupy the whole of China, he would have been able to conquer Korea and the greater part of Manchuria. When it became known that Hideyoshi was not coming to Korea, all the military leaders were so disappointed that their ambitions and their fighting spirit were lessened. Moreover, the Japanese leaders in Korea frequently disagreed among themselves and even took independent action. In consequence, on the one hand the Japanese army in Korea lost its unity, and on the other China completed her military preparations and poured vast numbers of fighting men into Korea, while that nation, also, greatly increased her military power, especially her fighting strength on the sea, thereby threatening all communication and transportation. The Japanese were victorious in most of the battles, yet, because of the constantly increasing numerical strength of the joint Chinese and Korean armies, all battles were fought in Korea and the Japanese were not able to set foot on Chinese soil. Thus the ambitious plan of Hideyoshi for continental conquest ended in a mere Korean campaign.

APPENDIX 39

Terms of Peace Dictated by Hideyoshi to the Chinese Representatives

IN JANUARY, 1593, the large Chinese army sent to Korea by the Ming emperor under the command of Li Ju-Sung, one of the most distinguished military leaders of the time, was completely routed by a Japanese force of comparatively small strength. The entire Chinese army then retreated into northern Korea. General Li was greatly discouraged and abandoned entirely his plan of driving the Japanese army from the national capital of Korea; he was strongly inclined, indeed, toward concluding a treaty of peace. Among the Japanese military leaders in Korea, ever increasing disagreements developed into enmity. They were conscious, too, of the seriousness of fighting without a commander-in-chief against China with her inexhaustible man power. Besides the perils of the severe winter weather, there was increasing difficulty in obtaining food supplies, so that the Japanese military men in Korea suffered physically as well as mentally. They became tired of war and longed for home and peace. A movement for peace was originated in Korea by both the Chinese and the Japanese at about the same time. In May, 1593, two Chinese representatives, Hsu I-Huan and Hsieh Yung-Tsu, came to the military headquarters at Nagoya, Japan, to have an interview with Hideyoshi on terms of peace. Not only did their overtures for peace lack sincerity, but even their official function was uncertain. However, Hideyoshi readily received them as imperial envoys from the Ming throne, sent by the Ming emperor to express his regret and to offer apologies for his having taken military action in Korea, and to sue for peace. Hideyoshi appointed Masuda, Otani, Ishida, and Konishi as his representatives and had them hand to the "Ming imperial envoy" the following terms of peace, with the statement that peace would be concluded only in the event that the Ming should agree to all the terms without modification. Hideyoshi's terms of peace consisted of seven articles. They read as follows:

"1. If the peace terms are agreed to and pledges exchanged, they must be faithfully adhered to. These pledges shall continue in force even though Heaven and earth shall pass away. As evidence of sincerity, the imperial families of the two nations [China and Japan] shall enter into marriage relations. The Ming emperor shall send one of his daughters to Japan to be married to the emperor of Japan as his empress.

"2. Because of the long period of misunderstanding between the two nations, trade in accordance with the Kango plan has been entirely discontinued. Henceforth, trade relations shall be renewed and both the government and the merchant ships of each nation shall be permitted to sail to the country of the other for trade purposes.

"3. International friendship and good will shall be permanent, misunderstandings and misinterpretations being eliminated. Duly authorized state ministers of the two nations shall make sworn statements to this effect in written form, and exchange these statements as evidence of good faith and mutual sincerity.

"4. The first division of our troops has invaded and conquered Korea. According to our present plan, we shall send military leaders of genius and ability to that country with instructions to control that nation and to provide a good administration for the people there. However, if all the foregoing terms are accepted by Tai-Min [China], notwithstanding the fact that Korea has been rebellious against our country, we are willing, in order to show our good will to Tai-Min, to divide the eight provinces of Korea into two main divisions, and to return four provinces, including the one in which the national capital is situated, to the King of Korea. Further details will be given by our four representatives.

"5. When we return the four provinces to Korea, that nation shall send one of her royal princes and one or possibly two of her statesmen of the rank of state minister across the sea to Japan and have them remain here as hostages.

"6. In 1592, the first division of our troops captured two royal princes of Korea and held them as prisoners of war. Because of their high birth, they have not been able to live as do the common people. Therefore, our four representatives shall arrange with Chin Yugeki with respect to the returning of these two royal princes to their home.

"7. The state ministers in power in Korea should make sworn statements in written form to the effect that henceforth Korea shall neither oppose Japan nor overlook her generosity, and shall remain faithful to Japan, generation after generation. These sworn statements should be sent to Japan. Our four representatives shall take up this matter in detail with the envoys of Tai-Min."[20]

In this way, Hideyoshi virtually dictated the terms of peace to both China and Korea as though he were a victor in war. Hideyoshi also prepared a paper entitled "Articles to be Presented to the Imperial Envoy of Tai-Min [China]" in which he outlined the causes and results of his military campaign. This paper was handed by his four representatives to the Chinese representative. It read as follows:

"1. Japan is a divine nation. Our Divinity is the Heavenly Emperor, the Heavenly Emperor is our Divinity, there being absolutely no difference between them. Our nation having thus been created by the Divinity, our national customs were originally modeled after those of the Divine Age. The laws of our kings of yore were revered. The lives and doctrines of our ancestors were in accordance with the teachings and commands of Heaven, and were dependent upon the direction and order of the earth.

"However, our nation has not been able to maintain this sort of existence generation after generation. It has undergone many changes. The imperial authority has been ignored, and the nation has disintegrated into many disorderly units. Military leaders have rivaled each other for superiority.

"When I was conceived my mother had a miraculous dream, in which the Sun entered her bosom. She was terror-stricken and requested physiognomists to interpret her dream. They told her that just as there are not two suns in Heaven, there would soon be born to her a male child who would have no duplicate and who would become the sole ruler of the world. They said that her dream portended joyful tidings of the birth of a man whose virtue would shine all over the 'four seas.'

"Because I was born with such a destiny, upon attaining manhood I began to take a keen interest in the affairs of the world, and I strove to put an end to national chaos, thus saving people from misery and suffering. On the whole, I made it my ambition to bring back the Divine Age and thereby to cause my name to live throughout a myriad generations. This ambition has never left me. In only eleven years, I conquered and vanquished all unruly peoples. The castles and strongholds attacked by me were always stormed and occupied. All the military leaders that opposed me faced inevitable annihilation. Those who fostered rebellious inclinations lost their standing and some of them their very existence. Now the national prosperity and wealth have reached the highest point. The people are enjoying safe and happy lives. Everything that I had hoped to achieve has been accomplished. But the credit for this great work is not mine; this prosperity has been conferred upon us by Heaven. I merely carried out my destiny.

"2. In past generations, the pirate ships of Japan frequently entered the waters of Tai-Min. The pirate bands overran the whole of that nation, ravaging the land and killing the people. Because I was born with the destiny that my virtues should shine in all the places under the heavens wherever the sun shines, I determined that protection and justice should be extended to all corners of the world, including Tai-Min. As all the pirates and their ships have either been put under control or entirely destroyed, there is no more piracy even in distant islands. Our laws prohibiting and punishing piracy have been strictly enforced, and all the water routes are now safeguarded. By reason of this, all your coast provinces and the inhabitants therein are enjoying safety and prosperity. Are these not the things for which you have been striving for generations without success? However, you have entirely ignored our great service and have expressed neither appreciation nor gratitude. Probably you have ignored our nation, believing she is too small

to take any action, no matter how she may be dealt with. Therefore, in order to manifest our power, we have decided to send a
punitive expedition to your country [China]. Fearing that she
might become involved in this trouble between Japan and Tai-
Min, Korea sent three envoys to our country with the hope of establishing relations such as are due to a neighboring nation. Korea
pledged to open her kingdom to us, obstructing neither the roads
on which our fighting men would advance nor the lines of communication and transportation, when we should be ready to invade Tai-Min.

"3. However, when the Korean envoys were about to return
home, they begged of us the privilege of acting as mediators between us and China, so that the two great nations might not go
to war. They said that within three years they would be able to report the results of this mediation. On our part, we acceded to their
request that we postpone our military campaign against China for
three years. In 1592 this three-year period terminated, but Korea
made no report to us. She thus deceived our country, and committed a serious international crime, for which she should not remain
unpunished. Because of this violation of her national pledge, she
has suffered at the hands of our punitive expedition. Korea made
all possible military preparation, building strongholds at strategic
points and throwing up extensive works of defense. Nevertheless,
our advance-guard, which was of but limited military strength, engaged in a series of battles with Korean forces of considerable man
power and dispersed them on every occasion. Although the Korean
fighting men were thus defeated and scattered, nevertheless, taking
refuge in thickly wooded districts, they resorted to guerrilla warfare. Every time they clashed with our men, they were routed.
Thousands upon thousands of Koreans thus lost their lives.
Finally, they set fire to their national capital, reducing it to ashes.

"4. Having heard of the great national disasters in Korea, Tai-
Min sent a large army to that stricken country in the hope of saving
it from complete destruction. Strange as it may seem, the armies
of Tai-Min were always defeated. Tai-Min suffered these military
defeats only because of the untrustworthiness and trickery of the
Koreans. Now, Tai-Min has sent two envoys to our military headquarters at Nagoya, Japan. Upon arriving, they explained the im-

perial desire with respect to terms of peace. We have therefore
prepared our peace terms as set forth on a separate sheet in reply
to the inquiry of the Emperor of Tai-Min. Further detail will be
given orally by our four representatives. In order to show due courtesy, we shall postpone the sending of additional troops to Korea
until there has been time for a reply to our proposal to reach us.

"[Dated] June 27, of the second year of the Bunroku era [1593]."[21]

The Conclusion of Peace Between China and Japan, In-cluding the Imperial Command and Edict Issued to Hideyoshi by the Ming Emperor

AFTER HIDEYOSHI had handed the seven articles of the peace terms
to the Chinese representatives on June 28, 1593, he ordered the military leaders in Korea to act in accordance with the provisions of
these articles. In fact, even before the arrival of the Chinese envoys
in Japan, the Japanese troops had withdrawn from the national
capital of Korea and made it possible for the Korean king and his
family to return to their home. The two royal princes who had
been prisoners in Japan were released and allowed to join their
family. The Japanese troops in Korea first retired to southern Korea, but later most of them returned to Japan although some of
them remained in Fusan in Korea. Although Hideyoshi's plan to
divide Korea into a Japanese section and a Korean section was discussed and strongly opposed in Korea, the other proposals contained in Hideyoshi's terms of peace were either overlooked or
ignored. Hideyoshi heard nothing on the attitude of either Korea
or China with respect to them, and naturally he therefore found
it necessary to prepare for both peace and war in dealing with
China. Under date of January 15, 1594, he issued special instructions to the Japanese army which still remained in Korea. These
instructions read as follows:

"1. Although it would be very desirable to renew military activities immediately, yet, acting upon the suggestions of the military
leaders in Korea, we have decided to suspend our military activities in that country throughout this year [1594].

"2. In the coming year [1595], if the pending international problem has not reached a solution, Kampaku Hidetsugu [the successor of Hideyoshi both in the family line and in official capacity] shall be requested to cross the water to Korea at the head of a large army. Therefore, all the strongholds in Korea must be well equipped and communication facilities provided.

"3. As to provisions for the troops, in addition to what we have already sent, we are now sending about thirty thousand *koku* of rice. It is to be stored in the military granary at Fusan in Korea. This rice shall be distributed among the various military divisions when war is renewed.

"4. Because Tai-Min has apologized and expressed regret for engaging in military activities in Korea, and has sued for peace, a truce is now in force. However, we have reason to question that nation's sincerity. We shall therefore prepare for a permanent military occupation of Korea by strengthening all the military castles and strongholds to the fullest degree. We regard Korea as a part of our domain, the same as Kyushu. Accordingly, in the near future the fighting men now stationed in Korea will be permitted to return home to Japan, and will be replaced by troops that have enjoyed a furlough in the homeland. The officers shall inform all the men of this arrangement so that the rank and file may not pine for home and become restless. All the men at home in Japan, including those in Kanto, Tohoku, Dewa, and other districts, are assigned to work of one kind or another in connection with the present campaign. In fact, our fighting men in Korea are doing less work than are the Japanese at home.

"5. Our fighting men in Korea are required to develop and cultivate all the land available around their strongholds and military stations. Further detail will be delivered orally by Terazawa Shima. In the near future, a selected man will be sent to Korea in the capacity of Ometsuke [military inspector-general]."[22]

This document is dated January 16, in the third year of the Bunroku era (1594). It is both signed and sealed by Hideyoshi.

In the conclusion of peace delay followed delay. This irritated Hideyoshi and he showed a strong inclination to renew military activities on the continent. There was a persistent rumor that Hideyoshi would cross the water at the head of an army 200,000 strong and invade both Korea and China. Under date of September 12, in the twenty-second year of the Wan-Li era (1594), Yi-Yen, the king of Korea, sent a memorial to the Ming throne in which he appealed to the emperor to grant investiture to Hideyoshi, thereby saving the kingdom of Korea in her critical situation. Shen-Tsung, the Ming emperor, thereupon issued an edict to the Department of War of his government. It read as follows:

"Among the documents laid before us, we find a memorial addressed to the throne by the King of Korea. The petition of the Korean king with respect to our granting of tributary status to Japan, thus making it possible for Korea to maintain her national existence, is both urgent and pressing. According to our recollection, Chung-Kuo [China] has from very ancient times controlled outside barbarians by making them fear her military power and by causing them both to revere and depend upon her virtuous and benevolent rule. Consequently, if we should use either our fighting strength or our controlling and ruling power in dealing with them, it would be in nowise contrary to our traditional custom. At present, Japan has sent an envoy to us beseeching our good will and grace.

"Our national dignity and solemnity is invariably and everywhere maintained. If our dependent state [Korea] is to be protected and her safe existence thus made possible, our troops in that far-off land may be relieved from service. Thus our controlling power may be manifested [to Japan]. We are merely making preparations and awaiting the outcome. The taking of this step is in nowise contrary to our national policy. Your department is always depended upon by the throne and is requested to transact the military affairs of the nation. In dealing with important national problems, the advantage or disadvantage, together with the profit or loss that might accrue to our nation, should be carefully weighed and taken into consideration. If any of you, by reason of fear of criticism or because of individual interests, should either hesitate or delay in the expression of his opinion and thus make it impossible for the nation to reach a satisfactory solution, he will be charged with neglect of duty and of responsibility. You are hereby instructed to grasp all opportunities and to consider every condition carefully. You must lay out your plans clearly and precisely. Statements that are either ambiguous or vague should be avoided. The throne expects you to devise definitely a plan by means of which the barbarian state [Japan] may be successfully controlled and ruled and by which the urgent desires and petition of the nation [Korea] may be responded to by us."[23]

This imperial edict had a marked effect upon both the Department of War and the entire imperial court. In January, 1595, a plan for the conclusion of peace with Hideyoshi was adopted and imperial envoys to Japan were appointed. Upon arrival at Fusan, Korea, where he saw a strong force of Japanese troops stationed, the senior envoy, Li Tsung-Cheng, became frightened. He abandoned his party and escaped to the Korean capital. In May, 1596, the Emperor Shen-Tsung appointed Yang Fang-Heng as senior envoy, and Shen Wei-Ching as junior envoy. In August of the same year, these two envoys, accompanied by the Korean envoy, arrived in Japan. In September, Hideyoshi granted an audience to the Ming envoys, who presented to him the imperial patent of investiture and the imperial edict of the Ming emperor, Shen-Tsung. The imperial patent of investiture read as follows:

"In accordance with the heavenly doctrine and following out our destiny, the Emperor hereby issues this imperial command, saying: 'Our imperial virtue and benevolence being sacred and holy, and our imperial mission being vast and extensive, nowhere in the world where Heaven covers and earth extends is there any person who does not know how to revere us and how to depend upon us. Our imperial command and power now extend to lands in the far-off sea where the sun rises. The people in these lands are ready to make joyful obeisance and submission to us.

"Of yore, our imperial ancestor brought the nations in various parts of the world under the imperial protection and bounty. The gift of Kui-nui Lung-Chang was then enjoyed in the land of Fu-Sao [Japan]. The mountain in that land was graced with Cheng-ming Ta-Chuan, and it was recognized as the radiating center of peace and tranquillity in that nation. However, in later years, sea waves rose high and wafted that nation away from the imperial bounty and protection of our forefathers. Now, in our glorious reign, the rites and ceremonies are revived. You, Toyotomi Hideyoshi, have risen in the island country and have learned how to revere Chung-

Kuo [China]. You have sent an envoy to the West in order to express your admiration of us and your devotion to us. After having crossed the great northern barrier, a myriad miles in length, your envoy has reached our imperial capital and has presented your petition to have your country become our dependent state. Your reverence and obeisance have been sincerely expressed. Our blessing and protection should be extended to the country that has shown such devotion. With our special grace, we hereby invest you as 'King of Japan'. The imperial patent of this investiture is hereby conferred upon you. You are now in our imperial favor; our imperial coronet and robes are herewith sent over the sea to you. It is an honor for a state to depend upon and revere the dignity and glory of our throne. You, Hideyoshi, are hereby instructed to comply with our commands and to stand ready to fulfill your obligations to our throne as a loyal subject. You are also instructed reverently to conform with the imperial desire and to maintain your everlasting existence by following the imperial guidance and by cheerfully obeying our imperial commands!"[24]

The imperial edict was presented to Hideyoshi together with the imperial patent of investiture by the Ming envoy.

The imperial edict read as follows:

"In accordance with the heavenly command, we have ascended the throne as sovereign over the myriad nations of the world. It is not our ambition to make Chung Hwa [China] alone a land of safety and prosperity, but our heart shall be satisfied only after we have made all the districts both within and without the sea and every spot of land upon which the sun and the moon shine, places where life may be enjoyed with neither suffering nor uneasiness.

"You, Hideyoshi of Japan, have recently sent troops to Korea, thus causing great disturbance there. Korea is a nation that has strictly adhered to her tributary duties and obligations to our throne. She has appealed to us in this, her national crisis. Your military acts in Korea have caused us great anger. We have therefore sent troops to Korea to rescue her from impending calamity. The bloody struggles and loss of life thus brought about are wholly contrary to our liking. Konishi, a military leader of your army in Korea, has sent Fujiwara Joan as an envoy to us and had him lay before us a full account of the present military trouble in Korea.

He has stated that you, Hideyoshi, were originally desirous of obtaining an investiture from our throne and that you had requested Korea to present your petition to our throne in your behalf. However, Korea, he said, had refused to comply with your request, thus obstructing your path in approaching our imperial authority and guidance.

"Thereupon you, Hideyoshi, made a desperate move, thus causing our imperial troops to act. Now that you have realized with regret how serious was your error, you have withdrawn your troops and have returned the royal capital of Korea to that nation. You have permitted the royal princes of Korea and their attendants to return to their homes. You have now reverently prepared in written form your former petition and have presented it to our court. Our trusted and experienced officers have taken one course after another in your behalf and have finally presented your petition to our throne. While matters have been thus proceeding in your favor, your troops in Korea have been causing much bloodshed in the district of Chin Chou. This untrustworthiness and duplicity finally caused us to cease proceedings in your case. However, Yi-Yen, King of Korea, has appealed to our throne in your behalf stating that Japanese troops have remained at Fusan in Korea for more than a year in a most quiet and orderly manner, solely for the purpose of awaiting the arrival of the imperial envoy charged with investiture. The King of Korea also said that these Japanese at Fusan have conducted themselves respectably in every way. We, therefore, have again summoned Fujiwara Joan to our imperial capital. Upon his arrival, civil and military officers of various ranks held a series of conferences with him. The entire situation having thus been fully discussed and clearly understood, the three following agreements were entered into.

"1. All the Japanese in Fusan, Korea, shall return to their homes in Japan. Henceforth, not a single Japanese shall be permitted to remain in that district.

"2. After the investiture has been granted, Japan shall not seek from us those trade privileges that are due to a tributary state. Possible misunderstandings will thereby be avoided.

"3. Japan shall never again invade Korea, thus to forfeit the good will of her neighboring nation.

"The facts of the whole matter have been discussed and are now understood to our satisfaction. We have at last discovered sincerity and loyalty in you. We no longer have any suspicion of your motives in our heart. We commend your doing good and practicing virtue. We have instructed Shen Wei-Ching to proceed to Fusan and to have all your men in that place return to their homes in Japan immediately. We have especially selected two men, appointing Li Tsung-Cheng as senior envoy and Yang Fang-Heng as junior envoy. These envoys have been provided with the imperial letter of credence. They are therefore qualified to hand you the imperial edict and to invest you as King of Japan, conferring upon you the imperial gift of the golden seal as well as the official coronet and robes. Our official titles and ranks will likewise be conferred upon a number of your subjects in recognition of their individual abilities and merits. Our imperial grace shall thus be more widely extended.

"We hereby instruct all the people in your country to respect and obey your commands and to adhere strictly to your regulations in order that both yourself and your descendants may maintain a prosperous existence in your country, generation after generation, and may rule the country well. In the past, our Cheng-Tsu Wen emperor conferred the investiture upon your country. Now, in our reign, your country has again been honored by the imperial investiture. Your country's having thus been twice so invested by us is a most glorious event that rarely takes place in this wide world.

"Now that our investiture has been conferred upon you, henceforth you shall faithfully adhere to our three-term agreement. You are instructed always to concentrate your mind upon and to manifest your loyalty and sincerity to our throne. You should always be faithful and just, thereby maintaining friendly and harmonious relations with neighboring nations. As to the barbarous class of people [pirate bands] who maintain their existence near your country, you must deal with them strictly and severely. You shall not allow them to approach our coast districts and the surrounding waters. The people in the sixty-six islands [Japan] have long been subjected to various sorts of requisitions and have been forced either to neglect or entirely to abandon their respective trades and occupations. You are hereby instructed to give your attention and care as well as your protection and sympathy to your people, so that fathers, mothers, wives, and children may enjoy a happy home life and cheerful gatherings.

By carrying out all these instructions, you will comply with our desires and at the same time you will fulfill the heavenly command. Concerning the sending of tribute to the throne, we fully realize your loyalty and sincerity in so cheerfully and promptly meeting this obligation incumbent upon a tributary state. However, our military officers who guard the coast district are always zealous in performing the work entrusted to them. Their sole attention is always turned toward warfare, as they know nothing else save to fight and to defend. On days of wind and storm, when the coast districts are swept by destructive gales, our coast guards may fail to differentiate between a jewel and a stone and may mistake tribute-bearing ships from Japan for pirate vessels. You have already strongly impressed us with your loyalty and sincerity. We shall therefore certainly not demand tribute from you. We hereby exempt you from this duty to the throne. This step is also taken to prevent possible misunderstandings and unfortunate happenings. You shall not deviate from our instructions, but you shall reverently obey and adhere to our imperial command. Heaven looks down on the earth below and the will and laws of Heaven are strict and severe. Our imperial words and codes are brilliant and effective. Always revere Heaven and the throne.

"This edict is issued to you for all these purposes."[25]

The period of truce which was also that of peace negotiations between China and Japan, covered three years and three months, beginning in June, 1593, when Hideyoshi handed the seven-article peace terms to the so-called imperial envoys of the Ming, and ending in September, 1596, when the Ming envoys conferred the investiture of "King of Japan" upon Hideyoshi in the name of the Emperor Shen-Tsung. Throughout this long period, the representatives of China and Japan not only deceived each other, as though cheating were the leading art of diplomacy, but they also deceived their respective governments. Their representations led the Emperor Shen-Tsung and Hideyoshi each to believe that he could dictate terms of peace to the other as if he were a victor in war. The Emperor Shen-Tsung was placed in an especially embarrassing position. As he said in his imperial edict to Hideyoshi, peace would be concluded by Hideyoshi's acceptance of the three-term agreement. The Chinese emperor considered Japan to be a part of the domain of his empire. He invested Hideyoshi as "King of Japan" and instructed him in the methods of ruling Japan domestically as well as diplomatically. He demanded that Hideyoshi be loyal to the Ming throne. Hideyoshi not only entirely ignored the three-term agreement, but he promptly refused investiture and drove the Ming envoys from Japan. Three months later, the Emperor Shen-Tsung was forced to engage in war. He sent hundreds of thousands of fighting men to Korea to aid the Korean king to meet the second invasion of Hideyoshi.

APPENDIX 41

Chinese Source Material on the Korean Campaign and Hideyoshi's Death; Their Effects upon China and Korea

HIDEYOSHI ORDERED the envoys of the Ming emperor, Shen-Tsung, to leave Japan immediately after he had granted them an audience. This was in September, but, because of weather conditions, they were unable to take ship until October. At the same time, Hideyoshi instructed his government to prepare for a second campaign. His army, 130,000 strong, began to set sail for Korea in January of the following year (1597) and effected, in February, the landing of all the troops and supplies. The second campaign was onesided, all the major battles ending in decisive victories for Japan. The campaign was abandoned because of the death, from old age, of Hideyoshi, on August 18, 1598.

The effect of Hideyoshi's death on the Korean campaign is described in the *Chinting Ming-Shih*, the standard historical work on China in that period. This elaborate work was compiled and edited, in compliance with an imperial request, by the Historical Bureau under the supervision of Chang Ting-Yu (1671–1755).

The following excerpts are translations from the *Chinting Ming-Shih:*

"Therefore, all the Japanese sailed home to Japan. From the

time [1592] that Japan started the military disturbance in Korea, that nation suffered calamity for seven years. During this period, several hundreds of thousands of fighting men [Chinese and Koreans] lost their lives in battle. Several million *shiang* of rice were consumed. Finally, Chung-Chao [China] and her dependent state [Korea] became convinced that they had absolutely no fighting chance against Japan. However, because of the death of the Kampaku [Hideyoshi], the warfare at last came to an end."

"In April, in the twenty-seventh year of the Wan-Li era [1599], the Emperor Shen-Tsung issued an imperial edict to the people of his empire, announcing the end of the war with Japan. At the same time, the Emperor issued to Yi Yen [King of Korea] an imperial edict in which he said: 'That contemptible Hideyoshi ignored both the laws of Heaven and of men and acted arbitrarily and brutally. He overran the kingdom, trampling down and devastating the whole of your land. We recollected that both yourself and your forefathers, generation after generation, have been loyal to our throne. We were therefore deeply impressed and moved because of the sufferings of your country. During the entire period of seven years, we made it our problem how we might deal with the robber nation [Japan]. . . . Although your former country has been restored to you, the kingdom that you have regained is not the one you lost. In fact, you must create a new nation out of the ruins and devastation, by lifting up and raising the downtrodden and the suffering and by giving hope and encouragement to those in desperate circumstances. . . .' "[26]

"Seven years passed. Hideyoshi died. All the Japanese sailed back to Japan. The military calamity in Korea at last came to an end. Since the Kampaku [Hideyoshi] invaded Tung-Kuo [Korea], seven years had passed, including the first and second invasions. During this period, several hundreds of thousands of fighting men [Chinese and Koreans] lost their lives in battle. Several million *shiang* of rice were consumed. Finally, Chung-Chao [China] and Chao Hsien [Korea] became convinced that they had absolutely no fighting chance [against Japan]. However, with the death of the Kampaku [Hideyoshi], the military calamity at last came to an end. After withdrawing from Korea, the Japanese returned to their islands and remained quiet without making any further trouble. Thenceforth, both the Chinese and the Koreans were able to spend their nights without worrying about military ventures from the southeast."

Hideyoshi was succeeded by his son, but his family terminated with the second generation. On the part of China, throughout the entire period of the Ming dynasty her people were strictly prohibited from having any connections or transactions with either Japan or the Japanese. "All the Chinese and the Koreans feared the Japanese even so greatly as to use the expression, 'The Japanese are coming', to conjure with and to silence crying children."[27]

NOTES TO DOCUMENTS—CHAPTER I

APPENDIXES 1–14

[1] Toneri, *Nihon Shoki*, vol. 5, pp. 116–17; vol. 4, pp. 118–19. Ariga, *Dai Nippon-Rekishi*, vol. 1, pp. 131–33. Tokugawa, *Dai-Nihon Shi*, vol. 237, pp. 719–21. Waseda University, *Dai-Nippon Jidai-Shi*, vol. 1, pp. 442–47.

[2] Kume, *Dai Nippon (Kodai) Jidai-Shi*, vol. 1, p. 442.

[3] Tokugawa, *op. cit.*, vol. 237, p. 720 (fu.).

[4] App. 5, above, p. 221.

[5] *Chinting Sung-Shu*, vol. 7, p. 8. *Chinting Nan-Chi Shu*, vol. 58, p. 3. *Chinting Liang Shu*, vol. 58, p. 11. *Chinting Nan Shih* (History of the Four Southern Dynasties, Imperial Authorized Edition), vol. 79, p. 3.

[6] Ono, Yasumaro, *Kojiki*, vol. 2, pp. 107–09.

[7] Waseda University, *op. cit.*, vol. 1, pp. 18–25.

[8] *Ibid.*, vol. 1, p. 26. Naka, Michiyo, *Naka Michiyo Iko* (Historical Manuscripts left by Dr. Naka to be Published After his Death), pp. 6–7, 20–21, 25–26, 34.

[9] Naka, *op. cit.*, pp. 10–12.

[10] *Ibid.*, pp. 41–43.

[11] *Ibid.*, pp. 45–47.

[12] *Ibid.*, pp. 35–40.

[13] Ota, *Nikkan Kodai-Shi Shiryo* (Documental Source Material with Regard to the History of the Ancient Period of Japan and Korea and Their National Relations), pp. 174–84.

[14] App. 4, above, p. 214.

[15] Waseda University, *op. cit.*, vol. 1, pp. i–vi; vol. 2, pp. 477–500. Ota, *op. cit.*, pp. 155–59.

[16] Hagino, *Dai-Nippon Tsushi*, pp. 209–11. Kume, *op. cit.*, p. 350. Yoshida, *Tojo Nippon-Shi*, vol. 10, pp. 424–26.

[17] *Chinting Wei-Chih* (History of the Three Kingdoms, Annals of the Wei Dynasty, Imperial Authorized Edition), vol. 30, p. 11.

[18] *Chinting Sui-Shu* (History of the Sui Dynasty, Imperial Authorized Edition), vol. 81, p. 7.

[19] Toneri, *op. cit.*, vol. 22, pp. 383–84. Kimiya, *Nisshi Kotsu-Shi*, vol. 1, pp. 104–08. Ota, *op. cit.*, p. 101. Shuho, *Zenrin Kokuho-Ki*, vol. 1, pp. 9–10.

[20] Ito, *Dai-Nippon Minzoku-Shi*, p. 238.

[21] Kume, *op. cit.*, vol. 2, p. 425.

[22] Hagino, *op. cit.*, p. 154.

[23] Kume, *op. cit.*, p. 423.

[24] Toneri, *op. cit.*, vol. 27, pp. 478–79.

[25] Yoshida, *Dai-Nippon Chimei Jisho* (Encyclopedia of the Geography of Great Japan), vol. 4, p. 3022.

[26] Holt and Chilton, *European History 1862–1914*, pp. 343–44. Hazen, *Modern European History*, p. 577. Latourette, *The Development of Japan*, pp. 167–68. Bryan, *The Civilization of Japan*, pp. 41–55, 151–83.

[27] Shidehara, *Chosen Shiwa* (Historical Account of Korea), pp. 23–25, 41.

[28] Holt and Chilton, *op. cit.*, p. 344.

[29] Kida, *Kankoku no Heigo to Kokushi* (Annexation of Korea and the Japanese Historical Accounts in Connection with It), pp. 89–91.

[30] Hagino, *op. cit.*, p. 155.

[31] Ariga, *op. cit.*, vol. 1, pp. 666–67.

[32] Ito, *op. cit.*, p. 238.

[33] Kuroita, *Kokushi no Kenkyu*, pp. 64, 98–100.

[34] *Rinji-Zokan Rekishi-Chiri, Chosen-go* (a special issue of the magazine *History and Geography*, Korean Number, published on November 3, 1910, in Commemoration of the Annexation of Korea to Japan), p. 506.

[35] *Rekishi-Chiri, Chosen-go*, pp. 9–21.

[36] *Ibid.*, pp. 38–39.

[37] *Ibid.*, pp. 280–83.

NOTES TO DOCUMENTS—CHAPTER II

APPENDIXES 15–18

[1] *Chinting Yuan-Shih,* vol. 208, p. 809. Shuho, *Zenrin Kokuho-Ki,* vol. 1, pp. 25–26. Miura, *Kamakura Jidai-Shi* (History of the Kamakura Period), pp. 441–42.

[2] Ko, S. M. (Ko, Shao-Min), *Hsin Yuan-Shih,* vol. 250, p. 1.

[3] *Ibid.,* vol. 250, pp. 1–3. Kimiya, *Nisshi Kotsu-Shi,* vol. 2, pp. 103–04.

[4] *Chinting Yuan-Shih,* vol. 208, p. 9. Ko, S. M., *op. cit.,* vol. 250, pp. 3–5. Tsuji, *Kaigai Kotsu Shiwa,* pp. 210–11. Kimiya, *op. cit.,* vol. 2, pp. 105–08. Kuroita, *Kokushi no Kenkyu,* p. 353.

[5] Tsuji, *op. cit.,* p. 231. Kuroita, *op. cit.,* p. 359.

NOTE.—In notes 1, 3, and 4 to this chapter, as well as in some of the notes to the other chapters, several references (a state paper, an imperial edict, or some other important document) are given as authority for the same fact. These references have been selected from standard works in the Chinese, Japanese, and Korean languages. This method has been adopted because there are sometimes slight differences in the respective wordings of the Chinese, the Japanese, and the Korean texts; the content is identical in every respect.

NOTES TO DOCUMENTS—CHAPTER III

Appendixes 19–30

[1] Ono Yasumaro, *Kojiki*, vol. 1, pp. 51–52. Minamoto Chikafusa, *Shinko Shoto-Ki* (Records of the Imperial Orthodoxy of Japan), pp. 24–27, 41–43, 46, 188, 190–91. *Koshitsu Tenhan* (The Imperial Household Law of Japan), Article X. Omori, *Kokushi Gaisetsu* (Essence of the National History of Japan, pp. 200–01. Yoshida, *Tojo Nippon-Shi*, vol. 5, pp. 320–37.

[2] *Chinting Ming-Shih*, vol. 2, pp. 2b, 3a–b, 4a; vol. 322, p. 1a. Kimiya, *Nisshi Kotsu-Shi*, vol. 2, pp. 272–73.

[3] *Chinting Ming-Shih*, vol. 322, pp. 1b, 2a–b. Kimiya, *Nisshi Kotsu-Shi*, vol. 2, pp. 280–83. Aoki, *Dai-Nippon Rekishi Shusei*, vol. 2, pp. 977–78. Tsuji, *Kaigai Kotsu Shiwa*, pp. 302–04.

[4] Shuho, *Zenrin Kokuho-Ki*, vol. 1, p. 32.

[5] *Ibid.*, vol. 1, pp. 32–33.

[6] *Ibid.*, vol. 2, p. 44.

[7] *Ibid.*, vol. 2, pp. 45–46.

[8] *Ibid.*, vol. 3, pp. 77–78.

[9] Zuikei, *Zenrin Kokuho-Ki*, pp. 8–9, 11–12.

[10] *Ibid.*, pp. 13–14.

[11] *Ibid.*, pp. 15–16.

[12] *Ibid.*, pp. 21, 24.

[13] Tsuji, *Kaigai Kotsu Shiwa*, p. 307.

[14] *Ibid.*, pp. 309–12.

[15] *Ibid.*, p. 308.

[16] Shuho, *op. cit.*, vol. 1, p. 37.

[17] *Ibid.*, vol. 1, p. 37.

[18] *Ibid.*, vol. 1, pp. 38–39.

[19] *Ibid.*, vol. 2, pp. 36–37, 40.

[20] Tsuji, *op. cit.*, pp. 246–47.

[21] Shuho, *op. cit.*, vol. 2, pp. 42–43.

[22] *Ibid.*, vol. 2, pp. 43–44.

[23] Tsuji, *op. cit.*, p. 247. *Chinting Ming-Shih*, vol. 322, pp. 2a–3a.

[24] Tsuji, *op. cit.*, p. 248.

[25] *Ibid.*, p. 249.

[26] *Ibid.*, p. 250.

[27] *Ibid.*, p. 250.

[28] Kimiya, *op. cit.*, vol. 2, p. 320.

[29] Tsuji, *op. cit.*, pp. 250–51.

[30] *Chinting Ming-Shih*, vol. 322, pp. 3a–b. Shuho, *op. cit.*, vol. 2, pp. 47–48.

[31] *Ibid.*, vol. 2, p. 49.

[32] *Ibid.*, vol. 3, pp. 66–72.

[33] *Ibid.*, vol. 2, pp. 62–63.

[34] *Ibid.*, vol. 2, p. 64; vol. 3, p. 75.

[35] *Chinting Ming-Shih*, vol. 322, p. 4a. Zuikei, *op. cit.*, p. 5.

[36] Zuikei, *op. cit.*, p. 5.

[37] *Ibid.*, pp. 6–8.

[38] Shuho, *op. cit.*, vol. 3, p. 77.

[39] *Ibid.*, vol. 3, p. 76.

[40] Zuikei, *op. cit.*, pp. 9–10.

[41] *Ibid.*, pp. 10–11. *Chinting Ming-Shih*, vol. 322, p. 3b.

[42] Hagino, *Nippon-Shi Kowa*, pp. 569, 572–73.

[43] Tsuji, *op. cit.*, pp. 262–63. *Shigaku Zasshi*, vol. 5, pp. 501–02.

APPENDIXES 31-41

[1] Kuroita, *Kokushi no Kenkyu*, p. 635. Tanaka, *Toyotomi Jidai-Shi*, pp. 44–45. Waseda University, *Dai-Nippon Jidai-Shi*, vol. 6, p. 302.

[2] Tokutomi, *Kinsei Nippon Kokumin-Shi*, vol. 7, pp. 145, 150, 153, 162–63, 186.

[3] Zuikei, *Zoku Zenrin Kokuho-Ki*, pp. 35–36. Tokutomi, *op. cit.*, vol. 7, pp. 194–97. Li Tan-Ka, *Senbyo Hokan* (History of Korea During the Reign of King Syong-Cho, 1569–1609).

[4] Tokutomi, *op. cit.*, vol. 7, pp. 227–31.

[5] Zuikei, *op. cit.*, p. 33.

[6] *Ibid.*, pp. 33–34.

[7] Tokutomi, *op. cit.*, vol. 7, pp. 135–37, 277–78.

[8] Tsuji, *Kaigai Kotsu Shiwa*, p. 429.

[9] *Shigaku Zasshi*, vol. 1, pp. 76–80; vol. 36, pp. 384–91. Tsuji, *op. cit.*, pp. 430–35.

[10] Tsuji, *op. cit.*, pp. 442–43.

[11] *Ibid.*, pp. 421–26.

[12] Tokutomi, *op. cit.*, vol. 7, pp. 435–42, 452–53. Hanawa, *Gunsho Ruiju* (Classified Collections of Japanese Standard Works and Documents), vol. 399, pp. 1475–78.

[13] Tokutomi, *op. cit.*, vol. 7, pp. 442–49.

[14] *Ibid.*, vol. 7, pp. 432–33.

[15] *Ibid.*, vol. 7, p. 466.

[16] *Ibid.*, vol. 7, p. 596. Aoki, *Dai-Nippon Rekishi Shusei*, vol. 2, pp. 1194–95. Kusaka, *Hoko Ibun* (Personal letters and private communications of Hideyoshi recently collected and published).

[17] Tokutomi, *op. cit.*, vol. 7, p. 471.

[18] *Ibid.*, vol. 7, pp. 481–82.

[19] *Ibid.*, vol. 7, p. 476.

[20] *Ibid.*, vol. 8, pp. 518–21. Zuikei, *op. cit.*, pp. 36–37.

[21] Tokutomi, *op. cit.*, vol. 8, pp. 522–28. Zuikei, *op. cit.*, pp. 37–38.

[22] Tokutomi, *op. cit.*, vol. 8, pp. 578–80.

[23] *Chinting Ming-Shih*, vol. 20, p. 6; vol. 320, pp. 7–8.

[24] Tokutomi, *op. cit.*, vol. 8, pp. 736–37; vol. 9, pp. 323–24. A document in the archives of Viscount Ishikawa.

[25] Tokutomi, *op. cit.*, vol. 8, pp. 731–35.

[26] *Chinting Ming-Shih*, vol. 320, p. 9b (lines 9–12).

[27] *Ibid.*, vol. 322, p. 8 b (lines 8–11).

BIBLIOGRAPHY

1. ONO YASUMARO. *Kojiki* (Record of Ancient Affairs), compiled in 712 A.D. (Tokyo, Keizai Zasshi Sha [Kokushi Taikei series], 1904), 170 pp.

2. TONERI. *Nihon Shoki* (Chronicle of Japan), compiled in 720 A.D. (Tokyo, Keizai Zasshi Sha [Kokushi Taikei series], 1904), 574 pp.

Kojiki and *Nihon Shoki* are the two oldest Japanese histories. Prior to the eighth century, all national affairs were transmitted solely by word of mouth. In the early part of the eighth century, the ruling emperor decided to put the national history into written form. In compliance with the imperial request, Yasumaro, a noted scholar, wrote a national history from the dictation of the court historians. At that time, Japan had no written characters of her own, and so Chinese characters were used exclusively. The completed work was called *Kojiki*. It resembles mythology rather than history. In 720 A.D., the second national history, *Nihon Shoki*, was compiled by the Imperial Board of History under the supervision of the imperial prince, Toneri. When the *Nihon Shoki* was written, all available historical material, including that of China and of Korea, was used. Unfortunately, because of the historians' lack of ability to sift and eliminate, Japanese and Chinese historical events are hopelessly confused and mixed. In the writing of the work, the Chinese classical language was used. In consequence, the work as a whole was compiled under the dominating influence of China. Although both the *Kojiki* and the *Nihon Shoki* are unreliable in respect to historical accuracy, they are the only works from which some knowledge of conditions in ancient Japan may be gleaned.

3. TOKUGAWA, MITSUKUNI. *Dai-Nihon Shi* (History of Great Japan), 243 volumes (pamphlet size) completed in 1715 (Tokyo, Koraku-Shoin, 1912), 5 vols. (translation).

Mitsukuni, 1628–1700, was one of the three Shinpan feudal lords of the Tokugawa. When he was 18 years of age, he was greatly inspired by a Chinese historical work, and decided to compile a reliable history of Japan. When he succeeded to the lordship, he invited noted historians from all parts of Japan and established an institute for the compilation of history. He sent scholars to various parts of Japan to search out documents and other historical materials. The history compiled by him was replete with footnote citations supporting all important statements. This was the first history written in Japan according to modern methods. The first seventy-three volumes dealt with Japanese history proper. They brought the record of the nation's history to the reign of Gokomatsu, the one-hundredth emperor, who ruled from 1395 to 1412. The remaining one hundred and seventy volumes gave accounts of the lives of military men, statesmen, literary men, artists, artisans, and other men who had contributed to the national development. It is said that Mitsukuni appropriated one-third of the state revenue for this historical work. The work was not completed until 1715, seventeen years after the death of Mitsukuni. In accordance with the custom of the time, the work was written in the Chinese classical language. It was not translated into modern Japanese until 1912 A.D. This translation consists of five volumes, each containing approximately eight hundred pages.

4. KIMIYA, YASUHIKO. *Nisshi Kotsu-Shi* (History of Communications Between China and Japan; Tokyo, Kinshi Horyu, 1928), 2 vols., approximately 700 pages each.

Kimiya, in his book, dealt with the national and trade relations of Japan and China up to the close of the nineteenth century. He stressed especially the international relationships between China and Japan in the Japanese feudal period of seven hundred years. Because of the inclusion of many important diplomatic events, his work was translated into the Chinese language by a Chinese scholar. It is now a standard work in both China and Japan.

5. TSUJI, ZENNOSUKE. *Kaigai Kotsu Shiwa* (A Historical Account of the Communications of Japan with Nations Beyond the Seas; Tokyo, Naigai Shoseki Kabushiki Kaisha, 1930), 816 pp.

The author has dealt with the national and the trade relations of Japan with China and Korea and with Spain and Holland, Mexico, and other Occidental nations. The book is especially valuable because all the important matters are supported by state papers and diplomatic notes.

6. SHUHO. *Zenrin Kokuho-Ki* (Records of National Papers of Great Value Exchanged with Friendly Neighboring Nations; 1466). Reprinted in Shiseki Shuran series (Tokyo, Kondo Shuppan-Bu, 1901), 3 vols.

7. ZUIKEI, ZOKU. *Zenrin Kokuho-Ki* (second series; original text with supplement, 1784), 2 vols. Reprinted in Shiseki Shuran series (Tokyo, Kondo Shuppan-Bu, 1901).

The *Zenrin Kokuho-Ki* contains all the state papers that Japan exchanged with China and with Korea in the Ashikaga period. The second series contains state papers exchanged with China and Korea and with other nations in the Orient and in the Occident. By reference to the state papers recorded in these two books, the standing of Japan and her relations with Korea and with China prior to the nineteenth century can be understood.

8. MIURA, CHIKAYUKI. *Nippon-Shi no Kenkyu* (Research in Japanese History; Tokyo, Naigai Shoseki Kabushiki Kaisha, 1930), 1338 pp.

9. KUROITA, KATSUMI. *Kokushi no Kenkyu* (Research in the National History of Japan; Tokyo, Bunkai-Do Shoten, 1918), 877 pp.

Miura and Kuroita are eminent historians in present-day Japan, and noted for their work in historical research. Miura made known, in his book, his findings with respect to widely discussed historical subjects such as the national relations of Japan with China and with Korea in the Ashikaga period, and with respect to many other political and national problems such as the cultural and social development of the people and the founding and development of cities. Kuroita, in his book, gave the history of Japan from the time of its founding up to the present century. In compiling this history, he did much valuable research and introduced many new considerations bearing on Japan's relations with the Asiatic continent and her political organization.

10. TOKUTOMI, SOHO IICHIRO. *Kinsei Nippon Kokumin-Shi* (A History of the Japanese People in Modern Times, 1918–; Tokyo, Minyu-Sha), 51 + vols.

Tokutomi's work is both the most nearly complete and the most noteworthy history of New Japan. His volumes begin with the second half of the sixteenth century, when the Dark Age had come to an end and restoration of national peace had been effected by Nobunaga, Hideyoshi, and Iyeyasu. His plan is to bring his work down to his own generation. He published his first volume in 1918, and since then he has published three volumes every year. Each of these volumes contains approximately five hundred pages. The latest volume is the fifty-first, and the completed work will total more than one hundred. Tokutomi has made extensive use of historical documents and other reliable materials in corroboration of the statements in his history. Judged by its size and thoroughness, Tokutomi's history excels any other history of Japan. Last year, the Imperial Academy of Japan recognized *Kinsei Nippon Kokuminshi* as the most noteworthy history ever written in Japan, and awarded a national prize to Tokutomi.

11. WASEDA UNIVERSITY. *Dai-Nippon Jidai-Shi* (History of Great Japan, Period by Period; Tokyo, Waseda Univ. Press, 1915), 12 vols.

Waseda University requested many noted historians each to write on some designated period of the ten periods into which the history of Japan might be divided. Upon the completion of these period histories, twelve volumes in all, the work was edited by Waseda University, and entitled *Dai-Nippon Jidai-Shi*. This is one of the most elaborate histories published in modern times. Because each volume was written by a historian who was a recognized authority on the special period assigned to him, ever since its publication this work has been accepted as one of the most reliable histories of Japan.

12. YOSHIDA, TOGO. *Tojo Nippon-Shi* (History of Japan in Reverse Order; Tokyo, Waseda Univ. Press, 1917), 10 vols.

13. YOSHIDA, TOGO. *Dai-Nippon Chimei Jisho* (Dictionary and Encyclopedia of the Geography of Great Japan; Tokyo, Fuzan-Bo, 1922–23), 7 vols., approximately 6000 pages.

Yoshida was a nationally recognized historian and geographer of New Japan. In the writing of history, he had ideas of his own that were quite different from those of other historians. He insisted that history should be both written and read with sympathy. He insisted also that it should be possible for the reader to trace readily the causes and effects of all important national events; hence, in the writing of an elaborate history, the first volume should deal with the modern period and the last volume should deal with the ancient period. Thus, Yoshida wrote his history of Japan in "reverse order." He thereby laid special emphasis upon the causes and effects of historical events and of national undertakings. At the end of his description of each historical period, he gave a summary of important national events in China and in Korea, thus facilitating the study of contemporaneous historical events in Oriental nations. His history runs to about 5000 pages. In his geography, Yoshida gives complete descriptions and historical accounts of all the places mentioned that are in Japan, including counties, cities, towns, and villages. His work thus provides authentication for such events as those of the seventh century, when the kingdoms of Kudara and Korai were destroyed and many thousands of Koreans fled to Japan and made it their permanent home.

14. AOKI, BUSUKE. *Dai-Nippon Rekishi Shusei* (Comprehensive History of Great Japan; Tokyo, Ryubun-Kan, 1913–17), 5 vols.

15. ARIGA, NAGAO. *Dai Nippon-Rekishi* (Unabridged History of Japan; Tokyo, Hakubun-Kan, 1907–08), 2 vols.

16. OMORI, KINGORO. *Dai-Nippon Zenshi* (Complete History of Japan; Tokyo, Fuzan-Bo, 1929–31), 3 vols.

Although these three histories have no outstanding characteristics, each of them is an elaborate work of from 3000 to 6000 pages, and because of their thoroughness they are used extensively by Japanese scholars. Within a few years after their original publication, several editions of each were issued, two of the histories running to fifteen editions.

17. HAGINO, YOSHIYUKI. *Nippon-Shi Kowa* (Lectures on Japanese History; Tokyo, Meiji-Shoin, 1920), 1018 pp.

18. HAGINO, YOSHIYUKI. *Dai-Nippon Tsushi* (Comprehensive History of Great Japan; Tokyo, Hakubun-Kan, 1899), 918 pp.

Hagino based the first of these two histories upon material in his lectures given in the Tokyo Imperial University. Because of his long connection with the highest educational institution in Japan, he had opportunity to avail himself of the best library in Japan in the preparation of his lectures, year after year; hence, in respect of material, and conciseness and clarity of statement, the *Nippon-Shi Kowa* is one of the best histories of Japan. In the past fifteen years, forty editions have been published. The *Comprehensive History of Great Japan* was more elaborately planned. When the first volume was published, it was the author's intention to write several additional volumes. It is to be regretted that he published only the one volume, for the *Dai-Nippon Tsushi* is a most noteworthy work.

19. TANAKA, YOSHINARI. *Nanboku-Cho Jidai-Shi* (History of Japan During the Period of the Northern and the Southern Imperial Dynasties; Tokyo, Meiji-Shoin, 1924), 280 pp.

20. TANAKA, YOSHINARI. *Ashikaga Jidai-Shi* (History of Japan During the Ashikaga Period; Tokyo, Meiji-Shoin, 1925), 358 pp.

21. TANAKA, YOSHINARI. *Oda Jidai-Shi* (History of Japan During the Oda Period; Tokyo, Meiji-Shoin, 1924), 286 pp.

22. TANAKA, YOSHINARI. *Toyotomi Jidai-Shi* (History of Japan During the Toyotomi Period; Tokyo, Meiji-Shoin, 1925), 290 pp.

The Dark Age in Japan, which lasted nearly two hundred years, was a transition period from Old to New Japan. It was marked by several important historical events. The Ashikaga entered into disgraceful international relations with China; Japanese pirates ravaged the coasts of both Korea and China; Catholicism was introduced, thus bringing Japan into touch with Occidental civilization. The Dark Age terminated with Hideyoshi's attempt to conquer the Asiatic continent. Tanaka wrote four periodical histories based on extensive research which covered the whole of the Dark Age. These histories are standard works.

23. HASEGAWA, SEIKI. *Wako* (Ravages of Japanese Pirates Along the Korean and Chinese Coasts; Tokyo, Toyo-Do, 1914), 216 pp.

24. HISTORICAL RESEARCH ASSOCIATION. *Zoku Shiteki Kenkyu* (Research in Historical Subjects, second series, being SHIDEHARA, TAN, *Wako ni Tsuite* [The Invasion of the Asiatic Continent by Pirates from Japan], Tokyo, Fuzan-Bo, 1916), 143 pp.

The ravages of Japanese pirates in the fifteenth and sixteenth centuries are a unique episode in the Orient. Hasegawa and Shidehara have done careful research on this subject. Hasegawa lived in China, and Shidehara had a long residence in Korea. Both have dealt especially with the pirate raids in their respective places of residence.

25. NAKA, MICHIYO. *Naka Michiyo Iko* (Posthumous historical work; Tokyo, Dai-Nippon Tosho Kabushiki Kaisha, 1915), 1083 pp.

26. NAKA, MICHIYO, *Shina Tsushi* (Comprehensive History of China; Tokyo, Dai-Nippon Tosho Kabushiki Kaisha, 1889–90), 4 vols.

Naka did much original research work. It was he who, through a careful comparative study of the histories of China, Japan, and Korea, was able to announce authoritative facts which proved that there was an error of more than six hundred years in the traditional date of the founding of the empire of Japan. The *Naka Michiyo Iko* is filled with findings that are equally valuable. Naka, in writing Chinese history, emphasized the Occidental methods of explanation by means of charts. He wrote his history in the Chinese classical language. Prior to the middle of the nineteenth century, most of the Japanese histories and other standard works were written in the Chinese classical language, just as, during the medieval period, English scholars wrote their works in Latin. Although this custom has now almost entirely died out, yet, like Naka, some Japanese scholars still write their research work in the Chinese classical language. Their purpose in so doing is the same as that of German scholars of the present day who write the results of their Oriental research in English instead of in German, namely, in order that their works may have a wider reading circle.

27. HAYASHI, TAISUKE. *Chosen Tsushi* (Comprehensive History of Korea; Tokyo, Fuzan-Bo, 1912), 608 pp.

28. SHIDEHARA, TAN. *Chosen Shiwa* (Historical Accounts of Korea; Tokyo, Fuzan-Bo, 1925), 531 pp.

These two works are nationally recognized histories of Korea written by Japanese scholars. Hayashi described the national development of Korea and the successive political changes. Shidehara's work is a collection of essays based on research concerning selected historical events in Korean history, and is published under the title, *Chosen Shiwa*.

29. OTA, RYO. *Nikkan Kodai-Shi Shiryo* (Historical Materials on the Ancient Periods of Japan and Korea; Tokyo, Isobe Koyo-Do, 1928), 187 pp.

Ota read with care all the Chinese and Korean histories. He gathered together historical facts concerning international relations between Japan and Korea that were not to be found in any history written in the Japanese language.

30. KIDA, SADAKICHI. *Kankoku no Heigo to Kokushi* (The Annexation of Korea and the National History of Japan in Connection Therewith; Tokyo, Sansei-Do Shoten, 1910), 182 pp.

Kida gave an account in this book of the three kingdoms into which Korea was divided prior to the seventh century, together with the relationships of these kingdoms to China and to Japan. He explained the ways in which Korea, after its unification by Shinra, was related to Manchuria, to China, and to Japan. Finally, Kida discussed all the important international events that took place in Korea, beginning in the nineteenth century, with respect to Japan and Russia and to China and Russia. He set forth clearly how and why Korea was annexed to Japan. Although his book contains fewer than two hundred pages, yet because of its clear and concise statements, its reliability and authenticity, it is extensively used.

31. OMACHI, YOSHIYE KEIGETSU. *Nippon Bunmei-Shi* (History of the Civilization of Japan; Tokyo, Hakubun-Kan, 1903), 302 pp.

32. ITO, GINGETSU. *Dai-Nippon Minzoku-Shi* (History of the Race of Great Japan; Tokyo, Ryubun-Kan, 1917), 754 pp.

Both Omachi and Ito made bold and unhesitating statements on the strong and weak national characteristics of Japan and of her people. Although these writers have often placed undue emphasis on some phases of the national life of Japan, they have not failed to point out many things that have been overlooked by historians in general. In this respect, these two works are especially noteworthy. Persons who know how to read books critically find them of great value.

The following-named books have no striking characteristics, yet are regarded as reliable and authoritative works on certain historical periods and particular historical subjects in which their respective authors have specialized. In the writing of the present volume, they have been frequently referred to in the verification of important historical events.

33. YOSHIDA, TOGO, and NISHIKAWA, K. *Nikkan Jokoshi no Rimen* (The Seamy Side of the Ancient Period of Japan and Korea and of Their National Relations; Tokyo, Kaiko-Sha, 1910), 1142 pp.

34. TANAKA, KEIJI. *Shiryo-teki Nippon-Shi* (History of Japan; based in large part upon documentary evidence; Tokyo, Meguro-Shoin, 1930), 580 pp.

35. RESEARCH ASSOCIATION IN HISTORY AND GEOGRAPHY. *Muromachi Jidai no Kenkyu* (Research in the Muromachi Period; Tokyo, Meguro-Shoten, 1923), 374 pp.

36. ASSOCIATION FOR JAPANESE HISTORY AND GEOGRAPHY. *Nippon Kaijo Shiron* (History of Japan on the Seas; Tokyo, Association for Japanese History and Geography, 1911), 492 pp.

37. KIYOHARA, SADAO. *Nippon Shigaku-Shi* (A History of the Japanese Histories and of Their Respective Emphases; Tokyo, Chubunkan-Shoten, 1928), 330 pp.

38. MINAMOTO, KITABATAKE CHIKAFUSA. *Shinko Shoto-Ki* (The Imperial Orthodoxy of Japan; Tokyo, Sheishi-Do, 1908, eleventh edition; the original text was written about the year 1339), 435 pp.

39. NATIONAL HISTORY RESEARCH ASSOCIATION. *Ashikaga Jugo-dai Shi* (History of the Rule of the Fifteen Shoguns of the Ashikaga; Tokyo, Daido-Kan, 1912), 404 pp.

40. RESEARCH ASSOCIATION IN HISTORY AND GEOGRAPHY. *Kamakura Jidai Kenkyu* (Research in the Kamakura Period; Tokyo, Hoshino-Shoten, 1925), 506 pp.

41. JAPANESE HISTORY AND GEOGRAPHY RESEARCH ASSOCIATION. *Sengoku Jidai-Shi* (History of the Period of War in Japan; Tokyo, Sansei-Do, 1910), 360 pp.

42. TAKAKUWA, KOMAKICHI. *Nippon Tsushi* (A Comprehensive History of Japan; Tokyo, Kodo-Kan, 1912), 1316 pp.

43. IHARA, G. *Tokugawa Jidai Tsushi* (A Comprehensive History of the Tokugawa Period; Tokyo, Daido-Kan, 1912), 1218 pp.

44. TOKYO IMPERIAL UNIVERSITY, ASSOCIATION OF HISTORICAL SCIENCE. *Shigaku Zasshi* (Magazine of Historical Science; Tokyo, 1889 ff.), 42 vols. (December 1889–December 1931).

45. JAPAN HISTORICAL AND GEOGRAPHICAL ASSOCIATION. *Rekishi-Chiri* (History-Geography; Tokyo, 1899 ff.), 59 vols. (October 1899–December 1933).

Of all the technical magazines in Japan, the *Shigaku Zasshi* and the *Rekishi-Chiri* are the most prominent. The members of all the leading universities in Japan, as well as leading scholars, are privileged to use them in making known the results of their respective lines of study. The first number of the *Shigaku Zasshi* was published in December, 1889. Forty-two bound volumes, ending in December, 1931, are obtainable. Of these, all the publications from Volume I to Volume XL are fully indexed according to subjects and authors. This index is published in a separate volume. The first number of the *Rekishi-Chiri* was published in October, 1899. Fifty-nine bound volumes, ending with that of December, 1933, are obtainable. All the publications from Volume I to Volume XXVI are fully indexed according to subjects and authors. The index of Volume II has gone to press. These magazines are reliable and authoritative.

46. *Documents in the archives of the Tokugawa, of the Mori, of the Mayeda, of the Asano, and of the Nabeshima families* are not available to the public. Nevertheless, these noble families extend ready courtesy to scholars doing research work. These formerly feudal families were founded in the sixteenth and seventeenth centuries, and their archives therefore contain valuable historical documents in connection with Hideyoshi's plan of continental conquest. Toku-

tomi, Tsuji, and other historians privileged to use them, have published those documents in their books.

47. *Chinting Erh-Shih-Ssu Shih (Imperial Authorized Edition of Twenty-four Histories;* Tu Shu Dzi Cheng Shu Ju, Shanghai, 1885), 3243 vols.

Beginning in very ancient times, there was a strong movement in China to select the most authoritative histories from among numerous dynastic histories written in different periods. Prior to the tenth century, only four histories had gained nation-wide recognition. By the Tien-Sheng era (1023–31) of the Sung dynasty, seventeen dynastic histories had gained recognition. In the Ming dynastic rule (1368–1644), the number of recognized histories was increased from seventeen to twenty-one. After the Ching (Manchu) dynasty had come to rule China, a reliable history of the Ming dynasty was written and added to the number of recognized histories.

During the Chien-Lung era (1736–95) of the Manchu rule, in compliance with a command from the throne, the Imperial Board of History made a careful study of all the existing histories of the different dynasties, and, basing their findings on the seventeen histories and the twenty-one histories, the members of the Board selected twenty-four histories, numbering 3243 volumes (*Chuan*). They presented these to the throne with their reasons for the selections made. The emperor not only approved of this work, but was also greatly pleased. The selections were published in 1739 in accordance with an imperial command, and are therefore known as the *Imperial Authorized Edition of Twenty-four Histories.*

48. Ko, Shao-Min. *Hsin Yuan-Shih* (New History of the Yuan [Mongol] Dynasty, edition of 1926–27), 257 vols.

Many years after the publication of the Twenty-four Histories in the imperial authorized edition, Ko Shao-Min completed an elaborate work known as the *Hsin Yuan-Shih.* This history was the finished product of his life's work. It was soon recognized as an authoritative history, and in more recent times has been accepted by Chinese scholars as the most reliable. For this reason, at the present time the *Imperial Authorized Edition of Twenty-four Histories,* together with the *New History of the Mongol Dynasty,* by Ko Shao-Min (Ho-Chao-Mon), are known as the Twenty-five Standard Histories of China. The dynastic histories referred to in this treatise—the Han, the Wei, the Sung, the Sui, the T'ang, the Yuan, and the Ming—are among these twenty-five standard histories of China.

49. Wang, Hsien-Chien. *Jihpen Yuan-Liu Kao* (History of Japan Based upon All Obtainable Sources; Chang-Sha, China, 1902), 22 vols.

In writing this history, Wang Hsien-Chien made use of standard Japanese histories written by Japanese authors, thus completing two thousand years of the History of Japan. At the same time, he cited all the accounts of Japan that could be found in the *Imperial Authorized Edition of Twenty-four Histories,* and that were not recorded in the Japanese histories, thus supplementing his work. By this arrangement, he made it possible for scholars to study Japanese history from both Japanese and Chinese sources.

50. Kin, Fu-Shiki. *Sangoku Shiki* (Chronicles of the Three Kingdoms in Korea), 50 vols.

In 1145, Kin Fu-Shiki, in compliance with a request by Jinso, the king of Korea, completed this, the oldest history of Korea. It is filled with accounts of Japanese invasions and military activities of the ancient period which are not recorded in Japanese history. The *Chronicles of the Three Kingdoms in Korea* has therefore proved a valuable source of material by means of which historians have been enabled to consider the so-called Korean conquest by the Empress Jingo as an event of possible actuality rather than as a page from mythology.

The names of all the Korean books and of their authors are always written in Chinese characters. These characters are pronounced differently in the three languages, Chinese, Japanese, and Korean. Since 1910, the Japanese government has adopted the policy of making Japanese the national language in Korea. For more than a quarter-century, all educational work in Korea, especially in secondary and collegiate institutions, has been conducted exclusively in the Japanese language, so that, at the present time, the Japanese language is now more predominant in Korea than the English language is in the Philippines. The Chinese characters employed in the title, *Chronicles of the Three Kingdoms in Korea,* are pronounced in the Korean language "Sankook Saki" and in the Japanese language "Sangoku Shiki." The names of all Korean books and all Korean authors are today given the Japanese pronunciation.

51. ICHIZEN. *Sangoku Iji* (Historical Incidents and Anecdotes Surviving the Three Kingdoms in Korea), 5 vols.

Ichizen completed this work in the reign of King Churetsu (1275–1308). The *Sangoku Shiki* and the *Sangoku Iji* are the two oldest histories in Korea. They are not wholly reliable, yet they are the only Korean works through which something of the national affairs in ancient Korea may be gleaned.

The *Sangoku Iji* contains very many accounts concerning national relations between Japan and Korea that are not recorded in any of the Japanese histories, including the *Sangoku Shiki.* The *Sangoku Iji* gives an account of Korea's having been a sort of tributary state of Japan in the ancient period. From these two Korean sources (nos. 50 and 51), historians have come to believe that early in her national life Japan made it her policy to extend her dominion to the continent.

52. SHUNJU-KAN (ed.). *Korai-Shi Setsuyo* (Essence of Korean History; Keijo), 37 vols.

It is not definitely known when this Korean history was written; the history extant today is that edited by the Shunju-Kan historical staff in 1452. It is one of the most complete and most reliable histories of Korea, and because of its usefulness the Korean government-general published the entire work.

53. RYU, SEI-RYO. *Chohi-Roku* (Records of the National Suffering for the Purpose of Giving Warning to the Koreans of Future Generations; Keijo), 16 vols.

Ryu Sei-Ryo was the prime minister of Korea when that kingdom was invaded by the army of Hideyoshi. After the capitulation of Seoul, the national capital, Ryu Sei-Ryo, in company with the king, wandered from place to place and saw the suffering of the people and the disgrace of the nation. After Japan had abandoned the Korean campaign, Ryu Sei-Ryo retired from public life and devoted himself entirely to writing the *Chohi-Roku,* in which he gave a detailed description of the seven years' campaign which ended in 1598. His statements are supported by various state papers and other documents. Ryu Sei-Ryo's purpose, in thus depicting the national suffering, was to warn future generations that they might protect the kingdom of Korea from again suffering national calamity and disgrace.

54. SHIN, KEI. *Saizo Hanpo-Shi* (Records of the Rehabilitation and Reorganization of the State After the Japanese Invasion; Keijo), 4 vols.

Shin Kei completed his work in 1649 but it was not published until 1693. In this work he described how Korea, a tributary state of China, had maintained its existence and had been rehabilitated through the military and political assistance of China under the Ming dynasty. As this work was written within half a century after Hideyoshi's invasion, its content is considered reliable.

55. KI, JI-KEN. *Senso Jitsuroku* (Authentic Record of the Rule of King Senso; Keijo), 221 vols.

This work gives a complete account of the rule of King Senso, who ruled over Korea for forty years, his reign ending in 1608. Ki Ji-Ken completed it in 1616. Because the invasion by Hideyoshi took place in the reign of King Senso, the work is of great value and importance in the study of the standing and attitude of Korea on this Japanese aggression.

56. RI, TAN. *Senbyo Hokan* (The Treasured Mirror Which Reflected the Rule of King Senso; Keijo), 10 vols.

After 1675, in compliance with the request of King Shukuso, Ri Tan spent ten years in compiling this work, which was centered upon the invasion of Korea by Hideyoshi. The histories listed herein under numbers 55–56 are of great value in conjunction with Japanese histories in the study of Hideyoshi's invasion.

57. CHOSEN SHI GAKKAI (Korean Historical Association). *Chosen-Shi Taikei* (A Series of Fundamental Histories of Korea; Keijo [Seoul], Korea, Chosen Shi Gakkai, 1927), 5 vols.

58. AOYAGI, NANMEI. *Richo-Shi Daizen* (A Complete History of Korea During the Rule of the Yi Dynasty; Keijo, Korea, Korea Research Association, 1922), 966 pp.

59. HIGASA, MAMORU. *Nissen Kankei no Shiteki Kosatsu to Sono Kenkyu* (Study and Research from the Historical Viewpoint on National Relations Between Japan and Korea; Tokyo, Shikai-Shobo, 1930), 250 pp.

60. WANG, YUN-SHENG. *Liu-Shih-Nien Lai Chung-Kuo yu Jihpen* (Relations Between China and Japan During the Past Sixty Years; Tientsin, China, Tai-kung-Pao Company, 1932), 6 vols.

61. RAI JO (SANYO). *Nippon Gaishi Rombun* (Essays on Japanese Historical Subjects; Tokyo, Nisho-Do, 1913), 276 pp.

Sanyo was the most notable Japanese historian of the nineteenth century. Like Macaulay, he was more an essayist than a historian. *Nippon Gaishi* is a widely read work; probably no other book has had so wide a circulation in Japan. Nevertheless, it is a well-known fact that it is lacking in historical accuracy. In this work, Sanyo has inserted brief historical essays and critical remarks, pointing out causes and effects. In all his comments he reveals a personal loyalty to the throne, and sympathy for the emperors during the military rule of the Shogunate. It is the consensus in Japan that Sanyo's essays, by arousing the Japanese to a nation-wide enthusiasm, were mainly instrumental in bringing about the Imperial Restoration in 1868. The first edition was published about 1827.

62. OMORI, KINGORO. *Kokushi Gaisetsu* (Essence of the National History of Japan; Tokyo, Sansei-Do, 1910), 568 pp.

The first 172 pages of Omori's book are given over to a history of Japan from the founding of the nation to the present time; the remaining 396 pages, to a discussion of various historical subjects. He states 310 historical problems relating to sources of historical materials, the nature and relative values of standard histories, and the origin and the workings of national laws and codes of both ancient and modern times, together with all known traditions and usages, and gives explanations of these. Although his work is not elaborate, it may be used as a reliable guidebook.

63. KUO-HSUEH LIBRARY. *Chia-Ching tung-nan ping-Wo tung-lu* (Records of

the Suppression of Japanese Pirates in Southeastern China During the Chia-Ching Era, 1522–66; Nanking), 63 pp.

This little volume gives brief descriptions of the activities of Japanese pirates in southeastern China, making note of their movements during the period 1552–64. According to the descriptions in the book, the field of the pirates' operations included Shantung, Chekiang, Kwangtung, Kwangsi, and Fukien. Not only did they plunder along the coast; they also marched far into the interior and attacked Nanking and several strongly fortified cities. They were far from being marauders; their fighting strength often numbered several thousands, sometimes reaching more than 10,000. Furthermore, pirate bands from Japanese waters were, as a rule, joined by discharged Chinese government officials, wild Buddhist priests, and young men who were either unemployed or dissatisfied with their situations. In the victory won by the Ming army in Fukien in December, 1564, as described in the book, more than 2200 Japanese pirates were beheaded, countless others were either burned or drowned, and more than 3000 Chinese men and women who had been caught by the pirates and held as prisoners were rescued. This gives some idea of the nature and magnitude of the battle between the Chinese army and the pirates from Japanese waters in the second half of the sixteenth century. A supplement to the book describes the inroads of the Japanese pirates in Kwangtung in 1568, four years after this famous victory.

The time being in the midst of the Dark Age of Japan, the Chinese government was well informed of the national chaos in Japan, and of the assassination of the "King of Japan" (the shogun) and of all his chief officers. Japan had no central ruling power. The military chiefs rivaled each other and engaged continually in petty warfare. China was therefore cognizant of the fact that Japan was wholly impotent in the control of pirates and of other outlaws. China realized that the inroads and plunderings of the Japanese pirates constituted a domestic affair within her own borders.

The book contains descriptions of pirate invasions and bloody fighting, as well as of imperial edicts, reports from local governments, and plans and proposals advanced by prominent statesmen in China for the suppression of Japanese pirates.

64. *Chao Wen-hua ping-Wo tsou-shu* (Memorials to the Throne Regarding the Suppression of Japanese Pirates by Chao Wen-hua, holder of a Chin-Shih degree of 1529; the original book, in one volume, was published *ca.* 1556–57).

This book contains twenty-eight memorials presented to the Ming throne by Chao Wen-hua, twenty-five of them dealing exclusively with plans for the suppression of the Japanese pirates. Chao's services and activities in connection with the suppression of the pirates are mentioned in various parts of *Chia-Ching tung-nan ping-Wo tung-lu*. According to descriptions in this book, in May, August, September, and December in the thirty-fifth year of Chia-Ching (1556), Chao Wen-hua personally commanded an army and defeated the Japanese pirates, thus rendering distinguished military service to the nation.

Numbers 63 and 64 deal exclusively with domestic affairs in China. Neither of them deals in any way with international transactions or with diplomatic relations between China and Japan. However, they give interesting accounts of how China suffered from, fought against, and to some degree succeeded in suppressing the Japanese pirates, in the second half of the sixteenth century, especially during the period beginning when the so-called tribute-bearing envoys ceased to go from Japan to China, and diplomatic relations were terminated entirely;

and ending in the time when the national unification of Japan was brought about by Hideyoshi, who in 1588 promulgated and enforced the law for the control and punishment of pirates and thereby freed the entire coast of China from the inroads of pirates in Japanese waters.

65. Hsu, Hsueh-Chu (holder of a Chin-Shih degree of 1583, comp.). *Kuochao tien-hui* (Documents in the National Imperial Archives, vol. 169), 15 pp.

This small volume of pamphlet size describes the international relationships and recounts the diplomatic transactions between China and Japan during the Ming and Ashikaga periods. It begins with a description of events that took place in 1369 when the Ming emperor, Tai-Tsu, sent an envoy to Japan informing that nation of his accession to the throne. He gave to Japan a national seal as a throne gift, thus dealing with Japan as a tributary state. The book ends with the entry of events in the twenty-seventh year of Chia-Ching (1548), when the twelfth Ashikaga shogun (the "King of Japan"), Yoshiharu, sent a tribute-bearing envoy to the Ming throne, and upon the return of the envoy, the Ming emperor, Shih-Tsung, gave silver, silk brocades, and other valuable things to the "King of Japan" and his "Queen" as throne gifts. Although stating them but briefly, this book gives full accounts of the inroads of the Japanese pirates, of the imperial edicts to the "King of Japan," of the arrivals of tribute-bearing envoys from Japan, and of the troubles consequent upon the evaluation of the tribute, and of the trade transactions with Japan. This book also describes the troubles occurring in China because discharged government officials, wild Buddhist priests, desperate and disappointed young men, and other disorderly Chinese joined the Japanese pirates, serving as spies or guides, and shared in the plundering, thus causing great harm to their own nation. It also mentions the appreciation and recognition by the Ming throne of the distinguished service of Yoshimitsu in having repeatedly suppressed and punished the Japanese pirates.

66. Fan, Hua. *Chinting Hou-Han Shu* (History of the Later Han Dynasty, Imperial Authorized Edition issued in the fourth year of the Chien-Lung era, 1739, reprinted at Shanghai), 120 vols.

67. Shen, Yao. *Chinting Sung Shu* (History of the Sung Dynasty, Imperial Authorized Edition, 1739, reprinted at Shanghai), 100 vols.

68. Hsiao, Tsu-Hsien. *Chinting Nan-Chi Shu* (History of the Southern Chi Dynasty, Imperial Authorized Edition, 1739, reprinted at Shanghai), 59 vols.

69. Yao, Ssu-Lien. *Chinting Liang Shu* (History of the Liang Dynasty, Imperial Authorized Edition, 1739, reprinted at Shanghai), 56 vols.

70. Li, Yen-Shou. *Chinting Nan Shi* (History of the Four Southern Dynasties, Imperial Authorized Edition, 1739, reprinted at Shanghai), 80 vols.

71. Wei, Cheng. *Chinting Sui Shu* (History of the Sui Dynasty, Imperial Authorized Edition, 1739, reprinted at Shanghai), 84 vols.

72. Ou Yang, Hsiu. *Chinting Tang Shu* (History of the Tang Dynasty, 1739, reprinted at Shanghai), 225 vols.

73. Sung, Lien. *Chinting Yuan Shih* (History of the Mongol Dynasty, Imperial Authorized Edition, 1739, reprinted at Shanghai), 210 vols.

74. Chang, Ting-Yu. *Chinting Ming Shih* (History of the Ming Dynasty, Imperial Authorized Edition, 1739, reprinted at Shanghai), 332 vols.

All these nine *Chinting* histories of different dynasties are works recognized internationally. However, although all the international relationships of China with Japan, existing in and after the seventh century, that are mentioned in some of these histories are identified with entries in Japanese history, yet international relationships and diplomatic transactions between China and Japan prior to the seventh century and mentioned in the histories of Hou-Han, of Sung, of Nan-Chi, and of Liang are entirely unknown and unrecognized events in Japanese histories. Nevertheless, in consequence of many historical evidences, and of extensive research, Japanese historians have come to concede that they all had actuality, and have concluded that Japanese military chiefs in Kyushu and Japanese governors-general in Korea sent envoys to the imperial court of China and entered into transactions with her of their own accord, without the knowledge of either the emperor or the imperial government of Japan. The *Chinting* history of Hou-Han, Vol. I, Pt. II, p. 10a, and Vol. 115, pp. 5–6, states that Japan, situated southeast of Korea, was divided into more than one hundred countries, at least thirty of which revered the suzerainty of China and sent tribute-bearing envoys to the Han throne. In the spring of the second year of the Chung-Yuan era (57 A.D.) the king of the southernmost district in Japan sent a tribute-bearing envoy to the Han throne. Upon his return, the emperor, through him, gave a golden national seal to the king as a throne gift. In February, 1784, in the district of Ito, Kyushu (the southernmost district in Japan), this same golden seal was accidentally excavated. The seal was only identified after careful study by historians and archeologists, who took into consideration designs, styles of Chinese character writing, and the wording and engraving on the seal. This golden seal is now in the possession of Marquis Kuroda. Its replica is kept in the Tokyo Imperial Museum. The excavation of the golden seal incidentally attests the reliability of the ancient history of China.

75. IKEUCHI, HIROSHI. *Genko no Shin-Kenkyu* (New Research on the Mongol Invasion; Tokyo, Toyo Bunko, 1931), 2 vols.

76. KUME, KUNITAKE. *Dai-Nippon (Kodai) Jidai-Shi* (Periodic History of Ancient Japan; Tokyo, Waseda University, 1915), 2 vols.

INDEX

Ainu: territory controlled by, 25, 27; plan to drive, from Honshu, 27–28; subjugation of, 28

Akamatsu: military family, 110; Yoshinori's plan for, 110; plan of head of, 110–11; murder of shogun by, 111; rebellion of, 111

Annam: edict of Tai-Tsu to ruler of, 82–83; state tributary to China, 83, 127

Armada. *See* Kublai Khan

Ashikaga: rivalry between, and Nitta families, 62–63; branch of Minamoto family, 63; head of, 63, 64; military government at Kamakura, 63, 64, 65, 109–10; head of, family made shogun, 67, 117; affairs of, family placed in hands of Yoriyuki, 74–75; rule of, family falls into two periods, 107

Ashikaga Period, 65–66; controlling elements during, 66–67; war between Northern and Southern dynasties in the, 69, 72; length of, 120; shoguns that exercised ruling power during, 120

Ashikaga shogun: first, 64, 67; second, 74, 109; third, 75, 90, 120; as "King of Japan," 107; fourth, 100, 109, 120; fifth, 109, 120; sixth, 109 *passim*; seventh, 111; eighth, 111–14 *passim*; ninth, 118; tenth, 115, 118, 120; not even a figurehead, 117; eleventh, 118, 120, 121; twelfth, 107, 118, 120, 121; thirteenth, 118, 123; fourteenth, 118, 123; fifteenth, 119, 123, 124, 132; last memorial sent to Ming throne by, 122

Ashikaga shogunate, 40, 66, 110; establishment of, 64, 65, 67, 77; situation during rule of, 67; authority of, 75, 77, 78, 117; degeneracy of, 115; provinces of, lost in chaos of Dark Age, 115; unable to meet obligations to imperial family, 115–16; remained a storm center, 117–18; ended with Yoshiaki, 120, 124; not able to equip tribute-bearing ships, 123; known as the Government of the King of Japan, 124; length of existence of, 129; length of ruling authority of, 129. *See also* "King of Japan"

Asiatic empire, Hideyoshi's plan for, 143

Azuchi, seat of third military government, 135. *See also* Nobunaga

Barbarian people, 42, 83; Eastern, 68

Board of National Trustees, 178

Buddhism: in Japan, 12, 13; influence of, 33; degenerated, stimulated, 130; deeply rooted Honganji, 136; final chapter of militant, in Japan, 136

Buddhist church, 133

Buddhist communities, 112; destruction of, 133, 135, 136

Buddhist monasteries: retired Japanese emperors at, 32, 36; use of trade licenses by, 97; establishment of military government by, 129, 136

Buddhist priests, 15, 52, 55, 82, 135, 142

Bunbu, king of Shinra, unification of Korea under, 20

Calendar: introduced from Korea, 15; Chinese national, sent to Kanenaga, 85; Ming national, sent to "King of Japan," 91, 105

Campaign for the Invasion of Japan, 55

Catholicism in Japan, 130, 133

Cha Ta-Shou: Yukinaga deceived by, 162; attack on Pyeng Yang by, 162–63

Chan-Cheng (Cochin China): edict sent to ruler of, 82–83; became state tributary to China, 83

Chao-Hsien. *See* Korea

[359]